THE
JUDICIAL
MIND

The Attitudes and Ideologies
of Supreme Court Justices
1946–1963

THE JUDICIAL MIND

The Attitudes and Ideologies of Supreme Court Justices

1946–1963

BY GLENDON SCHUBERT

NORTHWESTERN UNIVERSITY PRESS · *Evanston*

To
the Fellows of "the Class of '61" and to the Staff
of the
Center for Advanced Study in the Behavioral Sciences
this book is gratefully dedicated,
with affection and esteem

FOREWORD

HAROLD D. LASSWELL
Edward J. Phelps Professor of Law and Political Science, Yale University

THE MOST REMARKABLE FACT about modern political science is the intelligence and vigor with which the "method gap" is now being closed. The gap came into the picture when professional students of government, law, and politics failed to avail themselves of the modes of theory formation and the techniques of data processing that, though initiated by specialists in other fields, could be applied to the study of power values and institutions. Professor Schubert's volume is a brilliantly sustained extension of neglected methods to the analysis of the most distinctive institution of the American system of public order—the Supreme Court.

Specialists and laymen alike promptly want to know whether the results warrant the effort required to learn a new approach. An affirmative answer is not always welcome, especially among an established intellectual elite whose members are rather proud of their achievements. Hence novelties of method are met with so many manifestations of zeal for high standards of intellectual life that the casual observer might be led to assume that the intellectual achievements of the critics are even higher than they usually seem to be.

Some of Schubert's earlier work has been the target of perfectionist criticism of this kind; and doubtless the same fate will befall the present highly polished performance. As a methodologist Schubert has been subject to attacks of a different kind than met the work of such a scholar as Charles A. Beard, whose innovations were less in the relam of "procedure" than of "content." Beard's study of the Court was a clearcut application of research procedures common to historians. That the founding fathers could have had their feet on the ground and their minds on money was shocking to the American myth, as perceived by most of Beard's academic and activist cotemporaries. Schubert's findings are more likely to be dismissed as "obvious" or "not worth the trouble."

The severity of the criticism that meets the methodologist innovator is not too difficult to understand. The distinguished professors and practitioners of a profession at any given time have invested years in acquiring the perspectives and operational techniques regarded as conventionally acceptable by their teachers. Their capital, as intellectuals, is knowledge and skill, which are complex sets of predispositions to recall the right thing at the right time, and to exercise with facility a variety of skills that, in the case of political scientists and lawyers, are largely communicative. The successful career—distinguished by the acquisition of effective claims to respect, wealth, power and other values—depends on the strategies employed in managing the base values of conventional enlightenment and skill with which the career began. Striking innovations in methodological skill are often perceived as acutely deprivational, since they accelerate the obsolescence of yesterday's learning.

It is not universally true that striking innovations are met with defensive strategies by all members of an established profession. In many fields important elite elements have adapted themselves to permanent modernization. Drastic innovations are perceived as capital gains for the profession as a whole, hence for each ego whose self-system is identified with the value position of the corporate entity. Professor Herman Pritchett, whose initiative in the study of judicial process is continued and greatly intensified by Schubert, was fortunate to have acquired his professional formation in the environment created by Charles E. Merriam, who deliberately launched a program for the modernization of political—including legal—studies. The growing success of this program contributed opportunities and encouragement to the "take-off" in several sub-fields. It is greatly to Schubert's credit that he has contributed a benchmark study to research on the Supreme Court, and therefore to the understanding of the judicial process as it functions within the larger social process.

What can be said more concretely about the contribution that Schubert has made by adapting the techniques originated by Louis L. Thurstone, and subsequently developed by several important figures? To begin with the simplest observation: The research has produced an explicit analysis of the content of Supreme Court decisions between 1946 and 1963, and summarized the patterns of participation in these 1659 decisions by the eighteen justices who have been on the bench during the period.

The act of classification cannot fail to have a far-reaching influence on future discussion of how "decisions" are best classified for research purposes. Schubert now realizes that at first he classified decisions in the conventional categories employed in legal disputation. The litigant who obtains access to an authorized and controlling decision-maker uses conventional legal language to express his "claim" to the tribunal, and also to "justify" it. In reply, the tribunal uses similar language in phrasing its "decision" and providing "justifications" for the position taken. It was insufficiently apparent to the author at the beginning that the scientific observer must classify the conventional language of any legal order by means of independent functional categories for which he takes responsibility. Shall the observer classify according to the impact, whether indulgent or deprivational, on the value position of the litigants, or according to the identity of the institutional practices that are approved or disapproved by the Court? Whatever the analyst's choice it will now be possible to compare the results of any alternative system with Schubert's data.

The method of classifying decisions is crucial for interpreting the significance of alignments among decision-makers. The present research shows in careful detail how the alignments can be manipulated to disclose the perspectives of the justices individually and aggregatively. Since the correlations discovered depend on a defined mathematical configuration, the scientific observer must use his judgment when he attempts to label them in terms that refer to empirical events. In the present research the categories bring out the residual perspectives of the great revolutions of the eighteenth and nineteenth centuries.

Fruitful controversy will continue among scholars about the explanatory usefulness of the results. The research is intended to go beyond the classification of decisions and to disclose factor-combinations that account for the trend of Court response. One line of evaulation will hold that explanatory factors must provide a technique of showing how a decision response leaves the decider better or worse off. Is participation in the minority, for instance, to be treated as a deprivational experience that increases the predisposition to affiliate with majorities? Are the significant factors to be located outside the courtroom, so that the success or failure of the Court as a whole is to be measured by the rise or fall of its power when compared with the Congress or the Presidential office? Are the most satisfactory indices for individual justices to be found in the approval or disapproval expressed in journals of the professional bar and in the mass media? Are the rewards and penalties entirely internal, depending on self-perceived conformity to self-imposed criteria? Schubert's discussion of Mr. Justice Warren's "genuine shift" toward liberalism will focus and eventually clarify such questions, and provide grounds for assessing factorial techniques.

To say that a complex technique, when used in a new field, is "applied" conveys an incomplete evaluation. The peculiarities of the new configuration and the ingenuity of the investigator are likely to introduce changes, even corrections, in the technique. Schubert's treatment of certain features of Guttman's cumulative scaling procedure is probably an instance of this kind.

Another consequence of the research, forecast by the author, is that it will help to dissipate the mystique that has had an intimidating effect on the study of courts by social psychologists.

Professor Schubert has launched a mighty craft in intellectual competition. Even if it loses and sinks, the waves will carry many fragile vessels with it to the bottom, and permanently influence design.

PREFACE

No MAN is an island; and least of all, one who ventures to study and to inform others about the behavior of fellow humans. Especially is this true when the human behavior that we seek to understand consists of events that cannot be directly observed, and about which our knowledge must consist of inferences, in the validity of which our confidence must be based upon their capacity to predict behavior that we can observe. The acquisition of this kind of theoretical knowledge about the human mind is perhaps the most basic objective of research in the behavioral sciences; and one who labors in this field does so only with the cooperation and assistance of many other persons. On grounds of both general principle and discrete fact, I think that it is most appropriate that this particular book of mine should be dedicated to friends rather than to relatives, since there is no doubt in my own mind that the work that I shall discuss owes considerably more to the influence of nurture than to that of nature. More than any other single factor, the Center for Advanced Study in the Behavioral Sciences at Stanford has contributed to my own education as a social scientist.

The staff persons at the Center to whom I owe a special debt of gratitude are Preston Cutler, Miriam Gallaher, John Gilbert, Jane Kielsmeier, and Ralph Tyler, each of whom played an indispensable role in making it possible for me to do the bulk of the research for this book, during the year that I was at the Center. There was hardly one of my fifty colleagues from whom I did not learn, but there is one fellow in particular whose own research was indispensable to my construction of the theoretical model that guided my subsequent empirical research: this was Clyde Coombs, Professor of Psychology at the University of Michigan. Coombs's lectures and writings on the theory of data were instrumental in facilitating my own understanding of the fundamental psychometric relationships upon which I have based my theory and methodology in this work.

xi

The basic theoretical model, the methodology, and the research design all were worked out at the Center during the late fall and early winter of 1960–61. The collection and ordering of scale and factor data for the first fifteen of the seventeen terms (which the study now includes) were completed during the following spring and summer. The work was subsequently extended to include the 1961 Term, with the assistance of an academic quarter of released time for research, granted by the Department of Political Science and the College of Social Science at Michigan State University. The 1962 Term was added through the assistance of a grant-in-aid from the Social Science Research Council, during the summer of 1963; and at that time, work also was begun on the writing of the manuscript.

I also received aid in several other respects, from Michigan State University. I am particularly indebted to Joseph LaPalombara, former Chairman, and Charles R. Adrian, the present Chairman, of the Department of Political Science; and to Alfred L. Seelye, Dean of the College of Business, and Louis L. McQuitty, Dean of the College of Social Science, for their help in various administrative arrangements which facilitated my work on the project during the academic years 1960–64. A grant from the All-University Research Fund was used to pay for the photographic reproduction of some of the figures; and the Institute of Community Development aided me by providing the drafting services of John Edsall for several of the figures. The early chapters were typed through the courtesy of Mrs. Hazel Brickley, Supervisor of the Central Stenographic Office.

The writing and typing of the latter portion of the book were completed early in 1964 during my tenure as a Senior Scholar in Residence at the Institute of Advanced Projects of the Center for Cultural and Technical Interchange between East and West, at the University of Hawaii. I am grateful to Edward W. Weidner, Vice Chancellor of the Center, and to Arthur Feraru, Director of the Institute, for having provided the facilities that made it possible for me to complete the work on the book. I wish to thank also Hazel Tatsuno, Arline Uyeunten, and Jeannette Matsui for their help in typing parts of the manuscript and most of the tables; and Ilyong Kim, for assisting me in the preparation of the index.

I have had occasion to discuss various aspects of the theory and methods that I have employed in this work, either in person or in correspondence (or both), with several persons, including David Danelski, Louis L. Guttman, John E. Hunter, Fred Kort, Stuart S. Nagel, Harold J. Spaeth, Joseph Tanenhaus, and S. Sidney Ulmer; and to all of these friends, I wish to acknowledge my sincere appreciation. My elder son, Frank A. Schubert, has taken time from his own busy life as an undergraduate to assist me, upon more than one occasion, with some of the details of translating the output of the computer into the format of tables for the book. And my wife and younger children, though long since inured to living with a person who does much of his writing at home, have helped to make home a pleas- ant place in which to work, and just by being themselves.

There will be no doubt, in the mind of anyone who reads very far in this book, concerning who is to blame for that which follows.

GLENDON SCHUBERT

Honolulu, Hawaii
March, 1964

CONTENTS

LIST OF EQUATIONS

LIST OF FIGURES

LIST OF TABLES

THE
JUDICIAL
MIND

The Attitudes and Ideologies
of Supreme Court Justices
1946–1963

Chapter 1 · INTRODUCTION

A s CHILDREN, those of us who have reached middle age (at least) were taught that $2 + 2 = 4$, and that in the world of plane geometry, the whole is equal to the sum of its parts. In the process of growing up intellectually, we began to harbor suspicions—which were confirmed in our adulthood—that this neat model of reality, with its simple and absolute closure, did not explain (and *could* not explain) many of the empirical situations with which life confronted us. Organic processes of growth would transform our data in ways that could not be captured by methods of observation and measurement designed to map a static universe; and so we would frequently get for our answer a mutation, when we sought a *quod erat demonstratum*. Previous attempts to study either the ideology of liberalism, or the attitudes of Supreme Court judges, have been confined almost exclusively to what could be done with a theory of data (and associated measurement techniques) appropriate for surveying the flood-plain of the Nile; the few exceptions with which I am familiar are found in the recent work of a few social psychologists and one or two political scientists.[1] It is certainly true, at least for some purposes, that two feet plus two feet equals four feet; but we also know that two rabbits plus two rabbits may not (at least for very long) equal four rabbits, depending upon their sex, age, and condition. And the study of the ideology of liberalism and the attitudes of Supreme Court justices is more akin to working with rabbits

[1] See T. W. Adorno, Else Frenkel-Brunswik, Daniel J. Levinson, and R. N. Sanford, *The Authoritarian Personality* (New York: Harper, 1950); Hans J. Eysenck, *The Psychology of Politics* (London: Routledge and Kegan Paul, 1954); Herbert McClosky, "Conservatism and Personality," *American Political Science Review*, Vol. 52 (1958), pp. 27–45; Stuart S. Nagel. "Off-the-Bench Judicial Attitudes," ch. 2 in Schubert (ed.), *Judicial Decision-Making* (New York: The Free Press, 1963) and note particularly the references cited at pages 44–47; and Milton Rokeach, *The Open and Closed Mind* (New York: Basic Books, 1960). (McClosky and Nagel are the political scientists among the above group.)

than it is to the addition and subtraction of linear feet. No matter whether we perceive the effort as painful or as an adventure, we must (like Alice) go beyond the parlor of apparent reality and pass through the Looking Glass into an imaginary world of ideal relationships and hypothetical constructs, if we would understand people (such as judges) and their ideologies (such as liberalism). In this book we shall keep one foot planted on empirical reality, and the other will rest on theoretical ideality; and we shall alternatingly shift the weight of analysis and discussion back and forth, from one to the other.

Most books about the Supreme Court are addressed to quite different questions than the ones that I propose to discuss herein. Many such books take the form of commentaries upon the propriety of the public policy content of the Court's decisions. Writers express their agreement or disagreement with the policy norms that they associate with particular decisions of the Court. The Court is variously praised or condemned, for example, because the writers deem wise (or unwise) the Court's current policy line with regard to such matters as the reapportionment of state legislatures, or public school integration. A favorite tactic of academic dissenters from the Court's current policies is to decry the failure of the Court to follow its precedents; obviously, any change in policy necessarily involves a departure from *stare decisis,* so conservative commentators are in a particularly advantageous position to (and often do) mask their disagreement on the merits of the substantive issue behind a smokescreen of discussion about logical consistency, predictability in the law, the confusion of lower courts, the befuddlement of counsel, and the confounding of legal academicians. Closely related is the recent debate which has adorned the pages of legal and political science journals, concerning the ultimate wisdom of having the Court assume a posture of what is termed "judicial activism" as opposed to "judicial restraint." This particular formulation of the underlying issue of liberalism versus conservatism on the Court is personified by an explicit identification of activism with Justice Black and of restraint with the late Justice Frankfurter: these heroic antagonists are seen as having waged a mighty struggle, over the course of the past generation, with the fate of what is termed "our democratic way of life" hanging in the balance. (Other titans of yore, such as Holmes and Brandeis, look down from Olympus; and as in other wars among humans, the advocates of activism and those who favor restraint alike believe that the Olympians are on the side of *their* champion.) As in the case of the *stare decisis* isotope, conservatives stack the deck against liberals by converting to their own purposes what was good liberal dogma only thirty years ago: that courts should not make policies, because for them to do so is to usurp the functions of "popularly responsible" legislatures and chief executives, thereby subverting the basic premises of a democratic polity. The proper function of courts, under this conception, is to uphold traditional values only, and then primarily by enforcing the constitutional rules of the political game. One Harvard law professor created a modest commotion a few years ago, in law school circles and among a few political-scientist public-lawyers, by advocating that the Court follow what he termed "principles of neutrality in constitutional adjudication"; this was essentially an academic brief filed in support of the general position of restraint attributed to Justice (and former Harvard law professor) Frankfurter. I am aware that the interpretation that I have just suggested will be quickly discounted by those who would point to the indisputable facts that long before they joined the Court, Black was a member of the Ku Klux Klan, while Frankfurter was a defender of Sacco and Vanzetti. But I am not so much concerned, for present purposes, in defending my interpretation of the motivations that underlie the current disputations among professors; I do, however, wish to characterize the kind of discussion about the Court that remains in substantial, though diminishing, vogue. It is my hope that the present work may contribute to the further diminution of scholasticism in the study of courts and judges.

I have two primary objectives in writing the book, which is about the political ideologies and attitudes of Supreme Court justices, as manifested in their decision-making behavior. One objective is to explain a theoretical model that I have constructed. The theory is about how and why the justices arrive at the particular decisions that we can observe them to have made. The model of Supreme Court decision-making that I shall present is a logical consequence of the theory of motivation that I shall discuss, and the model has a demonstrable capacity to serve as the basis for making predictions about the future behavior of the justices. Moreover, the predictions that one would make on the basis of the model are in no sense idiosyncratic functions of the subjective intuitions of any particular student of the Court (including myself). Any reader who will go through this book with enough patience to try to understand it ought, logically, to make the same predictions on the basis of the model; and if this were not true, the model would have no scientific value, and I should expect any serious student either of the Supreme Court (or of human behavior more broadly defined) to entertain maximal skepticism about both my theoretical interpretations and my empirical findings. In order to relate the theory to the real-life events that occur in the day-to-day work of the Supreme Court, I have had to develop what may seem to some readers to be an unnecessarily complicated methodology, in order to bridge the hiatus between the raw empirical data of Supreme Court decisions and the abstract hypothetical constructs that social psychologists imply when they speak of political attitudes and ideologies. On this point, I can only ask that judgment be reserved until the reader is in a position to evaluate the results. Elaborate methodologies entail high social and fiscal costs in terms of time, money, and attention; and I hope that I shall be the first to acknowledge my indebtedness to anyone who suggests a simpler way to achieve similar results, with equivalent validity and reliability.

My second primary goal is to make available to other students of the Supreme Court a relatively concise and consistent analysis of the major trends in the Court's policy-making during the period since the end of World War II. In so defining the empirical range of the data that I would examine, to begin with the 1946 Term of the Court, I was consciously motivated to do this in order to articulate my own work with that of Professor C. Herman Pritchett in his book, *The Roosevelt Court: A Study in Judicial Politics and Values, 1937–1947.*[2] I hasten to add that I do this in no spirit of pretentiousness. I am quite aware that this particular book of Pritchett's is the most important and influential book to be published in the past two decades in the general field of constitutional law and politics, and that a whole generation of political scientists—of whom I am one—was compelled to modify, some more radically and others less so, their basic orientation toward the study of the Supreme Court, as a consequence of having read *The Roosevelt Court.* Pritchett's major contribution in that book is implied by the subtitle: "A Study in Judicial *Politics* and *Values.*" From a theoretical point of view, the significance of his work lies in his interpretation of the Court's policies in terms of a single major attitudinal dimension: liberalism and conservatism. By "values," he meant essentially the same thing as I shall discuss when I talk about "attitudes"; and by "politics," he meant the observable differences in the decisional behaviors of the justices, which he attributed to conflict in values among them, and which I shall discuss under the alternative concept of their attitudinal

[2] (New York: Macmillan, 1948.) Pritchett's work focuses upon the decade specified in his title, but his sample of data includes the sixteen terms from 1931 through 1946; hence, his study and mine overlap in the 1946 Term (in order to facilitate direct comparison of the similarities and differences in our theories and methods), and together they span a period of a third of a century: 1931–63.

differences. As he remarked in his preface, what he was attempting to do was "to examine into the *personal* foundations of judicial decisions" by which he meant "that the present justices are motivated by their own preferences"—no more so, he presumed, than had been their predecessors, but certainly no less so, either. This book of mine has the same objective, although I have the great advantage of being in a position to build, not only upon Pritchett's earlier work, but also upon that of many other scholars in the fields of psychology, social psychology, sociology, and cultural anthropology, as well as constitutional law, whose research on the theory and measurement of attitudes has appeared within the past fifteen years. To mention only a few of the most obvious examples from the field of social psychology, the following may suggest the scope of intervening developments: the work on cumulative scaling reported by Louis L. Guttman and others in *The American Soldier;* [3] the studies of the California group in *The Authoritarian Personality* [4] and the many commentaries upon this seminal work; [5] and the monumental *Handbook of Social Psychology.* [6] In the field of political science, I need only note that the political behavior movement was just beginning to emerge as a major influence within the profession at the time Pritchett's book was published, [7] and there was no recognized sub-field of judical behavior for yet another decade. [8]

From a methodological point of view, the importance of Pritchett's book lay in his systematic evaluation of judicial voting behavior, through the use of dyadic agreement matrices. Pritchett was able to array the justices along a dimension of liberalism-conservatism by the relatively simple means of observing the cell frequencies of the major diagonal of four-fold tables: *i.e.,*

[3] In Samuel Stouffer *et al., The American Soldier: Studies in Social Psychology in World War II,* Volume IV: *Measurement and Predication* (Princeton: Princeton University Press, 1950).

[4] Adorno *et al., op. cit.*

[5] *E.g.,* Richard Christie and Marie Jahoda (ed.), *Studies in the Scope and Method of "The Authoritarian Personality"* (Glencoe: The Free Press, 1954).

[6] Gardner Lindzey (ed.), (Reading: Addison-Wesley, 1954), 2 vols.

[7] David B. Truman, "The Impact on Political Science of the Revolution in the Behavioral Sciences," in *Research Frontiers in Politics and Government: Brookings Lectures, 1955* (Washington: Brookings Institution, 1955); Robert A. Dahl, "The Behavioral Approach in Political Science," *American Political Science Review,* Vol. 55 (1961), pp. 763–766; and David Easton, "Introduction: The Current Meaning of 'Behavioralism' in Political Science," especially at p. 21, in James C. Charlesworth (ed.), *The Limits of Behavioralism in Political Science* (Philadelphia: The American Academy of Political and Social Science, 1962); Evron M. Kirkpatrick, "The Impact of the Behavioral Approach on Traditional Political Science," pp. 1–31 in Austin Ranney (ed.), *Essays on the Behavioral Study of Politics* (Urbana: University of Illinois Press, 1962); and Heinz Eulau, *The Behavioral Persuasion in Politics* (New York: Random House, Studies in Political Science No. 42, 1963).

[8] Glendon Schubert, "From Public Law to Judicial Behavior," in Schubert, *op. cit.,* pp. 1–3.

how often pairs of justices agreed in voting together in the majority, and in dissent, in decisions of the Court. He was also able to denote the subsets of justices with relatively high shared interagreement, and by examining the content of opinions in specific decisions, to assign directionality to the continuum and hence also to categorize the ideological positions of the subsets (or "blocs") of justices who manifested high interagreement. Thus, for example, for the Court of the "Nine Old Men" during the 1931–35 Terms, he identified a left or liberal bloc (Brandeis, Cardozo, and Stone), a center or moderate bloc (Hughes and Roberts), and a right or conservative bloc (Van Devanter, Sutherland, Butler, and McReynolds); and for the eight-justice 1945 Term—while Jackson was on leave at Nuremburg—Pritchett identified a four-justice liberal bloc (Rutledge, Murphy, Douglas, and Black) and a four-justice conservative bloc (Reed, Burton, Stone, and Frankfurter). Pritchett was quite explicit that his designations were strictly relative to the membership of the Court at a particular time; therefore, the fact that Stone was identified with a left bloc in 1935 and with a right bloc a decade later did not signify that Stone necessarily had become more conservative in his attitudes; to the contrary, a preferable interpretation was that the set of justices constituting the Court in 1945 occupied a different and more liberal segment of the continuum than those of 1935. What had been the most liberal position in 1935 had become the position of the relatively most conservative members of the Court in 1945; and the liberals of 1945 represented an attitudinal position that was unrepresented on the Court of 1935, just as the conservatives of 1935 represented an attitudinal position that was unrepresented in 1945.

From a substantive point of view, by far the greater portion of Pritchett's book was allocated to his summarization of and commentary upon the opinions of individual justices in discrete cases. Most readers of *The Roosevelt Court* appear to have found this discussion of the cases to be the most useful and valuable part of the book. Pritchett himself seems to have appraised his methodological innovations primarily in instrumental terms: they were important to the extent that they provided clues to insights into the cases, and the "issues" that these raised, that might not otherwise have occurred to him. There is no doubt that the primary focus of his book is upon the political attitudes of the justices, and yet Pritchett was unwilling to base his interpretation of the cases upon such grounds. Cases are described in terms of their "facts," the ad hoc theoretical categories employed by the justices themselves in their opinions, legal doctrines, constitutional principles, and philosophical maxims of judicial parsimony (such as *stare decisis,* or judicial activism versus judicial restraint). Pritchett also made quite explicit the reason for his unwillingness to rely, other than partially and with caution, upon an attitudinal interpretation of judicial responses to the issues raised in cases decided by the Court: "The terms 'liberal' and 'conservative,' though they remain the labels most generally used to distinguish between opposed complexes of preferences in matters of public policy, have largely lost any precision they may once have had in describing the substance of political attitudes." [9] He thought this fundamental theoretical problem could be avoided by substituting, most of the time, the words "left" for liberal and "right" for conservative, and adding the caveat that left and right were "not intended to convey any fixed connotation or impute the possession of any definite set of political principles." [10]

I have thought it necessary to go into this much detail about *The Roosevelt Court,* both because of my own stated goal of articulating this present book to it, and also because the comparison would in any event occur to any reader familiar with the earlier book, and I therefore feel an obligation to be explicit about the respects in which the two books are similar and dissimilar. In theory and methodology, I shall in this book be moving in the same direction as Pritchett, but with considerably more emphasis upon the systematic development of both of these than one will find in the earlier book. From a substantive point of view, the divergence will be even more apparent. I shall undertake relatively little discussion of "the case law," and virtually none from the point of view of my own private views about what might be wise public policy for the Supreme Court to establish. By and large, I think that the political attitudes of Supreme Court justices are a matter of very considerable interest and importance, because of the political roles played by the justices in our polity. The political attitudes of professors, although frequently a matter of transitory concern to their own students, probably have—and I would add, certainly ought to have—less enduring consequences for the fate of the nation. As the late Herman Carey Beyle used to say to *his* students, political scientists have an obligation to their profession to do more for their students than to indoctrinate them with the liberal ethic. I should hope that my own position on the liberalism-conservatism dimension along which I shall array the justices would be as irrelevant to what I shall say in this book as would be my private views regarding, say, the

[9] Pritchett, *op. cit., supra,* pp. 33–34.
[10] *Ibid.,* p. 34.

advisability of taking a finesse or playing for the drop when the four trump out are Q-x-x-x, as declarer I hold K-J-x-x-x, and the Ace lies in dummy. I hasten to add, in all candor, however, that the same cannot be said concerning some of the more "psychological" dimensions that I shall discuss; and I doubt very much that a person with a very high score on dogmatism will read very far in this book.

Instead of venturing a discursive commentary upon individual cases, I shall attempt to provide a substantive interpretation of the major trends in the Court's policy-making during the past seventeen terms, on the basis of measurements of aggregate data relating primarily to the manifest voting behavior and inferred political attitudes of the justices. When I refer to discrete items, therefore, these usually will be justices rather than particular decisions. My view of decisions is that these are the products of sets of judicial attitudes that have been activated by particular stimuli; and from this perspective, the attitudes of the justices are of much more fundamental importance than the decisions. I can well understand that, at one level of analysis, decisions such as the School Segregation Case,[11] or the Tennessee Reapportionment Case,[12] or the New York Bible-Reading Case [13] might be considered to be the events of greatest importance, because it is the decisions which supply the norms which affect the political behavior of millions of Americans and the fortunes of giant corporations such as DuPont and General Motors. My argument is that such a level of analysis, although quite appropriate and adequate for many purposes, clearly is superficial once the question is raised: Why these outcomes instead of alternative or even opposite ones?

Everyone knows that behind the decisions stand the justices and behind the justices there hangs a purple curtain; and from John Marshall's day to our own, the question of real interest always has been: what is behind the curtain? Our generation has given up, as Max Lerner phrased it two decades ago, the notion that the purple curtain enshrouds a constitutional stork; we are all sufficiently legal and political realists to repudiate the mystique of a constitutional law spun in a seamless web. A way of thinking that is quaintly, and quite inaptly, dubbed "sociological jurisprudence" would have us believe that the justices function as a living Ouija board, mirroring in their decisions the "standards of decency" of a "civilized society"; no means of operationalizing this notion appears yet to have

[11] *Brown v. Board of Education*, 347 U. S. 483 (1954).
[12] *Baker v. Carr*, 369 U. S. 186 (1962).
[13] *Engel v. Vitale*, 370 U. S. 421 (1962).

been discovered, nor is it claimed that the justices are a representative sample of American society. An approach that might with greater propriety be termed sociological suggests that the group of justices comprising the Court is partitioned into subgroups, and shifting alignments among subgroups of essentially like-minded justices "explains" the decisions of the Court. This is an intermediate level of analysis which takes us much further than the transcendental casuistry of either mechanical or sociological jurisprudence; but it stops short of providing the answers we seek. In what sense are some justices "like-minded"? How and why do subgroups coalesce and then divide from one case to another on the same decision day? We are led ineluctably to conclude—as Pritchett concluded—that we must analyze the integrals and the differentials of the political attitudes of the justices in order to explain what lies behind the curtain.

There is, of course, a level of analysis beyond the one that we shall employ in this book: what causes a justice to have one syndrome of attitudes instead of another? Why does Black vote and write like Black instead of like Frankfurter? There has been considerable attention paid in recent years to the kind of data appropriate to attempts to come up with scientific answers to such questions as these,[14] and the related scholarship in judicial biography always has sought to provide explanations through the intensive examination of the character-shaping events in the life of the particular unique figure under examination. But I wish to make it clear that questions about the political socialization of judges are beyond the scope of the present endeavor, and cannot be answered on the basis of the kind of evidence that I shall discuss here.

It would be easier, in a way, if I were to employ the language of discourse of mathematical psychology and nonparametric statistics in describing my theory of the way in which the political attitudes of the justices affect their decisions. It would be easier because I have had to think in such terms in order to hypothesize an operationalized concept of judicial decision-making, and to design and carry out empirical research to provide a test of the theory. I shall try, however, to minimize recourse to a technical vocabulary, in order to make the book as accessible as I can for a larger number of readers. A certain amount of what some readers will feel is gobbledegook is inescapable; to them, I extend my apologies in advance with the assurance that the effect may seen to be scientism, but my intent is not.

[14] See Glendon Schubert (ed.), *Judicial Behavior: A Reader in Theory and Research* (Chicago: Rand McNally, 1964), ch. 3; and also *op. cit.* fn. 1, *supra,* Part III.

I start with the assumption that Supreme Court justices can, with very few exceptions, readily be assimilated to Harold Lasswell's category of "the political type." Lasswell identifies the political type with men who seek to play political roles that will permit them to enjoy the power they crave. Lasswell defines the political type as the man who displaces his private motives on public objects, for which he then provides a rationalization in terms of public interest.[15] Lasswell also defines a pair of character types, which he calls "compulsive" and "dramatizing," but which correspond closely to the attitudinal dimension that I shall later discuss as dogmatism-pragmatism. The specific examples that he then presents, for the purpose of illustrating the developmental links between character type, political type, and political role, are three trial court judges: X, Y, and Z.[16] A discussion of Lasswell's typology of roles (*i.e.,* agitator, bureaucratic, detached), which he derived from Freudian premises, would divert us from the point I am now trying to make. But it may be helpful, to those who are familiar with Lasswell's case studies of these three judges, if I anticipate the subsequent exposition of ideological dimensions in this book to the extent of pointing out that Judge X (as described by Lasswell) is traditionalist, authoritarian, individualist; Judge Y is equalitarian, libertarian, collectivist; and Judge Z is equalitarian, authoritarian, collectivist. Judge X is a conservative, Judge Y is a liberal, and Judge Z is a dogmatic liberal. Among recent justices of the Supreme Court, as we shall see, my data indicate that Whittaker is the most similar to Judge X, and Black to Judge Y; none has resembled Judge Z. Lasswell's political formula provides a succinct summary of a broader theoretical framework into which my own theory of attitudes and decision-making will fit. What he calls "private motives" can be explained only on the basis of detailed knowledge about the processes of growth and development of the individual justice beginning with his infancy; and Lasswell advocates the use of psychoanalysis (his term is "the psychiatric interview") in order to uncover information about this range of influences upon judicial character. (He carefully reports with regard to Judge X, for example, that "At the mother's instigation—and this was established from direct testimony—the nurse tried to force the pace of cleanliness training, and imposed a severe regimen on the infant and child"; and I need hardly add that, under a Freudian rather than a Lasswellian typology, X would be classified as an "anal" and Z as an "oral" personality type.) Now, this is not the kind of

[15] Harold D. Lasswell, *Power and Personality* (New York: Norton, 1948), p. 38.
[16] *Ibid.,* pp. 65–88.

relationship that has been investigated thus far by other political scientists who have studied the political socialization of judges; nor is this the kind of psychology with which my present book is concerned. Whatever the ultimate sources of the "private motives" of justices, the displacement of such motives upon "public objects" is a process analogous to the implementation of the attitudes of the justices toward issues of public policy through the act of voting in decisions on cases. Again, I must point out that the kind of example of displacement that Lasswell gives would be a justice who demands excessive exhibitions of deference from his colleagues, counsel, his office staff, his wife and children, etc., in his attempts to compensate for the felt deprivations he suffered as a child owing to what he perceived to be his mother's preference for a favored sibling or for his father. Projective psychology certainly provides one approach to theoretical understanding of the relationship between attitudes and decision-making, and I do not in the least mean to denigrate such an approach. It is not, however, the only psychological approach possible; and I wish to make clear that the kind of psychology that I shall employ is that sometimes denominated as "hard" (as distinguished from "soft," not from "easy") and associated with the use of psychometrics in relation to stimulus-response, cognitive and learning theory. This kind of psychology emphasizes the rational aspects of human thinking and choice-making; and although it seems probable that both rational and irrational processes are operative in the decision-making of Supreme Court justices, I am prepared to make the basic assumption that the former are the more important influences for men in their position. The reason for this is that the roles of Supreme Court justices are defined in such a way as to give maximal emphasis to the importance of rational factors. The legal training of the justices, the institutional traditions of the Court, the defined procedures for the establishment of a record in lower courts and for the exposure of the justices to both written and oral argument, the requirement that the decision of the Court be determined after group discussion and with a micropublic (*i.e.,* within the group) voting procedure, and that the group decision be supported by reasons which must be exposed to the critical scrutiny of dissident members of the group as well as to professional (and other) critics from "out-groups," all of these tend to encourage recourse by the justices to rational rather than irrational ways of thinking.

Not only does the use of such a psychology of rationality seem to provide a better fit for the work of Supreme Court justices; it also offers the advantage of providing a basis for considerably more precise and systematic measurements than would be possible for a researcher attempting to use the projective approach, at least at this time. And not least, data appropriate for the analysis of rationality in Supreme Court decision-making presently are accessible and readily available, while psychoanalytic data about the justices, to the extent that these may exist, neither are nor are likely to become a matter of public record. My interpretation of "displacement" is, therefore, different from Lasswell's, but it is not an unreasonable meaning to supply for the study of Supreme Court justices.

The third and final element in Lasswell's political formula—the rationalization, in terms of public interest, of decisions made because of the displacement of private motives onto public objects—requires little comment. Lasswell used "rationalization" in the Freudian sense, of substituting "for the record" an explanation of motivation acceptable to the ego, for the purpose of sublimating ("hiding from one's self") the actual libidinal reasons for one's acts. I conceive of "rationalization" in a similar but more general sense: a justice offers to his colleagues in conference, and to the general public through his written opinions, sets of reasons to support his votes, which he thinks will be publicly acceptable—and it should be noted that the kinds of reasons that he offers to the microcosmic public of the conference room are not necessarily identical to those that he makes available to the public-at-large, although I should expect the two sets of reasons offered by Supreme Court justices to be much more similar than in the case of almost any other American political decision-makers. The sets of reasons offered by the justices to their macropublic can be distinguished as "rationales"; the reasons that they give each other in conference are not generally accessible, and I have made no attempt to observe them for purposes of this study. However, it seems evident that the whole point of the opinion-writing ritual is to provide acceptable rationales which will protect the justices from personal criticism—and even from personal responsibility—for their decisions. (It was not the justices themselves who ordered racial integration of public schools; it was the Fourteenth Amendment, or the politicians who drafted it or voted for it, or the conscience of American society in mid-century, or the recent research of child psychologists—so say the rationales.) It is not, however, necessary to assume that there is any great amount of tension between the private ideologies of justices, and the public attitudes that are articulated in their written opinions; and my own assumption is that there generally will be very close correspondence between the private beliefs and the public voting and opinion behavior of the Supreme Court justices who comprise my sample of respondents.

My own interests, in undertaking the research upon which this book is based, were not primarily in the Court as an institution, or in the justices as a group of discrete humans, or even in the particular policy norms articulated in the opinions associated with their decisions. The question to which I address myself is this: When men (and, at least in principle, women) play political roles, to what extent are their public acts influenced by their personal beliefs? There is also a closely related methodological question: How can a social scientist study the relationship between political belief and political action, in such a way as to maximize the probability that his findings can be replicated by other scholars, and therefore also to minimize the probability that he is projecting his own predilections onto the political actors whose behavior he seeks to understand? Taken together, these two questions presume a socio-psychological approach to political behavior, in which the purpose of inquiry is to explore the motivational elements of choice in political decision-making. The subjects of such inquiry might be (among others) voters at the polls, legislators, administrators, judges, or lobbyists. Their activities might take place in relationship to any "level" of government, ranging from a rural town to the United Nations. The substantive policies at issue might range from the closing of the town dump to lunar exploration. And from the point of view of political development, the polities might vary from the Congo to the United Kingdom.

Wherefore, therefore, judges? And why, in particular, those of the United States Supreme Court?

This is a perfectly fair question, and one that deserves to be answered. Lawyers, political scientists, and historians already have favored the United States Supreme Court with an overweening emphasis, although they have provided neither extensive nor intensive analyses of the activities of judges of the so-called "lower" courts.[17] But psychologists and sociologists, with very few exceptions, have ignored judges in general and the United States Supreme Court in particular, as appropriate subjects for their own investigations into learning, cognition, motivation, interpersonal relationships, and other aspects of human behavior. Consequently, the Court

---

[17] Herbert Jacob and Kenneth N. Vines, "The Role of State Courts in the Political System," in Schubert (ed.), *Judicial Decision-Making,* pp. 245–256; and Kenneth N. Vines and Herbert Jacob, *Studies in Judicial Politics* (New Orleans: Tulane University Studies in Political Science, Vol. VIII, 1962).

may have been "overstudied," but certainly not from the perspective that I propose. In addition, there are important considerations of research strategy that support an empirical focus on the Court, in order to study attitudinal theory.

One of the major difficulties in studying the motivation of political decision-makers is that of obtaining access to the relevant raw data. In the case of popular elections, for example, we cannot ordinarily observe the decisions of the individual actors, since to do so would violate laws intended to assure the secrecy of the ballot; therefore, we study aggregates of voters, and attempt to relate statistical summarizations of the decisions of voters to aggregate data about the social characteristics and political attitudes of the voting population. The latter information usually is obtained by interviewing samples of voter populations.[18] In the case of legislators, it is possible to observe the decisions of individual legislators in a minority of the voting tallies, in which roll calls are used; otherwise, only nominal data about outcomes of aggregate decisions are available, as in the case of voters. In comparison to voter populations, legislator populations are much smaller and much more stable in composition; and it it not surprising that there is much more of a focus upon discrete individuals and their specific sets of attitudes and social interrelationships in studies of legislative behavior. Background data about legislators usually is readily available, and many legislators make frequent statements purporting to "explain"—to voters and lobbyists and administrators and other clienteles—the reasons for the legislators' own decisions on issues of public policy. Political scientists tended to conclude, long ago, that the validity of legislative rationales was low, and they recently have begun to make use of interviewing techniques in order to acquire more valid information about the attitudes of legislators.[19] Moreover, a commercial reporting service has been providing, for almost two decades, systematic analyses of the voting behavior of members of the Congress, in relation to such variables as political party affiliation, and geographic (*i.e.,* sub-cultural) differences such as Southern/Eastern-Northern-Western, or rural/urban.[20] But attempts to deal with the basic question I have posited—why do voters vote as they do? or why do legislators vote as they do?—have been confronted

[18] See Angus Campbell, Philip E. Converse, Warren E. Miller, and Donald E. Stokes, *The American Voter* (New York: Wiley, 1960).

[19] John C. Wahlke, Heinz Eulau, William Buchanan, and LeRoy C. Ferguson, *The Legislative System: Explorations in Legislative Behavior* (New York: Wiley, 1962).

[20] See *Congressional Quarterly Weekly Report* and *Congressional Quarterly Almanac*, published by Congressional Quarterly Inc., 1735 K St., N.W. Washington, D. C., 20006.

with many problems of theory and methodology, few of which have as yet been satisfactorily resolved. This is not to decry the very important work that has been done in the fields of electoral behavior[21] and legislative behavior;[22] to the contrary. But I do intend to direct attention to the great complexity that arises when one seeks to study individual relationships in a group of 435 congressmen, or even in an average-size upper house of a state legislature, which would be a group of about 35 senators.

What are some of the relative advantages that make it parsimonious to study political attitudes by using Supreme Court justices as a population of respondents? The Court consists of just nine justices, and the size of decision-making groups varies empirically from six to nine. The Court's dockets, and the outcomes of its decisions, are widely available as public records. Over two thousand cases are docketed each year, and over 90 percent of the Court's decisions nominally are refusals to decide the issues of public policy presented in particular cases. The Court does purport to make decisions on the issues in about a hundred and eighty cases a year; and for most of these decisions, formal opinions are written. The nominal function of such opinions is to provide what are intended to be profession-ally and publicly acceptable reasons which explain why each justice voted as he did in the decisions to which the opinions relate. Information about the previous careers and social characteristics of justices is available, and generally in greater depth than is true in the case of legislators; many of the incumbent justices, and almost all of their predecessors, have been the subject of published biographies.[23] Many justices also have written exten-sively *ex cathedra,* thus providing additional information concerning their political attitudes; Douglas and Frankfurter are recent examples. Al-though from some points of view this is a limitation, analysis in other

[21] Seymour M. Lipset, Paul F. Lazarsfeld, Allen H. Barton, and Juan Linz, "The Psychology of Voting: An Analysis of Political Behavior," in Gardner Lindzey (ed.), *op. cit.,* Vol. 2, pp. 1124–1175; Eugene Burdick and Arthur J. Brodbeck (ed.), *American Voting Behavior* (New York: The Free Press, 1959); Robert E. Lane, *Political Life* (New York: The Free Press, 1959); Anthony Downs, *An Economic Theory of Democracy* (New York: Harper, 1957).

[22] Stuart A. Rice, *Farmers and Workers in American Politics* (New York: Columbia Studies in History, Economics and Public Law, No. 253, 1924); Herman C. Beyle, *Identification and Analysis of Attribute-Cluster-Blocs* (Chicago: University of Chicago Press, 1931); Duncan MacRae, Jr., *Dimensions of Congressional Voting* (Berkeley and Los Angeles: University of California Press, 1958); David B. Truman, *The Congressional Party* (New York: Wiley, 1959); John C. Wahlke and Heinz Eulau, *Legislative Behavior: A Reader in Theory and Re-search* (New York: The Free Press, 1959).

[23] For the most complete list of biographical materials on the justices, see John R. Schmid-hauser, "The Justices of the Supreme Court: A Collective Portrait," *Midwest Journal of Po-litical Science,* Vol. 3 (1959), pp. 50–55.

respects is facilitated by the relative smallness of the universe population of justices; fewer than one hundred different individuals have been members of the Court since its establishment in 1790. (My sample of 18 respondents for the present study includes a fifth of all the justices who have ever been members of the United States Supreme Court.)

Other data are available, at least potentially, but little use has been made of them thus far. For example, systematic direct observation of the court-room behavior of the justices on the bench, in the reading of opinions when decisions are announced and, probably much more importantly, when oral argument is heard in cases under consideration, might add considerably to our knowledge about such matters as the personality differences among the justices, their interpersonal relationships, and their attitudes toward both their own roles and the issues raised for decision. In effect, the Court in public session provides a laboratory situation, main-tained on a more or less continuing basis and at public expense, which not a single social scientist appears thus far ever to have exploited for scientific purposes. The reason for this may well be that lawyers and political scientists have lacked the technical training in theory and methodology to do the job, while social psychologists, who know how to carry out much more complicated and difficult research relying upon direct observation as the primary source of data, have failed to perceive the Court (or courts generally) as relevant situses for their work. In a sense, social psychologists have perceived judges as "belonging" to lawyers and political scientists, notwithstanding the recognition of "law" and "lawyers" as appropriate subjects for certain types of sociological inquiry.[24] Perhaps the social psychologists have been anesthetized by the writings about judges and courts by lawyers and political scientists, who have tended to describe attitudinal and behavioral differences among justices in terms of meta-physical abstractions, such as the "philosophical systems" that are usually substituted for the human similarities and dissimilarities among justices.

There are, of course, limitations to the study of political attitudes via the justices. Certain data are largely or completely unavailable, because access to them is foreclosed. More than one "student of the Court" (as many legal scholars and political scientists classify themselves) doubtless has subli-mated libidinal yearnings for a range of data that could become available only by bugging the conference room, since the Court's observed customs

---

[24] Cf. the recent issue of *The American Behavioral Scientist,* on the "Frontiers of Legal Re-search," Vol. VII, No. 4 (December 1963); and particularly the article by Alfred de Grazia and Charles L. Ruttenberg: "Innovators in the Study of the Legal Process," pp. 48–52.

prescribe that no written record be kept of decision-making discussions among the justices as a group, nor are any persons other than the justices themselves even admitted to the conference room when they are in session. Such secret and—in terms of the prevailing professional ethos—lascivious thoughts do suggest, however, an awareness, even on the part of traditionalists, of the importance of socio-psychological dimensions to an adequate understanding of the work of the Court; one difference between traditionalists and behavioralists is that the former have "given up"—without ever having tried to acquire it—a kind of knowledge that, as I intend to demonstrate, is accessible by less direct methods of observation. For even if we could bug the Court's conference room—or better yet, install therein a televiewer (in the fashion of Big Brother in Orwell's *1984*) or best, station an observer or a team of social scientists in the conference room—in each situation we should have to cope with new problems of theory and methodology. As soon as the justices became aware that they were playing for a macro- instead of a micropublic audience, we might anticipate more or less extensive adaptations in their behaviors.[25] We should never expect to be able to "get at" whatever is now revealed, about the attitudes of individual justices, by their speech and demeanor at a conference that is secret both in principle and in practice. Even if we could, we might be disappointed: it is entirely possible that the role structure of the conference may be such that observation of its activities would develop data that reveal considerably more about the attitudes of the justices toward each other than toward the issues of public policy confronting them for decision. Informal conferences between subsets of justices, and particularly between pairs, probably would provide better data for getting at their political attitudes. Systematic interviews with the justices themselves, and with their administrative assistants ("law clerks") might be even more valuable. Most of these data probably will remain inaccessible, although occasional and limited interviewing might prove to be feasible. Memoranda exchanged among the justices provide a source of data that can be and have been utilized, although only after a considerable time lag, since the usual entree is through library deposits of the private papers of deceased justices,

[25] Cf. Max Gluckman's report of his own role as an observer of judicial proceedings, in his *The Judicial Process Among the Barotse of Northern Rhodesia* (New York: The Free Press, 1955), pp. 11–12, 35; and my own comment in the Introductory Note to ch. 2, "Cultural Anthropology and Judicial Systems," in Schubert (ed.) *Judicial Behavior: A Reader in Theory and Research;* and William J. Hanna, "Image-Making in Field Research: Some Tactical and Ethical Problems of Research in Tropical Africa," *American Behavioral Scientist,* Vol. 8 (January 1965), pp. 15–20.

with use restricted to items relating to other persons who also are dead. Such exploitation is further limited, typically, by the historical interests of the researchers, who have tended to fail to ask of the data the questions, about judicial decision-making behavior, for which they might have provided relevant evidence.[26]

The immediately preceding paragraphs may indicate that I am quite aware that a complete knowledge of the political attitudes and decision-making behavior of Supreme Court justices would require the observation of these many events, such as the hearing and the conference and the *tête-à-tête* and the subconscious minds of individual justices, that I have not observed. But partial knowledge, if based upon systematic observations and measurements, and related to other knowledge about human behavior, ought to be much more useful than guesses or intuitions. The fact that we cannot study everything that we would like to be able to study surely does not preclude our venturing the modest beginnings that may be possible now. The model of the Court which I shall discuss in this book certainly is incomplete, from a socio-psychological point of view; whether it is adequate unto its own day depends upon the extent to which it proves useful in extending our present knowledge about political attitudes and decision-making behavior. I anticipate that the theory of attitudes that I shall present is generalizable, and that with appropriate methodological modifications, it should be possible to replicate my findings about United States Supreme Court justices by similar studies of judges of other courts. Indeed, I assume that the theory of attitudes to be presented here rests upon even more fundamental communalities in human behavior, and that it should be applicable to the decision-making behavior of persons acting in adjudicatory roles in private as well as public social structures and irrespective of their formal status as "judges." Whether my anticipations and assumptions are correct can be demonstrated, of course, by further empirical research in the political attitudes of other judicial or adjudicatory respondent populations.

Thus, my objective is to investigate a theory of attitudes that is much broader in scope than an explanation of judicial decision-making. It is also my expectation that the specific methodology, which I have developed in

[26] There are, however, exceptions, as exemplified by Alexander M. Bickel, *The Unpublished Opinions of Mr. Justice Brandeis: The Supreme Court at Work* (Cambridge: Harvard University Press, 1957); and by Walter F. Murphy, "In his own Image: Mr. Chief Justice Taft and Supreme Court Appointments," *The Supreme Court Review* (1961), pp. 159–193, and also "Chief Justice Taft and the Lower Court Bureaucracy: A Study in Judicial Administration," *Journal of Politics,* Vol. 24 (1962), pp. 453–476.

order to study the Court as an empirical example, will prove useful for the analysis of the relationship between political attitudes and decision-making behavior in other relatively small groups, such as other appellate courts, administrative boards and commissions, legislative committees, municipal councils, and possibly the relatively small chambers that exist in some state legislatures. Indeed, the methodology is potentially useful whenever the empirical problem is that of measuring attitudinal differences among a small number of respondents who are presented with a large number of stimuli, under circumstances such that the group decision-making process is highly stylized and quite routine, and it is reasonable to suspect that the stimuli raise questions about a small number of basic values toward which the respondents' attitudes are functions of consistently high levels of cognition.

Chapter 2 · THEORY AND A MODEL

THERE ARE THREE principal sources that have functioned as the well-springs for my own work, both theoretical and methodological, in this book. These persons upon whose earlier theoretical work I have relied are all social psychologists who have made major contributions to the field of attitude measurement: Louis L. Thurstone, who pioneered in the development of multiple factor analysis;[1] Clyde H. Coombs, whose work in the theory of data and nonmetric factor analysis was critical to my own thinking about the possibility of combining multiple factor analysis and multidimensional cumulative scaling in a composite model;[2] and Louis Guttman, whose work in the theory of linear cumulative scaling and in the principal and elementary components of cumulative scales is of fundamental importance to both the theory underlying my model, and its empirical validation.[3] The work of all three of these men is well known among social psychologists, and for present purposes, I shall indicate only how it bears upon my own model.

Attitudinal Theory

VECTORS OF THE MIND

Thurstone developed both a geometric theory of and a statistical method for investigating the elementary components of a correlation matrix. His basic assumption was that if the behavior of a group of persons was intercorrelated, the correlations must reflect the extent to which the members of the group were individually correlated with the set of dimensions

[1] Louis L. Thurstone, *Multiple-Factor Analysis: A Development and Expansion of* The Vectors of Mind (Chicago: University of Chicago Press, 1947).

[2] Clyde H. Coombs, *A Theory of Data* (New York: Wiley, 1964).

[3] Louis Guttman, "The Principal Components of Scalable Attitudes" and "A New Approach to Factor Analysis: The Radex," ch. 5 and 6 in Paul F. Lazarsfeld (ed.) *Mathematical Thinking in the Social Sciences* (New York: The Free Press, 1954), pp. 216–348.

22

relevant to their behavior. The effect of this approach was to differentiate a correlation matrix into component parts, which Thurstone called factors. Such factors were assumed by Thurstone to be bi-polar, so that a person might be correlated in either of two directions with a dimension, the semantic polarity of which must be assigned—from a statistical or geometrical point of view, arbitrarily—by the investigator. In his own famous example, "minus cheerfulness" was equivalent to "plus grouchiness." The first factor to be "extracted" from the correlation matrix, by means of the standard statistical methods which I shall not discuss,[4] was assumed to represent the dimension for which the communality—the sum of the squares of the individual correlations with the dimension—was highest. In other words, the first factor represented whatever it was that the members of the group had most in common that affected the aspect of their behavior that had been observed. The second factor to be extracted represented the next most important dimension, in the defined sense, and so on. In general, the size of the correlations of the original matrix would be further reduced each time a factor was extracted; and assuming that there were n individuals in the group, the cells of the residual matrix all would equal zero after the $(n\text{-}1)$th factor had been extracted. (In practice, only approximations of zero would be anticipated at this stage, because of error variance in the observations of the raw data, the rounding of decimals during the computations, and other sources of chance variation.) It was possible, of course, that the first m factors to be extracted might account for so much of the communality in the behavior under investigation that the mth residual matrix would contain cell entries smaller than the expected range of error variance, in which case an investigator usually would cease factoring at that point. (There have been long-standing technical problems relating to the development of an objective criterion for determining the rank of a matrix or, which amounts to the same thing, when to stop factoring; a full understanding of this and some other statistical problems relating to factor analysis is unnecessary to a comprehension of my own use of the method.) One rough test of the sufficiency of the number of factors extracted is to sum the dyadic cross-products of the individual correlations (usually called "loadings") with each dimension, which should approximate the cell entries in the original correlation matrix. Whether any pair of individuals is positively or negatively correlated in the original matrix depends, of

[4] Thurstone, *op. cit.*, ch. 8; Benjamin Fruchter, *Introduction to Factor Analysis* (Princeton: Van Nostrand, 1954), ch. 5; Harry H. Harman, *Modern Factor Analysis* (Chicago: University of Chicago Press, 1960), ch. 10; and cf. ch. 3, *infra.*

course, upon whether, in general, their respective loadings on the common dimensions are in the same or in different directions. In addition to the dimensions common to at least two persons, there might be dimensions specific to each individual, as well as the error variance already mentioned; so the total variance for any individual's behavior would be the combination of his common variance (loadings on the shared dimensions) and his unique (specific plus error) variance.

An equivalent discussion of the same set of relationships can be made in geometric terms. Although such a discussion readily can be generalized for any finite set of common factors, I shall select a set of three factors for purposes of exemplification. This will keep the discussion simpler and more accessible to readers accustomed to thinking of spatial relationships in terms of the three-dimensional Euclidean (and apparent real) world; and there is the additional convenience that the model of the Supreme Court that I shall construct also will be three-dimensional. Factors are assumed to be lines of the same standard length, ranging from $+1.00$ to -1.00; and it is further assumed, for purposes of defining the genotypic space (*i.e.,* inferred and hypothetical, as distinguished from the phenotypic or empirical level of description), that each factor is orthogonal to each other factor. Factor I, therefore, intersects Factor II at right angles to form a square, since the point of intersection is at the zero or midpoint of each factor; and Factor III is perpendicular to that plane, intersecting at its own zero point the intersection of Factors I and II. (The statistical method of factor analysis, in the process of extraction, treats each factor as orthogonal to the others; and orthogonality is the geometric equivalent of statistical independence. It does not necessarily follow, however, that these orthogonal factors have a recognizable psychological meaning; to the contrary, it is usually assumed to be both unlikely and coincidental if they do. But the genotypic space is initially defined in terms of orthogonal factorial reference axes, since this is a computationally convenient way to determine the positions of the points representing the individuals in the space. The latter step is accomplished by using the set of loadings on the factors, for each individual; these are, it will be recalled, correlation coefficients which range, like the factors themselves, from $+1.00$ to -1.00, and they provide a set of Cartesian coordinates which uniquely locate each individual in the three-dimensional space. The set of points representing the individuals in the genotypic space is called the configuration, which remains invariant under any rotation of the factorial reference axes. Of course, when the position of the reference axes is changed, the loadings of the individual-points on the axes also are transformed, and hence the individual correlations with these axes change even though the positions of the points have not changed. The configuration of points may be viewed, alternatively, as a set of vectors which are imbedded in the space, and whose interrelationships may be measured by an infinite number of frames of reference (*i.e.,* sets of reference axes).

Three orthogonal reference axes define a unit sphere (*i.e.,* with a radius equal to one) and Thurstone discusses three-dimensional factorial space as spherical. This is, of course, the geometrically correct view. In my own model, I shall talk about three-dimensional relationships as though the genotypic space were a cube, with length, breadth, and width all equal to two units. My reason for doing this is that I hope thereby to facilitate reader perception of graphic portrayals of spatial relationships, but it should be remembered that all eight corners of my cube, and also of the planar perspectives of the cube, are quite imaginary vacua; the sphere is encased by a tangential cube, and it is the sphere which contains the psychological content.

The implication of rotating the reference axes is that, if they are no longer orthogonal in their rotated positions, then they must be correlated; and indeed, the cosine of the angle included by any pair of axes in the factorial space is the measure of the degree of their correlation.[5] Since the reference axes have defined polarity, correlations between them may be either positive or negative, and may range from +1.00 (in which case both the polarity and the lines of the two axes coincide) to −1.00 (coincident lines but with opposite polarity); and as we already have observed, a correlation of 0.00 signifies a right-angle intersection of the two axes. It is logically apparent that if any pair of reference axes for a three-dimensional factorial space are rotated to a position of coincidence (*i.e.,* maximum correlation), then the three-dimensional space has been in effect *folded* into a plane, the boundaries of which are defined by the joint axis (the two that have been rotated to a common position) and the third axis. It is also apparent that the third axis could be rotated to the same position as the joint axis, the effect of which would be to enfold the plane into a single line. The configuration of individual points, although itself invariant, can project orthogonally upon an infinite number of planes which pass through the origin and intersect the space of the sphere; the points themselves will lie upon such a plane only coincidentally, however. Simi-

[5] Thurstone, *op. cit.,* pp. 63, 126; Fruchter, *op. cit.,* p. 31; and Hans J. Eysenck, *The Psychology of Politics* (London: Routledge and Kegan Paul, 1954), p. 115.

larly, the individual points will project orthogonally upon any of an infinite number of lines which pass through the origin and intersect the space of the sphere; and the length of the line connecting any two points, which represents the distance between them, in the three-dimensional space, can be measured by computations based upon the known reference axis coordinates (*viz.,* the original set of factor loadings). Evidently, if the genotypic space is three-dimensional, and this corresponds to the dimensionality of the phenotypic level of behavior, then the effect of observing the point projections upon a plane necessarily will be to distort perception of the spatial relationships among the individual points. Such distortion would not occur if all points lay in the field of the plane, but in that event, the third dimension would be non-functional, because the correlation matrix would have a rank of only two and the relevant genotypic space would be two-dimensional. On the other hand, there might be empirical grounds for working with a three-dimensional space, in which there is reason to believe that a plane of particular psychological significance is imbedded, in order to recover the two-dimensional genotypic space of the plane. There are such empirical grounds for focusing attention upon an imbedded two-dimensional plane in the three-dimensional space of my model of the Supreme Court, although I shall reserve discussion of these grounds until a later point.

UNFOLDING MULTIDIMENSIONAL SPACE

In his general theory of data,[6] Coombs classifies the mapping and the analysis of the recorded observations of raw psychological data according to three criteria: whether (1) the observations are of one or two pairs of points; (2) a pair consists of an individual's ideal-point and a stimulus-point, or of two stimulus-points; and (3) the measurement relationship of the pair (or pairs) of points is one of ordinality or proximity. The joint application of these three criteria results, of course, in eight categories, and both factor analysis and cumulative scaling are mapped into the same octant of Coombs' classification chart: both involve ordinal measurement of the relationship between a pair of points drawn from distinct sets (*i.e.,* a pair consists of an individual's ideal-point and a stimulus-point). At the level of abstraction of Coombs' theory of data, both metric and nonmetric factor analysis and cumulative scaling are conceptualized as alternative approaches to the same basic measurement problem.

By an individual's "ideal-point," Coombs refers to that particular combi-

---

[6] Coombs, *op. cit.,* ch. 1.

nation of the relevant dimensions which best approximates the person's own syndrome of attitudes; such a point is, of course, an abstraction (to what may seem to be an extreme degree) of the real person, but it is an abstraction of those characteristics of the individual's personality that are most significant and relevant to the investigation of his choice-making in regard to questions of public policy. (It would doubtless hinder rather than facilitate the investigation if, for example, the dimensions along which the ideal-point is measured were to include such physiological characteristics as height, or length of nose, even though such aspects of personal physiognomy may well be correlated with individual personality.) What Coombs proposes is that the dimensions of human personality relevant to the population and question under investigation can be represented symbolically by a point in a postulated genotypic space of any dimensionality. Similarly, the questions to which individuals respond may, under appropriate decision-making circumstances, be termed stimuli and measured along the same dimensions as the attitudes of the individuals; and it follows that stimuli syndromes may also be represented by points in a genotypic space. Defining the subscript i as the generic category for an individual's ideal-point, and j as the corresponding category for stimulus-points, Coombs then defines a *joint* genotypic space as one which includes sets of both i- and j-points.

Although it is important, for certain psychological inquiries, to distinguish between an individual's personal *values* (*i.e.,* his beliefs or "accepted truths") and his *attitudes* (predisposition to respond to a stimulus in a particular way), it happens that this distinction is unimportant to my model of the Court. I shall refer to attitudes of the justices, and I shall mean by "attitude" their predisposition to respond in particular ways when measured along certain dimensions. But I shall use the term "value" to refer to the attributes of the *stimuli,* which raise particular questions that also can be measured along the same dimensions. Coombs hypothesizes that when an individual responds to a stimulus, his mental process may be conceptualized as that of making a comparison between his ideal-point and the stimulus-point, *in the genotypic space.* Coombs discusses two alternative models of the measurement relationship between an i-point and a j-point pair. According to the proximity model, the individual accepts (responds positively to) all stimuli whose j-points he perceives as being located within a critical distance from his own i-point (*i.e.,* the position with which he identifies himself—where he perceives himself to be located in the space); and he rejects (responds negatively to) all other stimuli that he perceives to be located elsewhere in the same space. According to the ordinal model, however, both the *i*-point and the *j*-point are compared in relation to the directionality of the dimensions which define the space: the individual responds positively if his own position equals or exceeds that of the stimulus, and otherwise he responds negatively. As I previously have stated, it is Coombs' ordinal model that is pertinent to measurement relationships in factor analysis and in cumulative scaling. His own precise definition of the "dominance" relationship for the ordinal choice function is:

(1) $$P_{hIJ} \geq 0 \leftrightarrow i > j.$$

In other words, "if, and only if, at the moment *h*, the point corresponding to the individual dominates the point corresponding to the stimulus, the individual responds positively to the stimulus," where P_{hIJ} is defined as the distance between the pair of points in the joint space of the relevant dimensions, and where $\leftrightarrow$ signifies "implies and is implied by." [7]

Coombs and his associates also have worked on methods and models for multidimensional extension of the linear Guttman model of cumulative scaling, and Coombs and Kao [8] have shown that metric factor analysis and multidimensional cumulative scaling (nonmetric factor analysis) may— given suitable data—provide alternative methods of data processing for the recovery of *i*- and *j*-points in the same genotypic space. Although the raw data for Supreme Court decision-making do not provide sufficient information to permit deterministic analysis of voting choices by means of multidimensional scaling techniques, it is useful to borrow a concept developed in the work in multidimensional unfolding, since I assume the theoretical equivalence of factor analysis, for which the data are adequate. The relevant concept is that of the *individual compensatory* composition model,[9] according to which (1) it is the individual (rather than the stimulus) who determines the weighting function, which is considered to be constant over all stimuli for the responses of that individual; and (2) it is not essential that the individual exceed the stimulus on all relevant dimensions, since it may be possible for him to compensate for his deficiency on one dimension with an excess on other dimensions—depend-

---

[7] *Ibid.,* p. 23.

[8] Clyde H. Coombs and Richard C. Kao, "On a Connection between Factor Analysis and Multidimensional Unfolding," *Psychometrika,* Vol. 25 (September 1960), pp. 219–231.

[9] Coombs, *op. cit.* fn. 2 *supra,* ch. 12; Warren S. Torgerson, *Theory and Methods of Scaling* (New York: Wiley, 1958), pp. 352–359.

ing upon the precise location of both the i-point and the j-point, and the number of dimensions, which obviously must be more than one.

CUMULATIVE SCALING

Guttman's model of the linear cumulative scale is as follows: a set of stimuli are hierarchically organized in a consistent relationship of dominance (as defined by Coombs), so that $a_j < b_j < c_j < d_j \ldots n_j$. An equivalent statement would be that the j-points are arrayed along a single dimension in the ordered sequence: $a, b, c, d, \ldots n$. Whatever the value represented by the dimension, a represents less of it than does b, which in turn represents less than c, and so on, with n representing the greatest quantity of the value of any of the points in the set; or, again, in relationship to the defined directionality of the dimension, a is the most negative and n is the most positive for this set of points. Guttman's own well-known example of a quantitative cumulative scale was a series of questions about height,[10] such as:

a. Are you at least four feet tall?
b. Are you at least four and a half feet tall?
c. Are you at least five feet tall?
n. Are you at least seven feet tall?

Several professional basketball centers might respond positively to the nth question; and if their replies were to be consistent, they ought also to respond positively to all other questions in the series. Most midgets, on the other hand, ought to respond negatively to all questions in the set, assuming that they intend their replies to be truthful; and in particular, having responded negatively to question a, they ought to respond negatively to all other questions in the set. A person of average height should, if he is to respond consistently, say yes to questions a–c and to one or more of the other questions between c and n in the set; but having replied negatively to any question, he should then reply negatively to all remaining questions. If we assign the directionality "tallness" to the scale, the dominance relationships then correspond to our previous mathematical example. We might substitute a less readily quantifiable variable, and measure individual perceptions of stimuli arrayed along a dimension with the assigned content

---

[10] As Bert F. Green has remarked, a more analogous set of questions, to the items used in attitudinal investigations by questionnaires, would be:
"Are you taller than a table?"
"Are you taller than the head of a pony?"
"Are you taller than a good-sized bookcase?"
See his article on "Attitude Measurement," chapter 9 in Gardner Lindzey (ed.), *Handbook of Social Psychology* (Reading: Addison-Wesley, 1954), Vol. 1, especially pp. 353–354.

and directionality of "sweetness." Or we might inquire about respondents' attitudes toward some political value such as "freedom of speech."

Guttman's linear cumulative scale may be classified, in terms of Coombs' theory, as a one-dimensional joint genotypic space—that is, both i- and j-points are arrayed along the same line. This implies an ordinal relationship among i-points as well as among j-points. If the positions on the scale of the j-points are known, then the ordinal (and the approximate metric) position of any i-point can be determined from the individual's responses to the stimuli. Conversely, *if* the position on the scale of the i-points of the respondents were known, then the ordinal ranking of the j-points could be determined, assuming that the i-points were sufficiently numerous and sufficiently scattered that each j-point lay between two i-points. In particular, and in the absence of error, it would be possible theoretically to predict an individual's responses to all stimuli, once his rank (*i.e.*, the ordinal position of his i-point on the scale) was determined. Empirically, a certain amount of error usually is found in cumulative scales, due to individual differences in cognition, in the perception of the stimuli, or due to errors in the observation and processing of the data by the analyst, or to several of these causes. Both the measurement of inconsistent responses in a linear cumulative scale, and the definition of a criterion of maximum acceptable error in such a scale, are essentially empirical rather than theoretical problems; and I shall discuss these matters in greater detail in the context of the chapter on methodology.

Although a linear cumulative scale is one-dimensional by definition, we can consider the relationships of such a scale in a space of two or higher dimensionality. I shall assume that the metric of the scale ranges from $+1.00$ to -1.00, and that its zero point coincides with the zero point (where the reference axes intersect) of the space. The scale then becomes an axis imbedded in the space; its position can be defined precisely in terms of its correlations (cosines) with the reference axes; or, alternatively, in terms of the Cartesian coordinates which locate the termini of the scale (on the rim of the sphere, if the space be three-dimensional): such coordinates are functionally equivalent to loadings on the orthogonal (unrotated) factorial dimensions. If the space were two- or three-dimensional, and the known positions of the i-points were scattered in the space, then the ranking of the individuals on the scale would be determined not by their positions *on* the scale—since the condition of scattering implies that most i-points would not lie upon any common line—but rather by the orthogonal projections upon the scale from the i-points. From a psychological point of view, the scattering of the *i*-points means that the individual attitudinal syndromes are combinations of *another* attitude (or other attitudes) in addition to the scale axis that we have been discussing. If a set of two or more scale axes were hypothesized to be located in a space of higher dimensionality, they would define a plane or hyperplane embedded in the factorial space. Moreover, if the imbedded space defined by the scale axes were assumed to include the most relevant psychological content that was of particular interest in an investigation, then we might say that the genotypic space was imbedded in the factorial space. Thus, for example, a set of two scale axes would define a genotypic plane which might be imbedded in a three-dimensional factorial space. Coombs has suggested that a factorial space always includes the genotypic space plus one extra dimension,[11] which he considers to be a measure of the distance separating all other (say, *i*-) points from the axis passing through the *i*-point that is closest to all of the others. I have considered this theory, but it does not appear to satisfy my own empirical data on the Supreme Court. In Chapter 8 I shall discuss an alternative theory of the psychological meaning to be attributed to the difference in dimensionality between the two-dimensional genotypic space of the plane bounded by a pair of scale axes, and the three-dimensional factorial space, in my model of the Court.

SCALE COMPONENT CURVES

Guttman has suggested a distinction between linear cumulative scales, which he termed "simplexes," and a more complex attitudinal structure which he designated the circumplex.[12] According to Guttman, the major structural basis of differentiation among stimuli whose points are arrayed along a simplex is the difference in their degrees of complexity, in the previously defined sense that for any given point, something has been added to whatever content is associated with points of lesser rank; hence points of low rank are relatively simple, while points of high rank are relatively complex. But two different simplexes, Guttman thought, would be of "equal rank," and would differ not in complexity but rather in the universes of content that they measured. In other words, the relationship between two linear scales in a plane—Guttman specifically used two-dimensional space for his example—would be circular rather than hierarchical. From this I hypothesize that *the i-point relationships in the genotypic space of the plane defined by the scale axes should be a circumplex.*

Guttman also has proposed that a distinction be made among the three

[11] Coombs and Kao, *op. cit.* fn. 8 *supra.*
[12] Guttman, *op. cit.,* ch. 6.

different sets of components which he associated with a perfect simplex—*i.e.,* with the correlation matrix for an error-free linear cumulative scale. The first set consists of the *semantic* components, which define the content to be observed. In my model of the Supreme Court, for which the correlation matrices are not perfect simplexes but rather are examples of what Guttman calls a "quasi-simplex," I shall define two major semantic components of the phi matrices, and subsets of semantic subcomponents for each scale; and I shall also postulate several minor semantic components. Chapter 5 will discuss both the major and the minor semantic components of the phi matrices; and Chapter 6 will discuss the semantic subcomponents of the two major scales. The second type distinguished by Guttman consists of a set of *elementary* components; these "represent a hypothesis as to why the observations are interrelated the way they are." [13] In my own model, the manifest relationships among joint-scale respondent types which are discussed in Chapter 7, in relationship to the *i*-points and scale axes within the factorial frame of reference, constitute one set of elementary components of the phi matrices. The third type of relationship, that represented by the principal components, constitutes (according to Guttman) a deeper and more fundamental basis for analyzing the structure of a linear cumulative scale. In Chapter 8 I shall discuss a theory of latent relationships among the elementary components of the phi matrices. This theory is derived from Guttman's theory of principal components and of how perfect simplex matrices (*i.e.,* linear cumulative scales) are interrelated in circumplex and radex structures.

Guttman gradually developed a psychological interpretation for the first four principal components of perfect linear cumulative scales after having initially identified their geometric characteristics on the basis of mathematical analysis. I shall now summarize Guttman's description of the geometric properties of the first three principal components and his psychological interpretation of these curves.

The first principal component consists of a monotone transformation of the cumulative scale ranks, in terms of the criterion of maximizing the internal consistency in the sense of least-squares. Maximizing differences between subgroups of respondents is equivalent to minimizing differences within such subgroups; or in other words, the effect is to minimize the variances within those segments of the continuum where subsets of *i*-points are densely clustered. Scores on the metric of the first component should be isomorphic with ranks on the cumulative scale; that is to say, when these

[13] *Ibid.,* p. 216.

are plotted against each other, the resulting curve should be a close approximation of a straight line (*i.e.,* one with *no* bends in it).

The second principal component has one bend, and is U- or J-shaped. The turning point of the bend is equivalent to the zero point of the cumulative scale; and according to Guttman, the bending point of a second principal component remains invariant with regard to empirical differences arising from sampling, provided that the procedures that he prescribes are employed to locate the "true" zero point. Since my data for the Supreme Court are not based upon the responses of the justices to a questionnaire with prefabricated questions about the psychological dimensions that I seek to investigate, I cannot employ Guttman's recommended procedures to locate the bending points of principal components. Hence, the bending points in curves that I shall subsequently discuss *are* functions of the particular sample of cases that were decided by the Court, and not the invariant points which (in theory) exist.

The third principal component has two bends, which must take place on opposite sides of the zero point, according to Guttman's mathematical calculations. The characteristic shape of the curve is that of the letter N, as though an inverted U segment were joined at the zero point with an upright U segment to form the curve.

The psychological interpretation that Guttman suggested for these three types of curves is as follows. The first component represents attitudes towards the content, and in effect is a reproduction of the cumulative scale, with the same directionality and the same rank order of points. The first principal component differs from the cumulative scale in that it groups the points on the line into subsets, thus providing information about which persons are closest together and which are furthest apart in their attitude toward the value which constitutes the scale variable. The second component measures intensity, with the point of the bend denoting the "zero" point of indifference or minimal intensity of attitude toward the scale variable, while the tails of the curve identify the persons who are most extreme and therefore most intense in their attitude. Guttman plots the cumulative scale (*i.e.,* the content variable) as the abscissa in a graph of the intensity curve, and therefore the content metric ranges from the minimal score (or rank), at the left, to the maximal score (or rank) at the right. The ordinate is a separate scale of items designed to measure how strongly a respondent believes in the replies he gives to substantive questions about the value, irrespective of the direction of his answers. The second principal component curve measures the intensity of attitude of those persons least favorable to the scale variable (to the left of the bending point), and also the intensity of attitude of those most favorable (to the right of the bending point). However, Guttman also has suggested that *"the zero point of an attitude acts as a pivot in U-shaped relations with other outside variables."* [14] It is this suggestion that I have found most stimulating in application to the present work.

The psychological meaning that Guttman associated with the third principal component was what he termed "closure," by which he meant the extent to which respondents had made up their minds about the questions of valuation raised by the scale variable. The second principal component defines its own zero point as that of the third component also, although the shape of the third component curve is such that its zero point is located near the median of the segment between the two bends. Guttman suggested that if a cutting line parallel to the content (abscissal) metric were drawn through the zero point, then all points on segments of the curve above the cutting line would be positive on closure, and all other points would be negative on closure, toward the attitude represented by the scale variable. Thus, persons in the left tail of the curve would be the most uncertain of all about their intense negative attitude toward the content, while persons in the right tail of the curve would be the most certain about their intense positive attitude toward the content. He went on to develop a psychological typology according to which persons in the left tail were even more "prejudiced" than were persons in the right tail of the "closure" curve. Guttman's psychological interpretation may make some sense for the data with which he worked in developing it—those data related to the extent to which Israeli soldiers had alternative plans to remaining in the army—but his theory of closure makes no sense as an interpretation of my own data on the Supreme Court.

For interpreting relationships between one scale variable and another ("outside") scale variable, I propose a substitute theory of the psychological meaning of third principal component-type curves, which seems to make better sense in application to my own data (as discussed in Chapter 8). My own hypothesis is based upon a logical extension of the rationale which supports the interpretation given by Guttman to the second component curve. If the second and third curves share (in a mathematical sense) the same zero point, and they relate to the same joint attitudinal content, then

---

[14] *Ibid.*, p. 230. Emphasis added. Cf. Uriel G. Foa, "Scale and Intensity Analysis in Opinion Research," *International Journal of Opinion and Attitude Research*, vol. 4 (1950), pp. 205–207.

perhaps the bends on opposite sides of the zero point distinguish further between those respondents who are less and those who are more intense in their attitude, both for those who are positive and also for those who are negative. Thus, the additional information that the third curve would provide would be a more precise differentiation between the two sets of extremists (in the tails) and the moderates.

This proposed alternative interpretation for third component-type curves seems to be much more consistent with the fundamental assumptions about the attitudinal structure of cumulative scales than does Guttman's own theory of closure. The basic notion, it will be recalled, is that an attitude is scalable because of its cumulative—that is, its hierarchical— structure: as one moves in the positive direction of the scale, each rank (or point) includes everything (in the way of relevant content) that any lesser rank or point includes, *plus* some additional content—and it is the additional content that accounts for the higher rank of the dominant point. This is precisely the way in which I am proposing it would be most useful to think about the set of *psychological* structural relationships among the principal component curves of a cumulative scale. The content scale itself provides certain manifest information: the dominance rank order of points in a (psychologically) arbitrarily specified direction. The curve for the first principal component provides that same information, *plus* additional information about the relative distance separating the points arrayed along the scale. The curve for the second principal compo- nent provides all of the information conveyed by the first, *plus* an iden- tification of the zero point for the attitude. The third curve provides all of the information conveyed by the second, *plus* a division into subsets of more and less intense, of both those with favorable and those with un- favorable attitudes toward the content. In short, I propose that *a cumu- lative theory of psychological structure be employed to interpret the psychological meaning of interrelationships between cumulative scales.*

If the theory is to be useful in the present research, however, it is necessary to determine how the elementary component (principal component-type) curves derived from the relationships between cumula- tive scale variables (*i.e.,* a pair of simplexes) can be related to the scale axes and configuration of points in the factorial space. The correlation of the scale axis for an attitudinal variable, with the cumulative scale for the same variable, ought to yield a curve equivalent to the first principal component curve—approximately, a straight line. Moreover, since the expected rela- tionship is linear, the comparison readily can be made statistically, as well as graphically, by computing the correlation coefficient for the two sets of i-point ranks, on the scale axis and on the cumulative scale. The demonstration of isomorphism between the axis and the scale would suggest that both are measuring the same attitudinal content.

A scattergram correlation graph of the two major cumulative scales (*i.e.,* the semantic components of the phi matrix) ought to yield two different elementary component curves, depending upon which scale is placed in the ordinate and which in the abscissal position. An intuitively plausible hypothesis might be that if the phi matrix is a quasi-simplex [15] and if the two scales represent what are quantitatively the most important components of the total semantic content in the data that has been observed for the computation of the original correlation matrix, then a graph with the scale for the most important content in the abscissal position and the second most important content scale in the ordinate position ought to resemble a second principal component curve. Similarly, when the most important content scale is the ordinate, and the second most important is in the abscissal position, the curve should resemble that of the third principal component. Moreover, we should expect to derive these second and third principal component-type curves from three differing types of data measurement: (1) directly from pairs of cumulative scale ranks or scores; (2) from pairs of scale axis ranks or scores; and (3) directly from the point configuration in the three-dimensional space. Only in the latter instance, however, could we expect to derive first component-type curves, by comparing cumulative scales with their analogue scale axes imbedded in the three-dimensional factorial space (which is a function of the phi matrix).

It is the projections from the i-points, it will be recalled, rather than the points themselves, that lie upon the scale axes. And by tracing the ordinal sequence of the points themselves, through the configuration, we should expect to observe elementary component curves similar to either second or third principal component curves, depending upon the relative importance of the semantic components (*i.e.,* the content of the scale variables being investigated). If, indeed, we were able in fact to make one set of observations of the raw data for the factorial measurements, and a quite independent set of observations of the same raw data for the cumulative scaling measurements, and then we were able to demonstrate that each set of measurements yielded the *same* set of elementary component curves, we might well infer that we had arrived at a basis for placing considerable

[15] *Ibid.,* pp. 278 and 294–314, especially pp. 311–314.

confidence in our capacity to denote the fundamental attitudinal content of the relationships we seek to understand.

A Psychometric Model

STRUCTURE OF THE MODEL

We are now in a position to construct the model of the Supreme Court that has guided the empirical research to be reported in this study. I assume that justices of the United States Supreme Court "correspond with, more than they differ from, people;"[16] and that "Judges are human, but they are a peculiar breed of humans, selected to a type and held to service under a potent system of governmental controls."[17] The processes employed for the selection of Supreme Court justices are such that it is reasonable to assume that each justice either comes to the Court with, or soon acquires as the result of the kind of task with which he is charged, relatively well-structured attitudes toward the recurrent major issues of public policy that confront the Court for decision. On the basis of an analysis of their content, it is possible to identify the common issues, and the relevant attitudinal dimensions that are functions of these issues. This content analysis provides the basis for systematic discussion of the set of attitudinal dimensions that is most important for a series of subsets consisting of the justices who comprise the Court at any particular time, even if there is considerable individual variation in the direction and intensity of judicial attitudes, as these are measured on the relevant dimensions over an extended period of time. The syndrome of attitudes for each justice can be symbolized and represented graphically as a unique point in spaces varying from one to three dimensions. I shall follow Coombs's terminology and call each such point the *i*-point of the justice.

The cases on the Court's dockets are conceptualized as complex stimuli, which (in effect) ask questions about issues to which the justices are asked to respond. The number of issues that survive in any case, after appellate review below and the Supreme Court's jurisdictional screening are completed, are few and refined, in sharp contradistinction to the multiplicity of issues that may have been raised during the trial and other earlier stages in the litigation of the case. Characteristically, the effect of what are called "the facts" of the case is to provide direction and intensity in

[16] James G. March, "Sociological Jurisprudence Revisited: A Review (More or Less) of Max Gluckman," *Stanford Law Review*, Vol. 8 (1956), p. 534.

[17] Felix S. Cohen, "Transcendental Nonsense and the Functional Approach," *Columbia Law Review*, Vol. 35 (1935), p. 843.

defining the nature of the issue; that is, the issue specifies which attitudinal dimension (or dimensions) is (or are) relevant, while the facts determine where a particular case is located on the dimension(s). The questions of valuation raised by cases are the counterparts of the attitudes of the justices, which mediate the external values (represented by issues in cases) and the internal values (which constitute the beliefs of the individual justices). Each case, therefore, also can be measured along the same dimensions that have been used for the attitudes of the justices, and each case can be represented by a j-point in the joint space with the i-points.

Assuming an individual compensatory composition model for spaces with a dimensionality greater than one, and Coombs' ordinal dominance definition of the individual choice function, it is clear that the decision of the Court in any case will depend upon whether the j-point for the case dominates, or is dominated by, a majority of i-points. In the simplest, one-dimensional case, all ten points are arrayed along the same continuum; and the justices are partitioned into two subsets (one pro and one con the issue) by the j-point. One such subset can, of course, be empty; and a unanimous decision upholding an issue will occur when the j-point is dominated by all i-points, while unanimous decisions in the negative will occur when all i-points are dominated by the j-point. In multi-dimensional space, the attitudinal variable will be an axis in the space, and both the j-point and the i-point will project orthogonally to analogue points upon the axis. Psychologically, this is equivalent to saying that each justice will perceive a dominant issue in the case, and that that perception determines for him the relevant axis to serve as a criterion for decision-making purposes. He then perceives a position on the axis as being that of the j-point; a position— usually, a different one—as being that of his own i-point; and his decision, as in the one-dimensional case, is based upon his comparison of the dominance relationship between these two points. Obviously, it is necessary for all justices to agree upon both the relevant criterion (axis) and the position of the j-point upon that axis in order for this theoretical model to fit the empirical decision of the group of justices. It is equally obvious that individual differences in perception, relating either to the relevant criterion or to the location of the j-point upon a consensual criterion axis, readily can account for occasional "errors" in the responses denoted in linear cumulative scales, if it is empirically true (as it seems to be) that such scales characteristically are imbedded in multidimensional psychological spaces, as the justices perceive the stimuli (cases). From this it follows that the model of the decision-making function of the Court is basically the same, irrespective of the dimensionality of the decision-making space; but the probability of observing empirically inconsistent responses is directly and positively correlated with the complexity of the psychological space relevant to the decision-making process. Since a three-dimensional space is postulated for the model of the Court, we should anticipate a larger amount of inconsistent response than we should expect to find in the decision-making of a group of judges with more specialized jurisdiction, such as the Court of Claims or the Tax Court of the United States, or any of the so-called independent federal regulatory commissions.

Justices who are attitudinally in close agreement with each other ought to be located close to each other in the three-dimensional space; and we should expect such justices to agree closely in their voting. Justices who hold opposing views on such fundamental issues as civil liberties, or the proper role of government in the national economy, ought to be located far apart in the space, and we should expect them to disagree often in their voting. Cases that raise questions of differing degrees of valuation about the same issue will by arrayed as a set of j-points along a single continuum, which I have hypothesized to be a scale axis imbedded in the space. If such a scale axis is orthogonal to one of the reference axes, this is equivalent to saying that this axis lies in a space that is only two-dimensional—with respect to whatever meaning may be associated with the reference axes. We should anticipate, however, that such orthogonality between scale and reference axes will be exceptional rather than usual; for if the contrary were empirically true, there would be little justification for carrying out the analysis in three-dimensional space—a plane or a line would do just as well and would be much simpler methodologically to work with. Moreover, the arrayal of j-points precisely upon a scale axis is empirically improbable, because the content analysis of Supreme Court cases makes it evident that rarely are they purely univariate. Instead, sets of j-points will be scattered, although not to the same extent as i-points, in nonlinear patterns in the space; it is the orthogonal projections from the j-points that lie upon the scale axes; and a scale axis is the centroid that is the line closest to all of the relevant j-points, with regard to the content of the particular value and attitude that have been attributed to that scale axis.

I shall speak presently of semantic subcomponents of the major attitudinal variables. These can be conceptualized, for present purposes, as a set of highly intercorrelated scale axes, each of which draws projections from only a subset of the set of j-points that consensually are perceived to project upon the major attitudinal scale axis. If all j-points in the set are partitioned into subsets of points which project upon such subcomponent scale axes, then the scale axis for the major attitude will be the centroid of the subcomponent scale axes. Each subcomponent axis will relate to a "field" of j-points which occupy a lesser segment of the space than the space-field of the scale axis for the major attitude. For example, an analyst can define issues narrowly or broadly, depending upon the purpose of his inquiry and also upon what seems to be reasonable, from an empirical point of view, based upon an examination of the value-content of the cases that are of interest. Thus, one might be interested in any or all of the following cases which appear upon the dockets of the United States Supreme Court: (1) F.E.L.A. (Federal Employers Liability Act) evidentiary cases; (2) all F.E.L.A. cases; (3) F.E.L.A. cases, Jones Act cases, Longshoremen and Harborworkers Act cases, maritime cases raising the question of seaworthiness, maintenance and care, etc.; (4) both federal and state cases involving workers' claims for monetary compensation for industrial accidents; (5) any cases involving workers' claims for monetary compensation; (6) any cases involving the rights of workingmen; (7) any cases which raise the fundamental issue of economic liberalism-conservatism. Any of these seven categories might constitute an issue which could be represented by a scale axis in my model of the Court; but these categories obviously are cumulative, and the seventh is far the most general, including many kinds of public policy issues beyond those involving the interests of injured laborers. We might well consider the seventh category to denote the semantic content of a major attitude, while each of the other categories represents an increasingly narrower subcomponent of the major variable. A set of scale axes representing those subcomponents will appear, geometrically, as a fan-like cluster of axes, whose respective fields of points occupy successively overlapping segments of the space. As in Guttman's basic conception of a cumulative scale, the scale axis for the major variable dominates all of the space which is dominated by its labor subcomponents, plus a considerably greater segment of space-content which these particular subcomponents do *not* dominate—because that space-segment is dominated by other subcomponents—each with a differing content—of the major variable.

I shall presently define two major semantic components: political liberalism and economic liberalism. The scale axes for these two variables will define the genotypic space of a plane imbedded in the three-dimensional factorial space. The psychological relationships of greatest interest are those between the configuration of i-points, which represent the attitudinal syndromes of the justices, and the political liberalism (C+) and economic liberalism (E+) scale axes, which represent the major issues raised for decision-making by the cases. The observation of isomorphic elementary component curves, in relation to the configuration of i-points and for the corresponding pairs of scales and of scale axes, will demonstrate that the configuration is primarily a function of the attitudes of the justices toward the issues of public policy defined by C+ and E+.

Finally, the observation of principal component-type curves in the phenotypic space of the plane defined by the C and E scales will support the inference that these two simplexes join to form a joint elementary component curve—a circumplex in the genotypic space. New reference axes will be defined for the plane, and these together with the elementary component curves will provide the basis for a theory of psychological types that applies to all of the justices who served on the Court during the period covered by the empirical study next to be discussed; ultimately it is these psychological types that determine the circumplex. Heretofore psychometric discussion of the attitudes of Supreme Court justices has assumed that there is a single linear continuum—liberalism-conservatism—along which such attitudes can be measured. Such a theory requires a model in which liberals are at one extreme, and conservatives are at an opposite extreme. I shall show that such a theory is not so much wrong as it is incomplete. The attitudes of Supreme Court justices are better represented as curvilinear functions, such as the geometric forms of the parabola, the circle, and the ellipse.

FUNCTIONS OF THE MODEL

My own interests in the model are as an imaginary replication of the set of psychological events that are most important to the making of official choices by the small group of humans who, at any given time, include the incumbent justices of the Court. I assume that these psychological events *are* taking place in the real world, in the minds of the individual justices and in the context of their social interrelations with each other and with many other persons. At least under presently obtaining circumstances, however, these psychological events cannot be observed directly; so we must seek to acquire knowledge about them by means of indirect observation—that is to say, by inferences based upon direct observations of the manifest behavior of the justices. The observation of consistent regularities in the behavior of the justices will lead us to infer, therefore, that such manifest consistencies are functions of consistent relationships among the underlying psychological variables with which the model is concerned. The model is the basis, therefore, for a theory of how and why the justices of the Supreme Court make whatever decisions they do make.

The model has descriptive, analytical, and normative implications. It is descriptive in the sense that one can infer from it a set of hypotheses about past decisions of the Court. From the descriptive point of view, one says that given a particular structure of attitudinal relationships among the justices, and a set of cases raising questions that correspond to degrees of valuation along the same dimensions as the attitudinal dimensions for the justices, it is then possible to specify (in theory) how each justice voted in each case—and therefore also, of course, how each case was decided by "the Court." From an analytical point of view, one says that the observable structure of attitudinal relationships among the justices best can be explained in terms of their individual correlations with the dimensions which represent the relevant fundamental psychological variables; and the theoretical interrelationships among these variables constitute the latent psychological structure which accounts for the decision-making behavior of the justices (and therefore of the Court). From a normative point of view, one says that if a given structure of attitudinal relationships among the justices and among the latent psychological variables evidently has manifested high stability over an extended period of time, then one may be willing (on the basis of extrinsic information about such real-life parameters of political importance as the age and health—and hence probability of retirement—of incumbent justices, and the political attitudes of the incumbent President, his own probable tenure in relationship to the national electoral cycle, etc.) to make the assumption that the structure specified by the model will remain substantially unchanged for some limited short-run period—the next term of the Court, for example. The model then can be used for normative purposes, but not in the sense that it permits one to say that the justices (or the Court) ought to decide cases one way or another because of the intrinsic preferability—necessarily, in terms of some extrinsic criterion of valuation that may or may not be quite independent of the structure of the model—of certain outcomes (for society, the public interest, the good life, civilization ideals, humanity, or whatever) as compared to other outcomes. The normative sense in which the model can be used is to specify how each justice ought to vote in any set of cases raising questions that correspond to degrees of valuation along the same dimensions as the attitudinal variables for the justices, if his voting behavior is to remain as consistent in the future, as it has been in the past, with the postulations of his attitudes.

It is obvious that there is a close affinity between what I have termed the descriptive and the normative implications of the model. In its descriptive implications the model makes possible what are in effect predictions about the past behavior of the justices, while in a normative sense the model makes possible predictions about the future behavior of the justices. In either case, the validation of the prediction consists of a comparison of the voting prescriptions deduced from the model, with the observable empirical voting data.[18] From a scientific point of view, it is not very important that in the descriptive case the data are available for examination without delay (other than for data collection and processing), while in the normative case there is a time lag until the data becomes available for collection and processing.

[18] For an example of validation of predictions based upon the present model and what turned out to be, in some respects, an inadequate subset of empirical data, see the concluding section, "Predictions for the 1962 Term," of my article, "Judicial Attitudes and Voting Behavior: The 1961 Term of the United States Supreme Court," *Law and Contemporary Problems,* Vol. 28 (1963), pp. 137–142, reprinted together with a new "Appendix: Report and Analysis of the 1962 Term Predictions" in my *Judicial Behavior: A Reader in Theory and Research* (Chicago: Rand McNally, 1964), pp. 575–587.

Chapter 3 · THE EMPIRICAL DATA AND METHODOLOGY

THE SAMPLE of decisions to be analyzed consists of all cases in which the Supreme Court divided on the merits during the period of the 1946–62 terms, *i.e.,* from October 7, 1946 to June 17, 1963. Both formal decisions (those for which an individual justice is assigned the responsibility of writing the opinion for the majority of the Court) and *per curiam* decisions (those for which the author of the opinion for the majority of the Court is anonymous) are included, but unanimous and jurisdictional decisions are excluded. The total set of 1,659 dissensual decisions is divided into seventeen subsets, since the analysis was made on the basis of the subsample of decisions for each term. As Table 1 indicates, the size of term subsamples ranges from 60 to 132, with an average of approximately a hundred (97) dissensual decisions per term. One or more justices dissented in a majority of the Court's decisions on the merits over the past seventeen terms, and there were only four terms in which this was not true. However the level of consensus appears to have been quite stable, ranging within the limits of ±10 units from the average of 68 on the index (I′, below).

The matrix for generating the index of consensus is given in Table 2. The formula for computing the cell entries is:

$$(2) \qquad\qquad I = \frac{X - Y}{X},$$

when I is the index, X the total of justices participating in the decision, and Y is the number of dissenting justices. The index is a simple ratio of the manifest to the possible agreement in each decision. The rules of the Court require that a quorum for decision-making on the merits shall consist of at

TABLE 1

Consensus in Supreme Court Voting Agreement, 1946–1962 Terms

Term	Dissensual Decisions (N)	Total Decisions (N)	Percentage of Decisions Unanimous	Index of Consensus
1946	125	232	46	65
1947	104	171	39	66
1948	113	188	39	59
1949	91	160	43	71
1950	88	159	45	67
1951	92	152	38	66
1952	112	163	31	60
1953	72	132	45	67
1954	60	141	57	76
1955	75	175	57	74
1956	114	203	44	68
1957	132	254	48	69
1958	88	180	51	67
1959	102	175	42	65
1960	99	174	43	66
1961	83	163	49	73
1962	107	265	60	78
Average	97	181	46	68

least six of the maximum of nine justices for whom positions are author-ized by statute, and evidently no more than three justices can be in the *minority* with quorums of six or seven; consequently, the 7:4 and 6:4 cells are empty, because they specify relations that cannot arise empirically un-der the rules which obtained during the period of this analysis. The empir-

TABLE 2

Matrix for Generating the Index of Consensus

		Number of Dissents (Y)				
		0	1	2	3	4
Total Participa-tion (X)	9	1.000	.889	.778	.667	.556
	8	1.000	.875	.750	.625	.500
	7	1.000	.857	.714	.571	
	6	1.000	.833	.667	.500	

ical data for each term were partitioned among the cells of the matrix, and the empirical cell frequencies were multiplied by the cell values specified by Table 2. The average index value for each term is a decimal, and the empirical range for these term index values is from .7938 to .8924; the theoretical range of the index in that form is .5000 to 1.000. In order to facilitate comparison with the "percent of Decisions Unanimous" column of Table 1, the term index values were converted from the theoretical range 0.50–1.00 to that of 0–100, by use of the formula:

$$(3) \qquad\qquad I' = 100(2I - 1),$$

and the latter values are the indices reported in the final column of Table 1.

It will be observed that all unanimous decisions receive the maximum weight (irrespective of nonparticipation), that 4–2 decisions are weighted the same as 6–3 decisions, and that both 3–3 and 4–4 decisions are weighted the same. Both 4–2 and 3–3 decisions are empirically rare, however, as are also 6–0 unanimous decisions.

The term series for the proportion of unanimous decisions evidently is positively correlated with the series of index values. The latter, however, provide a more complete and sensitive measure of consensus, since the percentage series ignores both nonparticipation and the degree of dissension in decisions. Both series agree, however, that 1948 and 1952 were terms of exceptionally low consensus, while 1954 and 1962 were terms of exceptionally high consensus. The average index value of 68 suggests that, in general, a high proportion of the votes of individual justices must have been made to express disagreement with the Court's majorities. This inference is confirmed by an examination of the gross raw data: of the total of 14,236 individual votes included in the total sample of dissensual decisions, 4,215 or 30 percent were dissenting votes.

Each case, to which the Court had assigned a unique docket number and for which the Court had made a disposition on the merits, was a unit for voting analysis; and for each case, one set of from six to nine votes was counted. As Table 3 shows, two-thirds (67 percent) of these decisions were made with the participation of a full Court of nine justices; another quarter (25 percent) were decided with eight participating justices; and less than 10 percent were decided by groups of seven or six. Table 3 also shows that there was a modest difference in the frequencies with which dissenting groups of differing size occurred. Under the hypothesis that it is just as likely to have two, three, or four justices dissent as to have only one do so, one would expect about 25 percent of the decisions to be partitioned among the groups of each size. In fact, three justices dissented in 29 percent of the decisions, with two dissenting in 27 percent, four in 23 percent, and with solitary dissenters in 21 percent of the decisions. None of these differences seems very remarkable, although they are quite statistically significant (with $X^2 = 30.55$, and a two-tailed p of $< .001$) because of the large number of cases in the sample. It might be interesting to explore the psychological and sociological reasons why dissenting subsets of three are most common, and those of one are least common—a task which has not been attempted for purposes of this study.

TABLE 3

Summary Matrix of Sample of Votes in Dissensual Decisions

		Number of Dissents				
		1	2	3	4	Σ
Total	9	190	269	331	321	1111
Participa-	8	109	128	117	57	411
tion	7	42	51	34	*	127
	6	3	4	3	*	10
	Σ	344	452	485	378	1659

* = cannot occur

Most of the 60 decisions in which the Court divided evenly could not be used in the analysis, because there was no objective means of identifying the voting positions of the participating justices. Therefore, the sample for analysis consisted of approximately 1,600 decisions and about 13,762 votes (including 3,978 dissents).

Eighteen justices participated in the decisions of the Court during the seventeen terms covered by this study. As Table 4 indicates, two persons (Black and Douglas) served throughout the entire period, although it should be noted that Douglas' participation during the 1949 Term was minimal, because of a horseback-riding injury which required him to miss most of the decisions of that term. Frankfurter participated in all except the last term, although his retirement *de facto* because of illness required him to miss all of the decisions of the 1961 Term that were announced after

TABLE 4

Sample of Judicial Respondents, in Term Subsets

	1946	47	48	49	50	51	52	53	54	55	56	57	58	59	60	61	62	Total
V	X	X	X	X	X	X	X											7
Wa								X	X	X	X	X	X	X	X	X	X	10
Bl	X	X	X	X	X	X	X	X	X	X	X	X	X	X	X	X	X	17
Re	X	X	X	X	X	X	X	X	X	X	X							11
F	X	X	X	X	X	X	X	X	X	X	X	X	X	X	X	X		16
D	X	X	X	X	X	X	X	X	X	X	X	X	X	X	X	X	X	17
Mu	X	X	X															3
J	X	X	X	X	X	X	X	X										8
Ru	X	X	X															3
Bu	X	X	X	X	X	X	X	X	X	X	X	X						12
C				X	X	X	X	X	X	X	X	X	X	X	X	X	X	14
Mi				X	X	X	X	X	X	X								7
H									X	X	X	X	X	X	X	X	X	9
Br											X	X	X	X	X	X	X	7
Wh												X	X	X	X	X	X	6
S													X	X	X	X	X	5
BW																X	X	2
G																	X	1
	9	9	9	9	9	9	9	9	9	9	10	9	9	9	9	10	9	155

April 9, 1962—and these were more than half of the total for the term. Clark participated in all except three of the terms. On the other hand, four justices—Murphy, Rutledge, White, and Goldberg—served for three terms or less during the period covered by this study. The average participation for this sample of respondents clearly was about half of the total period: nine of the eighteen justices served for eight terms or more, and the mean is 8.6 terms. It will be observed that two of the term subsets total 10 rather than 9 justices. Of course, no more than nine participated simultaneously, but both Reed and Whittaker (who replaced him) served part of the 1956 Term, and similarly, Whittaker and White each served part of the 1961 Term. In each of these instances, participation during the term was adequate to permit the inclusion of both respondents in the samples for factor analysis and cumulative scaling for these terms. This makes possible the seeming anomaly of discussing interrelationships among ten respondents when the known size of the decision-making group was nine. It also entails the somewhat unusual advantage of permitting direct comparisons, in these exceptional instances, between the decision-making behaviors of predecessor-successor pairs of justices who never actually sat together on the Court.

The Factor Analysis

Table 5 reports the correlation matrices together with the four-fold tables upon which they are based. Since the correlation matrices are symmetrical, the four-fold tables are shown above the major diagonal and the corresponding coefficients are shown below, in order to conserve space. The tables are based upon machine tabulations of the term sets of voting data described above. The tabulation was made on the basis of a nominal classification of votes in terms of (1) agreement, or (2) disagreement with the decision (disposition of the case) made by a majority of the justices. The vote of each justice in every case was compared with the vote of every other justice, and the frequencies were recorded for each pair of justices and cumulated for the total decisions in the sample for each term. For any pair of respondents, there are five possibilities in each decision: (1) both may agree in the majority; (2) both may agree in dissent; (3) the first member of the pair may vote with the majority, while the second dissents; (4) the second member of the pair may vote with the majority, while the first dissents; (5) either or both respondents may fail to participate in the decision, or vote only on the question of jurisdiction instead of the merits, or the vote of either or both may be indeterminate (as usually is true in

TABLE 5

Four-Fold Tables and Phi Correlation Matrices, 1946–1962 Terms

1946 TERM

		Mu		Bl		Ru		D		Re		V		Bu		J		F	
		+	−	+	−	+	−	+	−	+	−	+	−	+	−	+	−	+	−
Mu	+			63 04		52 15		49 14		47 19		48 16		42 25		34 26		31 35	
	−			13 35		14 37		21 29		49 02		49 02		49 02		38 10		45 06	
Bl	+	.697				54 22		53 19		56 19		59 41		53 23		41 28		35 40	
	−					13 29		19 22		40 02		17 01		38 04		32 08		41 01	
Ru	+	.501		.388				46 18		52 15		49 16		48 19		29 32		35 31	
	−							26 26		47 06		51 02		46 08		44 04		44 10	
D	+	.366		.273		.244				58 13		55 16		52 20		31 33		36 35	
	−									37 07		42 02		39 05		39 01		40 04	
Re	+	−.321		−.257		−.145		−.031				80 17		81 18		60 29		64 35	
	−											20 01		13 08		12 07		14 06	
V	+	−.288		−.266		−.288		−.241		−.136				83 17		64 29		73 26	
	−													09 09		08 05		05 13	
Bu	+	−.394		−.236		−.162		−.194		.184		.286				59 29		66 27	
	−															14 07		13 14	
J	+	−.237		−.211		−.466		−.509		.034		.051		.003				56 17	
	−																	17 19	
F		−.429		−.512		−.298		−.413		−.042		.352		.201		.295			

1947 TERM

	Ru + −	Mu + −	Bl + −	D + −	Re + −	V + −	Bu + −	F + −	J + −
Ru	+ / −	71 04 / 05 21	68 08 / 04 21	47 14 / 07 19	60 15 / 24 02	60 15 / 26 00	39 37 / 25 01	42 33 / 23 03	28 26 / 23 03
Mu	.764	+ / −	66 10 / 05 20	45 16 / 08 18	58 17 / 26 00	61 14 / 25 01	38 26 / 38 00	45 30 / 21 05	28 24 / 27 02
Bl	.701	.631	+ / −	44 13 / 10 20	58 13 / 26 04	60 11 / 26 04	37 35 / 27 03	37 34 / 28 02	22 28 / 29 01
D	.473	.403	.430	+ / −	39 14 / 32 02	40 14 / 33 01	34 20 / 31 03	21 32 / 32 02	21 23 / 30 04
Re	−.144	−.265	−.061	−.259	+ / −	78 07 / 09 07	58 27 / 07 10	54 30 / 12 05	42 21 / 09 08
V	−.246	−.182	−.028	−.298	.375	+ / −	60 27 / 05 10	56 30 / 09 06	42 24 / 09 05
Bu	−.404	−.451	−.364	−.313	.210	.262	+ / −	39 25 / 27 11	38 18 / 14 11
F	−.296	−.191	−.393	−.545	−.050	.038	−.102	+ / −	44 10 / 08 18
J	−.357	−.403	−.530	−.422	.118	−.005	.114	.498	

1948 TERM

	Ru +	Ru −	Mu +	Mu −	Bl +	Bl −	D +	D −	Re +	Re −	V +	V −	Bu +	Bu −	F +	F −	J +	J −
Ru	+		55	07	53	09	45	16	40	21	41	20	39	23	33	29	23	39
		−	11	31	17	28	14	31	43	02	44	01	44	01	40	05	38	05
Mu	.637		+		56	10	45	21	42	23	45	20	42	24	39	27	28	38
				−	14	24	14	23	38	00	37	01	38	00	31	07	32	06
Bl	.495		.493		+		49	21	48	22	50	20	47	24	40	30	29	41
						−	11	26	36	01	36	01	37	00	33	04	32	03
D	.424		.294		.386		+		42	17	43	16	38	22	34	25	24	35
								−	41	06	42	05	45	02	39	08	37	08
Re	−.360		−.410		−.333		−.193		+		75	08	70	14	55	28	50	31
										−	10	13	13	10	18	05	11	12
V	−.379		−.337		−.310		−.205		.485		+		74	12	59	26	55	28
												−	09	12	14	07	06	15
Bu	−.413		−.416		−.386		−.386		.264		.411		+		62	21	56	25
														−	11	13	05	19
F	−.378		−.231		−.327		−.272		−.107		.024		.259		+		52	19
																−	09	25
J	−.511		−.407		−.478		−.418		.117		.307		.411		.444			

1949 TERM

	+/−	D	Bl	Bu	V	C	Re	Mi	F	J
D	+	+	06 01	07 00	07 00	04 01	05 02	05 02	01 05	01 06
	−	−	01 15	15 01	16 00	15 00	13 03	14 01	15 01	14 01
Bl	+	.795	+	33 06	33 03	32 02	23 17	36 03	14 22	16 23
	−		−	47 03	49 01	40 00	43 07	44 03	36 14	38 10
Bu	+	.141	−.154	+	73 03	62 02	59 21	71 06	43 34	45 32
	−			−	08 01	09 00	06 03	08 00	07 01	09 00
V	+	.000	−.148	.104	+	65 01	62 20	72 06	45 33	52 27
	−				−	03 01	01 03	04 00	04 00	02 02
C	+	−.397	−.181	−.063	.327	+	52 20	65 05	47 22	48 21
	−					−	00 02	01 01	01 01	01 01
Re	+	−.110	−.320	.048	.241	.256	+	62 01	35 30	36 27
	−						−	18 05	15 06	18 06
Mi	+	−.297	.026	−.089	−.064	.255	.350	+	46 31	49 28
	−							−	03 03	03 03
F	+	−.771	−.331	−.188	−.186	.064	−.153	.051	+	43 05
	−								−	09 26
J		−.790	−.391	−.263	.071	.070	−.164	.073	.652	

1950 TERM

	D + −	Bl + −	C + −	V + −	Re + −	Mi + −	Bu + −	J + −	F + −
D		21 17 / 16 27	26 03 / 33 05	31 05 / 40 04	29 09 / 36 07	24 12 / 41 03	26 10 / 37 07	23 12 / 34 10	19 19 / 30 13
Bl	.181	+ / −	27 03 / 32 05	32 04 / 39 05	26 12 / 39 04	27 10 / 38 05	29 08 / 34 09	22 16 / 35 06	23 15 / 27 16
C	.043	.054	+ / −	55 03 / 05 03	50 09 / 06 02	48 10 / 07 01	46 13 / 06 02	40 18 / 06 02	33 26 / 06 02
V	−.076	.004	.367	+ / −	59 12 / 05 04	60 11 / 04 04	54 16 / 08 01	49 20 / 09 00	42 29 / 08 01
Re	−.093	−.279	.085	.218	+ / −	54 11 / 11 04	51 13 / 12 04	46 17 / 11 05	36 30 / 14 02
Mi	−.338	−.197	−.042	.265	.097	+ / −	53 11 / 09 06	45 18 / 11 04	40 25 / 09 06
Bu	−.144	−.008	.023	−.091	.046	.218	+ / −	44 17 / 13 04	39 24 / 10 07
J	−.128	−.306	−.043	−.212	.038	−.017	−.040	+ / −	39 18 / 10 12
F	−.202	−.023	−.125	−.194	−.268	.012	.026	.212	

1951 TERM

		D	Bl	F	J	C	V	Mi	Re	Bu
D	+	+	27 15	28 08	32 10	35 01	30 12	22 18	27 15	34 08
	−	−	13 27	24 07	34 07	38 00	40 03	34 04	31 12	37 06
Bl	+	.318	+	25 04	32 09	37 01	30 11	21 17	19 22	22 09
	−		−	27 11	34 06	34 00	37 05	33 05	36 06	37 05
F	+	.004	.180	+	43 08	44 01	38 15	28 18	32 21	45 08
	−			−	11 04	13 00	15 00	14 01	12 03	11 04
J	+	−.083	−.089	.119	+	56 01	52 15	43 19	47 20	56 11
	−				−	16 00	16 01	14 03	11 06	14 03
C	+	−.120	−.112	−.071	−.062	+	62 12	49 19	49 25	62 12
	−					−	00 01	00 01	01 00	01 00
V	+	−.283	−.189	−.283	−.169	.254	+	52 12	52 18	57 13
	−						−	05 10	06 10	15 01
Mi	+	−.383	−.384	−.302	−.119	.190	.419	+	42 15	46 11
	−							−	13 09	20 02
Re	+	−.084	−.416	−.170	.047	−.082	.305	.142	+	51 07
	−								−	21 07
Bu		−.069	−.134	.126	.013	−.051	−.130	−.123	.164	

1952 TERM

	D +	D −	Bl +	Bl −	F +	F −	J +	J −	C +	C −	V +	V −	Re +	Re −	Mi +	Mi −	Bu +	Bu −
D +	+		23	11	21	12	12	17	24	04	23	11	28	06	26	09	28	07
D −	−		27	39	42	26	56	04	61	02	58	10	61	04	61	07	61	07
Bl +	.253		+		36	14	32	13	37	04	36	13	40	08	39	11	39	11
Bl −			−		25	25	35	10	48	01	47	06	50	01	48	05	50	03
F +	.018		.226		+		48	08	50	06	45	18	52	08	49	15	53	11
F −					−		21	12	34	00	38	01	37	02	38	01	36	03
J +	−.573		−.076		.255		+		60	04	57	11	63	05	58	11	59	10
J −							−		16	01	19	04	21	02	20	03	20	03
C +	−.207		−.168		−.208		−.006		+		74	13	77	06	77	10	76	11
C −									−		00	05	05	01	04	02	04	02
V +	−.206		−.195		−.325		.014		.486		+		75	06	75	09	74	10
V −											−		16	04	15	06	17	04
Re +	−.181		−.256		−.133		.022		.088		.168		+		80	12	77	15
Re −													−		06	04	10	00
Mi +	−.202		−.173		−.280		−.035		.160		.204		.220		+		80	10
Mi −															−		11	05
Bu	−.134		−.238		−.134		−.018		.147		.084		−.137		.207			

1953 TERM

	±	D	Bl +	Bl −	Wa +	Wa −	C +	C −	Bu +	Bu −	Re +	Re −	Mi +	Mi −	J +	J −	F +	F −
D	+		23	04	21	05	21	04	13	14	12	15	19	08	14	10	20	07
	−		11	27	32	06	32	05	34	08	37	02	31	11	30	05	38	04
Bl	+	.555			26	04	26	07	17	17	17	16	24	10	18	12	27	07
	−				25	07	29	02	32	01	30	01	28	05	23	03	29	04
Wa	+	−.045	.112				46	03	36	19	41	11	38	17	35	12	45	10
	−						04	06	08	03	08	03	09	02	07	01	11	00
C	+	−.035	−.212		.562				44	11	39	13	41	14	35	13	44	11
	−								03	06	06	03	08	01	05	01	09	00
Bu	+	−.344	−.530		−.057		.367				40	06	38	11	32	10	41	08
	−										11	11	14	08	13	05	19	03
Re	+	−.567	−.512		.056		.067		.399				38	13	30	12	40	11
	−												13	04	13	03	17	00
Mi	+	−.038	−.171		−.105		−.118		.145		−.020				33	10	43	09
	−														12	05	17	02
J	+	−.309	−.321		−.108		−.075		.042		−.100		.064				40	05
	−																09	06
F		−.219	−.114		−.189		−.184		−.034		−.254		−.083		.323			

1954 TERM

	D +	D −	Bl +	Bl −	Wa +	Wa −	C +	C −	Mi +	Mi −	Re +	Re −	Bu +	Bu −	F +	F −	H +	H −
D +	+		30	04	31	01	31	02	20	14	10	24	18	16	24	09	08	06
D −	−		12	09	19	03	21	01	21	01	18	04	22	00	19	03	01	00
Bl +	.356		+		39	03	39	03	29	14	16	27	26	17	33	09	08	06
Bl −			−		11	01	12	01	12	01	11	02	13	00	10	03	00	00
Wa +	.197		.019		+		48	03	38	13	24	27	35	16	39	11	08	06
Wa −					−		03	01	03	01	03	01	04	00	03	01	01	00
C +	−.033		.009		.191		+		39	13	27	25	37	15	39	12	08	06
C −							−		03	01	01	03	03	01	04	00	01	00
Mi +	−.404		−.237		−.003		.000		+		26	16	30	12	31	10	05	04
Mi −									−		02	13	10	05	13	02	04	02
Re +	−.512		−.401		−.145		.139		.428		+		23	05	18	10	01	04
Re −											−		17	12	26	02	08	02
Bu +	−.509		−.363		−.179		−.022		.046		.257		+		33	06	06	02
Bu −													−		11	06	03	04
F +	−.162		.017		.019		−.148		−.119		−.348		.223		+		09	03
F −															−		00	03
H	−.218		.000		−.218		−.218		−.111		−.577		.327		.612			

1955 TERM

		D +	D −	Bl +	Bl −	Wa +	Wa −	C +	C −	Re +	Re −	Mi +	Mi −	Bu +	Bu −	H +	H −	F +	F −
D	+	+		46	01	46	00	40	06	26	21	27	20	22	24	16	25	23	22
D	−		−	10	17	13	14	23	03	25	02	27	00	25	02	19	04	21	06
Bl	+	.683		+		55	00	49	06	33	23	36	20	29	26	18	29	30	24
Bl	−				−	04	14	14	03	18	00	18	00	18	00	17	00	14	04
Wa	+	.636		.851		+		53	05	37	22	39	20	33	25	21	29	32	25
Wa	−						−	10	03	14	00	14	00	14	00	13	00	11	03
C	+	−.022		.087		.177		+		46	17	47	16	39	23	27	28	34	27
C	−								−	04	05	05	04	07	02	07	01	08	01
Re	+	−.388		−.381		−.320		.205		+		45	06	41	10	21	24	26	25
Re	−										−	09	14	06	16	14	05	18	03
Mi	+	−.461		−.345		−.299		.141		.512		+		43	10	25	20	31	22
Mi	−												−	04	16	10	09	13	06
Bu	+	−.451		−.425		−.358		−.104		.509		.569		+		23	17	28	19
Bu	−														−	12	12	16	09
H	+	−.420		−.547		−.471		−.257		−.248		.027		.073		+		28	06
H	−																−	11	18
F		−.265		−.197		−.183		−.227		−.324		−.090		−.043		.456			

1956 TERM

	+/-	D	Bl	Wa	Br	C	Re	F	H	Wh	Bu
D	+	+	61 03	69 01	59 05	45 25	11 10	32 27	31 39	16 13	26 39
D	−	−	13 28	25 14	28 08	37 03	11 00	36 05	40 01	15 00	40 01
Bl	+	.680	+	71 01	61 06	48 25	09 09	40 23	36 37	16 13	30 38
Bl	−		−	16 14	19 07	28 02	12 00	26 05	29 02	11 00	30 01
Wa	+	.480	.583	+	78 06	66 27	16 10	51 31	54 39	24 13	49 39
Wa	−			−	07 07	14 00	06 00	15 00	15 00	04 00	15 00
Br	+	.206	.233	.442	+	60 25	11 08	55 21	53 33	24 06	48 33
Br	−				−	12 01	06 01	07 06	09 04	13 00	11 02
C	+	−.312	−.285	−.225	−.167	+	21 06	42 30	46 36	23 12	54 28
C	−					−	00 04	25 01	24 04	08 01	11 11
Re	+	−.488	−.535	−.324	−.259	.558	+	11 11	15 07	— —	15 07
Re	−						−	04 03	05 05	— —	06 04
F	+	−.354	−.209	−.293	.142	−.359	−.061	+	58 10	23 02	44 18
F	−							−	13 18	08 04	15 17
H	+	−.536	−.418	−.302	−.053	−.268	.174	.446	+	24 00	50 15
H	−								−	07 13	16 24
Wh	+	−.466	−.427	−.224	−.265	−.205	.000	.322	.709	+	24 02
Wh	−									−	03 10
Bu		−.578	−.500	−.322	−.181	.134	.080	.236	.371	.707	

1957 TERM

		D		Bl		Wa		Br		F		H		Wh		Bu		C
		+	−	+	−	+	−	+	−	+	−	+	−	+	−	+	−
D	+			69 10		64 10		77 02		43 31		41 38		45 34		41 37		46 32
	−			12 36		19 31		29 19		46 04		48 02		48 02		47 03		50 00
Bl	+	.629				75 01		75 06		41 35		41 40		47 34		43 37		49 31
	−					08 38		29 15		46 00		46 00		44 02		43 03		45 01
Wa	+	.506		.845				75 08		43 35		44 39		49 34		43 39		55 27
	−							26 13		41 00		40 01		39 02		40 01		41 00
Br	+	.484		.341		.293				71 30		69 37		70 36		67 38		73 32
	−									16 05		18 03		21 00		19 02		21 00
F	+	−.369		−.493		−.468		−.049				80 09		70 19		64 24		63 26
	−											07 28		22 13		20 15		28 06
H	+	−.464		−.511		−.448		−.165		.688				74 15		70 18		67 22
	−													19 21		18 22		29 10
Wh	+	−.424		−.401		−.374		−.280		.162		.368				73 20		73 20
	−															15 20		23 12
Bu	+	−.436		−.411		−.454		−.214		.151		.346		.343				74 13
	−																	22 18
C		−.462		−.405		−.375		−.261		−.118		.010		.132		.325		

1958 TERM

		D	Bl +	Bl −	Wa +	Wa −	Br +	Br −	C +	C −	S +	S −	H +	H −	F +	F −	Wh +	Wh −
D	+		32 03		33 00		34 01		24 11		14 12		15 19		11 19		10 25	
	−		10 33		16 31		27 20		40 03		44 02		45 01		44 03		43 04	
Bl	+	.680			35 05		37 06		31 11		21 13		24 17		18 20		17 26	
	−				10 26		22 14		30 03		34 01		34 02		33 03		33 03	
Wa	+	.666	.607				47 02		36 12		29 12		28 19		24 22		21 28	
	−						12 19		26 02		29 01		31 00		31 00		31 00	
Br	+	.450	.286	.633					44 14		40 13		41 19		35 22		33 29	
	−								21 00		19 01		20 01		20 01		21 00	
C	+	−.317	−.218	−.222	−.279						44 11		52 12		45 16		43 22	
	−										11 03		06 08		06 07		07 07	
S	+	−.507	−.440	−.331	−.221	.014							47 10		44 14		48 11	
	−												08 06		07 05		03 11	
H	+	−.613	−.416	−.461	−.273	.337	.241								50 09		46 15	
	−														04 13		07 13	
F	+	−.615	−.478	−.519	−.329	.227	.149	.562									46 09	
	−																06 17	
Wh		−.651	−.539	−.584	−.426	.128	.514	.366	.557									

1959 TERM

	D +	D −	Bl +	Bl −	Wa +	Wa −	Br +	Br −	S +	S −	C +	C −	F +	F −	H +	H −	Wh +	Wh −
D	+		48	08	51	06	54	04	38	16	44	13	17	36	23	35	22	36
	−		16	27	24	17	28	15	38	04	42	00	41	02	39	03	40	03
Bl	.503		+		62	01	60	04	40	20	54	09	25	35	29	35	29	35
			−		11	22	20	15	34	00	30	04	31	03	31	03	33	02
Wa	.360		.724		+		70	05	51	20	66	09	35	36	38	37	37	38
					−		10	13	22	00	19	04	20	02	22	00	22	01
Br	.354		.444		.546		+		59	19	67	13	42	35	46	35	43	39
							−		17	01	19	00	16	03	16	03	19	00
S	−.246		−.391		−.291		−.181		+		62	12	50	23	53	22	54	22
									−		19	01	07	13	05	15	05	15
C	−.334		−.035		.067		−.190		−.133		+		53	29	53	32	54	32
											−		03	09	08	05	06	07
F	−.643		−.485		−.360		−.242		.282		.270		+		49	08	45	13
													−		11	27	16	22
H	−.541		−.448		−.425		−.222		.382		.006		.579		+		47	15
															−		14	24
Wh	−.560		−.484		−.401		−.382		.384		.115		.360		.388			

1960 TERM

	D	Bl +	Bl −	Wa +	Wa −	Br +	Br −	S +	S −	C +	C −	Wh +	Wh −	F +	F −	H +	H −
D +	+	41	05	42	04	44	02	31	14	23	22	20	26	16	23	20	25
D −	−	23	29	31	21	33	19	43	06	51	01	45	07	47	03	50	01
Bl +	.471	+		61	03	58	06	41	19	40	23	32	32	31	26	37	26
Bl −		−		12	22	19	15	33	01	34	00	33	01	32	00	33	00
Wa +	.363	.655		+		69	04	51	18	50	22	41	32	39	26	45	26
Wa −				−		08	17	23	02	24	01	24	01	24	00	25	00
Br +	.392	.403		.664		+		57	16	55	21	45	32	44	25	49	26
Br −						−		17	04	19	02	20	01	19	01	21	00
S +	−.230	−.337		−.195		−.029		+		56	18	52	22	51	15	56	17
S −								−		15	04	11	09	10	09	11	08
C +	−.551	−.410		−.273		−.175		−.031		+		56	18	55	14	59	14
C −										−		09	14	08	11	11	12
Wh +	−.455	−.474		−.367		−.319		.133		.331		+		51	12	53	11
Wh −												−		12	14	17	15
F +	−.578	−.481		−.390		−.287		.228		.343		.348		+		58	05
F −														−		04	20
H	−.602	−.441		−.362		−.322		.171		.317		.315		.745			

1961 TERM

	D +	D −	Wa +	Wa −	Bl +	Bl −	Br +	Br −	BW +	BW −	C +	C −	S +	S −	Wh +	Wh −	F +	F −	H +	H −
D	+		54 00		46 08		53 00		07 01		31 23		40 14		08 06		09 13		15 39	
	−		12 15		12 15		22 06		04 00		27 01		26 01		14 00		16 00		25 02	
Wa	.674		+		56 10		64 01		09 01		43 23		52 14		13 06		15 13		24 41	
			−		02 12		10 05		01 00		14 01		13 01		09 00		10 00		15 00	
Bl	.426		.600		+		56 01		09 01		36 22		44 13		11 05		13 11		17 40	
					−		18 05		02 00		21 02		21 02		11 01		12 02		22 01	
Br	.389		.471		.343		+		10 01		52 23		59 15		17 06		20 13		35 39	
							−		01 00		06 00		06 00		05 00		05 00		05 01	
BW	−.213		−.100		−.135		−.091		+		09 02		10 01		— —		00 00		03 08	
									−		00 01		01 00		— —		00 00		01 00	
C	−.407		−.240		−.289		−.178		.522		+		45 12		19 06		21 11		33 24	
											−		21 03		03 00		04 02		07 17	
S	−.270		−.137		−.164		−.137		−.091		−.100		+		18 04		22 09		34 31	
													−		03 02		02 04		05 10	
Wh	−.522		−.359		−.276		−.244		.000		−.181		.204		+		16 06		16 06	
															−		04 02		02 04	
F	−.615		−.431		−.321		−.281		.000		−.008		.291		.055		+		21 03	
																	−		02 11	
H	−.611		−.492		−.596		−.190		−.426		.262		.148		.337		.710			

1962 TERM

		D		Bl		Wa		Br		G		BW		S		C		H	
		+	−	+	−	+	−	+	−	+	−	+	−	+	−	+	−	+	−
D	+	+		68	12	73	07	75	05	71	08	60	16	44	36	40	39	18	61
	−		−	14	09	19	03	20	03	19	04	22	01	20	03	18	03	19	02
Bl	+	.249		+		78	03	78	04	71	10	63	16	44	38	46	35	19	62
	−				−	14	07	17	04	19	02	19	01	20	01	12	07	18	01
Wa	+	.068		.403		+		91	01	80	11	72	17	54	38	53	37	28	62
	−						−	03	07	09	01	09	00	10	00	04	05	09	00
Br	+	.106		.213		.762		+		84	10	74	17	56	39	54	39	30	63
	−								−	06	02	08	00	08	00	04	03	07	00
G	+	.094		−.035		−.019		.120		+		71	17	60	30	45	42	32	55
	−										−	10	00	03	09	12	00	05	07
BW	+	−.187		−.162		−.146		−.135		−.154		+		59	23	52	27	34	45
	−												−	03	14	04	13	02	15
S	+	−.274		−.345		−.254		−.227		.276		.423		+		35	26	31	30
	−														−	23	16	06	33
C	+	−.290		−.051		.084		.005		−.319		.327		−.016		+		26	32
	−																−	11	31
H		−.571		−.579		−.409		−.358		−.033		.247		.358		.191			

equal divisions of the Court), and in any of these three latter events, the voting of the pair in such a decision was recorded in an extended table but was excluded from the cells of the four-fold table, which are based upon the first four categories specified above. *In this tabulation of votes for factor analysis, no attention was given to the semantic content of the decisions.*

In the early stages of the planning of the research, I experimented both with tetrachoric and with phi/phi-max coefficients, as alternatives to phi correlation coefficients for the computation of the matrix for factor analysis. I was concerned about the well-known statistical property of phi coefficients: that the theoretical limits (to the statistic) of -1 to $+1$ can be attained empirically only if the marginal distributions are identical or reversed, since the maximum size of phi is a function of the proportionality of the marginals. Of course, it was not difficult to convert the empirically obtained coefficients so that they were transformed to base limits of -1 to $+1$.[1] However, the effect of such a transformation was to produce a correlation matrix that overestimated both agreement and disagreement—in effect, the tails of the distribution were stretched considerably, and the difference between the tails and the bulk of the curve was magnified. This is an undesirable effect to produce in a set of relations that evidently are quite bi-polar. The tetrachoric coefficient is extremely sensitive to the presence of zero cells in the four-fold tables, and consequently produced an effect similar to that of the transformed phis. For example, in the 1957 Term, there were no joint dissents between Douglas and Clark, Black and Harlan, Black and Frankfurter, Warren and Clark, Warren and Frankfurter, Brennan and Clark, and Brennan and Whittaker. On the other hand, the sums of the frequencies of the minor diagonal for the fourfold tables for these pairs of respondents was, respectively: 82, 86, 81, 68, 76, 53, and 57; while the total frequencies of agreement (necessarily, in the majority, since their common frequency of agreement in dissent was zero) for the same pairs in the same sequence were: 46, 41, 41, 55, 43, 73, and 70. (See Table 5.) Obviously, each of these pairs showed both substantial agreement *and* substantial disagreement; the first five pairs showed more disagreement than agreement, but the two Brennan pairs showed the opposite. Both the phi/phi-max coefficients and the tetrachoric coefficients, for all seven pairs, were -1.00. The ordinary phi coefficients for these same pairs, however, were: $-.46$, $-.51$, $-.49$, $-.38$, $-.47$, $-.26$, and $-.28$.

[1] Edward E. Cureton, "Note on ϕ/ϕ_{max}," *Psychometrika*, Vol. 24 (March 1959), pp. 89–91.

These findings are summarized in Table 6. Obviously, the phi coefficient is sensitive to differences in joint relationships that are blurred and distorted by the phi/phi-max coefficients and the tetrachorics, but the phis *do* take into consideration the ways in which agreement and disagreement are expressed (as manifested by the differences between the pair of cells in each diagonal, and therefore in the marginal frequencies), and this is the quality desired in the correlation metric.

There are also differences among these various measures, from the point of view of theoretical statistics, but I shall not dwell upon this matter. In

TABLE 6

Variance in Correlation Measures for Selected Pairs of Respondents, 1957 Term

Respondent Pair	Total Frequency of Disagreement	Agreement in the Majority	Agreement in Dissent	r_t	ϕ/ϕ_{max}	ϕ
Douglas/Clark	82	46	0	−1.00	−1.00	−.46
Black/Harlan	86	41	0	−1.00	−1.00	−.51
Black/Frankfurter	81	41	0	−1.00	−1.00	−.49
Warren/Clark	68	55	0	−1.00	−1.00	−.38
Warren/Frankfurter	76	43	0	−1.00	−1.00	−.47
Brennan/Clark	53	73	0	−1.00	−1.00	−.26
Brennan/Whittaker	57	70	0	−1.00	−1.00	−.28

brief, phi is supposed to be appropriate for the correlation of data for which the nominal classification of the variables reflects a "true" or natural dichotomy, such as sex (male/female); while tetrachorics are appropriate when two continuous normally distributed variables (such as height) have been compressed artificially into two categories (such as tall [equal to or over six feet] and short [under six feet]). It is certainly beyond the scope of this study to enter into epistemological controversy over the question whether sex, for example, is a continuous (rather than a discontinuous) variable "in nature." One readily can appreciate that, for many purposes, biologists might find it useful so to conceptualize that variable. With regard to my own data, the question also is one of the level of conceptualization: on the level of the manifest content of the voting data, the dichotomy is a "natural" one, since each respondent can be said, at a behavioral level, either to have agreed or disagreed with the majority decision in a case. On the other hand, all we have to do is to make the quite realistic assumption that there are intensity differences, in agreement and disagreement, that are perceived by the justices—and such differences frequently are manifest in the opinions associated with sets of votes, even though they cannot be perceived by an analyst in the manifest voting data alone—and the variable that we are measuring (agreement and disagreement in voting) should be conceptualized as a continuous variable. In limiting my observation to the voting data, I have not observed directly such intensity differences, however, so my preference for the use of the conventional phi coefficients, as distinguished from tetrachoric coefficients, appears in any event to be the more reasonable course to follow, in the light of the relevant statistical theory.

The usual term correlation table is a 9×9 matrix which reports coefficients for thirty-six different dyads, although as previously noted, for two terms (1956 and 1961) there is a 10×10 matrix for forty-five dyads. In regard to the latter two, it should be noted that there were no empirical data for the four-fold tables to represent the relationship between the two pairs of respondents who had no interaction, because one succeeded to the other's position on the Court (Whittaker/Reed in 1956, and White/Whittaker in 1961). In each of these instances, a coefficient of zero was inserted in the correlation matrix. Similarly, since White joined the Court after Frankfurter's *de facto* retirement late in the 1961 Term, there was no empirical possibility of interaction between this pair, although there might have been if Frankfurter's health had permitted him to participate until the end of the term. In this instance, zero entries were recorded for both the cells of the four-fold table and the correlation coefficient. All data were placed on punch cards, and the computation of the phi coefficients was programmed for computer analysis.

The initial product of a factor analysis is a set of derived correlations or "loadings" which purport to measure the extent to which each element, of whatever has been associated in the correlation matrix, is related to the reference dimensions into which the original correlation matrix has been partitioned. In the present study, the elements are the justices, and the factor loadings purport to express the correlation of each justice with the manifest structural dimensions of the phi matrix. The complete centroid method of factoring was employed, and all except the data for the last two terms—which were processed after they became available, subsequent to when the bulk of the research was completed—were programmed for the I.B.M. 650 at Stanford University, utilizing a program (SU-4524) developed at the Watson Scientific Computing Laboratory of Columbia University by Jonathan E. Robbins in April 1957, as modified by John P. Gilbert, Staff Statistician of the Center for Advanced Study in the Behavioral Sciences at Stanford University. I factored the correlation matrices for the two most recent terms, using a hand calculator, since a complete centroid program was not available for the former computer facility at Michigan State University. Communalities were estimated by using the highest loading in each column of the original correlation matrices. Although more factors were extracted and inspected, only the first three were used for the purpose of the primary analysis of this study. The correlations in the third residual matrices were smaller than the estimated error variance, a matter which I shall discuss presently in greater detail. The psychological distances between the justices (discussed in Chapter 9) can be computed from point configurations in a set of factorial spaces of three orthogonal dimensions, using the standard formula,

$$(4) \qquad d_{(i_1,\ i_2)} = [(X_1 - X_2)^2 + (Y_1 - Y_2)^2 + (Z_1 - Z_2)^2]^{\frac{1}{2}}$$

where d is the distance, i_1 and i_2 are the ideal-points for a pair of justices, and X, Y, and Z are the i-point loadings on the reference axes.

The factor loadings for all justices on the first three factors for each term are reported in Table 30. It will be observed that the highest loadings (both positive and negative) are on the first factor, and the mean magnitude of the absolute values of the third factor loadings is smallest. The first factor is the one to which the largest portion of the variance is attributed and I shall assume that it is the most important factor, that the second factor is next most important, and so on.

The usual procedure in factor analysis is to rotate the orthogonal factor reference axes, which are the direct product of a complete centroid routine, to oblique positions that are presumed to correspond to some criterion that is manifestly related to empirical reality, and thus to make possible a more meaningful psychological interpretation than would usually be possible if the orthogonal axes were retained for any purpose other than to determine the point configuration. Orthogonal axes are statistically independent, while oblique axes are correlated with each other; therefore, making a factor intepretation based directly upon a system of orthogonal axes implies an assumption that there is no correlation among the factors, which must be conceived to be statistically independent of each other.

I propose to use a somewhat unusual—indeed, so far as I am aware, a unique—criterion for the rotation of the reference axes. The theoretical possibility of using this criterion was suggested to me by Coombs' work, as I previously have acknowledged. However, I am also indebted to my own earlier work in cumulative scaling of judicial cases, and to the fact that my empirical data differ in many important respects from those with which social psychologists are accustomed to working and to thinking about. I am confident that the average professionally trained social psychologist, who knows far more about factor analysis and cumulative scaling and statistics generally than I do, would have come up with a similar proposal, if he had been confronted with the necessity of resolving an equivalent empirical problem in his research. It occurred to me that if cumulative scaling and factor analysis indeed are in theory alternative procedures for measuring the same psychological relationship, and appropriate alternative observations were made of the same raw data, then the cumulative scales themselves ought to provide the most appropriate criterion for the rotation of the factorial reference axes. If the first principal axis (which the first centroid factor approximates) [2] represents the most important way in which respondents agree and disagree, as this is represented in the correlation matrix, then it should correspond to the cumulative scale which measures the most basic attitudinal dimension along which the respondents are arrayed. Similarly, the second reference axis (centroid factor), which I shall assume represents the next most important respect in which the respondents agree and disagree, should correspond to the cumulative scale which measures the next most important attitudinal dimension.

The technique of cumulative scaling that I have used will be explained presently. Assuming for the moment that the cumulative scales have been constructed, each of them reports a rank order of the respondents' attitudes toward the semantic content measured by the scale. The theory outlined in the preceding paragraph suggests that somewhere imbedded in the factorial space, there are analogue axes that are functionally equivalent to the cumulative scales. I shall define "functional equivalence" to mean that the projections from the ideal-points of the respondents, upon the analogue scale axes, are in the same rank order as that of the corresponding

[2] Louis L. Thurstone, *Multiple-Factor Analysis* (Chicago: University of Chicago Press, 1947), p. 149.

cumulative scale. Because of the known error variance involved in both the factor analysis and cumulative scaling methods, it is not reasonable to expect perfect correlation between the rank order of respondents on cumulative scale and analogue scale axis pairs, but we should expect a high degree of positive correlation. I shall require the quite rigorous standard of a rank correlation of not less than $+.90$, at a confidence level of not more than .01. The identification of more than one analogue scale for the same fixed configuration of ideal-points will, of course, enhance confidence in the inference that the configuration is a function of respondent attitudes toward the scale variables; from a statistical point of view, such confidence is a result of the *product* rather than the average of the probabilities for a single scale pair alone. (If, for example, the confidence level for each of two pairs of cumulative scales and scale axes [for two different scale variables in relation to the same point configuration,] was .01 and each was correlated at an acceptable level of .01, the joint probability for the coincident chance occurrence of the set of interrelationships would be .0001, not .01.)

Louis L. Thurstone, the late pioneer in multiple factor analysis who developed the complete centroid method that I have followed, published in 1951 with J. W. Degan a factorial study of the 1943 and 1944 Terms of the United States Supreme Court. This study by Thurstone and Degan was very similar, from a methodological point of view, to the present undertaking; such minor differences as their practice of throwing away about a fifth of the data, by not including decisions with solitary dissenting votes, and of pooling the data for both terms, certainly should not result in any important differences in substantive findings or interpretation, as between their own factorial data and my own for, say, the 1946 and 1947 Terms. However, Thurstone and Degan rotated the obtained factorial reference axes to simple structure, and were unable to provide any interpretation for their findings. They did suggest that a re-examination of the raw data "with grouping according to the votes of the judges" should make it possible "to clarify just what the factors are that are common to the cases." In effect, the cumulative scaling constitutes just such a re-examination of the raw data. In any event, after the bulk of the research for the present study was completed, I undertook to re-analyze the Thurstone and Degan factorial study, using their own unrotated factor loadings, and estimates of cumulative scale ranks which I adapted from data published in 1948 in Pritchett's *Roosevelt Court*. I did this in part because I wanted to subject my own method of rotation to as rigorous a test as possible, and this seemed a unique opportunity to take advantage of factorial and scaling data that other researchers had computed and reported, in the intriguing context of a factorial space that a master theoretician confessed he could not satisfactorily interpret, in the absence of further work that he was not prepared to undertake. The results of my experiment have been published,[3] and an examination of them shows that the same method that I am now proposing, and which I shall exemplify in relation to my own data, produces very similar results when used to interpret data that were collected quite independently—and for other purposes—by other scholars.

I shall now describe the method for rotating the reference axes to positions for which the cumulative scales provide the criteria. The problem is essentially a mathematical one: to ascertain the set of weights which will locate an axis in the factorial space so that the rank order of projections upon the axis from the i-points is maximally correlated with the rank order of the respondents on the equivalent cumulative scale. The solution can be depicted geometrically, but it must be derived algebraically. The possibility of achieving a best solution for the problem by setting up a set of simultaneous equations has been explored, but I am informed by statisticians that the mathematical solution for the required set of equations is not known.[4] However, there is a relatively simple and straightforward procedure for computing an approximate solution, which is close enough (to the apparently unattainable maximal solution) to suffice for present purposes.

The distance from the origin of the factor space to the point which is

---

[3] Glendon Schubert, "A Solution to the Indeterminate Factorial Resolution of Thurstone and Degan's Study of the Supreme Court," *Behavioral Science*, Vol. 7 (October 1962), pp. 448–458.

[4] It may be possible to develop a least squares solution to the different problem of identifying the factorial axis rotation which results in an array of point projections, on the axis, that are most similar in dispersion to the array of points for scale scores. Professor Fred Kort of the University of Connecticut has done work on this problem, and he has written the sets of differential equations, including the partial derivatives, which must be solved simultaneously. Since these equations are non-linear, a direct algebriac solution is not possible; but using an iterative procedure based on Taylor's theorem, Professor Kort has written a computer program in FORTRAN, which he designed to produce a least squares solution. Of course, this procedure involves the direct comparison of the point positions (both scale and factorial) on the basis of the respective interval metrics. As I shall explain below, these two metrics are bounded by empirical range limits that vary, even for the same term sets of data; and for additional reasons that will be explored in the next chapter, the probable error variance in both the scaling and the factorial measurements is sufficiently large that I decided at the time of the designing of this research to rely upon the non-parametric test of rank correlation, rather than upon product-moment correlation, for the comparison of points on scales and point projections upon analogue axes. Therefore a least squares solution, which only coincidentally results in maximal rank correlation, does not provide a "best" solution for the problem described in the text.

closest to a given *i*-point, on any scale axis, is computed by use of the formula,

$$(5) \qquad d = \frac{\alpha x + \beta y + \gamma z}{(\alpha^2 + \beta^2 + \gamma^2)^{1/2}},$$

when *d* is the distance from the origin to the point on the scale axis where it is orthogonal to the projection from the *i*-point; x, y, and z are coordinates of the factorial reference axes for the *i*-point; and α, β, and γ are the coefficients which determine the position of the scale axis in the three-dimensional factor space, by serving as the reference axis coordinates for the positive terminus of the scale axis. These are the "weights" referred to above. Of course, it is a simple matter of plane geometry to compute from the weights the cosines for the rotated (viz., scale) axis, for the purpose of showing the apparent position of the rotated axis in sets of two-dimensional plots. Table 31 reports the weights and cosines for the scale axes for each term, and Figure 10 depicts the two-dimensional geometric representation of the scale axes, reference axes, and point configuration in the factor space, for each term.

The initial step in the procedure for determining the weights is to prepare a set of two-dimensional plots of the factor space, similar to those shown in Figure 10 except, of course, for the absence of scale axes. An examination of the point configuration from the three perspectives afforded by these plots makes possible an initial trial estimate of the probable weights. The next step is to prepare a table which simply lists, in parallel columns, the respondents and their loadings on each of the three reference axes. At this stage, formula (5) can be used without bothering to divide by the square root of the sum of the squares of the trial weights (since that division only serves the purpose of reducing the length of the scale axis to the unit radius of the factorial space); the rank order of *i*-points on the scale axis will be the same as that calculated from the set of numerator sums. The estimated weight for alpha is multiplied by each of the loadings for the first reference axis, the beta estimate is multiplied by the loadings on the second, and gamma by the third. These products are then summed by *rows,* and the ranking of the sums is compared with the scale ranks of the respondents. The analyst then can observe what adjustments in the weights may be necessary in order to improve the correspondence between the two sets of ranks. The sums are then recomputed, using the revised estimates of the weights, and the process proceeds by trial and error until no further improvement in the rank correlation appears possible. The denominator is then calculated, and also the final set of d's. Thus, both the projections of the i-points on the scale axis, and the position of the scale axis in the factorial space with the i-points, are the result of the same mathematical operation.

Since the rotational procedure is based upon the method of rank correlation, there can be no uniquely "best" fit to the configuration of i-points. There is, instead, a set of appropriate and approximately correct solutions, which may be conceptualized as follows: consider a cone which intercepts a relatively quite small circular area on the surface of a unit sphere. All axes lying within the cone will array the projections from the i-points so as to produce the same set of rankings of the justices as will be produced by any other axis within the cone. The rotation that is produced by the set of weights one should select, by the use of the empirical method that I have described, lies within that cone.

The Cumulative Scales

Cumulative scaling of the votes of the judicial respondents is based upon an independent observation of the same sets of raw data that are used for the factor analysis. But instead of tabulating votes by dyads according to agreement with the majority in each decision, for scaling purposes the individual votes that comprise the set for each decision are classified as being in support of, or in opposition to, the values associated with the scale variable, for which directionality previously has been assigned. I shall discuss below the semantic content of these scale variables, and I have discussed at some length, in an earlier work, the basic procedures for cumulative scaling of the votes of Supreme Court justices.[5] For present purposes, I shall summarize briefly the technique employed in this study.

In theory, as I have explained in the preceding chapter, the cases which the Court has docketed for decision-making on the merits of the issues presented are conceptualized as being equivalent to the items of a questionnaire. Each case asks the justices to respond to the question: is your attitude toward value X sufficiently favorable that you believe that a claim of degree Y should be upheld? (For example: Is your attitude toward political freedom sufficiently favorable that you believe that a witness before a congressional investigating committee cannot "constitutionally" be compelled to reveal his past associations, if any, with the Communist Party of the United States?) X defines the content of the scale variable which is

[5] Glendon Schubert, *Quantitative Analysis of Judical Behavior* (New York: The Free Press, 1959), pp. 269–290.

perceived by the respondents to be the relevant criterion for deciding the case; Y is the perceived verbal statement which specifies the location of the stimulus-point on the scale (or, alternatively, of the j-point's projection upon the scale axis in the factorial space). In my parenthetical example, above, X = "political freedom;" and Y = "a witness before . . . Communist Party of the United States." I am quite aware that many traditional public lawyers among political scientists,[6] and doubtless most law professors, will object to such a conceptualization of what transpires in the minds of Supreme Court justices, when they make decisions, as constituting vast oversimplification and distortion of both the "legal issues" and also "the facts" of the cases typically decided by the Court. But surely such other scholars cannot *know*, any more than I, what goes on in the minds of the justices. The public lawyers and law professors engage in the artistic enterprise of confusing their own personal values with those of the justices whom they seek to understand, as they make subjective inferences which they purport to base upon the data provided by the opinions written by the justices. Such scholars usually accept as a form of unquestionable truth the manifest content of judicial opinions, directing their own critique not to the reliability and validity of such verbalisms as articulations of underlying judicial attitudes, but instead to the logical consistency of the statements of values, or to the normative question whether such values as a judge espouses in his opinions are the ones in which—according to the personal preferences of the scholar—the justice *ought* to believe. I think it is clear that such scholarship requires an astounding degree of psychological naivete, on the part of both the scholar and his audience, if it is to be taken seriously. In any event, it seems to me that the question whether cumulative scaling involves "vast oversimplification" of the process of judicial decision-making is an empirical question, which best can be resolved on the basis of the usefulness and reliability of the knowledge to which it leads. When one compares the bulk and manifest complexity of the opinion and voting data in the typical Supreme Court decision, with the example I have suggested of the case transformed into a scale stimulus, it is evident that great simplification has taken place. If the results produced are not useful and reliable, then it has indeed been *over*simplification. If the contrary can be demonstrated, then this is the very kind of simplification

[6] *E.g.,* John P. Roche, "Political Science and Science Fiction," *American Political Science Review*, Vol. 52 (December 1958), pp. 1026–1029; Walter Berns, "Law and Behavioral Science," *Law and Contemporary Problems*, Vol. 28 (Winter 1963), pp. 185–212; Wallace Mendelson, "The Neo-Behavioral Approach to the Judicial Process: A Critique," *American Political Science Review*, Vol. 57 (September 1963), pp. 593–603.

for which social scientists ought to strive, if they are to achieve scientific understanding of human relationships, which usually are pretty complicated under any circumstances. After all, it has not been too long a time since physical scientists could debate whether the model of the atom was not a vast oversimplification of the rich complexity of natural phenomena.[7] Democritus laughed.

If a judicial respondent accepts the defined valuation, he is scored as having voted affirmatively; if he rejects it, he is scored as having voted negatively. The scale matrix consists of scores for the votes of the respondents, with each column consisting of the set of votes of a single justice for all decisions in which he participated, and each row consisting of the set of votes for all justices who participated in a particular decision. Since some nonparticipation is usual, even when the data are collected in term sets and there have been no changes in the set of respondents during the term, it is necessary to use special symbols to distinguish nonparticipation from voting scores. In constructing the scale, the objective is the usual one of maximizing the internal consistency of the voting patterns for the respondents; that is, if there were no inconsistency, the voting scores in all columns would be one of three types: (1) all affirmative responses; (2) one or more affirmative responses in one subset which consists exclusively of affirmative responses, and one or more negative responses in a second subset which consists exclusively of negative responses; or (3) all negative responses. From an empirical point of view, a limited amount of inconsistent voting can be anticipated, and the practical problem is to rearrange rows and columns of the scale matrix until the number of such inconsistent votes is minimized.

In Figures 1 and 3, consistent votes in support of the scale variable are denoted by the symbol x, and inconsistent positive votes by x̲. A blank space indicates a consistent negative vote, and the symbol — is used to signify an inconsistent negative vote. An asterisk signifies nonparticipation, and a slash bar indicates that a respondent was not a member of the Court at the time of the decision. Scale scores are simple functions of scale positions, and a respondent's scale position is defined as being fixed by his last consistent positive vote. When one or more asterisks or slash bars intervene between a respondent's consistent positive and negative votes, his scale position is assumed to be at the mean of the decisions for which his response could not be measured. The rationale underlying such a rule for

---

[7] Lancelot Law Whyte, *Essay on Atomism from Democritus to 1960* (Middletown: Wesleyan University Press, 1961).

handling nonparticipations is that in the absence of objective information about what his response might have been, it is most reasonable to assume that it was equally likely that he might have responded in either way in such decisions—hence they are so partitioned as to assimilate half with the set of his positive responses, and the other half with the set of his negative responses. The chief advantage of this rule is its simplicity. An alternative rule, which I have not used because of its greater complexity, but which might be preferred for some judicial scaling work, would partition the nonparticipations and absences according to the ratio of columnar marginal totals of positive and negative responses, or—if there were an unusual amount of inconsistent voting—according to the ratio of the frequencies of the items included in the two subsets of *consistent* positive and negative votes. The latter rule, in particular, conforms best to probability theory. If I had more confidence than I do entertain in the precise validity of the scale scores denoted in the scales reported in Figures 1 and 3, I should have followed the better but more complicated procedure. Since, however, I doubted that changes resulting from having followed the complex rule would be great enough to exceed the probable range of error variance in the scalar measurements, I chose to follow the simpler procedure of splitting the difference.

A respondent's scale score is computed by use of the formula,

$$(6) \qquad\qquad s = \frac{2p}{n} - 1,$$

where s is his scale score, p his scale position, and n equals the number of decisions measured by the scale. Scale scores, like correlation coefficients and factor loadings, can range in value from -1 to $+1$, with the difference that in practice, scale scores frequently attain these extreme values; the factor loadings cannot do this, irrespective of the extremity of the attitudinal position of a justice, because of the empirical limitation that the marginals place upon the range of the phi coefficients.

One of the weaknesses of cumulative scaling, from a statistical point of view, is the lack of any really uniform criterion for testing significance. Guttman himself proposed the use of a coefficient of reproducibility to measure the degree of consistency in cumulative scales, and various rules of thumb have been conventionally associated with the use of his coefficient.[8] I

[8] Warren S. Torgerson, *Theory and Methods of Scaling* (New York: Wiley, 1958), p. 324; Bert F. Green, "Attitude Measurement," ch. 9 in Gardner Lindzey (ed.), *Handbook of Social Psychology,* (Reading: Addison-Wesley, 1954), Vol. 1, p. 356; James C. Lingoes, "Multiple Scalogram Analysis: A Set-Theoretic Model for Analyzing Dichotomous Items," *Educational and Psychological Measurement,* Vol. 23 (1963), pp. 504–510.

have followed the conventions in the use of Guttman's coefficient in the scales reported in Figures 1, 3, and 4, but it should be understood that the lower limit of the coefficient is an empirical function of the extremity and distribution of the marginal frequencies, and that for the scales that I report of Supreme Court decisions, the lower limit is frequently quite high—varying from .60 to as high as .85. Since Guttman proposed that an R of .90 should be accepted as satisfactory evidence of "unidimensionality" in a scale—that is, that the scale actually was measuring a single attitudinal dimension—it should be noted that .90 would not be a very remarkable improvement in consistency if the least consistency possible, for the same marginals of decisions and respondents, were .85.[9] Consequently I have used an alternative measure of consistency that has been suggested by Menzel,[10] in addition to computing the limit of inconsistency for the more conventional R.

The formula for Guttman's coefficient is:

$$(7) \qquad R = 1 - \frac{e}{n},$$

when R is the coefficient of reproducibility, e is the total of inconsistent responses, and n is the total of all responses. One of the rules of thumb that I have followed, in computing R, is that decisions with only a single dissent have been excluded; hence, e for the formula may be less than the total of inconsistent responses evident in the scale, just as n will almost always be smaller than the combined sum for either the columnar or row marginal totals—which must, of course, be equal, since the total of affirmative responses is the same for justices as for cases, as is also the total of negative responses. All of the R's reported in the scales (Figures 1 and 3) are higher than .900, which signifies that, in terms of Guttman's criterion, the two major attitudinal variables scaled for seventeen terms in succession, without an exception.

The empirical lower limit of R for a scale readily can be determined by computing the coefficient,

$$(8) \qquad \text{MMR} = \frac{1}{N}\left(\sum_{1 \to N}^{i} \frac{m_a}{m_a + m_b} \right)$$

---

[9] The average actual difference between the observed consistency and the least possible consistency, for the scales in this study, is about .15 (.14 for C, and .15 for E). The smallest actual difference is .09 for C (in 1946) and .10 for E (in both 1946 and 1948); the greatest actual difference was .20 for C (in 1956) and .18 for E (in 1955, 1957, and 1961). See Table 7.

[10] Herbert Menzel, "A New Coefficient for Scalogram Analysis," *Public Opinion Quarterly*, Vol. 17 (1953), pp. 268–280.

TABLE 7

Measures of Consistency for the Cumulative Scales, 1946–62 Terms

Term	C Scale				E Scale				R-MMR$_{max}$	
	MMR$_j$	MMR$_i$	R	S	MMR$_j$	MMR$_i$	R	S	C	E
1946	.63	.82	.91	.52	.65	.85	.95	.68	.09	.10
1947	.64	.80	.91	.56	.70	.80	.96	.78	.11	.16
1948	.62	.81	.95	.72	.64	.87	.97	.79	.14	.10
1949	.68	.85	.98	.85	.73	.82	.95	.75	.13	.13
1950	.71	.78	.92	.69	.73	.73	.90	.68	.14	.17
1951	.72	.73	.91	.69	.74	.79	.96	.82	.18	.17
1952	.70	.87	.98	.80	.74	.69	.90	.62	.11	.16
1953	.66	.79	.92	.64	.70	.76	.92	.68	.13	.16
1954	.72	.77	.96	.82	.71	.81	.94	.67	.19	.13
1955	.64	.84	.95	.70	.71	.75	.93	.74	.11	.18
1956	.74	.76	.96	.86	.66	.82	.93	.60	.20	.11
1957	.68	.79	.96	.84	.70	.81	.99	.90	.17	.18
1958	.65	.86	.97	.82	.67	.79	.95	.80	.11	.16
1959	.67	.82	.95	.71	.70	.81	.97	.90	.13	.16
1960	.66	.83	.94	.71	.70	.77	.93	.74	.11	.16
1961	.71	.82	.98	.80	.74	.76	.94	.79	.16	.18
1962	.72	.82	.97	.83	.76	.74	.91	.75	.15	.15
Average	.68	.81	.95	.74	.70	.78	.94	.75	.14	.15

MMR$_i$ = Minimal Marginal Reproducibility for respondents (justices)
MMR$_j$ = Minimal Marginal Reproducibility for stimula (cases)
MMR$_{max}$ = The larger of each MMR$_i$, MMR$_j$ pair
R = Guttman's Coefficient of Reproducibility
S = Menzel's Coefficient of Scalability

when MMR is the minimal marginal reproducibility, N is the total cases or respondents, m_a is the more populous of the two marginal frequencies for each column (or row), and m_b is the less populous. In other words, MMR is the mean of the ratios of the modal frequency to the sum of the marginals for each respondent (or case).[11] MMR must be computed independently for both columns and rows, since the higher index will be the lower limit for R, for any given scale. Table 7 lists the MMR and R in parallel columns for both major variables for all seventeen terms, together with the S scores for Menzel's coefficient of scalability. This table shows that, although there is some variation, of course, from term to term, the

[11] See Allen L. Edwards, *Techniques of Attitude Scale Construction* (New York: Appleton-Century-Crofts, 1957), pp. 191–193.

corresponding averages for the C and E scales on these indices are very similar, the largest difference being only three percent.

S provides a more rigorous standard than does R, because S (unlike R) does not capitalize upon the spurious contribution to consistency that arises from the inclusion in the scale of either decisions or respondents with extreme marginal distributions. The formula for Menzel's coefficient is:

$$(9) \qquad S = 1 - \frac{e'}{\sum_{1 \to N}^{i} m_b},$$

when e' is the total of *all* inconsistent responses (including the decisions with solitary dissents), N is the number of respondents, and m_b is the less populous of the two marginal frequencies for each column. There is an alternative computing formula for S (just as for MMR) for measuring the row marginals; but its use is not applicable for any of the scales reported in the appendices, since without exception, the differences in the marginal distributions for the judicial respondents were more extreme than the equivalent differences for the decisions.[12] By using the more extreme set of marginals the value of S is minimized, and the value for MMR is maximized. Menzel has suggested that the appropriate level of acceptance for S is "somewhere between .60 and .65;" as Table 7 indicates, only two of the S coefficients reported for the scales in the appendices are below the suggested criterion level, and for most of the scales, S is considerably above that level.

In order to measure the correlation between the sets of ranks on cumulative scales and their analogue scale axes, Kendall's rank correlation coefficient, tau, was used. If ties are present in either ranking, the formula is :

$$(10) \qquad \tau_b = \frac{S}{[\tfrac{1}{2}n(n-1) - T]^{\frac{1}{2}} \ [\tfrac{1}{2}n(n-1) - U]^{\frac{1}{2}}};$$
$$T = \tfrac{1}{2}\, t(t-1); \ U = \tfrac{1}{2}\, u(u-1);$$

when τ_b is tau, S is the absolute difference between the sums of the consistent and inconsistent rankings for all pairs, *n* is the number of items

---

[12] Although there are no exceptions for S, there are two for MMR: in both 1952 and 1962, the row marginals for the E scale were more extreme than the column marginals. There is no anomaly here; the computation of S is based on the sum of the non-modal frequencies, while that of MMR is based on the mean of ratios of modal to marginal sum frequencies. Although both measures usually agree in their evaluation of the relative extremity of columnar and row marginals, it is possible for them to diverge when the difference is small; and this is what happened in regard to the two terms under discussion.

in each set of ranks, *t* is the number of items with the same rank in the first ranking, and *u* is the number of items with the same rank in the second ranking. If no ties are present in either set of ranks, then the formula reduces to the simpler form:

$$(11) \quad \tau = \frac{S}{\frac{1}{2}n(n-1)}.$$

For most of the computations in this study, *n* was nine, and therefore $\frac{1}{2}n(n-1)$ equaled 36; for the 1956 and 1961 Terms when *n* was ten, the denominator for tau was 45 (although this had to be corrected by the use of formula (9) for the C Scale in 1956, which contains one tie). Examination of Tables 1, 3, 4, and 32 shows that the differences among many scores, on either the scale axes or the cumulative scales, are quite small; and it might be thought that it would be preferable to consider to be tied all scores for which the difference is less than .050, since the probable error variance is greater than this difference. However, a sample of alternative computations using formula (9) and considering all such close differences to be ties resulted in even higher correlations. As a further check, Spearman rank correlation coefficients also were computed for a sample of the data; but rho also was consistently higher than tau for the same pairs of rankings.[13] So I have preferred the more conservative course and I have reported in Table 33 the lower tau correlations that result from the observed scores. I assume that whatever error variance there may be in the sets of rankings is unsystematic. The statistical significance of tau coefficients is determined by consulting published probability tables for the distribution of S, when *n* ≤ 10.[14]

It will be recalled, from the preceding chapter, that the objective of the rank correlation test that I have just described is to demonstrate the recovery of the linear first principal component-type curve for each cumulative scale, in the factorial space. An alternative geometric procedure would be to plot the scale axis ranks on an ordinate reference axis, against the cumulative scale ranks on an abscissal reference axis: the resulting curve should be a straight line extending diagonally at an angle of 45 degrees from the point representing the *n*th rank on both the scale axis and

---

[13] Coombs, *A Theory of Data,* pp. 457–458.

[14] Maurice A. Kendall, *Rank Correlation Methods* (London: Charles Griffin, 1955, 2nd ed.), p. 171; Sidney Siegel, *Nonparametric Statistics for the Behavioral Sciences* (New York: McGraw-Hill, 1956), p. 285 (Table Q). When *n* is greater than 10, tables of areas under the normal curve are used as an approximation to the exact values based on the distribution of S.

the cumulative scale, to the point which represents the first rank on both. If scores were to be used instead of ranks, then the curve should be a straight line extending from the point $(-1, -1)$ through the point of the origin $(0, 0)$ to the point $(+1, +1)$, providing that the correlation were both positive and perfect, and that the extreme respondents were maximally extreme on both the scale axis and the cumulative scale.[15] Empirically, such plots for either ranks or scores produce approximations of linear curves, and those for scores are shorter than the theoretical line for perfect product-moment correlation. I have not reproduced such curves, notwithstanding the ease of their construction, because the taus provide a more concise description of the same set of relationships.

The theory also states that one should be able to observe higher component curves, which pass through the configuration of i-points in the factorial space. Again, in theory, such curves might be compared with the component curves that result from plotting cumulative scale scores (or ranks) against each other. The mathematics required in order to make directly such curvilinear correlations is beyond my competence; and I am similarly precluded, by the lack of both the requisite engineering skills and sufficient funds, even from presenting photographs of three-dimensional geometric representations of the component curves in the factorial space. It is readily possible to compare the component curves for two-dimensional plots of cumulative scale scores, with the equivalent two-dimensional plots of scale axis scores. Such a demonstration is essentially trivial, however, since it is evident that if there is a high degree of positive linear correlation both between a C Scale and its analogue axis, and an E Scale and its analogue axis, then plots of the C and E Scales, and of their analogue scale axes, must result in similar component curves. I have prepared such plots for both C against E, and E against C, for both the cumulative scales and the scale axes, for all terms, in order to make the observations necessary to the classification of respondent attitudinal types upon which the discussion in Chapters 7 and 8 is based. In Figure 12, however, I report only the curves for two sample terms, in order to exemplify the method. Any interested reader can reconstruct the curves for any other term, or for the complete set, since all of the necessary data are reported in Figures 1 and 3 and Table 32.

---

[15] The empirical difference in the range of the metrics of the scale and for the scale axis precludes such a possibility from occurring. See pp. 67, 78, *supra*.

Chapter 4 · AN EXPERIMENTAL FACTOR ANALYSIS OF SIMULATED DATA

B EFORE ANY of the empirical data for this study were processed, except for a pilot analysis of the 1957 Term, and soon after the major outlines of the theory had been worked out, I decided to conduct an experiment which I would design on the basis of the theory and for which I would use simulated data. The purpose of the experiment was to investigate the amount of error variance inherent in the method that I proposed to use for factor analysis of real data. Since I knew, from the pilot study of the 1957 Term, what might be hypothesized as typical locations for the ideal-points, and I could estimate from other research the probable average volume of dissensual decisions for a typical term, and how these might be partitioned among the major scales, it was not difficult to define the simulated data. I decided to work with only two factors, in order to simplify the computations, since the effect upon the error variance of the addition of a third factor readily could be estimated. Nine i-points and 100 j-points were plotted in a two-dimensional space with orthogonal reference axes (I and II). The nine respondents, whose i-points I shall identify with the abbreviation of the names of the justices whose attitudinal syndromes I assumed the points to represent, were assigned factor loadings (reference axis coordinates) as follows:

84

TABLE 8

Actual Factor Loadings for Judicial Respondents (Simulated Data)

	Respondent	I	II
D	(Douglas)	.800	.300
Bl	(Black)	.800	−.100
Wa	(Warren)	.700	−.200
Br	(Brennan)	.500	.100
C	(Clark)	−.100	−.300
S	(Stewart)	−.300	.500
Wh	(Whittaker)	−.800	.300
H	(Harlan)	−.700	−.200
F	(Frankfurter)	−.600	−.500

Henceforth, I shall refer to these as the actual factor loadings.

By definition, the communality for each respondent consists of the sum of the squares of his factor loadings:

$$(12) \qquad h^2 = a_{i1}{}^2 + a_{i2}{}^2,$$

when h^2 is the communality, a is a factor loading, the subscript i identifies the respondent, and the subscript number identifies the factor ($1 = I$, and $2 = II$). Reference to the preceding table shows that Black's communality, according to Equation 10, is $(+.800)^2 + (−.100)^2 = .64 + .01 = .65$. The other true communalities (as I shall refer to them) are given in Table 14 below. The r matrix readily can be determined, since the correlation between any pair of respondents is equal to the sum of the cross-products of their factor loadings:

$$(13) \qquad r_{ik} = a_{i1}a_{k1} + a_{i2}a_{k2},$$

when i is the first respondent and k is the other respondent, r is the equivalent of the product-moment correlation coefficient, and other symbols are defined as in Equation 10. For example, the correlation between Douglas and Black is $[(.800)\ (.800)] + [.300)\ (−.100)] = .64 − .03 = .61$. All of the cell entries for the complete r matrix are listed in Table 15 below.

Several criteria affected the choice of locations for the set of one hundred j-points. First, positions were defined for three scale axes in the space. I assumed these axes to be the equivalent of the two major scale variables (C+ and E+) and one of the minor scale variables (F+, to be defined in the next chapter) so I shall identify the axes with those symbols here. The table below gives the coordinates for the positive termini of the axes:

TABLE 9

Reference Axis Coordinates for Scale Axes

		Scale Axes		
Coordinates		*C+*	*E+*	*F+*
	I	1.00	1.00	− .14
	II	.50	− .50	−1.00

The j-points then were partitioned as follows: 41 to C, 40 to E, and 19 to F. All points were assumed to be located on one of the scale axes, in order to simplify calculations. The projections from each i-point upon each scale axis were determined, as a control over the density of j-points in various segments of the scale axes, and to identify voting responses. At least one, and up to a maximum of ten, j-points were plotted so as to fall between each pair of adjacent projections upon every scale axis. No points were plotted beyond the most extreme projections, either positive or negative, upon any of the scale axes, since such points would represent unanimous decisions, and I already had decided not to include unanimous decisions in my sample of raw data; they would be of no help in distinguishing among positions on cumulative scales, and their only effect upon the phi correlations would be to increase the positiveness of all correlations by adding (in effect) a constant to the majority-agreement cells of the four-fold tables.

There was a third criterion which affected the location of the j-points. With the i-point projections plotted upon the scale axes, the decision regarding any j-point was readily ascertainable: if a majority of the projections were more extreme (in the positive direction of the scale axis) than the j-point, the decision was pro, and otherwise con. In either event, projections equally or more extreme (in the defined sense) than the j-point would be + votes, from the point of view of cumulative scaling, and the remaining projections would be − votes. However, for purposes of compiling the four-fold tables and the identification of majority-agreement and dissenting votes, projections equally or more extreme than the j-point will be majority votes if the decision is pro, and dissents if the decision is con. The j-points were so plotted as to establish what I then assumed to be a typical pattern in the number of decisions which generated one, two, three, or four dissents, respectively (cf. Table 3). The distribution of dissenting votes among the scale axes is given in the following table.

TABLE 10

Size of Dissenting Groups in Relation to Scale Axes (Simulated Data)

		Number of dissents:				
		1	2	3	4	*Total*
	C	5	13	11	12	41
Scale Axes:	E	7	10	11	12	40
	F	6	5	3	5	19
	Total	18	28	25	29	100

The coordinates assigned to the *j*-points, on the basis of the stipulated criteria of selection, are listed in Table 11.

Four-fold tables were compiled directly from observation of the relationships between *i*-point projections upon and *j*-points on the scale axes, as these had been plotted in the two-dimensional space, in the manner already described. It should be noted that my assumption was that when I directly observed these point relationships among the simulated data, this was functionally equivalent to the process that I went through when I read a decision of the Court and classified the votes according to whether the justices voted in the majority or dissented, except that I was limited to indirect observation of the psychometric relationships when working with real data, since then the location of the points and scales—and indeed, the entire reconstruction of the frame of reference—must be inferred *after* the processing of the complete sets of data for the term sample. It would be trivial to reproduce the cumulative scales, since these necessarily all are perfect (free of inconsistencies), although I shall briefly specify the scale ranks, in the order from most positive to most negative (+1.00 to −1.00): C is (D, Bl, Wa, Br, S, C, Wh, H, F); E is (Bl, Wa, D, Br, C, F, S, H, Wh); and F is (F, C, H, Wa, Bl, Br, Wh, D, S). Table 12 lists the four-fold tables that were compiled from these simulated data; the corresponding phi correlation coefficients are listed in Table 15, *infra.*

The phi correlation matrix based upon Table 12 was factored twice by the complete centroid method: once, using the largest loading in each

TABLE 11

Reference Axis Coordinates for Stimulus-points, as Partitioned Among Scale Axes

	C (1–41)			E (42–81)			F (82–100)	
j-point	I	II	j-point	I	II	j-point	I	II
01	750	375	42	650	−325	82	057	400
02	700	350	43	625	−312	83	050	350
03	650	325	44	600	−300	84	043	300
04	600	300	45	588	−294	85	036	250
05	575	288	46	575	−288	86	029	200
06	562	281	47	550	−275	87	022	150
07	550	275	48	525	−263	88	014	100
08	538	269	49	500	−250	89	007	050
09	525	262	50	475	−238			
10	512	256	51	450	−225			
11	500	250	52	425	−212			
12	488	244	53	400	−200			
13	450	225	54	375	−188			
14	400	200	55	350	−175			
15	350	175	56	300	−150			
16	300	150	57	250	−125			
17	250	125	58	200	−100			
18	200	100	59	150	−075			
19	150	075	60	100	−050			
20	100	050	61	050	−025			
21	050	125						
22	−050	−025	62	−050	025	90	−007	−050
23	−100	−050	63	−100	050	91	−014	−100
24	−150	−075	64	−150	075	92	−022	−150
25	−200	−100	65	−200	100	93	−029	−200
26	−250	−125	66	−250	125	94	−036	−250
27	−275	−138	67	−300	150	95	−043	−300
28	−300	−150	68	−325	162	96	−050	−350
29	−325	−162	69	−350	175	97	−057	−400
30	−350	−175	70	−375	188	98	−064	−450
31	−375	−188	71	−400	200	99	−072	−500
32	−400	−200	72	−438	219	100	−079	−550
33	−425	−212	73	−450	225			
34	−450	−225	74	−462	231			
35	−500	−250	75	−475	238			
36	−525	−262	76	−500	250			
37	−550	−275	77	−550	275			
38	−575	−288	78	−600	300			
39	−600	−300	79	−650	325			
40	−625	−312	80	−700	350			
41	−650	−325	81	−750	375			

TABLE 12

Four-fold Tables for Judicial Respondents (Simulated Data)

		Wa +	Wa −	Bl +	Bl −	Br +	Br −	C +	C −	S +	S −	Wh +	Wh −	H +	H −	F +	F −
D	+	52	11	51	19	59	23	49	41	48	34	25	38	21	41	23	41
	−	7	30	8	22	0	18	10	0	11	7	34	3	38	0	36	0
Bl	+			61	9	60	22	53	37	45	37	26	37	25	37	27	37
	−			2	28	3	15	10	0	18	0	37	0	38	0	36	0
Wa	+					67	15	62	28	52	30	33	30	34	28	36	28
	−					3	15	8	2	18	0	37	0	36	2	34	2
Br	+							72	18	67	15	48	15	44	18	46	18
	−							10	0	15	3	34	3	38	0	36	0
C	+									72	10	57	6	61	1	64	0
	−									18	0	33	4	29	9	26	10
S	+											58	5	54	8	51	13
	−											24	13	28	10	31	5
Wh	+													53	9	46	18
	−													10	28	17	19
H	+															55	9
	−															7	29

column of the matrix as an estimate of the communality [i.e., of the respondent's total correlation with both of the two common factors]; and the second time, with the true communalities inserted in the major diagonal. The *r* matrix also was factored by the complete centroid method, using, of course, the true communalities in the diagonal. Although factoring was carried out, in each instance, through the computation of the second residual matrix, no attempt was made to extract more than two factors; it was known, of course, that two and only two factors should account for all of the variance in the correlation matrices, and consequently, any values other than zero in the cells of the second residual matrices had to represent error variance. (The largest value—or otherwise stated, the greatest error variance—appearing in the second residuals was for Brennan and Warren: this was —.162 for the phi matrix with estimated communalities, and it was even larger [—.188] for the phi matrix with true communalities.)

I shall present first a comparison of the relative success with which each of the three factor analyses was able to reproduce the locations of the i-points in the space. Otherwise stated, I shall compare the factor loadings for each respondent, as determined by analysis variously of true and estimated correlations and of true and estimated communalities, with the known (or criterion) factor loadings for these respondents. Ideally, we should like to be able to reproduce perfectly the i-point configuration in the two-dimensional space. The realistic empirical question, however, is: how close can we come? Even with a perfect (r) matrix and true communalities, we cannot avoid rounding errors inherent in the computational procedures of factor analysis; and phi correlation of dichotomized (nominally classified) data yields only an approximation of the product-moment correlation coefficient. The phis are based upon observations of a small as well as finite number of points, whose discontinuities distort the relationships between i-points and the continuous variables represented by the scale axes. Clearly, a different sample of j-points would lead to a different approximation of the actual locations of the i-points in the space.

It is evident in Table 13 that the r matrix, with true communalities in the diagonal, which was constructed directly from the actual point coordinates, yields factors that are very close approximations of the actual reference axes, and does the best job of recovering the known configuration of i-points. However, it is also evident that even working with a "perfect" matrix which is itself free of error variance, there is a combined mean error variance of about 5 percent in the coordinates for the i-points. Unlike the two phi matrix factor loadings, the loadings extracted from the r matrix have more error variance on *II* than on *I*—twice as much, in fact—and none of the individual factor loading error variances is as large as 5 percent. When true communalities can be inserted in the diagonal of the phi matrix, the combined mean error variance is $2\frac{1}{2}$ times as large as for the r matrix with the same communalities, which suggests that from 7 to 8 percent of the error variance should be attributed to the distortion produced by the phi approximation of the product-moment correlation matrix. On the other hand, the use of estimated communalities in the phi matrix—and in this experiment, the factoring was *not* iterated in order to stabilize the communality estimates—adds only another 3 percent to the

TABLE 13

Actual and Estimated Factor Loadings for Judicial Respondents (Simulated Data)

i	Factor I (a) Criterion	(b) r matrix, true h^2	(c) ϕ matrix, true h^2	(d) ϕ matrix, est. h^2	Absolute differences: $(|a-b|)$	$(|a-c|)$	$(|a-d|)$	$(|c-d|)$
D	.800	.816	.798	.772	.016	.002	.028	.026
Bl	.800	.793	.876	.881	.007	.076	.081	.005
Wa	.700	.688	.715	.745	.012	.015	.045	.030
Br	.500	.505	.523	.567	.005	.023	.067	.044
C	−.100	−.117	−.275	−.331	.017	.175	.231	.056
S	−.300	−.271	−.237	−.236	.029	.063	.064	.001
Wh	−.800	−.782	−.672	−.637	.018	.128	.163	.035
H	−.700	−.710	−.783	−.793	.010	.083	.093	.010
F	−.600	−.627	−.689	−.686	.027	.089	.086	.003
				Means:	.016	.073	.095	.023
i	Factor II (a)	(b)	(c)	(d)	$(|a-b|)$	$(|a-c|)$	$(|a-d|)$	$(|c-d|)$
D	.300	.254	.310	.277	.046	.010	.023	.033
Bl	−.100	−.145	−.218	−.249	.045	.118	.149	.031
Wa	−.200	−.239	−.278	−.323	.039	.078	.123	.045
Br	.100	.071	.132	.121	.029	.032	.021	.011
C	−.300	−.294	−.428	−.413	.006	.128	.113	.015
S	.500	.517	.517	.526	.017	.017	.026	.009
Wh	.300	.345	.320	.308	.045	.020	.008	.012
H	−.200	.160	−.196	−.187	.040	.004	.013	.009
F	−.500	−.466	−.449	−.425	.034	.051	.075	.024
				Means:	.033	.051	.061	.021
			Sum of Means for *I* and *II:*		.049	.124	.156	.044

combined mean error variance, which is considerably less than appears to be inherent in either the factoring process or the use of phi coefficients instead of product moment coefficients. As a practical matter, of course, in empirical work, there is no alternative to using phi coefficients as an approximation for the *r* matrix, when the data is (like mine) based upon observations that are classified nominally. Neither, in empirical work, is it possible to know the true communalities. The point that I am making is that the great concern that statisticians seem to have expressed over the effect of communality estimates would seem, at least in terms of these data, to have better been focused upon other sources of greater error variance that appear to be inherent in the correlational and factoring processes. In any event, I concluded that, since the computer program most readily available to me at the time I was processing the data did not provide for automatic iteration of the communalities, the probable reduction in error variance that might be expected to result from such iteration was so relatively small that it was not worth the costs that this extra step would entail.

One might make the hasty inference from Table 13 that there is likely to be an average error variance of from 15 to 20 percent (allowing for the third factor) in the factorial measurements alone in the empirical findings that I shall discuss in subsequent chapters. Nevertheless, it is obvious that all three of the factor analyses *do* succeed in recovering a point configuration that unmistakenly is recognizable as the one which I plotted. What I shall henceforth refer to as the empirical technique (the phi matrix with estimated communalities) does least well in recovering Clark's ideal-point, for a very good reason that will become apparent when we turn presently to a discussion of Table 14; however, the distance that Clark's estimated i-point would be from the point that was plotted for him would not be the sum of the two error variances: it would be the square root of the sum of their squares, or about 25 percent rather than 35 percent, since the error variance on the factors is measured orthogonally, and the shortest distance between the actual and estimated points is the hypotenuse of the triangle for which the individual factor error variances for Clark form the legs. Similarly, the inference of from 15 to 20 percent average error variance, based upon the summation of the mean error variance for the individual factors, is too large; the hypotenuse for a right trihedron with legs of .095, .061, and (an estimated) .030 would be .117, and from 11 to 12 percent average error variance probably is a more reasonable estimate of the amount inherent in the empirical technique.

The error variance for Douglas is less than 3 percent, and the reason for this is the same as the reason why Clark's is about 25 percent. Table 14 shows that Douglas has a maximal (true) communality of .730, while Clark has a minimal communality of .100. Although, as I already have pointed out, there are other considerations relevant to the error variance, the proportion of a respondent's total variance that is loaded upon the common factors certainly is a relevant consideration, too, and in general, we can anticipate that there will be an inverse relationship between the amount of error variance in an estimated *i*-point and the respondent's communality with the factorial reference axes. Table 14 also shows that the factor loadings extracted from the *r* matrix reproduce almost perfectly the criterion communality, with only the most trivial of rounding errors for

TABLE 14

Actual and Estimated Communalities for Judicial Respondents (Simulated Data)

i	(*a'*) Criterion	Computed from Table 13, column: (*b*)	(*c*)	(*d*)	Absolute differences: ($\|a'-b\|$)	($\|a'-c\|$)	($\|a'-d\|$)	($\|c-d\|$)
D	.730	.730	.733	.673	.000	.003	.057	.060
Bl	.650	.650	.815	.838	.000	.165	.188	.025
Wa	.530	.530	.588	.659	.000	.058	.129	.071
Br	.260	.260	.291	.336	.000	.031	.076	.045
C	.100	.100	.259	.281	.000	.159	.181	.022
S	.340	.340	.323	.333	.000	.017	.007	.010
Wh	.730	.731	.554	.501	.001	.176	.229	.053
H	.530	.530	.651	.664	.000	.121	.134	.013
F	.610	.610	.677	.652	.000	.067	.042	.025
				Means:	.000	.089	.116	.036

[NOTE: Using formula (11), column *a'* is calculated directly from the actual factor loadings; column *b* is calculated from the factor loadings resulting from the *r* matrix; column *c* is calculated from the factor loadings resulting from the ϕ matrix with column *a'* in the diagonal; and column *d* is calculated from the ϕ matrix with estimated communalities in the diagonal.]

Whittaker, one of the two respondents with the highest true communality. Otherwise, this table confirms that in general, although by no means invariably, the use of the true communalities instead of estimates in the phi matrix—if this were empirically possible—would improve only slightly what can be done using the empirical technique, which tends to overestimate the communality for most respondents, with an average absolute error of about 10 percent.

The third comparison that we can make is of the extent to which the phi correlations deviate from the actual correlations, and also the extent to which the factor loadings extracted from the phi matrix, using both true

TABLE 15

Actual, Estimated, and Reproduced Correlations for Pairs of Judicial Respondents (Simulated Data)

			Reproduced from factor loadings of phi matrix with:		Absolute differences:		
	Calculated:						
i_1, i_2	r	ϕ	true h^2	est. h^2	$\lvert r-\phi \rvert$	$\lvert r-t.h^2 \rvert$	$\lvert r-e.h^2 \rvert$
D,Bl	.610	.625	.631	.611	.015	.021	.001
D,Wa	.500	.430	.485	.486	.070	.015	.014
D,Br	.430	.562	.458	.472	.132	.028	.042
D,C,	−.170	−.278	−.252	−.270	.108	.082	.100
D,S	−.090	−.020	−.029	−.036	.070	.009	.016
D,Wh	−.550	−.513	−.437	−.407	.037	.113	.143
D,H	−.620	−.653	−.686	−.664	.033	.066	.044
D,F	−.630	−.625	−.689	−.648	.005	.059	.018
Bl,Wa	.580	.764	.687	.736	.184	.107	.156
Bl,Br	.390	.450	.429	.470	.060	.039	.080
Bl,C	−.050	−.255	−.148	−.189	.205	.098	.139
Bl,S	−.290	−.359	−.321	−.339	.069	.031	.049
Bl,Wh	−.670	−.587	−.659	−.638	.083	.011	.032
Bl,H	−.540	−.600	−.643	−.652	.060	.103	.112
Bl,F	−.430	−.575	−.506	−.498	.145	.076	.068
Wa,Br	.330	.545	.337	.383	.215	.007	.053
Wa,C	−.010	−.073	−.078	−.114	.063	.068	.104
Wa,S	−.310	−.307	−.313	−.346	.003	.003	.036
Wa,Wh	−.620	−.502	−.569	−.574	.118	.051	.046
Wa,H	−.450	−.423	−.506	−.531	.027	.056	.081
Wa,F	−.320	−.400	−.368	−.374	.080	.048	.054
Br,C	−.080	−.156	−.200	−.238	.076	.120	.158
Br,S	−.100	−.016	−.156	−.070	.084	.056	.030
Br,Wh	−.370	−.197	−.309	−.324	.173	.061	.046
Br,H	−.370	−.367	−.436	−.473	.003	.066	.103
Br,F	−.350	−.351	−.419	−.440	.001	.069	.090
C,S	−.120	−.156	−.156	−.139	.036	.000	.019
C,Wh	−.010	.021	.048	.084	.031	.058	.094
C,H	.130	.357	.299	.339	.227	.169	.209
C,F	.210	.444	.381	.403	.234	.171	.193
S,Wh	.390	.342	.324	.312	.048	.066	.078
S,H	.110	.169	.085	.089	.059	.025	.021
S,F	−.070	−.080	−.049	−.062	.010	.021	.008

TABLE 15 (*Continued*)

Actual, Estimated, and Reproduced Correlations for Pairs of Judicial Respondents (Simulated Data)

i_1, i_2	Calculated:		Reproduced from factor loadings of phi matrix with:		Absolute differences:		
	r	ϕ	true h^2	est. h^2	$\|r-\phi\|$	$\|r-t.h^2\|$	$\|r-e.h^2\|$
Wh,H	.500	.595	.463	.447	.095	.037	.053
Wh,F	.330	.245	.319	.306	.085	.011	.024
H,F	.520	.658	.627	.623	.138	.107	.103
				Means:	.086	.059	.073

and estimated communalities, will reproduce the actual correlations between respondent pairs. Table 15 reports the results of this test. The range of the mean error variances is quite small, extending from 6 to 8½ percent. It is interesting to observe that the phi matrix itself is not as good an approximation of the r matrix as the reproduced matrices calculated from the factor loadings extracted from the phi matrix, and the estimation of communalities has little effect—only about 1½ percent—upon increasing the error variance. One's general impression, that the 7 percent mean variance (between the actual correlations and the correlations reproduced from the loadings extracted by the empirical technique) does not preclude a reasonably close fit, is confirmed by the computation of the product-moment correlation coefficient for the two sets of correlations. Pearson's r is $+.98$, and it is statistically significant at far beyond the .001 probability level: the observed t is 28.5717, while the t required for the .001 level, with two variables and $df = 35$, is only 3.59.

To summarize, factor analysis of the phi matrix, with estimated communalities which are *not* iterated, reproduces the point-configuration within an error variance of 11.3 percent in two-dimensional space, and within an estimated error variance of 11.7 percent in three-dimensional space; the equivalent error variance in the communalities of the respondents (for two-space) is an almost identical 11.6 percent; the reproduced correlations are within a mean error variance of 7.3 percent of the actual correlations; and the Pearsonian correlation between the reproduced matrix and the actual matrix is $+.98$ and very highly statistically significant. I infer from these measures that the empirical technique that I shall employ in this study is capable of reproducing with considerable success the postulated genotypic relationships that are assumed to exist among the attitudinal syndromes of the respondents. In interpreting our empirical data, however, we should bear in mind that error variance of about 12 percent is inherent in the computational procedures of the correlational and factor analysis.

Chapter 5 · LIBERALISM, POLITICAL AND ECONOMIC

TWO-THIRDS of the Supreme Court's dissensual decisions on the substantive merits of the issues presented in cases, during the seventeen term period extending from October 1946 through June 1963, raised questions to which the justices responded on the basis of their acceptance of relatively liberal or relatively conservative ideologies. The total of dissensual decisions was 1,657; of the 1,099 which evoked liberal/conservative voting responses, about half (562) related to political issues while the other half (537) raised economic issues for decision. For some justices, there is such a high positive correlation between their attitudes toward political and economic issues that a single dimension of liberalism/conservatism would serve quite adequately as a basis for scaling their voting behavior in this large subsample of relevant cases. If only all justices were alike in this respect, my task of analysis would have been greatly simplified: a single scale variable would have sufficed for cumulative scaling, and there would have been no need for factor analysis. But a few justices have been considerably more liberal in their attitude toward political than toward economic issues; and others have been the opposite. Such justices would manifest many inconsistent responses, even when the responses of their colleagues were quite consistent, if we were to combine cases raising political issues with those raising economic issues and attempt to measure the attitudes of all of the justices constituting the Court (at any given time) with a cumulative scale of liberalism/conservatism. In other words, such justices would appear to be quite inconsistent in the structuring of their attitudes toward the major issues of liberalism, even if they entertained quite consistent—but consistently *different*—attitudes toward each of the two issues. For this reason, general liberalism may have been a relevant ideology, but it was not a scalable variable for the voting behavior of Supreme Court justices during the period of this study.[1]

Two of the major issues of general liberalism, however, can be defined as scale variables which evince a high degree of consistency, from several points of view. As Table 7 (Chapter 3, *supra*) shows, both the political and the economic variable scaled year after year, for seventeen terms in succession. In some terms, C scales better than E, as in 1952 when R is .98 for C and only .90 for E; in other terms, E shows the higher internal consistency, as in 1951 when R is .91 for C but .96 for E; while in still other terms, both may be alike and relatively high (as in 1957–59: .96 and .99, .97 and .95, .95 and .97) or alike and relatively low (as in 1950, .92 and .90, and in 1953, .92 and .92). But the means for the two variables are almost identical: R is .94–.95; S is .74–.75; and the average improvement from both scales, over minimal marginal reproducibility, is .14–.15. These scales, in short, are consistent internally, the series for each variable shows considerable consistency through time; and the two scales consistently are similar in their statistical characteristics.

As I mentioned above, the total number of cases, for each set of scales, is about the same: each scale measures about a third of the total of approximately sixteen hundred and fifty cases in the sample of dissensual decisions. The average number of cases, for term scales, is 33 for C and 32 for E. There is, of course, fluctuation in frequencies from term to term, similar to that which we described above for the coefficients of reproducibility. The term frequencies for C range from a minimum of 21 to a maximum of 55 cases; while those for E range from 14 to 45. Our interest lies primarily elsewhere than in the parametric statistics for the distribution of the term frequencies for these scales, so I have not calculated such indices as standard deviations, coefficients of variation, skewness, kurtosis, and so forth. What is more pertinent, for present purposes, is the observation that except for two terms when C includes over 50 cases, and two other terms when E includes less than 20, for the remaining thirty term scales both C and E range between a minimum of 21 and a maximum of 47 cases, which indicates a deviation of about plus or minus a dozen cases from the average. In short, the Supreme Court seems to place about the same amount of emphasis upon both issues, since the justices disagree in their

---

[1] Any interested reader readily can test the validity of this assertion. The term scales for C and for E are reported in Figures 1 and 3, *infra;* take the pair of scales for any term, and try to combine them in a single L scale which meets the criteria for scalability discussed in ch. 3.

decisions regarding about the same number of cases raising political, as those raising economic, issues.

The statistical evidence demonstrates, therefore, that political and economic liberalism have a great deal in common, as attitudinal dimensions of Supreme Court decision-making. But if separate cumulative scales are required for these two variables in order to obtain maximal insight into the degrees of liberalism and conservatism among the justices, then it must follow that the two scales differ in at least two important respects: (1) in the substantive content to which each relates; and (2) in the relative degrees of liberalism (or conservatism) that are manifest, in the responses of at least some of the justices, toward political as distinguished from economic issues. We shall discuss first political liberalism, and then economic liberalism, from the point of view of both of these differences.

Political Liberalism

The discrimination of political liberalism as a major component of the attitudes of Supreme Court justices, in the technical sense that this attitudinal dimension could be represented by a cumulative scale variable, came as the result of a lot of hard work on the part of several persons; it is not the result of anybody's brainstorm. Earlier work by Tanenhaus[2] and by Kort[3] suggested to me the possibility of attempting to scale some samples of recent decisions of the Supreme Court relating to the claims of criminal defendants to the constitutional right to counsel under the Fourteenth Amendment; and this became one of several projects that were explored by a graduate seminar that I led in the autumn of 1957.[4] It was a lucky hit: the subsample of eight cases, for the period 1940–47, scaled without a single inconsistent vote. The reason it was lucky is because the observation of this rare empirical event encouraged me to look further into the structuring of judicial attitudes; in the dozens of cumulative scales of the voting behavior of Supreme Court justices and of other judges, which I have constructed since that time, I have yet to encounter another perfect scale. Subsequent experimentation resulted in cumulative scales of Supreme Court voting behavior in such diverse (and substantively discrete, in terms of legal

[2] Joseph Tanenhaus, "The Uses and Limitations of Social Science Methods in Analyzing Judicial Behavior" (American Political Science Association Annual Meeting, September 1956, mimeographed), pp. 1–22.

[3] Fred Kort, "Predicting Supreme Court Decisions Mathematically: A Quantitative Analysis of the Right to Counsel Cases," *American Political Science Review*, Vol. 51 (1957), pp. 1–12.

[4] Glendon Schubert, *Quantitative Analysis of Judicial Behavior* (New York: The Free Press, 1959), pp. xiii, 23, and *passim*.

criteria) sets of cases as those relating to the claims of criminal defendants that they had been subjected by the police to unreasonable search and seizure (which raised issues under the Fourth and/or Fourteenth Amendments); miscellaneous claims of defendants, all of whom were aliens; the monetary claims of injured railroad workers; and, most significantly—although the significance was not apparent to me at the time—a single scale of all of the dissensual decisions for the 1936 Term of the Court.[5] (I did think, and say, that the latter scale seemed to be measuring general liberalism and conservatism; and the scale variable was defined in terms of agreement with the majority, which is the same variable that underlies the factor analysis of the present study; but I did not then understand the implications of being able to observe a scale which appeared to show isomorphism between scaling majority agreement/disagreement and scaling liberalism/conservatism.) Soon thereafter, Ulmer began to publish a series of articles, in which he reported scales of all civil liberties decisions of the Supreme Court for each of several successive terms beginning with the 1956 Term.[6]

Consequently, when I began to work upon the present project, in the autumn of 1960, an obvious first step was to investigate the scalability of all civil liberties decisions for each term, in lieu of attempting to scale less comprehensive subsets of decisions. The 1957 Term was selected for a pilot investigation, after the initial formulation of the theoretical model and the methods (discussed in Chapters 2 and 3, *supra*), because this was the most recent term with the data of which I had more than a reading acquaintance, so to speak, and also because Ulmer then recently had reported a scale of all civil liberties decisions for this term. (It happens that the 1957 Term was not a very typical term, from the point of view of volume of content, because of the unusually large number of both civil liberties and total dissensual decisions that it included; but it was an excellent choice for purposes of the pilot scaling investigation.)

In order to construct a cumulative scale of all of the civil liberties

[5] *Ibid.*, ch. 5. Cf. the scales reported in Figures 25–29 of Schubert, *Constitutional Politics* (New York: Holt, Rinehart, and Winston, 1960).

[6] S. Sidney Ulmer, "Supreme Court Behavior and Civil Rights," *Western Political Quarterly*, Vol. 13 (1960), p. 288 [1956 and 1957 C Scales]; Ulmer, "The Analysis of Behavior Patterns on the United States Supreme Court," *Journal of Politics*, Vol. 22 (1960), p. 629 [1958 C Scale]. Cf. Ulmer, "Scaling Judicial Cases: A Methodological Note," *American Behavioral Scientist*, Vol. 4, No. 8 (1961), p. 31 [1959 C Scale]; Ulmer, "A Note on Attitudinal Consistency in the United States Supreme Court," *Indian Journal of Political Science*, Vol. 22 (1961), p. 195 [1960 C Scale]; and Ulmer, "Quantitative Analysis of Judicial Processes: Some Practical and Theoretical Applications," *Law and Contemporary Problems*, Vol. 28 (1963), p. 170 [1961 C Scale].

decisions of the 1957 (or any other) Term, it is necessary to select from among the set of dissensual decisions on the merits, for the term, those cases which raised for decision civil liberties issues. In the absence of a detailed set of rules for the analysis of the content of judicial opinions and/or case records, which to the best of my knowledge no one who has undertaken to scale judicial decisions has developed, the criteria of scale relevance depend upon the subjective judgment of the analyst. From the points of view of scientific validity and reliability, and methodological elegance, it would undoubtedly be preferable to partition among scales the set of dissensual cases for an entire term, on the basis of an objective content analysis.[7] However, my own interests were primarily theoretical rather than methodological; and the costs of such a content analysis, in terms of both time and money, would have been so great that I preferred to risk whatever additional error variance might be entailed by subjective partitioning of the decisions.

The concept of civil liberties with which I started, in selecting the cases for the C scale of both the 1957 pilot investigation and the other sixteen terms, was the usual understanding of a teacher of constitutional law. I defined civil liberties to consist of claims to personal (as distinguished from property) rights and freedoms. In terms of constitutional norms, these included primarily claims based upon the personal freedoms (of speech, press, religion, assembly, and petition) cited in the 1st Amendment; the general and particular specifications of fair procedure in criminal trials (in federal courts) that are listed in Amendments 4–8; and the analogous freedoms and rights (in relationship to state governments) that are associated with Amendment 14; plus the norms relating to racial equality that the Court has associated with Amendments 14 and 5.[8] My concept of civil liberties differed from the usual understanding of teachers of constitutional law in that I also included decisions that related to equivalent claims of personal freedom and of procedural right that were based upon statutory or avowedly judicial rather than constitutional norms.

Deportation cases, for example, typically raise questions of claims to personal freedom *and* to procedural rights; and during part of the period covered by this study, the position of the dominant majority of the Court was that such claims related exclusively to statutory norms, while during

---

[7] See Robert C. North, Ole R. Holsti, M. George Zaninovich, and Dina A. Zinnes, *Content Analysis* (Evanston: Northwestern University Press, 1963).

[8] My understanding of these norms is exemplified, in considerably more depth and detail, in the textual discussion and the organization of materials included in ch. 9–12 of *Constitutional Politics, op. cit.* fn. 5, *supra.*

the later part of the period the Court has considered many such claims to evoke both statutory and constitutional questions. Similarly, during the first three terms of the period, the majority position was that there was no federal legal right to support a claim against an unreasonable search and seizure by state officials, in a trial in a state court; for the next twelve terms, the majority position was that such a right existed, and it was a constitutional right based on the 14th Amendment, but the enforcement procedures (that made the analogous 4th Amendment right meaningful in federal court trials) were based upon the Supreme Court's policy-making authority over lower federal courts and *not* upon the 4th Amendment; the majority position during the final two terms of the period covered was that such a right included the enforcement procedure, in both federal and state courts, and both the substantive right and the enforcement procedure now were considered to be based upon constitutional norms, which were equivalent for both the 4th and the 14th Amendments. It would be easy to multiply examples, but I hope that I have said enough to make clear why I concluded that it would be impossible to work with a consistently defined body of substantive content, *if* one were to accept, as the major basis for classification, the various categories of norms which Supreme Court justices characteristically manipulate in the process of providing verbal rationalizations for their decisions. There is no evident reason why it should be assumed that the understanding of civil liberties—even among a group of generally elderly politicians who have been trained in their youth to think like lawyers—should be limited to what happens to be the language of the Constitution of the United States, as amended from time to time.

In short, any case for which the major question that the Court purported to decide related to a claim of personal freedom was classified as a civil liberties case. Such cases, included, therefore, both claims to freedom as a substantive value, and claims relating to the procedures according to which claims of the substantive value were determined. A research assistant aided me in the coding of many of the cases, for purposes of both partitioning decisions among the several scales (including the C scale), and also of specifying the individual votes of the justices. I personally constructed all of the scales, using pencil and paper methods of analysis. Since my concept of the scale variable which I called civil liberties was largely based upon legal notions and modes of thought, it is understandable that when I needed a label for the scale—as I did just as soon as a different scale variable had been identified—I simply called it the C scale: C for civil liberties. The scales for the first fifteen terms were all constructed and reproduced photographically during the winter and spring of 1961. Since then, I have committed myself in print, in about a dozen places, to the "C scale" label. Nevertheless, it is better that insight come late than not at all; and I am now aware that it is more appropriate for this variable to be named according to the psychological content of the attitude, rather than according to the legal content of the value, to which it relates.

If we consider the substantive content of the C scale, from the point of view of the history of political philosophy, it seems clear that the political values with which the scale is concerned all are among the core concerns of the long-standing dispute between liberal and conservative philosophers. Consequently, it seems appropriate to consider the attitudinal dimension measured by the scale to be that of political liberalism and conservatism. Since the polarity of the dimension must be arbitrarily assigned, I shall define liberalism as the positive value, and conservatism as the negative value. A shorthand way of referring to the scale is to call it by the name assigned to the positive value, and hence C+ (or "the C scale") measures the attitude of political liberalism.

THE 1946–1948 TERMS

An examination of the C scales in Figure 1 shows that during the period of the 1946–48 Terms, when Murphy and Rutledge were still on the Court, these two were the justices most sympathetic to political liberalism. Out of his total of 70 participations during these three terms, only four of Frank Murphy's responses were negative, and three of the four were inconsistently so. Wiley Rutledge's scale position and scores indicate that he was only slightly less extreme in his attitude than was Murphy; Rutledge had nine negative responses (six of which were inconsistent) out of a total of 70 participations. Douglas and Black were the only other justices with positive scale scores during this period, and their attitude was somewhat less extreme than that of either Rutledge or Murphy. The average scale score for Douglas and Black for these three terms (.63) was about two thirds of the average for Murphy and Rutledge, and the total of negative responses for Douglas and Black was over three times that for the other pair. At the other end of the scale, Vinson, Burton, and Reed clearly appear as political conservatives, with average scale scores (for these three terms) of −.87, −.83, and −.82, respectively; and each of these justices made only seven or eight positive responses out of his total of 80–81 participations. The apparent differences among these three respondents are so slight, and so inconsistent from term to term, that on the basis of this evidence alone, we should have to conclude that they are all about equally extreme political

1946 TERM

C Scale

Justices

Cases	Mu	Ru	Bl	D	J	Re	Bu	F	V	Totals
0/631	x									1-8
1/532	-	x								2-7
2/174:535	x	x						x̲	x̲	3-6
2/174:840	x	x						x̲	x̲	3-6
0/127	•	x	x						.	2-5
9/14:12	x	-	x		x̲					3-6
2/1	x	x	x	•						3-5
0/645	x	x	-	x						3-6
1/789:793	x	x	-	x						3-6
9/173	x	x	x	x						4-5
9/459	x	x	x	x						4-5
2/46	x	x	x	x						4-5
2/134	x	x	x	x						4-5
2/145	x	x	x	x						4-5
2/261:377	x	x	x	x						4-5
2/261:452	x	x	x	x						4-5
0/75	•	x	x	x	•					3-4
1/145	x	x	-	-	x					4-5
9/187	x	x	x	x	x	x				6-3
1/367	x	x	x	x	-	x	x			6-3
0/1	-	x	-	-	x	-	x	x		4-5

										74-110
Totals	17-2	19-2	13-8	12-8	4-16	2-19	2-19	5-16	0-20	184
Scale positions	21	20	17	14½	4½	3	2	1	0	
Scale scores	1.00	.90	.62	.38	-.57	-.71	-.81	-.90	-1.00	

$$R = 1 - \frac{16}{175} = .909 \qquad S = 1 - \frac{16}{33} = .515$$

1947 TERM

C Scale

Justices

Cases	Mu	Ru	D	Bl	F	J	V	Bu	Re	Totals
4/314			x	*						1-7
3/571	x	x		x						3-6
5/188	x	x		x						3-6
3/95	x	x	x							3-6
5/252	x	x	x	*						3-5
3/18	-	-	x	x						2-7
2/442:66	x	x	x	x						4-5
2/442:67	x	x	x	x						4-5
2/442:68	x	x	x	x						4-5
3/565	x	x	x	x						4-5
3/640	x	x	x	x						4-5
4/728	x	x	x	x						4-5
5/160	x	x	x	x						4-5
4/266	x	x	x	x			x			5-4
4/558	x	x	x	x		x̲				5-4
3/507	x	x	x	x		x̲		x		6-3
2/596	x	x	x	x	x					5-4
4/672	x	x	x	x	x					5-4
2/633	x	x	x	x	x		x̲			6-3
5/1	x	x	-	-	x	x				4-5
5/77	x	x	-	-	x	x				4-5
3/10	x	x	x	-	x	x				5-4
4/699	x	x	x	-	x	x				5-4
2/708	x	x	x	x	x	x				6-3
4/736	x	x	x	x	x	x				6-3
4/410	x	x	x	x	x	-	x	x		7-2
3/203	x	x	x	x	x	x	x	x		8-1
2/581	x	x	x	-	x	x	-	x	x	7-2
3/28	x	x	x	x	x	-	-	x	x	7-2
3/257	x	x	x	x	-	-	x	x	x	7-2

										141-127
Totals	28-2	28-2	26-4	22-7	12-17	9-21	6-24	6-24	4-26	268
Scale positions	29	29	27	26½	14	11	5	5	3	
Scale scores	.93	.93	.80	.77	-.07	-.27	-.67	-.67	-.80	

$$R = 1 - \frac{22}{251} = .912 \qquad S = 1 - \frac{23}{52} = .558$$

FIGURE 1. The C Scales of Political Liberalism and Conservatism, 1946–1962 Terms

1948 TERM

C Scale

Cases	Mu	Ru	D	Bl	F	J	Re	V	Bu	Totals
				Justices						
8/160	.			x	x					3-6
5/469	x	x								2-7
7/241	x	x								2-7
5/464	x	x	x							3-6
6/684	x	x	x							3-6
6/695	x	x	x							3-6
8/25:17	x	x	x							3-6
8/25:18	x	x	x							3-6
6/704	x	x	x				x			4-5
5/281	x	-	x	x						3-6
6/77	x	x	x	x						4-5
6/155	x	x	x	x						4-5
6/901	x	x	x	x						4-5
7/901:679	x	x	x	x						4-5
5/601B	x	x	x	x						4-5
5/601A	x	x	x	x				x		5-4
7/1	x	x	x	x		x				5-4
5/410	x	x	x	x	x					5-4
8/62	x	x	x	x	x					5-4
8/68	x	x	x	x	x					5-4
8/74	x	x	x	x	x					5-4
8/84	x	x	x	x	x					5-4
5/345	x	-	-	x	x	x				4-5
5/355	x	-	-	x	x	x				4-5
5/497	x	-	x	-	x	x				4-5
6/613	x	x	-	-	x	x				4-5
5/451	x	x	x	x	x	x				6-3
6/806	x	x	x	x	x	x				6-3
8/49	x	x	x	x	x	x				6-3
6/440	x	x	x	x	x	x	x	x		8-1
										126-144
Totals	30-0	25-5	24-6	19-11	14-16	9-21	2-28	2-28	1-29 / 126-144	270
Scale positions	30	29	27	21	13	8	1	1	0	
Scale scores	1.00	.93	.80	.40	-.13	-.47	-.93	-.93	-1.00	

$$R = 1 - \frac{14}{261} = .946 \qquad S = 1 - \frac{14}{50} = .720$$

1949 TERM

C Scale

Cases	Bl	D	F	J	Mi	Bu	V	C	Re	Totals
				Justices						
9/660	x	*								1-7
9/276	x	x								2-7
9/763	x	x			x					3-6
9/9	-	*	x							1-7
8/491	x	*	x							2-6
9/162	x	*	x					*		2-5
9/323	x	*	x					*		2-5
9/349	x	*	x					*		2-5
8/521:3	x	*	x	x				*		3-4
8/521:82	x	*	x	x				*		3-4
8/537	x	*	x	x				*		3-4
8/680	x	*	x	x						3-5
9/56	x	*	x	x						3-5
9/200	x	*	x	x						3-5
9/846	x	x	x	x				*		4-4
9/382:10	x	*	x	x	*			*		3-3
9/382:13	x	*	x	x	*			*		3-3
9/901:373	x	*	x	x	x	x				5-3
9/33	x	*	x	x	x	x	x	*		6-1
9/1	x	*	x	x	x	-	x	x		6-2
9/282	x	*	x	-	x	x	x	x	x	7-1
										67-92
Totals	20-1	3-0	18-3	12-9	4-15	4-17	3-18	2-9	1-20 / 67-92	159
Scale positions	21	20½	18	13	5	4	3	2½	1	
Scale scores	1.00	.95	.71	.24	-.52	-.62	-.71	-.76	-.90	

$$R = 1 - \frac{2}{128} = .984 \qquad S = 1 - \frac{4}{27} = .852$$

FIGURE 1. (continued)

1950 TERM

C Scale

Cases	D	Bl	F	J	Bu	C	Mi	V	Re	Totals
1/367	x									1-8
1/937:713	x									1-8
0/162	x					*				1-7
0/462	x	x				*				2-6
1/494	x	x				*				2-6
1/651	x	x		x̲						3-6
0/315	x	x				x				3-6
1/58	-	x	x							2-7
1/901:376	x	x	x							3-6
0/193:35	x	x	x			*				3-5
0/193:36	x	x	x			*				3-5
0/367	x	x	x			*				3-5
1/223	-	x	x	x						3-6
1/97	-	x	x	x		x̲				4-5
1/70	-	x	x	x		x̲	x			5-4
1/716	x	x	x	-	x					4-5
1/123:7	x	x	x	x	x	*				5-3
1/123:8	x	x	x	x	x	*				5-3
1/123:71	x	x	x	x	x	*				5-3
1/479	x	x	x	x	x	x	x	x		8-1
0/332	x	x	x	-	x	*	-	x	x	6-2
0/290	x	x	x	-	x	x	x	x	x	8-1
										80-108

| Totals | 18-4 | 19-3 | 15-7 | 7-15 | 8-14 | 2-10 | 5-17 | 4-18 | 2-20 | 80-108 / 188 |

| Scale positions | 22 | 19 | 15 | 10 | 7 | 4 | 3 | 3 | 2 | |

| Scale scores | 1.00 | .73 | .36 | -.09 | -.36 | -.59 | -.73 | -.73 | -.82 | |

$$R = 1 - \frac{12}{144} = .917 \qquad S = 1 - \frac{13}{42} = .690$$

1951 TERM

C Scale

Cases	Bl	D	F	J	Bu	C	V	Re	Mi	Totals
3/341	x									1-8
2/117	-	x						•		1-7
2/277	-	x			x̲					2-7
2/580:43	x	x				•				2-6
2/580:206	x	x				•				2-6
2/580:264	x	x				•				2-6
2/899:421	x	x								2-7
2/900:422	x	x								2-7
2/55	x	x						•		2-6
3/148	x	x						x̲	x̲	4-5
2/485	x	x	•							2-6
2/951:312	x	x	•							2-6
3/451:224	x	x	•							2-6
3/451:295	x	x	•							2-6
3/790	x	-	x			•				2-7
3/1	x	x	x							3-5
3/181	x	x	x			•				3-6
3/130	x	x	x				x̲			4-5
2/337	x	-	x	x						3-6
3/169	x	-	x	x		•				3-5
3/306	x	-	x	x						3-6
3/250	x	x	-	x			x̲			4-5
2/524:35	x	x	x	-	x					4-5
2/524:136	x	x	x	-	x					4-5
3/747	x	x	x	-	x					4-5
2/134	x	x	x	-	x	x				5-4
2/48	x	x	x	x	x	x				6-3
3/768	x	x	x	x	x	x		•		6-2
3/944:666	x	•	x	x	x	x		x̲		6-2
3/717	x	-	•	-	x	•	x			3-4
2/225:20	x	x	x	-	-	x	x			5-4
2/225:162	x	x	x	-	-	x	x			5-4
2/76	x	x	x	-	•	x	x	•		5-2
2/104:95	x	x	•	x	x	x	x	x		7-1
2/104:96	x	x	•	x	x	x	x	x		7-1
2/104:375	x	x	•	x	x	x	x	x		7-1
2/881:80	x	x	x	x	x	x	x	x		8-1
2/881:81	x	x	x	x	x	x	x	x		8-1
2/881:82	x	x	x	x	x	x	x	x		8-1
3/918:442	x	-	•	x	x	x	-	x		6-2
3/918:461	x	x	•	x	-	x	-	x		6-2
										163-184

| Totals | 39-2 | 33-7 | 20-11 | 16-25 | 16-25 | 14-20 | 12-29 | 9-32 | 4-33 | 163-184 / 347 |

| Scale positions | 41 | 40 | 29 | 23 | 19 | 16 | 12 | 8 | 2 | |

| Scale scores | 1.00 | .95 | .41 | .12 | -.07 | -.22 | -.41 | -.61 | -.90 | |

$$R = 1 - \frac{26}{279} = .907 \qquad S = 1 - \frac{28}{91} = .692$$

FIGURE 1. (continued)

1952 TERM

C Scale

Cases	D	Bl	F	J	Bu	C	V	Re	Mi	Totals
4/86	x									1-8
4/199	x									1-8
4/424	x	*					x			2-6
4/43	-	x								1-8
5/192	x	x								2-7
5/242	x	x	ʲ							2-7
5/395	x	x								2-7
5/229	-	x	x							2-7
4/443:20	x	x	x							3-6
4/443:22	x	x	x							3-6
4/443:32	x	x	x							3-6
4/561	x	x	x							3-6
5/22	x	x	x							3-6
5/83	x	x	x							3-6
6/137	x	x	x							3-6
6/156:391	x	x	x							3-6
6/156:392	x	x	x							3-6
6/156:393	x	x	x							3-6
6/273	x	x	x							3-6
5/979:750	x	x	x	*						3-5
6/1:540	x	x	x	*						3-5
6/1:573	x	x	x	*						3-5
6/235:634	x	x	x	*						3-5
6/235:635	x	x	x	*						3-5
6/235:636	x	x	x	*						3-5
4/604	-	x	x	x						3-6
5/206	x	x	x	x						4-5
5/286	x	x	x	x		*				4-4
5/565	x	x	x	x			*	x		5-3
4/133	-	x	x	x	x				x	5-4
5/979:549	x	x	x	*	x	*				4-3
6/209	x	x	x	*	x	*				4-3
4/590	x	x	x	x	x	x	x	x		8-1
5/461	x	x	x	x	x	x	x	x		8-1
4/94	x	x	x	-	x	x	x.	x	x	8-1
										117-185

| Totals | 31-4 | 32-2 | 28-7 | 7-20 | 6-29 | 3-29 | 4-30 | 4-31 | 2-33 | 117-185 |
| | | | | | | | | | | 302 |

| Scale positions | 35 | 32½ | 28 | 13 | 6 | 4 | 3 | 3 | 1 |

| Scale scores | 1.00 | .86 | .60 | .26 | -.66 | -.77 | -.83 | -.83 | -.94 |

$$R = 1 - \frac{6}{248} = .976 \qquad S = 1 - \frac{8}{39} = .795$$

1953 TERM

C Scale

Cases	D	Bl	F	J	Mi	C	Wa	Re	Bu	Totals
6/545	x									1-8
7/62	x	x								2-7
7/439:557	x	x								2-7
7/439:558	x	x								2-7
7/522	x	x								2-7
7/906:501	x	x					*	x		3-5
7/1	x	x						x		3-6
7/442	x	x	x							3-6
7/128	x	x	x					x		4-5
6/502	x	x	x				x	x		5-4
6/906:241	x	x	-	x						3-6
7/612	x	x	-	x						3-6
7/381	x	x	-	x	x					4-5
6/441:14	x	x	x	x	x					5-4
6/441:40	x	x	x	x	x					5-4
6/441:41	x	x	x	x	x					5-4
7/388	x	x	x	x	x	x	*			6-2
7/637	x	x	x	x	-	x	x			6-3
7/556	x	x	x	*	-	x	x			5-3
7/260	x	x	x	-	-	x	x			5-4
6/389	x	x	x	-	-	x	x	x		6-3
										80-106

| Totals | 21-0 | 20-1 | 11-10 | 8-12 | 5-16 | 5-16 | 4-15 | 3-18 | 3-18 | 80-106 |
| | | | | | | | | | | 186 |

| Scale positions | 21 | 20 | 14 | 11 | 9 | 5 | 4½ | 1 | 0 |

| Scale scores | 1.00 | .90 | .33 | .05 | -.14 | -.52 | -.57 | -.90 | -1.00 |

$$R = 1 - \frac{14}{177} = .921 \qquad S = 1 - \frac{14}{39} = .641$$

FIGURE 1. (continued)

1954 TERM

C Scale

Cases	D	Bl	F	H	Wa	C	Bu	Mi	Re	Totals
8/84	x			/						1-7
8/160	x			/						1-7
8/904	-	x		/	*					1-6
8/37	x	x		/						2-6
8/375	x	x		/						2-6
9/58	x	x		*						2-6
9/280	-	x	x	*						2-6
8/419	x	x	x	/						3-5
9/302	x	x	x	*						3-5
8/1	x	x	x	/	*	*				3-3
8/11	x	x	x	/	x	x				5-3
8/407	x	x	x	/	x	x				5-3
9/48	x	x	x	x	x	x				6-3
9/133	x	x	x	x	x	x				6-3
9/190	x	x	x	-	x	x	x			6-3
9/219	x	x	x	-	x	x	x			6-3
8/385	x	x	x		x	x	x			6-2
8/397	x	x	x	/	x	x	x			6-2
9/81	x	x	x	x	-	x	x			6-3
9/375	x	x	x	x	x	-	x			6-3
9/331	x	x	x	x	x	x	-	x		7-2
9/155	x	x	x	x	x	x	x	x		8-1
										93-88

	D	Bl	F	H	Wa	C	Bu	Mi	Re	
Totals	20-2	20-2	16-6	6-2	11-9	11-10	7-15	2-20	0-22	93-88 181
Scale positions	22	20	16	16	12½	12½	8	2	0	
Scale scores	1.00	.82	.45	.45	.14	.14	-.27	-.82	-1.00	

$$R = 1 - \frac{6}{149} = .960 \qquad S = 1 - \frac{7}{40} = .825$$

1955 TERM

C Scale

Cases	D	Bl	Wa	F	C	H	Bu	Mi	Re	Totals
1/454	x			x		x				3-6
0/422	x	x								2-7
1/131	x	x								2-7
0/91:32	x	x	x							3-6
0/91:36	x	x	x							3-6
1/215:643	x	x	x							3-6
1/215:704	x	x	x							3-6
1/513:202	x	x	x		x					4-5
1/513:320	x	x	x		x					4-5
1/470	x	x	x	*						3-5
1/487	x	x	x	*						3-5
1/916:555	x	x	-	x						3-6
1/345	x	x	x	x						4-5
0/214	x	x	x	x	x					5-4
0/551	x	x	x	x	x					5-4
1/12	x	x	x	x	x					5-4
1/91	x	x	x	x	x	*				5-3
0/11	x	x	x	x	x	x				6-3
0/497	x	x	x	x	x	x				6-3
0/3	x	x	*	x	-	x	x			5-3
1/115	x	x	x	x	-	x	x			6-3
1/536	x	x	x	x	-	x	x			6-3
										89-105

	D	Bl	Wa	F	C	H	Bu	Mi	Re	
Totals	22-0	21-1	17-4	12-8	8-14	6-15	2-20	1-21	0-22	89-105 194
Scale positions	22	21	19	12	9	5½	2	0	0	
Scale scores	1.00	.91	.73	.09	-.18	-.50	-.82	-1.00	-1.00	

$$R = 1 - \frac{9}{194} = .954 \qquad S = 1 - \frac{9}{30} = .700$$

FIGURE 1. (continued)

1956 TERM

C Scale

Cases	D	Bl	Wa	Br	F	H	Wh	Bu	Re	C	Totals
				Justices							
3/427	x									/	1-8
4/271	x									/	1-8
4/476:61	x	x								/	2-7
3/373:430	x	x								/	2-7
3/373:834	x	x								/	2-7
3/685	x	x								/	2-7
3/692	x	x								/	2-7
3/72	x	x				*				/	2-6
4/476:582	x	x			x					/	3-6
2/407	x	x		x						/	3-6
4/931:835	x	x	*	*						/	2-5
2/432	x	x	x							/	3-6
2/567	x	x	x						/		3-5
4/393	x	-	x	x						/	3-6
2/330	x	x	x	x						/	4-5
2/354	x	x	x	x						/	4-5
2/385	x	x	x	x						/	4-5
3/569	x	x	x	x						/	4-5
3/583	x	x	x	x						/	4-5
4/436	x	x	x	x						/	4-5
3/252	x	x	x				*	x		/	5-3
2/1	x	x	x	/			/		x	x	5-3
2/232	x	x	-	x	x			/			4-5
2/191	x	x	x	x	x		/		x		6-3
2/985	x	x	x	x	x	x	/				6-3
3/194	x	x	x	x	x	x	*				6-2
3/346	x	x	x	x	x	x	*				6-2
4/1:701	x	x	x	x	x	x	*				6-2
4/1:713	x	x	x	x	x	x	*				6-2
4/234	x	x	x	x	x	x	*				6-2
4/156	-	x	*	x	x	x	x				5-3
4/178	x	x	x	x	x	x	*	*			6-1
4/929:206	x	x	x	x	x	x	x	*		/	7-1
4/929:306	x	x	x	x	x	x	x	*		/	7-1
4/929:462	x	x	x	x	x	x	x	*		/	7-1
4/930:742	x	x	x	x	x	x	x	*		/	7-1
4/930:884	x	x	x	x	x	x	x	*		/	7-1
4/521	x	x	x	x	x	-	x	x		/	7-2
4/298:6	x	x	x	*	x	x	x	x		/	6-1
4/298:7	x	x	x	*	x	x	x	x		/	6-1
3/53	x	*	x	x	x	x	x	x		/	6-1
4/931:9M	x	x	x	x	x	x	x	x		/	8-1
4/351	x	x	x	x	x	x	*		x	/	7-1
2/322	x	*	x	x	x	x	/	-	x	x	7-1
											204-165
Totals	43-1	39-3	31-11	28-12	23-21	20-24	8-13	6-32	2-8	4-40	204-165 / 369
Scale positions	44	42	33½	31	22	20	19	10	10	2	
Scale scores	1.00	.91	.52	.41	.00	-.09	-.14	-.55	-.55	-.91	

$$R = 1 - \frac{10}{258} = .961 \qquad S = 1 - \frac{12}{88} = .864$$

1957 TERM

C Scale

Cases	D	Bl	Wa	Br	F	H	Wh	Bu	C	Totals
				Justices						
5/570	x									1-8
5/107	x				x					2-7
7/549:561	x				x	x				3-6
7/549:562	x				x	x				3-6
5/286	x	x								2-7
5/393	x	x								2-7
7/426	x	x								2-7
5/66	x	x	x							3-6
5/233	x	x	x							3-6
6/405	x	x	x							3-6
7/371	x	x	x							3-6
6/44	x	x	x				x			4-5
6/464	x	x	x	*						3-5
7/504	x	x	x	*						3-5
6/148	x	x	x	x						4-5
6/165	x	x	x	x						4-5
6/390	x	x	x	x						4-5
6/571	x	x	x	x						4-5
7/185	x	x	x	x						4-5
7/193	x	x	x	x						4-5
7/386	x	x	x	x						4-5
7/399	x	x	x	x						4-5
7/433	x	x	x	x						4-5
7/468	x	x	x	x						4-5
5/155	x	x	x	x			x	x		5-4
5/184	x	x	x	x			x	x		5-4
6/86	x	x	x	x			x			5-4
5/225	x	x	x	x					x	5-4
6/691	x	x	x	x			x	x	x	6-3
7/214	x	x	x	x	*			x	x	6-2
5/392	x	x	x	x	x			x		6-3
5/115	x	x	x	x	x					5-4
7/116	x	x	x	x	x					5-4
7/144	x	x	x	x	x					5-4
6/363	x	x	x	x	x	x				6-3
6/660	x	x	x	x	x	x				6-3
6/670	x	x	x	x	x	x				6-3
7/348	x	x	x	x	x	x				6-3
7/480	x	x	x	x	x	x				6-3
7/576	x	x	x	x	x	x				6-3
6/576	x	x	x	x	x	x		*		6-2
5/80	x	x	x	x	x	x	x			7-2
6/560	x	x	x	x	x	x	x			7-2
7/301	x	x	x	x	x	x	x			7-2
7/493	x	x	x	x	x	x	x			7-2
7/573	x	x	x	x	x	x	x			7-2
6/129	x	x	x	x	x	-	x	x		7-2
5/313	x	x	x	x	-	x	x	x		7-2
7/513:483	x	x	*	x	x	x	x	x		7-1
7/513:484	x	x	*	x	x	x	x	x		7-1
7/545:382	x	x	*	x	x	x	x	x		7-1
7/545:385	x	x	*	x	x	x	x	x		7-1
7/568	x	x	*	x	x	x	x	x		7-1
5/579:80	x	x	x	x	x	x	x	x		8-1
5/579:141	x	x	x	x	x	x	x	x		8-1
6/24	x	x	x	x	x	x	x	x		8-1
										280-215
Totals	56-0	52-4	44-7	44-10	28-27	21-35	20-36	13-42	2-54	280-215 / 495
Scale positions	56	52	49	43	26½	22	15	10	0	
Scale scores	1.00	.86	.75	.54	-.05	-.21	-.46	-.64	-1.00	

$$R = 1 - \frac{17}{419} = .959 \qquad S = 1 - \frac{17}{105} = .838$$

FIGURE 1. (continued)

1959 TERM

C Scale

Cases		D	Bl	Wa	Br	S	H	F	Wh	C	Totals
	Justices										
2/257		x									1-8
1/220		x	x								2-7
2/474		x	x								2-7
3/420:549		x	x								2-7
3/420:550		x	x								2-7
4/51		-	x	x					x		3-6
2/525		x	x	x							3-6
3/144		x	x	x			*				3-5
2/1		x	x	*	x						3-5
2/217		x	x	x	x						4-5
2/390		x	x	x	x						4-5
2/511:111		x	x	x	x						4-5
2/511:122		x	x	x	x						4-5
2/610		x	x	x	x						4-5
3/370		x	x	x	x						4-5
3/405		x	x	x	x						4-5
4/59		x	x	x	x						4-5
1/281:21		x	x	x	x					x	5-4
1/281:37		x	x	x	x					x	5-4
3/370		x	x	x	x				x	x	6-3
4/263		x	x	x	x	*			x		4-4
4/206		x	x	x	x	x					5-4
4/253		x	x	x	x	x					5-4
2/384		x	x	x	x	x		x			6-3
1/234		x	x	x	x	x			x	x	7-2
2/60		x	x	x	x	x	x				6-3
3/697		x	x	x	x	x	x	x			7-2
1/278		x	x	x	x	-	x	x		x	7-2
1/98		x	x	-	x	x	x	x	x		7-2
1/147		x	x	x	x	x	-	x	x	x	8-1
4/282		x	x	x	x	x	x	-	x	x	8-1
4/283		x	x	x	x	x	x	-	x	x	8-1
											147-138
Totals		31-1	31-1	25-6	24-8	10-21	6-25	5-27	7-25	8-24 / 147-138	285
Scale positions		32	31	27	24	11*	7	6	4	3	
Scale scores		1.00	.94	.69	.50	-.28	-.56	-.62	-.75	-.81	

$$R = 1 - \frac{12}{249} = .952 \qquad S = 1 - \frac{15}{52} = .712$$

FIGURE 1. (continued)

1960 TERM

C Scale

Cases	D	Bl	Wa	Br	S	Wh	F	H	C	Totals
5/762	x									1-8
6/308	x									1-8
6/420	x									1-8
6/582	x									1-8
7/820	x	x								2-7
5/265	x	x						•		2-6
4/507	-	x	x							2-7
4/611	-	x	x							2-7
5/458	x	-	x							2-7
4/388	x	x	x							3-6
7/486	x	x	x							3-6
7/556	x	x	x							3-6
5/381	x	-	x	x						3-6
4/372	x	x	x	x						4-5
4/426	x	x	x	x						4-5
5/43	x	x	x	x						4-5
5/301:70	x	x	x	x						4-5
5/301:179	x	x	x	x						4-5
5/399	x	x	x	x						4-5
5/431	x	x	x	x						4-5
6/36	x	x	x	x						4-5
6/82	x	x	x	x						4-5
6/117	x	x	x	x						4-5
7/203	x	x	x	x						4-5
7/1	x	x	x	x						4-5
7/386	x	x	x	x						4-5
6/617	x	-	-	x	x					3-6
6/599	x	-	-	x	x		x			4-5
4/587	x	x	x	-	x					4-5
4/479:14	x	x	x	x	x					5-4
4/479:83	x	x	x	x	x					5-4
5/85	x	x	x	x	x					5-4
5/551	x	x	x	x	x					5-4
6/1	x	x	x	x	x					5-4
7/456	x	x	x	x	x					5-4
7/568	x	x	x	x	x		x			6-3
5/715	x	x	x	x	x					6-3
7/643	x	x	x	x	x			x	x	6-3
4/631	x	x	x	x	x	x				6-3
5/312	x	x	x	x	x	x				6-3
6/213	x	x	x	x	x	x				6-3
6/418	x	x	x	x	•	x				5-3
7/421	x	x	x	x	-	x				5-4
7/740	x	x	x	x	-	x				7-2
6/712	x	x	x	x	-	x		x	x	6-3
4/350	x	x	x	x	-	x	x	x		6-3
5/534	x	x	x	x	-	x	x	x		7-2
4/454	x	x	x	x	x	-	x	x		7-2
7/433	x	x	x	x	x	-	x	x		7-2
5/610	x	x	x	x	x	x	x	x		8-1
5/167	x	x	x	x	x	x	x	x	x	8-1
										221-236
Totals	49-2	43-8	43-8	38-13	20-30	10-41	7-44	6-44	5-46	457
										221-236
Scale positions	51	47	45	39	25	13	6	6	1	
Scale scores	1.00	.84	.76	.53	-.02	-.49	-.76	-.76	-.96	

$$R = 1 - \frac{22}{403} = .945 \qquad S = 1 - \frac{23}{79} = .709$$

1961 TERM

C Scale

Cases	Bl	D	Wa	Br	S	BW	Wh	F	H	C	Totals
9/402	x					/	/				1-7
0/530:481	x	x				•	/	•			2-5
0/41	x	x	•			•	/	•			2-5
9/599	•	x	x			•	/	•			2-4
9/541	x	x	x			•	/	•			3-4
8/139	x	x	x				/				3-6
8/19	x	x	x	x			/				4-5
8/231	x	x	x	x			/				4-5
8/424	x	x	x	x			/				4-5
8/448:56	x	x	x	x			/				4-5
8/448:57	x	x	x	x			/				4-5
0/650	-	x	x	x		•	/	•	x		4-3
0/49	x	x	x	x		•	/	•			4-3
0/230	x	x	x	x		•	/	•		x	5-2
0/660	x	x	x	x	x		/	•	x		6-2
9/367	x	x	x	x	x	/	/				5-3
9/186	x	x	x	x	x	/	•			x	6-2
9/429	x	x	x	x	x	x	/	•	x	x	7-1
0/190	x	x	x	x	x	x	/	•	x	x	7-1
9/438	x	x	x	x	x	•	/	•			5-2
9/749:8	x	x	x	x	x	•	/	•			5-2
9/749:9	x	x	x	x	x	•	/	•			5-2
9/749:11	x	x	x	x	x	•	/	•			5-2
9/749:12	x	x	x	x	x	•	/	•			5-2
9/749:28	x	x	x	x	x	•	/	•			5-2
0/288	x	x	x	x	x	•	/	•			5-2
0/375	x	x	x	x	x	•	/	•			5-2
0/717	x	x	x	x	x	•	/	•			5-2
0/724	x	x	x	x	x	•	/	•			5-2
9/661	x	x	x	x	x	x	/	•			6-2
9/662	x	x	x	x	x	x	/	•			6-2
9/749:10	x	x	x	x	x	•	/	•			4-2
8/487	x	x	x	x	-	/	x				6-3
8/439	x	x	x	x	-	/	x	x			6-3
9/705	•	x	x	x	x	•	/	•	x		6-1
0/478	x	x	x	x	x	•	/	•	x		6-1
9/141:64	x	x	x	x	x	/	•	x	x		7-1
9/141:65	x	x	x	x	x	/	•	x	x		7-1
0/421	x	x	x	x	-	•	/	•	x	x	6-1
											187-110
Totals	37-1	38-1	36-2	32-6	23-16	4-2	2-6	3-10	7-32	5-34	297
										187-110	
Scale positions	39	38	36½	33	25	23	17½	6	5	1	
Scale scores	1.00	.95	.87	.69	.28	.18	-.10	-.69	-.74	-.95	

$$R = 1 - \frac{6}{236} = .975 \qquad S = 1 - \frac{9}{45} = .800$$

FIGURE 1. (continued)

1962 TERM

C Scale

Cases	D	Bl	Wa	Br	G	BW	S	H	C	Totals
					Justices					
3/420					x		x			2-7
1/75	x									1-8
3/83	-	x						x		2-7
3/179	x	x								2-7
1/341	x	x	x							3-6
3/647	-	x	x	x						3-6
1/392	x	-	x	x						3-6
3/427	x	-	-	x	x					3-6
4/23	x	-	x	x	x					4-5
1/471	x	x	x	x	x					5-4
2/144:2	x	x	x	x	x					5-4
2/144:3	x	x	x	x	x					5-4
2/293	x	x	x	x	x					5-4
2/487	x	x	x	x	x					5-4
2/539	x	x	x	x	x					5-4
2/734	x	x	x	x	x					5-4
3/503	x	x	x	x	x					5-4
4/449	x	x	x	x	x					5-4
4/469:39	x	x	x	x	x					5-4
4/469:293	x	x	x	x	x					5-4
4/109	x	x	x	x	x					5-4
1/415	x	x	x	x	x	x				6-3
2/353	x	x	x	x	x	x				6-3
2/391	x	x	x	x	x	x				6-3
3/487	x	x	x	x	x	x				6-3
2/710	x	x	x	x	x	•	x			6-2
2/477	x	x	x	x	x	x	x			7-2
2/708	x	x	x	x	x	x	x			7-2
2/709	x	x	x	x	x	x	x			7-2
2/711	x	x	x	x	x	x	x			7-2
2/713	x	x	x	x	x	x	x			7-2
2/771	x	x	x	x	x	x	x			7-2
3/1	x	x	x	x	x	x	x			7-2
3/242	x	x	x	x	x	x	x			7-2
3/243	x	x	x	x	x	x	x			7-2
3/723	x	x	x	x	x	x	x			7-2
4/498	x	x	x	x	x	x	x			7-2
4/499	x	x	x	x	x	x	x			7-2
4/490	x	x	x	x	x	x	x			7-2
4/509	x	x	x	x	x	x	x			7-2
2/58	x	x	x	x	x	x	x	x		8-1
2/229	x	x	x	x	x	x	x	x		8-1
2/522	x	x	x	x	x	x	x	x		8-1
3/113	x	x	x	x	x	•	x	-	x	7-1
3/668	x	x	x	x	x	x	x	-	x	7-1
4/203:119	x	x	x	x	x	x	-	x	x	8-1
4/203:142	x	x	x	x	x	x	-	x	x	8-1
Totals	44-3	42-5	42-5	42-5	41-6	24-21	21-26	6-41	4-43	266-155
										266-155
										421
Scale positions	46	45	43	42	40	26	22	7	4	
Scale scores	.96	.91	.83	.79	.70	.11	-.06	-.70	-.83	

$$R = 1 - \frac{9}{350} = .974 \qquad S = 1 - \frac{13}{76} = .829$$

FIGURE 1. (continued)

conservatives in their attitude. The remaining two justices, Frankfurter and Jackson, appear during these three terms to be moderate conservatives, with average negative scale scores less than half as great as the average score for the three extreme conservatives. Both the scale scores and the marginals for 1947 and 1948 indicate that Frankfurter is less conservative in his attitude than Jackson; and the marginals for 1946 would support such a finding but the scale scores would not, since four of Frankfurter's five affirmative responses in that term appear as inconsistent. Moreover, these same Frankfurter inconsistencies (plus Black's four) account for the minimal level of acceptability of the 1946 scale, although it should be noted that the acceptability of the 1947 scale is little better, and in 1947 it is primarily Black and Vinson (rather than Frankfurter) who are most inconsistent in their responses. We would certainly want more evidence before we could have such confidence in our evaluation of Frankfurter's attitude.

THE 1949–1952 TERMS

Murphy and Rutledge both died during the summer vacation following the 1948 Term, and they were replaced by Clark and Minton. The resulting group was stable in its composition during the next four terms (1949–52). Douglas and Black now *appear* to be as extremely liberal as Murphy and Rutledge had been during the preceding three terms. Douglas would have had a maximal positive score in all four terms, except for a single vote in the 1951 Term and the effect in the 1949 Term of my arbitrary rule for scoring nonparticipation; but on the other hand, Douglas had twice as many negative responses—and necessarily, inconsistent ones—as did Black (disregarding the 1949 Term, in which Douglas' participation was very low, due to the long period of his recuperation from an injury). I infer from these data that there is no adequate basis for distinguishing between the attitude of Douglas and that of Black during these four terms, and that both should be considered extreme liberals. But extreme in what sense? Is it reasonable to assume that Douglas and Black suddenly changed their attitude, and became (in terms of absolute position on the hypothetical attitudinal dimension) the *same* as Murphy and Rutledge had been during the preceding three terms? If we recall that the scale scores are an arbitrary metric which is a function of scale positions, and that scale positions are uniquely determined by the parameters of a particular scale, then we realize that scale scores are strictly a relativistic statistic. The comparison suggested, as between Douglas-Black and Murphy-Rutledge, is comparable to giving different tests—for which the difficulty, validity, reliability, and standard scores are unknown and, indeed, unknowable—to two different groups; and then asking whether those who ranked highest in the first group performed more or less well than those who ranked highest among the second group. So long as the group remains the same, we can make comparisons between term scales on the basis of rank order, in a gross sort of way, providing that even here we make allowance for the relatively large amount of error variance that is either manifest or latent in the data. Since Douglas and Black consistently ranked below Murphy and Rutledge during the three terms in which they participated jointly in the same decisions, the more reasonable inference to make is that Douglas and Black have not changed their attitude during the 1949–1952 Terms; rather, it is the character of the stimuli to which they are responding that has changed during this period. We know, for example, that the process of jurisdictional decision-making for the Court (*i.e.,* the selection of stimuli) is such that at least four justices must vote affirmatively in order for the Court to agree to decide any case on the merits. The scales for 1946–48 indicate that Murphy, Rutledge, Douglas, and Black had the necessary votes to bring before the Court cases that were relatively "way out"—only a political liberal would want the Court to decide such cases, and only a political liberal would vote to uphold the libertarian claims when these cases were decided on the merits. The extremity of many of the stimuli, then, would account for the high proportion of negative responses from Frankfurter and Jackson, whom we tentatively have classified as moderate conservatives. On the other hand, in 1949–52, when Douglas and Black would have to combine with justices more conservative rather than more liberal than they themselves were, in order to get civil liberties cases before the Court for decision on the merits, it seems quite plausible that they could gain the necessary support only for the selection of less extreme stimuli. And most likely, that support would have to come from Frankfurter and Jackson. Consequently, when the Court was being provoked to consider relatively extreme issues of political liberalism by Murphy and Rutledge, then Black and Douglas may frequently have responded, and Frankfurter and Jackson probably usually responded, that they were not *that* liberal in their attitude. But when the jurisdictional compromise had to be made to the right of Black and Douglas, then *they* could appear to be favorable to almost all of the questions that were raised, while Frankfurter and Jackson, responding to generally much more moderate sets of stimuli, could accept such claims much more frequently. (According to this hypothesis, Frankfurter and

Jackson were responding, in 1946–48, to questions that they usually had voted against having to decide; while in 1949–52, they were responding to questions that they had voted to have the Court decide.)

The scales for the 1949–52 terms confirm that Frankfurter and Jackson are indeed the only ones (other than Douglas and Black) who have positive scale scores, and who therefore gave preponderant affirmative support to the claims raised in these cases. These data also permit us to resolve, with some confidence, the question that we could not answer on the basis of the scales for the preceding three terms: Who is the more liberal, Frankfurter or Jackson? During these four terms, Frankfurter's average scale score was .50, while Jackson's was .05; and similarly, examination of the marginals shows that 74 percent of Frankfurter's responses, but only 38 percent of Jackson's, were affirmative. Accordingly, we might well revise our earlier judgment, based upon only the first three terms, in which we inferred that Frankfurter and Jackson appeared to be moderate conservatives in their attitude. It now would appear more correct to say that Douglas and Black are more politically liberal than Frankfurter, and Frankfurter is more politically liberal in his attitude than Jackson; but whether either Frankfurter or Jackson should be considered to be a moderate liberal, or a moderate conservative, or simply a moderate, we would be less certain—although we could be pretty sure that the most likely choice would be between (Frankfurter: moderate liberal; Jackson: moderate) and (Frankfurter: moderate; Jackson: moderate conservative).

When we examine the three respondents whom we grouped together as extremely conservative on the basis of their scores during the earlier period, we find that we can readily discriminate among them for the period 1949–52. They are consistently in the rank order Burton, Vinson, and Reed, with average scale scores of —.43, —.67, and —.79, respectively, for these four terms. Moreover, we can now account for our failure to be able to discriminate among them during the earlier period: when confronted with sets of relatively extreme liberal stimuli, as they were during the 1946–48 Terms, all three of them were so much more conservative in their attitude than the stimuli that we could not expect such questions to differentiate among them; in most cases, they all had to respond negatively. But the more moderate sets of questions raised in 1949–52 made possible the differentiation among them that is evident in these scales.

The two new justices were Clark and Minton. Clark's rate of nonresponse was high but diminishing during this period: it was 48 percent in

1949, and then successively 45, 17, 9 and finally 0 percent in the 1953 Term; this was due to the fact that he was appointed to the Court directly from the office of Attorney General, and under the custom of the Court, he felt obligated to disqualify himself from participation in the many cases, on the scales during these four terms, which the Department of Justice had prosecuted in the lower federal courts during Clark's tenure as department head. Except in the first term, when Clark participated in barely half of the decisions, he ranked consistently as more liberal than Minton. The average scale scores and proportions of affirmative votes for this period suggest that Clark's attitudinal position is closest to Burton's, and Minton's is closest to Reed's, on issues of political liberalism; and Burton and Clark do occupy adjacent ranks during the last three of these four terms, while Reed and Minton occupy the lowest ranks in 1951 and 1952. We need, however, further information before we can be very confident about the relative degrees of conservatism of Clark and Minton in relation to Burton, Vinson, and Reed, although we now are relatively confident about the rank order for the latter three.

THE 1953–1955 TERMS

A new Chief Justice, Warren, replaced Vinson at the beginning of the 1953 Term. The only other personnel change during the period of the 1953–54 Terms came when Harlan replaced Jackson early in the 1954 Term, and an examination of the scales indicates that Harlan moved directly not only into Jackson's vacancy, but also into the same rank position that Jackson had been occupying on the C scales for preceding terms: more conservative than Frankfurter, but less conservative than Burton, Reed, or Minton. Jackson, however, had also been more liberal than Clark; and we could not be certain, on the basis of the evidence of the 1954 and 1955 scales, whether the same relationship obtains between Harlan and Clark. Harlan ranks higher than Clark in 1954, but only as a consequence of the rule for scoring non-response; and although Clark ranks higher than Harlan in 1955, Clark alone is responsible for more than half of the inconsistent votes denoted in this scale, so we can hardly avoid making allowance for the apparent possibility that this scale may not be measuring validly Clark's attitudinal position, even though it may be measuring the remaining respondents quite well. An examination of the subsequent terms, however, ought to permit us to resolve this question, which we now leave open.

The much more interesting question is: how should we evaluate Warren's position, on the basis of the evidence of these three scales? Before attempting to answer this question, however, we had better examine the stability of the rank order for the other justices, in relationship to our findings for the preceding terms. The scales for the two preceding periods did not permit us to distinguish between Douglas and Black, but we now can observe that Douglas is slightly but consistently more extreme than Black on each of these three scales. Except during the 1953 Term, when Minton had four inconsistent votes—and with one more, he might have been assigned a minimal instead of a median rank—and when Clark had none, Clark continued to rank as more liberal than Minton; and on the basis of the 1953 and 1954 scales, we should have to say that Clark appeared considerably more liberal than Minton. Again with the exception of a single decision in the 1953 Term, when both had several inconsistent votes, Burton continues to rank as less conservative than Reed; Minton ranks more liberally than Reed on all three scales; and particularly, in view of the consistent relationships denoted in the 1954 and 1955 scales, we should probably infer that Minton is slightly less liberal than Burton, and slightly more so than Reed, thus establishing the rank order Burton, Minton, Reed for these relatively conservative justices. Such an inference is generally confirmed by a re-examination of their relative rank positions throughout the seven terms (1949–55) that they were together on the Court: Burton preceded Minton in rank in five of these seven terms, and Burton preceded Reed six times out of seven, while Minton preceded Reed in five of the seven terms. We now have two partial rank orderings which involve Burton and Reed: Burton, Vinson, and Reed (for the period 1946–52); and Burton, Minton, Reed (for the period 1949–55). We must now consider the relationship between Vinson and Minton, who were together during the four terms 1949–52. In the 1949 Term, Minton appears slightly more liberal than Vinson; in the 1952 Term, it is the other way around; and in 1950 they are tied. In the 1951 Term, however, the sample of decisions is sufficiently large and diverse that there are several decisions that clearly distinguish between Vinson and Minton, with Minton ranking as the more conservative of the two. We can, therefore, combine the two partial rankings, as follows: Burton, Vinson, Minton, Reed.

We can now reconsider, also, the relative ranking of Clark and Burton. Burton had preceded Clark in rank, although the difference in their scores was slight, during the period 1949–52. During the 1953–55 Terms, however, Clark consistently preceded Burton in rank, and on the basis of larger differences than had obtained during the earlier four terms. We may explain differences in scales scores—such as the shift from negative to positive scores for Frankfurter and Jackson, beginning in the 1949

Term—on the basis of changes in the extremity of the stimuli; but this kind of explanation cannot account for intransitivities of rank order. I therefore infer that either Clark or Burton did change his attitude, beginning in the 1953 Term, which was when Warren joined the group as the new Chief Justice.

As we have seen, the rank sequence of the justices (other than Clark and Warren) for this period was as follows: D Bl F J/H Bu Mi Re. During the preceding four-term period (1949–52), Clark and Chief Justice Vinson had ranked immediately below Burton; and during Warren's first term, Clark and he ranked 6th and 7th. This put Clark in the same position that he had occupied during the immediately preceding terms, and put Warren directly into the rank position that Vinson had vacated. I already have commented upon the dubious validity of Minton's observed rank in the 1953 scale; and if we are prepared to assume that Minton's actual rank was much lower, as shown in the rank sequence suggested above, then there was no change in the relative positions of either Warren or Clark, as between the 1953 and 1954 Terms. It is true that both of their scale scores are much higher in 1954 than in 1953 (by .71 and .66 points, respectively); but for reasons that we already have discussed, such a differential in scores probably reflects changes in the relative values of the stimuli more than changes in the attitudes of the two respondents. The changes in scores did not bring about any meaningful change in ranks, and both Warren and Clark reacted almost identically to the respective sets of stimuli in both 1953 and 1954.

As Figure 2 shows, Clark's scores had also moved in a pattern isomorphic with that for Vinson during the preceding four terms. This figure also shows that the divergence between Warren and Clark, which began in the 1955 Term, was not a function of any peculiarities in the sample of stimuli accepted for decision in that term; to the contrary, this term served as the transition to the even greater difference in their attitude which is manifest from the 1956 Term on. The curves for both justices for the period 1956–62 show the relatively slight variations, from term to term, which characteristically can readily be attributed to sampling variance. The evidence provided by the marginals, and by rank order changes, tends to confirm the inference that *both* Warren and Clark changed their attitude toward political liberalism during the 1955 Term, but that they changed in opposite directions. The pairs of marginals for Warren and Clark are almost identical in 1953 and 1954 (4–15/5–16, 11–9/11–10), while in 1955 they are reversed (17–4/8–14) and remain so thereafter. From the time he joined the Court (in 1949) until 1954, Clark's rank either coincided with or was adjacent to that of the Chief Justice—Vinson until 1952, and Warren in 1953 and 1954. In 1955, however, Warren was in the third rank, preceding Frankfurter (who had occupied the third rank from 1949 to 1954); Clark is assigned the fifth rank in the scale, although his numerous inconsistent votes tend both to cast doubt upon the validity

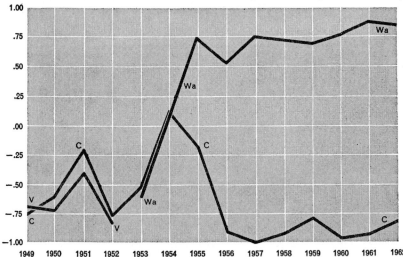

FIGURE 2. Political Liberalism Scale Scores for the Chief Justices and Justice Clark, 1949–1962 Terms

of his assigned rank, and also to confirm the inference that Clark was in the process of changing his attitude during this term—we should expect that a person who is changing his mind will be less consistent in his responses than a person whose attitudinal position is stable. After 1955, Warren without exception ranks third, and Clark ninth, for the next seven terms. The change, however, was of much greater magnitude for Warren than for Clark; Warren (in effect) jumped over three other justices (F, H, and Bu) to move into position between Black and Frankfurter, while Clark slipped back below Burton, where he had been in 1949–52. There were really, therefore, two different changes that involved these two justices: Clark became temporarily slightly more liberal during Chief Justice Warren's first three terms on the Court; while Warren, who had moved directly into former Chief Justice Vinson's position of moderate conservatism, moved steadily towards the political left, and after his second term on the Court reached and remained in the third rank.

We have by now concluded that as the Court entered this fourth period and the 1956 Term, the rank order of the incumbent justices (except for Clark) was:

D Bl Wa F H Bu Mi Re

Clark, as we have just discussed above, was about at this time in the process of changing his attitude back to the relatively more extreme political conservatism reflected in his minimal rank, during the 1956 Term and thereafter. Minton resigned just before the 1956 Term began, thus eliminating him as an item in the ordered set; he was replaced by Brennan, who moved at once into the fourth rank, which he occupied without exception during the next seven terms. Reed also retired, but during the middle of the term; he was replaced by Whittaker, whose political attitude appeared to be slightly more liberal than that of the man he replaced, since Whittaker moved into the rank preceding that of Burton, while Reed had followed Burton in rank. Consequently, at the close of the 1956 Term, the rank order of the incumbent justices was:

D Bl Wa Br F H Wh Bu C

With two qualifications, it can be said that this was a stable structure for the next half dozen terms. One qualification relates to the transpositions among the ranks of Frankfurter, Harlan, and Whittaker; but since the ordinal relationship of these three justices, as a group, to the others remains unchanged throughout this fourth period, and the transpositions typically depend upon such a small decisional margin in each term set, we attribute such changes to sampling variation in the stimuli, and we infer that the points representing these three justices, on the underlying attitudinal continuum, are densely clustered. The other qualification relates to changes in the structure—but not in the rank order sequence—that occurred as the result of the replacement of three of the incumbents by new respondents: without exception, these three new justices were more politically liberal than the men whom they replaced. In 1958, Stewart replaced Burton; and Stewart moved into the median rank position, preceding the F-H-Wh group, whom Burton had followed in rank. In 1961, Whittaker retired, to be replaced by White, who moved (as became evident in the 1962 scale) into the rank preceding that of Stewart; and when Goldberg joined the Court at the beginning of the 1962 Term in place of Frankfurter, who had retired during the preceding summer, Goldberg assumed a rank position preceding White's. Thus, when Brennan joined the group in 1956, his assumption of the fourth rank moved Frankfurter down to the fifth; when Stewart joined in 1958 and assumed the fifth rank, Frankfurter moved down to the sixth; and when Goldberg and White moved into the fifth and sixth ranks in 1962, Stewart moved down to the seventh; but in none of these instances of rank change is there evidence to support the inference that there was any change in the attitudes of the justices who were pushed down to lower ranks. To the contrary, the changes that were occurring in the group composition, as a consequence of the consistent replacement of relatively conservative justices by relatively liberal ones, had the effect of making it appear that justices like Frankfurter and Harlan—whose political attitudes may have remained (as I am assuming) perfectly stable—were becoming more conservative. But Frankfurter and Harlan were becoming "more conservative" only in the strictly relativistic sense of "as compared to their colleagues." As the group attitude became *absolutely* more liberal (in an aggregational sense), Frankfurter and Harlan, remaining constant, could only appear to be *relatively* more conservative; and the liberalization of the group probably also resulted in more liberal samples of stimuli, of which Frankfurter and Harlan could accept increasingly smaller proportions.

This is a fundamentally important point, which bears a critical relationship to an understanding of the Supreme Court's policy-making role within the national political system during the middle and late fifties and the early sixties. These, it will be recalled, were the years of racial integration and legislative reapportionment—both national policies of basic importance that were formulated in sets of decisions of the United States Supreme Court. Both a necessary and a sufficient condition to the formulation, by the Court, of more politically liberal policies, is that the collective attitude of the decision-making group should become more politically liberal. To what extent did the aggregate attitude of the group change, during this period when its policies were becoming manifestly more politically liberal in content? An examination of the C scales for this period, from the point of view discussed in the preceding paragraph, provides an answer to this question.

In 1954, Frankfurter ranked third on the term C scale, below Douglas and Black, of course; and there were, therefore, six justices who were more politically conservative than he. By 1962, five justices had moved into ranks between Black and Frankfurter (where there had been none in 1954); Frankfurter himself had left the Court; and there remained only two of the justices who were more conservative than he in 1954. Thus, a Court which in 1954 already was sufficiently political liberal to make the basic decision regarding racial integration in public schools had become even more liberal eight years later. Relative to Frankfurter, the proportion of political liberalism had shifted from 2–6 (in 1954) to 7–2 (in 1962). Some of the details already have been discussed, but I shall briefly summarize them all. First, Warren changed to a relatively and consistently more liberal position after 1954. (Could the experience of making the school integration decision, which was announced on May 17, 1954, have functioned as a major influence in helping to change Warren's attitude?) Second, Brennan replaced Minton. Third, Stewart replaced Burton. Fourth, White replaced Whittaker (who had replaced Reed in 1956). And finally, Goldberg replaced Frankfurter.

My general conclusion is that, except for Warren and Clark, there is little evidence to suggest that the attitudes of individual justices changed at all during this seventeen-year period. But there were very sweeping changes in the collective attitudinal structure of the group, during this period. These changes may be briefly summarized, as follows. (For convenience in making this summary, I shall characterize White, Stewart, Frankfurter, Jackson, Harlan, and Whittaker as "moderates"; respondents of higher rank [than the moderates] as "liberals"; and respondents of lower rank as "conservatives"; it being understood, of course, that these adjectives are imputed only relational significance, in the context of the present discussion.) During the first period (1946–48) the Court was balanced in structure, with four liberals, two moderates, and three conservatives. During the second period (1949–1952), the collective attitude of the group became more conservative, as the group's composition included only two liberals, two moderates, and five conservatives. The third period (1953–1955) was a period of transition; and Warren's change as this period drew to a close changed the balance to make it somewhat more liberal in orientation with three liberals, two moderates, and four conservatives. Throughout the fourth and final period, the shift in the direction of a more politically liberal orientation of the Court accelerated, so that by the close of the 1962 Term, there were five liberals, three moderates (White, Stewart, and Harlan), and one conservative (Clark).

The explanation for these changes in the structure of the group attitude of the Supreme Court must be sought in the political process by means of which Supreme Court justices are selected. There is a time lag between presidential preference and judicial performance; and the fundamental explanation for the relative liberalism of the Court during the immediate postwar period must be sought in the political factors that brought Frank-

TABLE 16

Summary of the C (Political Liberalism) Scale

Rank Order of Justices:	1946–48	1949–52	Term Periods: 1953–55	1956–61	1962
+ Mu	X				
Ru	X				
D	X	X	X	X	X
Bl	X	X	X	X	X
Wa			X[a]	X	X
Br				X	X
G					X
0 BW					X
S				X[d]	X
F	X	X	X	X	
J,H	X	X	X[c]	X	X
Wh				X	
[Wa]			X[b]		
[C]			X		
− Bu	X	X	X	X[d]	
C		X		X	X
V	X	X			
Mi		X	X		
Re	X	X	X		

NOTES

[a] Wa, 1955
[b] Wa, 1953–54
[c] J, 1953; H, 1954–55; J and H are tied in rank. (J was replaced by H.)
[d] Bu, 1956–57; S, 1958–61. (Bu was replaced by S.)

Scale Types:	1946–48	1949–52	Term Periods: 1953–54	1955	1956–57	1958–61	1962	Average
C+	4	2	2	3	4	4	5	3.3
Co	2	2	4	3	3	4	3	2.9
C−	3	5	3	3	2	1	1	2.8

lin Roosevelt to the White House and kept him there for the longest tenure of any American President to date. The relative conservatism of the second period must be explained in terms of the political factors—which obviously are highly correlated with the structure of the American political party system since the Civil War—which made it necessary for Franklin Roosevelt to accept Truman as Vice President in 1946—and in lieu, let it be remembered, of Henry A. Wallace! (What would the political attitude structure of the Supreme Court have been, during the period 1949–1952 if, instead of Burton and Vinson and Minton and Clark, there had been four justices chosen by Henry Wallace? Would this have resulted in an even more extremely liberal Court, by 1952, than obtained in fact in 1962? And, if so, with what political consequences?) The more liberal orientation of the Court, which began with the appointment of Warren (and notwithstanding the two terms that were required for him to define his political attitude as Chief Justice—instead of as governor or as public prosecutor) and which continued throughout the remaining two periods, is a direct reflection of the political choices of Eisenhower and Kennedy, and therefore of the political forces which put these two men in the White House.

Table 16 presents the general set of rankings that I have inferred, on the basis of the preceding analysis of ordinal relationships among the justices during the periods of relatively stable composition of the Court. I have explained, in the course of this analysis, why variations among scale scores, from one term to another, generally reflect variation in the extremity of the sets of stimuli presented for decision, and rarely should be construed to imply any significant change in the attitudes of the respondents. It is possible, of course, to compute the average scale scores of respondents, and to use these as an alternative summary scale if we are willing to assume that the variation among stimuli extremity—which I do not think are random—would tend to affect all respondents in the same way. The effect of stimuli variation could be ignored if we took the average scores of justices such as Black and Douglas, whose tenure extended throughout the seventeen terms of the analysis; and to the extent that a few justices served only for short periods of time, we would be entitled to repose less confidence in their average scale scores than we would entertain for respondents with longer tenure. As Table 4 shows, the average length of tenure of respondents was between 8 and 9 terms; and this seems to be a long enough period to justify the computation of a general scale of political liberalism based upon average scale scores. We should expect some differences in the rank order of respondents in such a scale, as compared to the rank order reported in Table 16, and we might interpret such differences as errors in the average scale scores resulting from sampling variation. However, if the two sets of rankings were in close agreement, the set based upon average scale scores would have one considerable advantage over the scale of Table 16: it would provide a metric that would discriminate the *degree* of difference, among respondents, and facilitate the differentiation of moderate from relatively extreme respondents (in either direction); and these advantages would become even more important if we should wish to make comparisons—as we subsequently shall, in Chapter 8—between the political and the economic liberalism scales. In order to assure that the amount of error, in the set of rankings based upon scale score averages, remains sufficiently small so that it does not undercut the cited advantages, I shall require that the rank correlation between the two scales be not less than +.90.

Table 17 shows that the rank correlation between these two scales is indeed quite high. No importance can be attached to the trivial scale score

TABLE 17

The General Scale of Political Liberalism

	Criterion (from Table 16)	Mean Scale	Scores
Mu	1	1	.98
Ru	2	3	.92
D	3	2	.93
Bl	3	4	.84
Wa	5 *	5 *	.73
Br	6	7	.56
G	7	6	.70
BW	8	8	.15
S	9	11	−.22
F	10	9	−.06
J	11.5	10	−.16
H	11.5	12.5	−.43
Wh	13	12.5	−.43
Bu	14	14	−.62
C	15 **	15	−.66
V	16	17	−.75
Mi	17	16	−.72
Re	18	18	−.82

* 1955–1962 Terms   Tau = .93
** 1949–52, 1956–62 Terms

differences between Douglas and Rutledge, or between Minton and Vinson, which account for two of the transpositions in ranks. The Goldberg-Brennan transposition results from the fact that we are able to observe only one term for Goldberg; this is the kind of error in the mean scale score ranks that we anticipated would result for some justices with limited tenure, and Goldberg's was the least tenure of all of the respondents. (As Figure 1 shows, in the 1962 Term C Scale, Brennan's score was .79 while Goldberg's was .70, but Brennan's mean score was reduced by his lower scores during the 1956–60 Terms; presumably, Goldberg's mean score would have been lowered to an equivalent extent, if he had participated in those decisions with Brennan.) In the case of Warren, the mean score is based on only the last eight terms of his tenure, after he had assumed a stable position; Clark, however, is shown in the position appropriate for 11 of his 14 terms of tenure, since his change (in 1953–55) involved ordinally only a single rank transposition (with Burton), and therefore I have computed the mean score for the entire period of Clark's tenure. The most important differences between the two scales relate to the most moderate respondents in the middle ranks, because they are the respondents most sensitive to sampling variation (i.e., to changes in stimuli extremity in either direction). Thus, Stewart and Jackson are transposed; we can observe that these two justices never participated together in decisions, and that Stewart was confronted with, generally, considerably more extremely positive stimuli than Jackson had been—if Jackson had lived for another decade, his mean scale score probably would have been considerably lower, just as Stewart's would have been higher if he had been on the Court for the entire period of seventeen terms. Thus, Frankfurter's mean score for the period of Jackson's tenure (1946–1953) was +.16 (rather than −.06, as compared to −.16 for Jackson); and during the four terms that they jointly participated (1958–61), Stewart's average score was −.12, as compared to Frankfurter's −.69. So I am confident that the criterion ranking is correct, and the transpositions in the mean scale score ranks are strictly due to sampling variation. On the same basis, I explain Harlan's tie with Jackson in the criterion scale, and his tie with Whittaker in mean scale score: Harlan took Jackson's seat on the Court, and they never participated together. However, since I assume the criterion-tied rank to be correct, we can estimate the probable mean score, for the entire period, for both of these two justices: since Jackson's tenure was eight terms and Harlan's was nine, their estimated joint score for all seventeen terms was −.29. Thus, I assume that Stewart's probable score for the total period would be higher than that shown in Table 17, and most likely would be positive but low; I accept as valid Frankfurter's mean score, since he served for fifteen and one-half of the seventeen terms and I have just assumed that the probable mean score, for the total period, for Jackson and Harlan would be about —.29. My conclusion is that the criterion scale is the more valid, but that the scale of mean scale scores is sufficiently valid to be useful in subsequent multivariate analysis, for which purposes ordinal measurement would lack the advantage of discriminating the degree of differences among respondents.

Economic Liberalism

The selection of the 1957 Term for the pilot investigation was most fortunate, because at the time the research was begun I had no concept of economic liberalism as a scalable attitudinal universe. As Table 7 indicates, 1957 happened to be the term with the highest consistency in voting behavior toward economic issues for the entire period of seventeen terms (the coefficient of reproducibility was .99 and the coefficient of scalability was .90—both exceptionally high indices for empirical data). The reason this was important is that it undoubtedly made it easier for me to recognize that the same response patterns were being produced for stimuli whose content—from a legal point of view—had nothing in common. Initially, I grouped sets of decisions according to categories which I adapted from Pritchett's earlier work in *The Roosevelt Court*.[9] Thus, I grouped together sets of cases which involved disputes between unions and employers; governmental regulation of business activities; fiscal claims of workers against employers; and disputes between small businessmen and their large corporate competitors. There was such a high degree of consistency manifest in the attitudes of the justices toward these issues, in this particular term, that I felt compelled to consider the issues to be isomorphic, which required me to consider the question: What did they all have in common, which would cause Supreme Court justices to disregard the many obvious empirical and—from a legal point of view—doctrinal differences among them? The inference that I made was that all of these cases involved an underdog economic relationship:[10] that is, the economic scale (or "E Scale," as I soon called it) related to conflicts of interest between the

[9] C. Herman Pritchett, *The Roosevelt Court* (New York: Macmillan, 1948), p. 257, Table XXIV.

[10] Cf. Jessie Bernard, "Dimensions and Axes of Supreme Court Decisions: A Study in the Sociology of Conflict," *Social Forces*, Vol. 34 (1955), pp. 19–27, especially the "superior-inferior litigant" scales.

economically affluent and the economically underprivileged. The economic liberal would support the claims of the economically underprivileged, while the conservative would stand pat and resist economic change that would benefit the have-nots. Hence the economic liberal would uphold the fiscal claims of injured workers (or their widows); he would support unions, who could be assumed to function (in general) as the agents of workingmen to improve their economic status; he would support government regulation of business, in order to maintain competition and protect consumers; and he would uphold state taxation, both because state tax laws often have the direct function of regulating enterprise, and also because an adequate program of state financing is a precondition to an effective state program of economic controls and services.

Prior to 1937, any of these sub-issues of economic liberalism—which I shall discuss in considerably greater detail in the next chapter—would have been considered to involve the decision of "constitutional questions"; but after the New Deal revolution, both on and off the Court, only the issue of state taxation was considered by a majority of the justices to raise questions of constitutional interpretation—the other issues now raised questions of statutory interpretation. For the same reason that I already have discussed in regard to the political liberalism variable, the first step toward enlightenment in the scientific study of judicial attitudes is to give up reliance upon legal concepts for classifying the data of judicial decisions. Indeed, I think it is precisely because a whole generation of political scientists continued to be brain-washed by the legalists, that they could continue to interpret the policy-making of the United States Supreme Court almost exclusively in terms of civil-liberties decisions (the political liberalism variable), and could virtually ignore the Court's decisions on economic issues—which by any quantitative standard, and by any reasonable qualitative standard, is just as important to the shaping of American political society—on the grounds that such cases involved "merely statutory" interpretation. This is not the place to develop the argument, but we can note that both legal and political science text-casebooks in "constitutional law" treat the subject of the Supreme Court's policy-making in regard to economic issues as though nothing of consequence had happened since 1937, when decisions in these matters *on constitutional grounds* largely disappeared. Perhaps this explains why it was not until after a quarter of a century that anyone ventured even to suggest, as I did in 1962 in a preliminary report on this research, that the Court's economic and political policy-making are of equivalent importance—and at that, the suggestion appeared in print only over the strong protests of the editor of the journal, who was trying, in a quite friendly and most benevolent way, to prevent me from appearing as a fool in the eyes of the whole profession.

I was convinced, however, that if the economic issues for the 1957 Term scaled even more consistently than the political issues, and there were such differences between the respondent scales that these issues could not be combined without a drastic increase in scale error, then it was quite likely that these were the two major attitudinal variables that one could expect to discover in the other sixteen terms of the sample. Work that was then contemporaneously in progress by another scholar [11] substantiated my own findings for the 1957 Term. The following discussion summarizes the scales of economic liberalism that I subsequently constructed, for each of the seventeen terms in the sample, as shown in Figure 3.

1946–48 TERMS

An inspection of these term scales shows that four justices (Murphy, Rutledge, Black, and Douglas) are much more liberal than the others. There is very little difference among these four; and there would be no lowering of the consistency of the 1947 scale if two cases (3/437, 3/445) were transposed, putting Douglas in the fourth instead of the first rank. Even without such a change, Murphy consistently dominates Rutledge, and Douglas ranks fourth in two of the three terms. Murphy precedes Black except in 1947, where the difference between them (under either version of this scale) would be Black's solitary dissent in a single case (4/249). Black precedes Rutledge in two terms, and is tied with him in 1948. I infer that the most consistent ordering of ranks, for these four justices, is: Mu, Bl, Ru, D. As among the next three justices (Reed, Burton, and Vinson), Reed's precedence over Burton seems clear, but the placement of Vinson cannot be determined on the basis of the data for these three terms. The two justices of lowest rank are consistently Frankfurter and Jackson; and since the single vote differential in the 1947 Term is much less persuasive than the larger margins by which Frankfurter precedes Jackson in the other two terms, the sequence F-J seems probable. We can, therefore, make a necessarily final inference about the rank positions of two justices (Murphy and Rutledge), and a tentative inference about the

[11] Harold J. Spaeth, "Warren Court Attitudes toward Business: The 'B' Scale," ch. 4 in Schubert (ed.), *Judicial Decision-Making* (New York: The Free Press, 1963), especially pages 79–84.

1946 TERM — E Scale

Cases	Mu	Bl	Ru	D	Re	Bu	V	F	J	Totals
1/17	x	x								2-7
0/545	x	x	x							3-6
0/649	x	x	x							3-6
1/256	x	x	x				x			4-5
2/218	x	-	x	*						2-6
2/126:731	x	x	-	x						3-6
2/126:732	x	x	-	x						3-6
1/704:312	x	x	-	x						3-6
9/637	x	x	x	x						4-5
0/258:759	x	x	x	x						4-5
0/258:760	x	x	x	x						4-5
0/258:781	x	x	x	x						4-5
0/258:782	x	x	x	x						4-5
0/258:811	x	x	x	x						4-5
0/743	x	x	x	x						4-5
1/586	x	x	x	x						4-5
1/704:673	x	x	x	x						4-5
2/155	x	x	x	x						4-5
2/319:89	x	*	x	x				*		3-4
2/319:90	x	*	x	x				*		3-4
2/319:91	x	*	x	x				*		3-4
9/394:70	x	x	x	x			x	x		5-4
9/394:71	x	x	x	x			x	x		5-4
9/402	x	x	x	x						5-4
1/29	x	x	x	x		x			x	6-3
0/552	-	x	x	x	x					4-5
1/416	x	x	x	x	x					5-4
0/485	x	x	x	-	x					5-4
9/531	x	x	x	x	x			x	x	6-3
0/395:6	x	x	x	x	x			*		5-3
0/395:7	x	x	x	x	x			*		5-3
0/395:8	x	x	x	x	x			*		5-3
0/395:9	x	x	x	x	x			*		5-3
0/395:10	x	x	x	x	x			*		5-3
1/398	x	x	x	x	x	x				6-3
0/567	x	x	x	x	x	x	x			7-2
0/585	x	x	x	x	x	x	x			7-2
1/40	x	x	x	x	x	x	x			7-2
9/607	x	x	x	x	x	x	x		x	8-1
0/469	x	x	x	x	-	-	x	x		7-2
9/452	x	x	x	x	-	x	x			6-3
9/324	x	x	x	x	x	x	x	x		8-1
1/432	x	x	x	x	x	x	x	x		8-1
9/1	x	x	x	x	x	-	x	x	x	8-1
										210-174
Totals	43-1	40-1	40-4	38-5	18-26	7-37	11-33	8-36	5-31	384
Scale positions	44	44	43	40½	19	10	9	5	1	
Scale scores	1.00	1.00	.95	.84	-.14	-.55	-.59	-.77	-.95	

$$R = 1 - \frac{17}{348} = .951 \qquad S = 1 - \frac{19}{60} = .683$$

1947 TERM — E Scale

Cases	D	Bl	Mu	Ru	V	Re	Bu	J	F	Totals
3/411:130	x									1-8
3/411:131	x									1-8
4/249	-	x								1-8
3/437	x	x	x	*						3-5
3/445	-	x	x	x						3-6
2/422	x	x	x	x						4-5
2/625	x	x	x	x						4-5
2/827:18	x	x	x	x						4-5
3/771	x	x	x	x						4-5
4/304	x	x	x	x						4-5
4/495	x	x	x	x						4-5
5/211	x	x	x	x						4-5
3/287	x	x	x	x		x			*	5-3
3/426	*	x	x	x		*		x	x	5-2
2/392	x	x	x	x	x				x	6-3
2/689	x	x	x	x	x		x			6-3
4/446:366	*	x	x	x	x	x				5-3
4/446:367	*	x	x	x	x	x				5-3
3/46	x	x	x	x	x	x				6-3
3/127	x	x	x	x	x	x		x		7-2
4/37	x	x	x	x	x	x	x			7-2
4/219	x	x	x	x	x	x	x			7-2
4/100	x	x	*	x	x	x	x	x		6-1
3/56	x	x	x	x	x	x	x	x		8-1
3/169	x	x	x	x	x	x	-	x	x	8-1
3/683:23	*	x	x	x	x	x	-	*	x	6-1
										124-100
Totals	20-2	24-2	22-3	22-3	12-13	11-15	5-21	4-19	4-22	224
Scale positions	26	24	23	22½	12½	10	6	3½	2	
Scale scores	1.00	.85	.77	.73	-.04	-.23	-.54	-.73	-.85	

$$R = 1 - \frac{7}{165} = .958 \qquad S = 1 - \frac{10}{46} = .783$$

FIGURE 3. The E Scales of Economic Liberalism and Conservatism, 1946–1962 Terms

1948 TERM

E Scale

Cases	Mu	Ru	Bl	D	Re	V	Bu	F	J	Totals
5/538	x									1-8
6/577:109	x	x	x							3-6
6/577:188	x	x	x							3-6
6/577:209	x	x	x							3-6
6/577:212	x	x	x							3-6
6/525	x	x	x					x		4-5
6/465	-	x	x	x						3-6
7/217	x	x	-	x						3-6
5/303:1	*	x	x	x					*	3-4
5/303:2	*	x	x	x					*	3-4
7/498	*	x	x	x						3-5
5/329	x	x	x	x						4-5
5/359	x	x	x	x						4-5
5/865:206	x	x	x	x						4-5
6/207	x	x	x	x						4-5
6/245:14	x	x	x	x						4-5
6/245:15	x	x	x	x						4-5
6/511	x	x	x	x						4-5
7/86	x	x	x	x						4-5
7/783	x	x	x	x						4-5
7/801	x	x	x	x						4-5
7/810:360	x	x	x	x						4-5
7/810:430	x	x	x	x						4-5
7/163	x	x	x	x		x				5-4
5/377	x	x	x	x	x					5-4
7/293	x	x	x	-	x		x			5-4
5/560:7	x	x	x	x	x	x				6-3
5/560:8	x	x	x	x	x	x				6-3
5/560:48	x	x	x	x	x	x				6-3
7/426	x	x	x	x	x	x				6-3
7/952:749	x	x	x	x	x	x				6-3
6/187	x	x	x	x	x	x	x			7-2
6/226	x	x	x	x	-	-	x	x		6-3
6/53	x	x	x	x	x	-	x	x		7-2
7/755:128	x	x	x	x	x	x	x	x		8-1
7/755:196	x	x	x	x	x	x	x	x		8-1
										161-158
Totals	32-1	35-1	34-2	29-7	11-25	9-27	5-31	6-30	0-34	161-158
										319
Scale positions	36	35	35	30	12	10	5	4	0	
Scale scores	1.00	.94	.94	.67	-.33	-.44	-.72	-.79	-1.00	

$$R = 1 - \frac{9}{292} = .969 \qquad S = 1 - \frac{9}{42} = .786$$

1949 TERM

E Scale

Cases	Bl	D	Bu	V	C	Mi	Re	J	F	Totals
8/267	x	*								1-7
8/338	x	*		*		x				2-5
9/470:309	x	*				x	x			3-5
9/470:364	x	*			x	x				3-5
9/827	x	x							*	2-6
8/304	x	*	x							2-6
9/643	x	x	x	x	x					5-4
8/384	x	*	-	x	x	*		x	*	4-2
8/430	x	*	x	x	x	x		x	*	6-1
9/96	x	*	x	x	x	x			*	5-2
9/142	x	*	x	*	x	x				4-3
8/294	x	*	x	x	x	x	x			6-2
8/464	x	*	*	x	x	x	x			5-2
9/113	x	*	x	x	x	x	x	*		6-1
9/485	x	x	x	x	*	x	x		*	6-1
9/497:58	x	*	x	x	*	x	x			5-2
9/497:79	x	*	x	x	*	x	x			5-2
9/497:96	x	*	x	x	*	x	x			5-2
9/542	x	*	x	x	x	x	x			6-2
9/563	x	x	x	x	x	x	x			7-2
9/577	x	x	x	x	x	x	x			7-2
9/594	x	x	x	x	*	x	x			6-2
										101-66
Totals	22-0	6-0	15-6	15-6	11-5	16-5	14-8	2-18	0-18	101-66
										167
Scale positions	22	20	17	16	16	14½	11	0	0	
Scale scores	1.00	.82	.55	.45	.45	.32	.00	-1.00	-1.00	

$$R = 1 - \frac{7}{138} = .949 \qquad S = 1 - \frac{8}{32} = .750$$

FIGURE 3. (continued)

1950 TERM — E Scale

Cases	Bl	D	C	V	Re	Mi	Bu	J	F	Totals
0/36:23	x									1-8
0/36:24	x									1-8
1/277:473	x									1-8
1/277:474	x									1-8
0/76	x		*					*		1-6
1/674	-	x			X		X			3-6
1/694	-	x			X		X			3-6
1/707	-	x			X		X			3-6
0/474	x	x								2-7
0/543:204	x	x								2-7
0/543:218	x	x								2-7
0/593	x	x								2-7
0/573	x	x		*				*		2-5
1/622	x	x		X						3-6
0/349	x	x				X				3-6
1/6	x	x				X				3-6
1/322	*	x							x	2-6
0/534	x	x	x							3-6
0/602	x	x	x							3-6
0/1:15	x	x	x	x						4-5
0/1:16	x	x	x	x						4-5
0/504	x	x	x	x	x				x	6-3
0/231	x	-	-	x	x	*				3-5
1/593	x	x	*	x	x	x	*			5-2
0/523	x	x	-	x	x	x	x			6-3
0/511	x	x	x	*	x	x	x			6-2
0/520	x	x	x	*	x	x	x			6-2
0/336:211	-	x	x	x	x	x	x	*		6-2
0/336:212	-	x	x	x	x	x	x	*		6-2
1/290	x	-	x	x	-	x	-	x	x	6-3
1/267	-	x	x	x	x	x	*	x	x	7-1
										106-160
Totals	24-6	24-7	11-18	11-18	12-18	10-20	5-24	5-23	4-26	266
Scale positions	31	26	14	12	10	8½	7½	3	2	
Scale scores	1.00	.68	-.10	-.23	-.35	-.45	-.52	-.81	-.87	

$$R = 1 - \frac{22}{228} = .904 \qquad S = 1 - \frac{23}{71} = .676$$

1951 TERM — E Scale

Cases	Bl	D	Mi	V	Re	C	Bu	F	J	Totals
3/326	x					*				1-7
2/512	x									1-8
3/470:448	-	x						*		1-7
2/187	x	x								2-7
3/112	x	x								2-7
2/570:15M	x	x				*				2-6
2/197	x	x						X		3-6
2/25	x	x	*							2-6
2/451:6	x	x	*		X				*	3-4
2/451:7	x	x	*		X				*	3-4
3/395	x	x	x							3-6
3/427:401	x	x	x	x						4-5
3/427:414	x	x	x	x						4-5
3/236	x	x	x	x	x	x		X		7-2
2/421	x	x	x	x	x	x	x	x		8-1
3/779	x	x	x	x	x	x	x	x		8-1
										54-82
Totals	15-1	14-2	6-7	5-11	5-11	3-11	3-13	3-13	2-13	136
Scale positions	16	14	7½	5	3	3	2	2	0	
Scale scores	1.00	.75	-.06	-.38	-.62	-.62	-.75	-.75	-1.00	

$$R = 1 - \frac{4}{93} = .957 \qquad S = 1 - \frac{5}{28} = .821$$

FIGURE 3. (continued)

1952 TERM

E Scale

Cases	D	Bl	V	Mi	Bu	C	Re	J	F		Totals
4/218	x										1-8
5/653	x						*				1-7
4/149	x	x									2-7
4/298:26	x	x									2-7
4/298:35	x	x									2-7
4/298:36	x	x									2-7
5/629	x	x									2-7
6/61	x	x					x				3-6
5/571	-	x				*					1-7
4/25	-	x						x			2-7
5/46	x	-	x			*					2-6
4/254	x	x	x								3-6
5/153:28	x	x	x								3-6
5/153:29	x	x	x								3-6
5/71	x	x	-	x							3-6
5/594:374	x	x	-	x	x						4-5
5/594:375	x	x	-	x	x						4-5
4/407	x	x	x	x	x	x					6-3
4/583:187	x	x	x	x	x	*	x				6-2
4/583:274	x	x	x	x	x	*	x				6-2
4/48	x	x	x	-	-	x	x				5-4
4/392	x	x	x	-	-	x	x	x			7-2
5/13	-	x	x	x	x	x	x	x			7-2
5/19	-	x	x	x	x	x	x	x			7-2
5/379	x	x	x	x	x	x	x	x			8-1
4/344	-	x	-	-	x	x	x	x	x		6-3
5/100	-	x	-	x	x	-	x	x	x		6-3
5/117	x	x	-	x	x	-	x	-	x		6-3
5/344	x	x	-	x	x	x	-	*	x		6-2
6/119	x	x	-	x	-	x	x	*	x		6-2
6/249	x	x	-	x	x	x	*	*	x		6-1
											128-142
Totals	25-6	28-3	12-19	15-16	13-18	10-17	12-17	7-21	6-25 / 128-142		270
Scale positions	31	29	21	17	16	14	13	10	6		
Scale scores	1.00	.87	.35	.10	.03	-.10	-.16	-.35	-.61		

$$R = 1 - \frac{26}{263} = .901 \qquad S = 1 - \frac{27}{72} = .625$$

1953 TERM

E Scale

Cases	Bl	D	Wa	C	Mi	Re	F	J	Bu		Totals
6/932:128	x										1-8
6/537	x	*									1-7
6/891:393	x	x									2-7
7/17:5	x	x									2-7
7/17:6	x	x									2-7
7/17:7	x	x									2-7
7/201	x	x									2-7
7/222	x	x									2-7
7/656	x	x					*				2-6
6/464	x	x				x					3-6
7/239	x	x			x						3-6
7/334	x	x			x						3-6
7/409	x	x	x		x						4-5
7/645:480	x	x	x					*			3-5
7/645:481	x	x	x					*			3-5
7/89	x	-	x	*				*			2-5
7/340	x	x	x	x							4-5
7/359	x	x	x	x							4-5
6/406	x	x	x	x	x		x				6-3
7/396	x	x	x	x	x	x					6-3
7/984:471	x	x	x	x	x	x					6-3
7/672:280	x	-	x	-	x	x	x	*			5-3
7/672:281	x	-	x	-	x	x	x	*			5-3
7/672:418	x	-	x	-	x	x	x	*			5-3
7/186	x	-	x	x	-	x	x	x	x		7-2
7/198	x	-	x	x	-	x	x	x	x		7-2
7/590	x	x	x	x	x	x	-	-	x		7-2
											99-135
Totals	27-0	19-7	15-12	8-18	10-17	8-19	7-20	2-18	3-24 / 99-135		234
Scale positions	27	25½	15	11½	9	8	6	4½	3		
Scale scores	1.00	.89	.11	-.15	-.33	-.41	-.56	-.67	-.78		

$$R = 1 - \frac{18}{217} = .917 \qquad S = 1 - \frac{18}{56} = .679$$

FIGURE 3. (continued)

1954 TERM

E Scale

Cases	D	Bl	Wa	C	Mi	Re	F	Bu	H		Totals
8/437	x	x							*		2-6
8/933	x	x								/	2-6
8/511	x	x	x						*		3-5
8/272	x	-	x			x				/	3-5
9/85	x	x	x	x	£				*		5-3
8/341	x	x	x	x	x	x	x			/	6-2
9/254:357	x	x	x	x	x	x	x				6-3
9/254:358	x	x	x	x	x	x	x				6-3
9/408	x	x	x	x	x		x				6-3
9/427	x	x	x	x	-	x		x	*		6-2
8/310	x	x	x	x	x	-	x			/	6-2
9/122	x	x	x	x	x	-	x		*		6-2
9/129	x	x	x	x	x	-	x		*		6-2
8/960	x	x	x	x	x	-	x	x		/	7-1
											70-45

	D	Bl	Wa	C	Mi	Re	F	Bu	H		
Totals	14-0	13-1	12-2	10-4	9-5	5-9	5-9	2-12	0-3	70-45	115
Scale positions	14	14	12	10	10	9	4	1	0		
Scale scores	1.00	1.00	.71	.43	.43	.29	-.43	-.86	-1.00		

$$R = 1 - \frac{7}{107} = .935 \qquad S = 1 - \frac{8}{24} = .667$$

1955 TERM

E Scale

Cases	D	Bl	Wa	C	Re	Mi	Bu	F	H	Totals
1/79	x		x							2-7
0/537	x							x	*	2-6
1/159	x								x	2-7
0/415	x	x	x							3-6
1/266	x	x	x							3-6
1/959	x	x	x							3-6
0/61	x	x	x					x	x	5-4
1/377	x	x	x	*						3-4
0/124	x	x	x	x						4-5
0/502	x	x	x	x		x				5-4
0/318	x	x	x	x		x		*		5-3
0/898:436	x	x	x	x		x	*	*	*	5-1
0/523	x	x	x	x			*	*	x	5-3
0/162:6	x	x	x	x				x	x	6-3
0/162:7	x	x	x	x				x	x	6-3
0/162:11	x	x	x	x				x	x	6-3
0/162:12	x	x	x	x				x	x	6-3
0/222	x	x	x	x	x					5-4
0/956:209	x	x	x	x	x					5-4
1/49:162	x	x	x	x	x					5-4
1/49:163	x	x	x	x	x					5-4
1/49:164	x	x	x	x	x					5-4
1/305	x	x	x	x	x	x				6-3
0/270	x	x	x	x	x	-	x			6-3
1/149	x	x	x	-	x	x	x			6-3
0/409	x	x	x	x	x	x	x			7-2
1/321:117	x	x	x	x	x	x	x			7-2
1/321:118	x	x	x	x	x	x	x			7-2
1/321:119	x	x	x	x	x	x	x			7-2
1/321:332	x	x	x	x	x	x	x			7-2
1/321:333	x	x	x	x	x	x	x			7-2
1/321:334	x	x	x	x	x	x	x			7-2
1/62	x	x	x	x	x	x	x	*		7-1
1/40:158	x	x	x	x	x	x	x	x		8-1
1/40:159	x	x	x	x	x	x	x	x		8-1
1/40:160	x	x	x	x	x	x	x	x		8-1
1/40:161	x	x	x	x	x	x	x	x		8-1
0/488	x	x	x	x	-	x	x	-	x	8-1
1/493	x	x	x	x	-	x	x	-		7-2
										217-125

	D	Bl	Wa	C	Re	Mi	Bu	F	H		
Totals	39-0	36-3	36-3	30-8	22-17	19-20	16-22	10-27	9-25	217-125	342
Scale positions	39	36	36	31*	22	17	16	6	2		
Scale scores	1.00	.85	.85	.62	.13	-.13	-.18	-.69	-.90		

$$R = 1 - \frac{21}{283} = .926 \qquad S = 1 - \frac{22}{85} = .741$$

FIGURE 3. (continued)

1956 TERM

E Scale

Cases	D	Bl	Wa	Br	C	Re	Bu	F	H	Wh	Totals
3/138	x					/				*	1-7
2/270	x	x					x			/	3-6
3/151:36	x	x	x			/				*	3-5
3/151:82	x	x	x			/				*	3-5
3/151:114	x	x	x			/				*	3-5
2/457	x	x	x	*						/	3-5
4/284	x	x	x			/				*	3-5
2/128	x	x	x				x		x	/	5-4
3/586	x	x	x	x	*	/			x	*	4-2
2/957	x	x	x	x	x					/	5-4
3/112	x	x	x	x	x	/				*	5-3
3/325	x	x	x	x	x	/					5-4
4/147	x	x	x	x	x	/				*	5-3
4/91	x	x	x	x	x	/					5-4
4/414	x	x	x	x	x	/					5-4
4/917	x	x	x	x	x	/					5-4
3/360	x	x	x	x	x	/		*			5-3
3/920:743	x	x	x	x	x	/		*			5-3
3/925	x	x	x	x	x	/		*			5-3
4/517	x	x	x	x	x	/		*			5-3
3/313	x	x	x	-	x					x	5-4
2/862	x	x	x	/	x				x	/	5-3
2/202	x	x	x	x	x	x				/	6-3
2/370	x	x	x	x	x	x				/	6-3
2/112	x	x	x	*	x	x			x	/	6-2
2/282	x	x	x	*	x	x	x			/	6-2
2/445	x	x	x	-	x	x	x				6-3
4/457	x	-	x	x	x	/	x			x	6-3
4/901	x	x	x	-		/	x	*			5-3
3/920:782	x	x	x	x	x	/	x	*			6-2
3/926:321	x	x	x	x	x	/	x	*			6-2
2/500	x	x	x	x	x	-	x	*		/	6-2
2/512	x	x	x	x	x	-	x	*		/	6-2
2/521	x	x	x	x	x	-	x	*		/	6-2
2/1027:122	x	x	x	x	x	/	-	x		/	6-2
3/81	x	x	x	x	x	/	-	x		*	6-2
3/436:408	x	x	x	x	x	/	-	x			6-3
3/436:424	x	x	x	x	x	/	-	x			6-3
2/315:45	x	x	x	x	-	-	x	x	x	/	7-2
2/315:47	x	x	x	x	-	-	x	x	x	/	7-2
											202-132

	D	Bl	Wa	Br	C	Re	Bu	F	H	Wh	
Totals	40-0	38-2	38-2	27-10	28-10	5-10	12-28	7-23	5-34	2-15	202-132 / 334
Scale positions	40	39	38	32	31½	13	15	9	2	0	
Scale scores	1.00	.95	.90	.60	.58	-.10	-.25	-.55	-.90	-1.00	

$$R = 1 - \frac{22}{326} = .933 \qquad S = 1 - \frac{22}{55} = .600$$

1957 TERM

E Scale

Cases	D	Bl	Wa	Br	C	Bu	Wh	H	F	Totals
6/595	x									1-8
7/357:81	x	x								2-7
6/617	x	*	x							2-6
6/634	x	*	x							2-6
5/131	x	x	x							3-6
5/415:616	x	x	x							3-6
5/415:617	x	x	x							3-6
5/415:618	x	x	x							3-6
7/93:127	x	x	x							3-6
7/93:273	x	x	x							3-6
7/93:324	x	x	x							3-6
7/345	x	x	x							3-6
7/357:289	x	x	x							3-6
5/373	x	x	x	x						4-5
5/389	x	x	x	x						4-5
5/396	x	x	x	x						4-5
5/426	x	x	x	x	x					5-4
6/412	x	x	x	x	x					5-4
6/421	x	x	x	x	x					5-4
6/342	x	x	x	x	-	x				5-4
6/1	x	x	x	x	*	x				5-3
6/282:106	x	x	x	x	x	x				6-3
6/282:118	x	x	x	x	x	x				6-3
6/525	x	x	x	x	x	x				6-3
7/221	x	x	x	x	x	x				6-3
6/252	x	x	x	x	x	x			*	6-2
6/271	x	x	x	x	x	x			*	6-2
6/481:73	x	x	x	x	x	-	x			6-3
6/481:74	x	x	x	x	x	-	x			6-3
6/326	x	x	x	x	x	x	x			7-2
7/155	x	x	x	x	x	x	x			7-2
5/83	x	x	x	x	x	x	x	x		8-1
5/253	x	x	x	x	x	x	x	x		8-1
5/62	x	x	x	x	x	-	x	x	*	7-1
6/41	x	x	x	x	x	x	x	x	*	7-1
6/320	x	x	x	x	x	-	x	x		8-1
										171-146

	D	Bl	Wa	Br	C	Bu	Wh	H	F	
Totals	36-0	33-1	34-2	23-13	18-17	14-22	7-29	5-31	1-31	171-146 / 317
Scale positions	36	35	34	23	20	17	9	5	2	
Scale scores	1.00	.94	.89	.28	.11	-.06	-.50	-.72	-.89	

$$R = 1 - \frac{3}{265} = .989 \qquad S = 1 - \frac{6}{61} = .902$$

FIGURE 3. (continued)

1959 TERM

E Scale

Cases	Justices									Totals
	D	Bl	Wa	Br	C	S	H	F	Wh	
1/39	x									1-8
1/733:12	x									1-8
1/733:27	x									1-8
1/733:88	x									1-8
4/280	x	x								2-7
2/99:63	x	x	x							3-6
2/99:66	x	x	x							3-6
3/207	x	x	x							3-6
1/138	x	x	x	ẋ						4-5
2/310	x	x	x	x						4-5
3/603	x	x	x	x						4-5
3/666	x	x	x	x						4-5
2/330	x	x	x	x			x̲			5-4
1/340	x	x	x	x	x					5-4
2/145	x	x	x	x	x					5-4
2/373	x	x	x	x	x					5-4
2/482	x	x	x	x	x					5-4
3/166	x	x	x	x	x					5-4
4/137	x	x	x	x	x					5-4
4/170	x	x	x	x	x					5-4
2/274	x	x	x	x	x		x̲			6-3
3/299	x	x	x	x	x.			x̲		6-3
1/15	x	x	x	x	x	*				5-2
4/140	x	x	x	x	-	x			x̲	6-3
1/129	x	x	x	x.	x	x				6-3
1/314	x	x	x	x	x	x				6-3
1/477	x	x	x	x	x	x				6-3
2/29	x	x	x	x	x	x				6-3
2/293	x	x	x	x	x	x				6-3
2/539	x	x	x	x	x	x				6-3
1/354	x	x	x	x	x	x		*		6-2
2/396	x	x	x	x	x	x		*		6-2
2/411	x	x	x	x	x	x	x			7-2
2/605	x	x	x	x	x	*	x	*		6-1
1/288	x	-	x	x	-	x	x	x		6-3
3/574:443	x	*	x	x	x	x	x	x		7-1
3/574:538	x	*	x	x	x	x	x	x		7-1
1/388	x	x	x	x	x	x	x	x		8-1
2/207	x	x	x	x	x	x	x	x		8-1
2/365	x	x	x	x	x	x	x	x		8-1
Totals	40-0	33-5	35-5	32-8	25-15	16-22	10-30	7-29	1-39	199-153
										199-153 · 352
Scale positions	40	36	35	32	17½	8	6½	0		
Scale scores	1.00	.80	.75	.60	.35	-.12	-.60	-.68	-1.00	

$$R = 1 - \frac{7}{266} = .974 \qquad S = 1 - \frac{7}{67} = .896$$

FIGURE 3. (continued)

1960 TERM

E Scale

Cases	D	Bl	Wa	Br	C	H	S	F	Wh	Totals
6/169	x									1-8
5/320	x	x								2-7
4/441	x	x					•			2-6
6/731	x	x								2-7
6/745	x	x								2-7
7/374	x	x								2-7
7/886	x	x	x	x						4-5
5/705	x	x	x	x				•		4-4
4/325	x	x	x	x	x			•		5-3
4/520	x	x	x	x	x		x			6-3
5/1:45	x	x	x	x	x			x	x	6-3
5/1:46	x	x	x	x	x			x	x	6-3
5/336	x	x	x	x	x			x	x	6-3
6/316	x	x	x	x	•	•				4-3
6/276	-	x	x	x	x	x				5-4
5/731	x	x	x	x	x					6-5
4/642	-	x	x	x	x	•				5-3
5/160	x	x	x	x	x	-	x	•		6-2
5/667:64	x	x	x	x	-	x	x	•		6-2
5/667:85	x	x	x	x	-	x	x	•		6-2
5/695	x	x	x	x	-	x	x	•		6-2
5/705	x	x	x	x	-	x	x	•		6-2
5/651	x	x	x	x	x	x	x	•		7-1
6/28	x	x	x	-	x	x	x			6-3
Totals	23-2	24-1	18-7	17-8	11-13	9-15	6-18	2-14	3-22	113-100 213
Scale positions	25	24	18	18	16	10½	7½	4	0	
Scale scores	1.00	.92	.44	.44	.28	-.16	-.40	-.68	-1.00	

$R = 1 - \frac{13}{196} = .934$ $S = 1 - \frac{13}{49} = .735$

1961 TERM

E Scale

Cases	D	Wa	Bl	C	Br	BW	S	F	H	Wh	Totals
9/95			x		/			•		/	1-8
0/76			x				•		•	/	1-6
0/451			x				•		•	/	1-6
9/60	x				/						1-8
9/134	x				/			•	•	•	1-6
0/173	x							•		/	1-7
8/403	x	x			/	•					2-6
8/20	x	x	x		/						3-6
9/153	x	x	x		/				•		3-5
0/165	x	x	x					•		/	3-5
0/626	x	x	x				•		•	/	3-4
8/324	x	x	x	x							4-5
8/464	x	x	x	x	x	/					5-4
9/463	x	x	x	x	x		•		•	/	5-2
9/482	x	x	x	x	x		•		•	/	5-2
9/527	x	x	x	x	x		•		•	/	5-2
8/81:17	x	x	x	x	x	/			x	x	6-3
8/81:18	x	x	x	x	x	/			x	x	6-3
9/355	x	x	x	x	x	/		x		7	6-2
0/114	x	x	x	x	x	x		•		/	6-2
0/195	-	x	x	x	-	x	x			/	5-3
8/360	x	x	x	x	x	/	x				6-3
9/404:77	x	x	x	x	x	/	x			/	6-2
9/404:94	x	x	x	x	x	/	x			/	6-2
9/643	-	x	x	x	x	•	x	•		/	5-2
9/698	x	x	x	x	x	•	x	•		/	6-1
0/31	x	x	x	x	x	•	x	•		/	6-1
0/254	x	x	x	x	x	x	x	•		/	7-1
0/460	x	x	x	x	x	x	x	•		/	7-1
8/370:23	x	x	x	x	x	/	x	x			7-2
8/370:24	x	x	x	x	x	/	x	x			7-2
0/607	-	-	x	x	x	•	-	x	x	/	4-3
8/208	x	x	-	x	x	/	-	x	x		6-3
8/35	x	x	x	x	x	/	x	x	x		8-1
Totals	28-6	27-7	29-5	23-11	21-13	4-2	12-21	4-14	4-29	2-11	154-119 154-119 273
Scale positions	31	28	27	23	22	19½	14	7½	3	0	
Scale scores	.82	.65	.59	.35	.29	.15	-.18	-.56	-.82	-1.00	

$R = 1 - \frac{11}{187} = .941$ $S = 1 - \frac{14}{66} = .788$

FIGURE 3. (continued)

1962 TERM

E Scale

Cases	Bl	D	Wa	Br	C	BW	G	S	H	Totals
				Justices						
1/156:27	x									1-8
1/156:28	x									1-8
1/195	x									1-8
3/64	x				x̲					2-7
1/94	-	x								1-8
1/69	x	x								2-7
1/555:14	x	x			•				•	2-5
1/555:15	x	x			•				•	2-5
3/33	x	x			•		x̲			3-6
1/296	-	-	x	x	•				•	2-5
3/294:72	x	-	x	x	x					4-5
3/294:73	x	-	x	x	x					4-5
3/294:74	x	-	x	x	x					4-5
2/658	x	-	x	-	x					3-6
2/253	x	-	x	-	x	•				3-5
2/84	x	x	x	x	x	•				5-3
4/321	x	x	x	x	x	•				5-3
3/132	x	x	-	-	x	x				4-5
2/29	-	x	x	x	x	x		x̲		6-3
2/108	x	x	x	x	x	x				6-3
4/1	x	x	x	x	x	x				6-3
3/546	x	-	•	x	x	x	x			5-3
1/84	x	x	x	x	x	-	x			6-3
1/184	x	x	x	x	x	-	x			6-3
1/38:42	x	x	x	x	x	x	x			7-2
1/38:43	x	x	x	x	x	x	x			7-2
1/38:44	x	x	x	x	x	x	x			7-2
1/505	x	x	x	x	x	x	x			7-2
2/633	x	x	x	x	x	x	x			7-2
3/341	x	x	x	x	x	x	x			7-2
3/410	x	x	x	x	x	x	x			7-2
4/398	x	x	x	x	x	-	x	x		7-2
2/368	x	x	x	x	x	x	x	x		8-1
2/699	x	x	x	x	x	x	x	x		8-1
3/206	x	x	x	x	x	x	x	x		8-1
3/262	x	x	x	x	x	x	x	x		8-1
3/267	x	x	x	x	x	x	x	x		8-1
3/374	x	x	x	x	x	x	x	x		8-1
3/375	x	x	x	x	x	x	x	x		8-1
4/16	x	x	x	x	x	x	x	x		8-1
4/174	x	x	x	x	x	x	x	x		8-1
3/690	x	-	x	x	-	x	•	x	x	6-2
3/701	x	-	x	x	-	x	•	x	x	6-2
1/132	x	x	x	x	-	x	x	x	x	8-1
4/167	x̲	x	x	x	x	x	x	-	x̲	8-1
										240-153
Totals	42-3	32-13	34-10	33-12	34-8	24-18	23-20	13-32	5-37	393
Scale positions	45	41	36	36	35½	30	24	14	4	
Scale scores	1.00	.82	.60	.60	.58	.33	.07	-.38	-.91	

$$R = 1 - \frac{23}{258} = .911 \qquad S = 1 - \frac{26}{102} = .745$$

FIGURE 3. (continued)

sequence for six other justices: Mu, Bl, Ru, D, Re, Bu, F, J; in regard to the remaining justice, Vinson, we can only say that he ranks below Douglas and above Frankfurter.

1949–55 TERMS

Although Black appeared, on the basis of the data for the 1946–48 Terms, to precede Douglas, and he continued to do so during four of the next seven terms, a glance ahead shows that the situation was reversed during all of the next half-dozen terms (1956–61). Only in 1955 and 1959, however, was there more than one or two votes difference between the rankings for these two justices; in one term (1954) they were tied and in another the choice of ranking was completely arbitrary (1952)—indeed, the preference of Douglas for the first rank in 1952 was probably not only arbitrary but also mistaken, since the marginals support the designation of Black. In 1955 and 1959, however, there is no room for choice, arbitrary or otherwise: Douglas' marginals are 39–0 and 40–0, while Black's are 36–3 and 33–5. On the other hand, in 1953, Black's precedence seems to be equally clearly supported by his marginals of 27–0 and 42–3, as compared to Douglas' 19–7 and 32–13. Throughout the period 1949–62, either Black or Douglas ranked first, and the other ranked second; and I do not infer that the transpositions reflect any change in the attitudes of either respondent. I think, rather, that the changes reflect sampling variation: more specifically, variation in the content of the issues that were extreme in their demand of liberal support. This remark will become more meaningful after we have discussed the subcomponents of the E scale, in the next chapter; but let us consider an example for present purposes. If Black were more sympathetic than Douglas to the fiscal claims for compensation of injured workers, while Douglas were more sympathetic than Black to the claims of unions, then it is clear that with a sample of cases consisting of both of these issues, either (or neither) respondent might appear to be the more extreme liberal in the scale, depending upon the characteristics of the stimuli. If, as I further assume, there is relatively little difference between the attitude of Douglas and that of Black toward either issue, then not many cases of either category can be expected to discriminate between them. Both of them will reject really extreme claims, and both of them will accept almost all claims that have any chance of clearing the Court's jurisdictional screening, even though some other of their colleagues may view such cases as "really extreme" in their demand of sympathy for liberal support. Only those few cases in any term, of either or both categories, that are more extreme than one of these two justices (in the multidimensional space of the decision-making model sketched in Chapter Two) and less so than the other, can be the basis for a choice in ranking one or the other as first. If there are no such cases, then the two respondents appear to be tied in rank; and if there are the same number in both categories, then choice is arbitrary in a double sense: one arbitrarily is ranked first, and the other arbitrarily is imputed a number of inconsistent votes equivalent to the number of cases which discriminate between the two ranks (see the scale for the 1952 Term).

I conclude that the most reasonable inference to make is that if Douglas and Black are to be ranked on a single linear scale which extends over the entire period, they should be considered tied.

There are also transpositions among Vinson, Clark, Minton, Reed, and Burton, but the clear preponderance of the evidence supports the indicated sequence for these five justices. I do infer from the transpositions that the points for these justices are relatively densely clustered on the underlying attitudinal continuum, and that Vinson is not very close to the Douglas-Black pair—if he were, it could be assumed that he would have ranked immediately below them more consistently than he did, on the term scales. Warren, it readily can be observed, moved immediately into the third rank upon joining the Court in 1953, and remained in that rank without exception until 1961, when he ranked second (but due to the same explanation that I already have given for the differences between Douglas and Black). This is in sharp contrast to Warren's behavior in regard to the political variable, toward which (it will be recalled) he appeared to be a conservative in his first term on the Court, but changed to a liberal position after the end of his second term. So I infer that Warren should precede his predecessor, Vinson, in rank in the sequence indicated above.

There is no consistent differential between Jackson and Frankfurter during the 1949–53 Terms; indeed, the 1952 Term seems to support Jackson's precedence just as much as the 1946 and 1948 Terms had seemed to support Frankfurter's. Hence it is necessary to reconsider our tentative finding in regard to Jackson and Frankfurter, which was based on the data for only three terms. Similarly, there is no consistent difference between Frankfurter and Harlan during the subsequent 1946–61 Terms: Harlan ranks below Frankfurter in four terms, and Frankfurter below Harlan in the other four. I assume that the explanation is similar to that for Douglas and Black: variation in the sampling of relatively extreme stimuli, which represent subcomponent issues of the economic variable, and toward one (or more) of which Frankfurter is more conservative than Harlan, and vice versa. And I conclude that there is no adequate basis for distinguishing among Jackson, Harlan, and Frankfurter, all of whom should be considered tied in rank. Our revised scale sequence, then, would be as follows:

$$\text{Mu, Bl/D, Ru, Wa, V, C, Mi, Re, Bu, J/H/F}$$

1956–61 TERMS

Brennan joined the Court in the 1956 Term, and moved immediately into the fourth rank, between Warren and Clark, retaining the same position except for his transposition with Clark in 1961, which hinges upon a single vote. Stewart joined the Court in 1958, and assumed a position between Clark and Harlan—since Minton, Reed, and Burton all had retired by this time. Since Clark invariably ranked before Stewart, and Stewart preceded Harlan in four of the five terms, I infer that the correct sequence for these three justices is: C, S, H. Whittaker had joined the Court in 1956: he ranked last in five of the six terms that he remained on the Court, and in each of these five instances with a maximal negative scale score of −1.00. I infer that he should be assigned the lowest rank.

THE 1962 TERM

White had joined the Court during the 1961 Term, and his limited participation in that term suggests a probable placement between Clark and Stewart. This inference is confirmed by the 1962 scale, which also indicates that Goldberg ranks between White and Stewart.

We now have identified two subsets of three justices each—Mi, Re, Bu; and BW, G, S—who rank between Clark and the J-H-F triplet. The first group was classified as conservatives on the C scale, while the second group consists of the justices who rank at the top of the moderate range, or the bottom of the liberal range, on the C scale. We have no adequate basis, however, in terms of the data we have considered thus far, for discriminating between the ordinal positions to be assigned to these two groups on the E scale: we can order them within the subsets, but not as between subsets, since all of the justices in the first group had retired before any of the justices in the second group joined the Court. Consequently, we can only conclude that both groups lie somewhere within a common segment on the continuum, whose range is defined by Clark and by the J-H-F triplet. The general scale for economic liberalism is, therefore, as indicated in Table 18.

My interpretation has been that there were no significant changes in the attitudes of individual justices toward economic liberalism during the

TABLE 18

Summary of the E (Economic Liberalism) Scale

Rank Order of Justices:		Term Periods		
	1946–48	1949–55	1956–61	1962
+ Mu	X			
Bl/D ᵃ	X,X	X,X	X,X	X,X
Ru	X			
Wa		X ᵇ	X	X
Br			X	X
0 V	X	X ᵇ		
C		X	X	X
Mi, BW ᶜ		X		X
Re, G ᵈ	X	X	X	X
Bu, S ᵉ	X	X	X	X
− J, H/F ᶠ	X,X	X,X	X,X	X
Wh			X	

NOTES

ᵃ Bl-D, 1949–53, 1962; D-Bl, 1954–61.

ᵇ V, 1949–52; Wa, 1953–55 (V was replaced by Wa).

ᶜ Mi, 1949–55; BW, 1961–62 (Mu and Ru were replaced by Cl and Mi; Mi was replaced by Br).

ᵈ Re, 1946–56; G, 1962 (Re was replaced by Wh, who was replaced by BW).

ᵉ Bu, 1946–57; S, 1957–62. (Bu was replaced by S).

ᶠ J, 1946–53; H, 1953–62. J, H, and F all are tied in rank (J was replaced by H; F was replaced by G).

Scale Types:	1946–48	1949–52	Term Periods: 1953–55	1956–61	1962	Average
E+	4	2	3	4	4	3.4
Eo	3	5	4	2	4	3.4
E−	2	2	2	3	1	2.3

period of analysis. There were changes in the group attitude, resulting from changes in the respondents who comprised the decision-making group, although these changes seem to be confined within a somewhat narrower range than was true for the political scale—primarily, it appears, because there were never more than three economic conservatives at any one time, while there were as many as five political conservatives (four of whom had been appointed by Harry S. Truman) during the period 1949–52. However, the general pattern of change was the same for both variables. Employing, for present purposes, the same *ad hoc* categorization that was used to characterize the groupings of positions on the political scale, we can observe that there was a slight liberal bias in the structure of the Court during the initial period, with four liberals, three moderates, and two conservatives. The next period (1949–52) was the low period of liberal support and attitudes towards the economic variable (as was also true for the political variable), with a balanced Court consisting of two liberals, five moderates, and two conservatives. From then, on, however, the Court changed consistently in the direction of a more liberal group attitudinal structure; during 1953–55, Warren's replacement of Vinson meant that the liberal group increased to three while the moderates decreased to four; while during 1956–61, the group was further polarized, as the substitution of another liberal (Brennan) for a moderate (Minton) was matched by the substitution of another conservative (Whittaker) for a moderate (Reed), resulting in subsets of four, two, and three. It might well be argued that the latter change was recessive, since Whittaker was a much more extreme conservative than Brennan was liberal; but I do not agree with such an interpretation, because of the technical consideration that a group of four liberals can control the selection of the stimuli sample, but a group of three cannot.[12] In the 1962 Term, the Court had the strongest liberal bias of any time during the period of our study, with four liberals, four moderates, and only a single conservative.

To recapitulate, the general pattern of change, in the group attitude toward both variables, was the same: a liberal bias during the initial period, followed by an abrupt shift (due to the deaths of Murphy and Rutledge, and the accession of Clark and Minton) to the most conservative bias evident during the total period of analysis, followed by a gradual increase in liberal sentiment which reaches a maximum at the end of the period, in the 1962 Term.

By comparing Tables 16 and 18, we can also make some general observations about the relationship, in regard to both scales, of subsets of respondents, although this is a subject that we shall explore at much greater length in Chapter 8. (1) The liberal set is the same—and in substantially

---

[12] Schubert, *op. cit.* fn. 4, *supra*, pp. 210–214, and 266–267; and Schubert, "Policy without Law: An Extension of the Certiorari Game," *Stanford Law Review*, Vol. 14 (1962), pp. 284–327.

the same rank order—for both scales, except that Goldberg is added in the lowest liberal rank for the political scale. (2) The subset of four economic conservatives is politically moderate. (3) One sub-subset of five economic moderates (V, C, Mi, Re, Bu), all of whom were appointed to the Court prior to the 1949 Term, is politically conservative. (4) The other sub-subset of economic moderates, all of whom were appointed to the Court much later, beginning in the 1958 Term, is located on the political scale between the groups whom we have identified as *economic* liberals, and conservatives; that is, G, S, and BW are economic moderates whose range on the political scale includes the lowest liberal rank (G) and the two highest moderate ranks (S, BW). Evidently there is a considerable amount of consistency and stability, not only in the structuring of the attitudes of individual justices and that of the group as a whole toward the variables (individually considered), but there also is considerable consistency and stability manifest in the manner in which subsets of justices align themselves toward these issues.

The fact that respondents are aligned toward these two scales in groups, rather than as individuals, suggests two hypotheses of fundamental importance: (1) that there is a latent structure in which the attitudes underlying both scales have a consistent and stable relationship; and (2) that the subsets of respondents represent basic attitudinal types (or ideological points of view) in such a latent structure. We shall explore both of these hypotheses in Chapters 7 and 8.

There remains the task of comparing the ordinal economic scale, which I reported in Table 18 on the basis of my analysis of the term scale rankings, and the interval economic scale which can be computed from average scale scores. As in the case of the similar analysis that was made for the political scale, I shall require that the rank correlation between these two isomorphs of the latent attitudinal scale be at least .90, in order to support my use of the interval scale in lieu of the ordinal scale as a basis for subsequent bivariate analyses. In view of my inability to establish a common ordinal ranking for the two subsets of economic moderates (V, C, Mi, Re, Bu; and BW, G, S), I can require now only that (1) the internal rankings for these two sequences be consistent, and that (2) all eight of these respondents be assigned ordinal ranks within the range from #7 to #14, thus following the liberals and preceding the conservatives. I recognize that the computation of a rank correlation coefficient, with this degree of indeterminacy in one set of ranks, could affect the value of the expected tau, depending upon the "true" ranks for both subsets on the underlying attitudinal con-

TABLE 19

The General Scale of Economic Liberalism

	Criterion (from Table 18)		Mean Scale Scores	
Mu	1	1.5	.92
Bl	2.5	1.5	.92
D	2.5	3	.90
Ru	4	4	.87
Wa	5	5	.67
Br	6	6	.44
V	7	11	−.13
C	8	8	.20
BW	9	7	.24
G	10	9	.07
Mi	11	10	−.02
Re	12	12	−.17
S	13	13	−.25
Bu	14	14	−.39
F	16	15	−.71
H	16	16	−.73
J	16	17	−.81
Wh	18	18	−.92

Tau = .94

tinuum. The maximum effect would occur if all respondents in one subset preceded all in the other subset, on the latent continuum (*i.e.,* if the true sequence were either [V, C, Mi, Re, Bu; BW, G, S] or [BW, G, S; V, C, Mi, Re, Bu]), and if the opposite ordering of subsets obtained according to the mean scale scores: this could result in an overestimation of tau by almost .20. It is clear, from Table 19, that that degree of error cannot be present, since members from the two subsets intermesh, in the following sequence, for the mean scale scores: *BW,* C, *G,* Mi, V, Re, *S,* Bu. The only transpositions of ranks evident in the table involve the members of these two subsets; but Clark's transposition with White, which involves a point difference of only .04, must be considered insignificant, particularly in view of the small subsample of responses upon which White's scale score for the 1961 Term necessarily was based. Vinson's low mean scale score can well be explained on the basis of sampling variance, since he was the first of his subset to leave the Court; had he participated, with the others in his subset, in the decisions of 1953–55, both his and their mean scale scores would doubtless have been different. During 1949–52, when Vinson and Clark did participate together, for example, Vinson's mean scale score was .05, while Clark's was —.09. The general correspondence between the two sets of ranks in Table 19 is so close, as evidenced by the high tau of .94 notwithstanding the error in regard to Vinson and the various ties, that I conclude that we can accept the mean scale scores as a close enough approximation of the ordinal criterion scale—which I assume to be closer to the latent scale—for subsequent analyses where an interval scale is needed.

The Minor Scales

Political and economic liberalism are the only variables which scaled in all seventeen terms, but I do not believe that they represent the only attitudes that are relevant to the decision-making of Supreme Court justices. There are four other variables which I regard as potentially scalable, in the sense that I think these would scale providing that there were enough respondents who considered the issues these variables represent to be of sufficient importance to increase the quantities of relevant decisions per term.[13] It would not be necessary that the Court decide as many cases for these variables as for C or E, but there would have to be from fifteen to twenty decisions for each of several successive terms before it would be possible to resolve, with some confidence, the question whether these variables represent scalable attitudes. It may also be possible to pool cases for several terms (as I shall do for the subcomponents of C and E, in the next chapter), when turnover among the respondents is low; such an approach was not included in my research design, and I have not attempted this for purposes of the present study.

The reason why an average of fifteen or twenty decisions per term would be necessary involves the technical requirements of the cumulative scaling technique; unanimous decisions and those with a single dissent are of little or no help in testing scalability and reproducibility, and it usually takes at least twice as many decisions (with two to four dissents) as there are respondents in order to distinguish among their ranks. In fact, there have been more than enough decisions for the two major variables, in most terms, but only rarely has there been an adequate volume for any of the four minor variables. I shall identify these minor variables as F, N, A, and J; and I shall define their content presently. The relationship between term volume and scalability is suggested by Table 20:

[13] Usually, this would require that there be at least three justices who were interested in actively pushing the issue. See *idem*.

TABLE 20

Sample Size and Scalability for Six Attitudinal Variables

Variable	Total Decisions	Average number of decisions per term	Number of terms with ten or more decisions	Number of scales	Number of quasi-scales
C	572	34	17	17	0
E	551	32	17	17	0
F	201	12	9	4	11
N	98	6	4	1	4
A	86	5	3	0	0
J	50	3	0	0	0

As this table shows, there seems to be a high positive correlation between sample size and the scalability of these variables. In particular, it should be noted that F is only marginally scalable, even though it is the third most important variable. Since F scales in four terms, and produces quasi-scales in eleven of the remaining thirteen terms, it seems plausible to assume that if F had averaged twenty decisions per term instead of twelve, many of the eleven quasi-scales would have become scales. (In each of the two terms, 1953 and 1961, in which F yielded neither a scale nor a quasi-scale, there were only three relevant decisions.)

Table 21 reports the proportion of the total content that was partitioned among the variables that scaled (or resulted in quasi-scales) for each term. The two major variables each pre-empted, on the average, about a third of the total content, so the remaining third necessarily was divided among the four minor variables. Only in two of the terms did the ratio of the total content, for either of the two major scales, fall below .20; and in two terms (E in 1955 and C in 1960), over half of the total content was assigned to one or the other of the major variables. However, in the 1946 Term, there were more decisions on F than on C; and in the 1949 Term (when Black was the only justice whom I have classified in the liberal subset, for both the C and E scales, participating in decisions throughout most of the term), there were as many cases for F as for either C or E. There are several reasons why F does not quite appear to scale, during the first four terms when the volume of decisions relevant to this variable appears to be adequate to support scalability. In 1949, for example, F does "scale" if one were to judge exclusively on the basis of coefficients, since R is .98 and S is .90; but sixteen of these twenty-two decisions consisted of cases in which

TABLE 21

Ratio of Scales to Total Content of Samples, by Terms

Term	C	E	Other Scales	Quasi-Scales	Other Content	Sample Size	C + E
1946	.17	.35	....	F .22	.26	125	.52
1947	.29	.36	....	F .14	.16	104	.64
1948	.26	.31	....	F .21	.15	118	.57
				N .08			
1949	.23	.24	....	F .24	.20	91	.47
				N .09			
1950	.25	.36	N: .11	F .09	.18	87	.61
1951	.46	.18	....	F .10	.27	90	.63
1952	.31	.28	F: .10	N .09	.21	112	.59
1953	.29	.38	....	....	.33	72	.67
1954	.35	.22	....	F .13	.29	62	.58
1955	.30	.53	....	F .07	.10	73	.84
1956	.41	.37	....	N .09	.06	108	.78
				F .06			
1957	.44	.28	F: .10	....	.18	128	.72
1958	.35	.41	....	F .13	.11	83	.76
1959	.34	.40	F: .13	....	.15	101	.73
1960	.52	.25	F: .14	....	.09	99	.77
1961	.47	.41	....	....	.12	83	.88
1962	.44	.42	....	F .07	.07	107	.86

Sub-sample			[Other and Quasi]				

Totals	572	551	241	279	1643	1123
Ratios	.35	.34	.15	.17	1.00	.68

NOTE: There is slight variation, for about half of the terms, between the sample sizes reported here and in Table 1. The reason is that the data were coded independently for the factor and for the scale analysis. The sample sizes reported in Table 1 are based upon machine tabulation of cards that were punched for the factor analysis. The data in this table were taken from the scaling code sheets, and the scaling operations and related tabulations were performed manually. So the discrepancies are due to either coding or punching errors; however, the average, for the seventeen terms, of the absolute sum of the differences between the two sets of sample sizes is less than two cases per term, and the means for the two distributions are identical (97). So there is an average error difference of less than two percent in the content of the samples used for scale, as compared to factor, analysis.

either Black or he and Douglas together dissented against the rest of the Court; and in view of Douglas' low participation in this term, I decided that the evidence to support a decision of scalability was inadequate. The quasi-scales for F in the 1947 and 1948 Terms are marginal scales; and I strongly suspect that part of the inconsistency manifest in the F quasi-scales for these terms (and for 1946 as well) reflects errors committed not by the justices but by myself. There was some conceptual confusion on my part concerning the boundaries between E and F when the cumulative scaling was done in 1961, and particularly was this true of the early terms, which were scaled first. I did not finally resolve this problem to my own satisfaction until almost a year and a half later, when a graduate seminar explored with me the relationship between F and the subcomponents of E; and by that time, I was long since committed, by the extensive machine and other analyses that had been completed, to the scales in the form in which they are reproduced herein. Of course, if I thought that such empirical errors would seriously affect the theory or the findings, then I should have to do all of the work over, or else give up the project. But they are not of that magnitude. What it amounts to is that I now think that the F quasi-scales for the early terms probably include some cases which should have been apportioned to E; as E-scale cases, these decisions would result in little or no additional scale inconsistencies, while as F-quasi-scale cases, they are responsible for numerous inconsistencies, and probably are the direct cause for F not appearing to scale in 1946–48. Taking cases away from F would not improve its scalability after 1949, however, because the problem thereafter is low volume; nor would the reclassification of the F quasi-scales for 1946–48 as scales lead to any important change in the theoretical interpretation presented in this and in the next three chapters.

Although the size of the term samples for F diminishes after 1949, it is notable that three of the four terms in which F scales are among the six most recent terms. For N, to the contrary, there has been a marked decline in volume of decisions during the past half-dozen terms. I assume that this reflects the virtual elimination of the political conservatives, as a group, after 1956, with just Clark and Burton left in 1957, and only Clark thereafter; the reason for my assumption will not make much sense until after we consider Chapter 7, but it relates to the factorial correlations of the political conservatives, and the probable factorial correlations of N (if it were a scalable variable).

Table 21 also shows that only about one-sixth of the data is neither scalable, nor virtually so. The proportion of this "other content" is never more than one-third, and it decreases sharply after Warren's conversion: during the first nine terms, the average ratio of other content is .21, while during 1955–62, it is only .11. Evidently, as the final column of Table 23 indicates, the drop in the ratio of "other content" was reciprocal to the increase in the combined ratio for the two major variables. So one result of the increase in the size of the liberal group, due to Warren's change in 1955 and Brennan's appointment in 1956, was that about 90 percent of the Court's non-unanimous decisions on the merits involved only three variables: C, E, and F.

THE F VARIABLE AND SCALES: GOVERNMENTAL TAXING AUTHORITY

On *a priori* grounds, one might make various assumptions about how Supreme Court justices might be likely to respond in their voting to cases raising questions about governmental taxing authority. Given what we already know about the two major variables, for example, one might assume that economic liberals would uphold the authority of the government, and economic conservatives would be in opposition. The logical basis for such an assumption might be that economic liberals and conservatives alike would recognize the necessity for increasing governmental income in order to support expanding programs of controls over the economy and of social services, and the implications of taxation for the redistribution of economic benefits among the populace generally. As Oliver Wendell Holmes, Jr., reputed to be among the most liberal of Supreme Court justices of an earlier period, is said to have remarked once to his law clerk (who is supposed to have commiserated with the justice over a tax bill) : "Sonny, I never object to paying taxes, because with taxes I buy civilization."

The chief objection to such a logical theory is that it doesn't seem to fit the psychological facts. As Figure 4 shows, the justices do not respond to the issue of taxation in the same way that they respond to the E scale, and certainly not in the same way that they respond to the C scale. We know, for example, that Douglas and Black shared adjacent ranks on the scales for each of the two major variables throughout the seventeen terms of this study; but in the 1959 and 1960 F scales, Black ranks first and Douglas ranks last; and in the 1952 F scale, Black and Douglas voted alike in only one of the eleven cases—in 1959 they agreed in two of thirteen cases, and in 1960, in one of fourteen cases. I already have indicated my opinion that these are much less satisfactory scales; and the frequent sets of tied ranks, in all four of these term F scales, can be attributed directly to the marginality of the sample sizes. An examination of the columns of marginals for

1952 TERM
F Scale

Cases	Bu	V	C	Mi	Re	Bl	J	F	D	Totals
4/167:79	x								x	2-7
4/167:80	x								x	2-7
5/639	x	x	x			*	*			3-4
6/15	x	x	*	x	x				*	4-3
4/6	x	x	x	x	x	x				6-3
4/82	x	x	x	x	x	x				6-3
4/66	x	x	x	x	x	x			x	7-2
5/183	x	x	*	x	x	x	x			6-2
5/544	x	x	x	-	-	x	x	x		6-3
5/278:76	x	x	x	x	x	x	x	x		8-1
5/278:138	x	x	x	x	x	x	x	x		8-1
										58-36

Totals: 11-0 9-2 7-2 7-4 7-4 7-3 4-6 3-8 3-7 | 58-36 94

Scale positions: 11 9 9 8 8 7 4 3 0

Scale scores: 1.00 .64 .64 .45 .45 .27 -.27 -.45 -1.00

$$R = 1 - \frac{5}{76} = .934 \qquad S = 1 - \frac{5}{25} = .800$$

1957 TERM
F Scale

Cases	Bl	Wa	C	Br	D	F	H	Bu	Wh	Totals
7/28	x	x								2-7
7/39	x	x							x	3-6
6/274	x	-	x					x		3-6
5/587	x	x	x	x		x				5-4
5/489:18	x	x	x	x	x					5-4
5/489:36	x	x	x	x	x					5-4
6/21	x	x	x	x	x					5-4
7/51:395	x	x	x	x	x	x		x		7-2
7/51:410	x	x	x	x	x	x		x		7-2
5/466	x	x	x	x	x	x	x			7-2
5/484:37	x	x	x	x	x	x	x			7-2
5/484:38	x	x	x	x	x	x	x			7-2
7/63	x	x	x	x	x	x	x	x		8-1
										71-46

Totals: 13-0 12-1 11-2 10-3 9-4 7-6 4-9 2-11 3-10 | 71-46 117

Scale positions: 13 12 11 10 9 6 4 1 0

Scale scores: 1.00 1.00 .69 .54 .38 .08 -.38 -.85 -1.00

$$R = 1 - \frac{6}{108} = .944 \qquad S = 1 - \frac{6}{24} = .750$$

1959 TERM
F Scale

Cases	Bl	C	F	Wa	Br	H	Wh	S	D	Totals
3/509	x						x			2-7
3/522	x						x			2-7
1/87	-	x	x				x			3-6
3/237:137	x	x	*	x						3-5
3/237:183	x	x	x	x						4-5
3/709	x	x	x	x						4-5
4/92:141	x	x	x	x	x					5-4
4/92:143	x	x	x	x	x					5-4
1/304	x	x	x	x	x	x				7-2
3/257:546	-	x	x	x	x	x	x			7-2
3/257:376	x	x	x	x	x	x	x	x		8-1
4/122	x	x	x	x	x	x	x			8-1
4/130	x	x	x	x	x	x	x			8-1
										66-50

Totals: 11-2 11-2 10-2 10-3 7-6 8-5 5-8 4-9 0-13 | 66-50 116

Scale positions: 13 11 11 10 7 5 5 4 0

Scale scores: 1.00 .69 .69 .54 .08 -.23 -.23 -.28 -1.00

$$R = 1 - \frac{5}{89} = .944 \qquad S = 1 - \frac{5}{29} = .828$$

1960 TERM
F Scale

Cases	Bl	Wa	C	Br	F	H	S	Wh	D	Totals
4/443	x									1-8
5/624	x	x						x		3-6
4811:288	x	x	x	x	x					5-4
4/361	x	x	x	x	x	x				6-3
5/467	x	x	x	x	x	x	*			6-2
4/310	x	x	x	x	x	x	x			7-2
4469:533	x	x	x	x	x	x	*	x		7-1
4/289	x	x	x	x	x	x	x	x		8-1
4/446	x	x	x	x	x	x	x	x		8-1
5/753	x	x	x	x	x	x	x	x		8-1
3381:629	x	x	x	x	x	x	x	x		8-1
3381:843	x	x	x	x	x	x	x	x		8-1
4/410	x	x	-	-	x	x	x	x		6-3
6/199	x	x	x	x	x	-	x	x	x	8-1
										89-35

Totals: 14-0 13-1 11-3 11-3 12-2 10-4 8-4 9-5 1-13 | 89-35 124

Scale positions: 14 13 12 12 11 9½ 8 1

Scale scores: 1.00 .86 .71 .71 .71 .57 .36 .14 -.89

$$R = 1 - \frac{3}{53} = .943 \qquad S = 1 - \frac{4}{23} = .826$$

FIGURE 4. The Minor Scales (F and N), 1946–1962 Terms

1950 TERM

N Scale

				Justices						
Cases	Re	D	C	V	Bl	J	M1	Bu	F	Totals
1/446:298	x		*					x		2-6
1/446:314	x		*					x		2-6
1/329	-	x							x	2-7
1/609	-	x	x	x	x			x		5-4
0/383:329	x	x	x	x	x	x				6-3
0/383:438	x	x	x	x	x	x				6-3
0/411	x	x	x	x	x	x				6-3
1/384:442	x	x	x	x	-	x	x			6-3
1/384:443	x	x	x	x	-	x	x			6-3
0/581	x	x	x	x	x	x	*	x		7-1
										48-39

Totals	8-2	8-2	7-1	7-3	5-5	6-4	2-7	4-6	1-9	48-39	87
Scale positions	10	8	7	7	7	6	3	1	0		
Scale scores	1.00	.60	.40	.40	.20	.20	-.40	-.80	-1.00		

$$R = 1 - \frac{8}{79} = .899 \qquad S = 1 - \frac{8}{24} = .667$$

FIGURE 4. (continued)

the distribution of votes, by cases, confirms the visual impression that the 1959 F scale does the best job of discriminating among the respondents; and this scale shows that in relationship to the respondent types that I have suggested for C and E, it is not merely a question of Black and Douglas: all three respondent types are split by this scale. As for the liberals, not only do Black and Douglas occupy oppositely extreme ranks, but also Warren and Brennan occupy the middle ranks; Frankfurter, with a high positive scale score, is split from Harlan and Whittaker, who have negative scores; and Clark, with a high positive score, is split from Stewart (the only other economic moderate in this term) who has a negative scale score.

In both the 1959 and 1960 scales, the three most negative respondents are Douglas, Stewart, and Whittaker; and as Figure 9 (in Chapter 7) will show, the only three respondents with positive loadings on the second factor during the 1958–60 Terms (while the composition of the respondent group remained unchanged) were Douglas, Stewart, and Whittaker. The observation of this kind of a pattern, in both the scales and the factor spaces, demands an attempt to answer the question: why should the issue of governmental taxing authority so divide the respondent groups (as these were identified on the E scales) that an economic liberal, an economic moderate, and an economic conservative should consistently appear to comprise the most negative group on this issue? The answer that I suggest is this: these three, and the other respondents, perceived different facets of the issue, and each responded according to his own valuation of what he saw as significant. Douglas opposed government taxation because of his general hostility to governmental regulation and control over individuals, and because of his concern for fair procedure—in short, Douglas tended to perceive this as an issue related to political liberalism, and he responded accordingly. It may be relevant to recall that Douglas, for years, was a professor of tax law at Yale University before he was appointed to the Supreme Court; and we can assume, I think, that he was (among the justices) uniquely sensitized to many of the technical and procedural aspects of governmental control through taxation. Robert Jackson was (like Whittaker) an economic conservative, and possibly a more extreme one, although it is impossible to be certain, since they did not participate together; Jackson also had a particular interest in and hostility toward federal taxation, and during the eight terms (of this study) during which he and Douglas participated together, this was the only issue upon which they were in substantial agreement. But I think that the economic conservatives such as Jackson and Whittaker perceived a different significance in F than did Douglas: they were strongly negative to governmental taxing authority because of their pronounced sympathy for business interests and "the private enterprise system," which is frequently the interest opposed to that of the government in F-scale cases. If we look ahead to the factor spaces for the first and second axes for 1958–60 (Figure 10), we can see that only persons who were either very negative on E or else very positive on C could project negatively on an F-scale axis which is practically identical to the second factorial axis (with $F- = II +$). In short, the factorial space suggests that this is an issue upon which the extremes of political liberalism and economic conservatism can meet in their common opposition to the exercise of governmental authority in what has been, historically, perhaps the most fundamental of conflicts between rulers and their subjects.

Whatever the merits of the above speculation, the objective fact is that the justices respond with what appears to be consistency, on the basis of the marginally adequate evidence available in this study, in a different rank order for F than for either C or E. I infer from this that their attitudes toward this issue are different from their attitudes toward political or economic liberalism, and that F represents the third most important issue in Supreme Court decision-making during the period of my analysis. We shall see in Chapter 7 that, except during the period 1949–53 (when the factorial structure was different), both C and E are maximally positively correlated with the first factor, and C is positively but E is negatively correlated with both the second and third factors. During the three of these same terms when F scales, it is generally neutral to the first (or general liberalism) factor, maximally negatively correlated on the second factor, and (like E) negatively correlated with the third factor. (During the 1952 Term, when the factorial structure was different, and the first and second factors were ideologically equivalent to the second and third factors in the later terms when F scaled, it was maximally negatively correlated with the first factor and negatively correlated with the second factor; so the F scale correlates in a consistent relationship to both the C and E scales on what are psychologically the same factorial axes, in all terms that the variable scales and such measurement is possible.) This observation confirms the interpretation, suggested in the preceding paragraph above, that F is not distinguishable from E on the third factor, but that it is distinguishable in the factor space defined (in 1957, 1959, and 1960) by the first and second factors. As the discussion in Chapter 7 will develop in detail, the ideological content of this second factor is primarily related to a belief in personal freedom and strong opposition to the authoritarian imposition of restraint upon personal freedom of choice. So I conclude that to be negative on the F scale requires that a justice have a strong latent belief in personal freedom and strong hostility to authoritarianism.

I mentioned above some early confusion, on my own part, regarding the definition of the content boundaries between F and E. This uncertainty related to state taxation challenged on constitutional grounds, and various kinds of fiscal claims to which the government may be a party (such as tort claims and eminent domain actions). After completing the analysis of the semantic subcomponents of the E scale, I concluded that these issues were more highly correlated, in the attitudes of most of the respondents, with the E scale than with the F scale; in multidimensional space, such cases would be represented by j-points that would be located in the space between the E and F scales. We shall return to this question in the next chapter, where the discussion focuses upon the subcomponents of political and of economic liberalism.

THE N VARIABLE AND SCALE: FEDERALISM

The positive direction I have assigned to this variable is to favor the interest of the national government, when conflicting national and state governmental interests constitute the major issue in a case. This variable represents one of the major issues which, in the opinion of students of the

Supreme Court, has affected the decision-making of the Court. During the recent period of this study, however, attitudes toward federalism appear to have been much less important than attitudes toward the three variables already discussed. It may be that, during the long period prior to 1937, N was an attitudinal variable of greater relative importance, but the only published study which provides relevant evidence casts doubt upon such an assumption. This was an article on the relative importance of attitudes toward slavery, the regulation of commerce and corporations, and regional differences between North and South.[14] The method used was linear cumulative scaling, and the author also had written a monograph on the subject of federalism in Supreme Court decision-making, from the point of view of constitutional history; so it can be assumed that he was adequately sensitized to the significance of federalism as an issue. It is readily possible to analogize, to C, attitudes toward slavery; attitudes toward governmental regulation of commerce and corporations, to E; and regional conflict between the North and South, to N. The author's conclusion, although stated by him in terms of the political party affiliations of the justices, clearly supports the finding that it was the attitudes of the justices toward C and E, rather than toward N, that dominated their voting behavior. His data were so classified that to be "pro-Northern" in attitude was to be C+ and E−, while to be "pro-Southern" was to be C− and E+; his analysis showed, however, that the basic distinction in judicial voting behavior was between Whigs and Democrats rather than between Northern and Southern justices; the sectional distinction was secondary, relating to the *extremity* of the attitudes of Whigs and of Democrats. (Northern Whigs and Southern Whigs were both "pro-Northern" in attitude, but the Northern Whigs were more extremely so; conversely, Southern Democrats were more extremely "pro-Southern" than Northern Democrats.) Even for the Taney Court in the decades immediately preceding the Civil War, according to the evidence of Schmidhauser's article, it was the attitudes of the justices towards issues which (for that time) characterized C and E that were of primary importance in the attitudes of the justices.

The only term in which N scaled was 1950. Even this was a marginal scale, in terms of criteria of reproducibility, scalability, and sample size. What it shows is that Reed and Douglas were the most nationalistic of the justices at that time, and that Frankfurter was the justice most sympathetic to states' rights. Since deference to the states is a constantly iterated theme

---

[14] John R. Schmidhauser, "Judicial Behavior and the Sectional Crisis of 1837–1860," *Journal of Politics*, Vol. 23 (1961), pp. 615–640.

in Frankfurter's opinions, and his reputation among scholars is consistent with his own advertisement of his views, the N scale is, at the very least, not in conflict with what generally has been accepted as true in recent years about the attitudes of Supreme Court justices toward federalism. In the factorial space for the 1950 Term, the N scale appears to be highly correlated with E on the first two factors; but on the third factor, N is maximally loaded while the C and E scales have quite small loadings, so III in this single term seems to be a factor very closely related to N. It is not possible to say with certainty what the effect might have been, upon the factorial structure, if N had scaled in other terms, but I think that it might have been considerable. This would follow logically, because if N does represent an attitude independent of C and E and F, then it might require an additional factor (and ideology), beyond those normally adequate for the representation of the first three scales, in order to define a statistical and/or psychological space into which N could fit.

THE A AND J VARIABLES: JUDICIAL ACTIVISM AND JUDICIAL CENTRALIZATION

The two remaining minor variables can be discussed much more briefly. Neither variable was represented by a term sample adequate for scaling in any of the seventeen terms of this study. In lieu of more adequate information about their statistical and psychological characteristics, I have defined these variables in terms of their semantic content, using category labels that correspond to the conventional legal scholarship and understanding of these issues. The positive direction for A corresponds to an attitude favoring a judicial check by the courts over the policy-making of Congress, the Presidency, and administrative agencies; the negative direction corresponds to an attitude of judicial deference (or of "judicial restraint," as it usually is called). Therefore, the judicial activism variable corresponds to what has been a major part of the subject matter of the field that lawyers call "administrative law," and of an aspect of constitutional law which, with very few and quite specialized exceptions also involving the C scale, largely has lain dormant since 1937.[15]

The judicial centralization variable, which I hypothesize to relate to a J scale, involves the relationship, within the judicial hierarchy, between the Supreme Court and lower courts. I have defined the positive direction to correspond to an attitude favoring the centralization of policy-making at the level of the Supreme Court, while the negative attitude corresponds to an attitude of deference toward lower courts. Obviously, this, too, is an

---

[15] On the constitutional aspects of judicial activism, see Part II of *Constitutional Politics*, *op. cit.* fn. 5, *supra*.

issue upon which Justice Frankfurter's reputation, both as based upon his own avowals in his opinions and upon the opinions of scholars who have read his opinions, is well known: Frankfurter is reputed to be J—.[16] Unfortunately, the volume of decisions in which, as I have analyzed them, J has presented the dominant issue for disposition is so much smaller than the quantity of *obiter dicta* about J, in the opinions in these same cases, that neither Frankfurter's nor any other respondent's position can be specified, on the basis of my term samples of data.

I do think that J and A, like N and F, may represent attitudes which are potentially scalable, if one were to employ a different research design and perhaps to study other periods of the Court, in which (as I did not) the attention of the analyst focused explicitly upon an attempt to measure them. Although these minor variables represent attitudes which, in recent years, have been much less important than either political or economic liberalism, the four minor variables do, in combination, represent on the average almost a third of the semantic content of Supreme Court decision-making. They certainly are of sufficient importance, therefore, to warrant further investigation into the tentative and very preliminary findings about them which it has been possible to venture here, on the basis of the evidence made available through the present research.

[16] Wallace Mendelson, *Justices Black and Frankfurter* (Chicago: University of Chicago Press, 1962); Harold J. Spaeth, "Judicial Power as a Variable Motivating Supreme Court Behavior," *Midwest Journal of Political Science,* Vol. 6 (1962), p. 62; Joel B. Grossman, "Role-Playing and the Analysis of Judicial Behavior: The Case of Justice Frankfurter," *Journal of Public Law,* Vol. 11 (1963), pp. 285–309; and Harold J. Spaeth, "The Judicial Restraint of Mr. Justice Frankfurter—Myth or Reality," *Midwest Journal of Political Science,* Vol. 8 (1964), pp. 22–38.

Chapter 6 · THE SUBCOMPONENTS
OF LIBERALISM

M

Y ORIGINAL research design made no provision for an investigation of the subcomponents of political and economic liberalism; and it was only after the bulk of the work had been completed—through the 1960 Term—that I realized the importance of such an inquiry, in order to clarify certain empirical problems that had arisen relating to the relationship between the two major scales in the factor spaces, and also certain theoretical problems concerning the relationship between attitudes and ideologies. In subcomponent scales, the attitudes of the justices ought to be even more consistently structured than they had proved to be for the scale variables. According to the model, as Chapter 2 points out, such subcomponent scales (or, stated otherwise, such more sharply differentiated subattitudes) were postulated by the theory; the question now was whether they could be observed empirically. The size of the term C and E scales was not great enough, however, to make it possible to undertake such subscale analysis simply by partitioning the term scales; most of the resulting subsets would be too small to meet the technical requirements for scale construction. The alternative was to pool the data for each set of the scales (C or E) for several successive terms: the partitioning of these data would provide subsets that would be scalable, from a technical point of view; but they might also result, in view of the increasing proportion of non-response (because of personnel turnover), in decreased reliability—and probably in decreased validity as well—for the subscales. It would be possible that all such subscales, assuming that the psychologically valid subcomponents of the attitude could be isolated, would manifest higher consistency than the scale; but it would also be empirically possible, in view of the additive structure by means of which a cumulative scale is constructed and its error is measured, that some scales for subsets of the data would manifest lower consistency— the higher proportion of error for which they were responsible might be compensated for by the much lower proportion of error of most of the other subscales.

On the basis of the known manifest content of the C scale, I hypothesized that there were five semantic subcomponents of political liberalism:

1. political equality
2. political freedom
3. religious freedom
4. the right to fair procedure
5. the right to individual privacy

Political equality was defined to include such legal issues as the white primary, public school and other forms of racial integration, legislative reapportionment, and citizenship status. Political freedom included freedom of speech, association, and press, and loyalty dismissals. Religious freedom included both free exercise and separation of church and state issues. The right to fair procedure related to claims based upon most of the Fifth, the Sixth, and the Eighth Amendments, or the analogous claims based upon the Fourteenth Amendment. The right to privacy included claims that one's person—in either a physiological or a psychological sense—had been violated by agents of the government; thus it subsumed both Fourth Amendment issues and also such Fifth Amendment issues as those of coerced confessions and other forms of self-incrimination. So far as I am aware, this set of categories, for classifying the content of the attitude of political liberalism (or, alternatively, of the Supreme Court's civil liberties decisions), reflects my own personal judgment, when I was induced to think about the materials—and probably for the first time—from an attitudinal point of view. The categories certainly do not correspond to those employed by constitutional law scholars, who classify the content of the Court's decisions as an exegesis upon the text of the Constitution. (For example, political equality is not a recognized category, since it lumps together constitutional sheep and goats, plus what some might well consider to be rabbits; political freedom almost invariably is joined with religious freedom—for do they not both stem from the First Amendment?—and the right to privacy is considered to be a subdivision of the right to fair procedure.)

A seminar that I taught in the spring term of 1963 investigated in considerable depth the scales corresponding to these five hypothesized semantic components of political liberalism, but the results were hardly what I had anticipated them to be; and in order to discuss them meaningfully, it is first necessary to take up the results of an earlier investigation, in the spring term of 1962, of the scale subcomponents of economic liberalism.

It had been hypothesized that the primary content of the economic liberalism attitude involved a broad sympathy for the economic underdog, and empathy for the collectivistic interests of the socio-economic underprivileged in preference to affluence, opulence, and *private* oligopolies and monopolies of economic power. The postulation of semantic subcomponents for this scale was easier than in the case of the C scale, since the latter had been conceived (at the time I undertook the pilot investigation of the 1957 Term) as a universe, while I constructed the universe for E, inductively, by associating together several subuniverses which I had initially assumed to be distinct scale variables. (Part of Ulmer's work on the C scale had been published by the autumn of 1960, so I was in the position of being able to build directly upon it. Therefore, from my point of view, the conceptualization of the universe for E was *more* difficult, and that of the subuniverses of E *less* difficult, than for C.) There were five such semantic subcomponents, which (as I assumed) together defined the general content of economic liberalism:

1. fiscal claims
2. governmental regulation of business
3. union-management disputes
4. freedom of competition
5. the constitutionality of state taxation

The first subcomponent included the claims for compensation that were made in behalf of injured railroad and maritime workers, as in F.E.L.A. and Jones Act cases; or of claimants under state workmen's compensation systems, in cases that got into the federal courts under diversity of citizenship jurisdiction; or of tort (and other small, inferior) claimants against either the national or state governments. The economically liberal position is to favor the inferior litigant, in all of the above instances. On the other hand, when the conflict is between the national government (acting in what is conceived to be its representational capacity in behalf of an aggregate of many inferior individual interests) and large corporate claimants (such as banks, railroads, utilities companies, and gold mines), then the economically liberal position is to uphold the government; hence in these cases, too, the parties are partitioned according to the judicially perceived inferiority/superiority status of the economic interests represented by the litigants.

The second semantic subcomponent deals with cases of government regulation of business, and the liberal position is to uphold the government, i.e., to be anti-business.[1] This generalization must be qualified immediately by the observation that governmental agencies charged with the authority to regulate business do not necessarily or always uphold "the public interest," or support freedom of competition in their decisions; and the Interstate Commerce Commission, particularly, is reputed to have followed a conservative economic policy in recent decades. Consequently, a more correct statement about the second component would be that it means to uphold governmental regulation of business, in those cases in which the governmental agency's decision was to uphold freedom of competition or to uphold consumer or other underdog interests, and otherwise it means to reverse the agency's decision. From the point of view of the Supreme Court, this requires primarily a distinction between the I.C.C. and the other federal regulatory agencies, as other analysts have pointed out [2] and as a brief analysis of the relevant data will demonstrate. The discussion that follows applies to a sample of fifteen decisions of the Supreme Court, reviewing the decisions of five federal regulatory agencies; this is a subsample of almost half of the cases on the scale for the second subcomponent, the remainder consisting of cases of judicial regulation (including anti-trust suits) and state regulation of business, and a few cases from other agencies (such as F.H.A.) whose major function is considered to be managerial rather than regulatory.

Table 22 shows the ratio of agreement of the justices, with decisions of the Interstate Commerce Commission, and with decisions of four other federal regulatory agencies that were reviewed by the Supreme Court during the four-year period of the 1957–60 Terms. An analysis of the outcomes of the decisions at the agency level shows that of the seven I.C.C. decisions, one (which favored truckers over railroads, and was pro-competition) was E+ and the other six were E—; for the eight decisions of the other agencies, six (three for the F.T.C., two for F.P.C., and one for

[1] See generally Harold J. Spaeth, "Warren Court Attitudes toward Business: The 'B' Scale," ch. 4 in Schubert (ed.), *Judicial Decision-Making* (New York: The Free Press, 1963), pp. 79–108.

[2] *Ibid.*, pp. 99–100; C. Herman Pritchett, *The Roosevelt Court* (New York: Macmillan, 1948), pp. 190–191. Cf. Joseph Tanenhaus, "Supreme Court Attitudes toward Federal Administrative Agencies, 1947–1956; An Application of Social Science Methods to the Study of the Judicial Process," *Vanderbilt Law Review,* Vol. 14 (1961), pp. 473–502.

S.E.C.) were E+, and two (one for F.P.C. and one for the Secretary of Agriculture) were E—. The outcomes of the decisions of the agencies in these cases, as compared to the decisions of the Supreme Court, are summarized in Table 23. The Court affirmed the E+ decision of the I.C.C., and reversed three and affirmed three of the I.C.C.'s E— decisions. In regard to the decisions of the other agencies, the Court reversed the E— decision of the Secretary of Agriculture, and affirmed two of the E+ F.T.C. decisions, two of the E+ F.P.C. decisions, and the E+ S.E.C. decision; the Court reversed one E+ F.T.C. decision, and it affirmed the

TABLE 22

Ratio of Agreement by Supreme Court Justices, with Decisions of Interstate Commerce Commission and of Other Federal Regulatory Commissions

Justice	I.C.C.	Other
Douglas	.14	.75
Black	.28	.75
Warren	.28	.75
Brennan	.56	.88
Clark	.42	.56
Stewart	1.00	.50
Burton	.75	.00
Harlan	.86	.25
Frankfurter	1.00	.25
Whittaker	.70	.25

$$tau = -.562$$

E— F.P.C. decision. Hence, the Court affirmed four and reversed three of the I.C.C. decisions, and affirmed six and reversed two of the decisions of other agencies. The net effect was to change three of the I.C.C.'s E— decisions to E+; and it seems clear that the Supreme Court, like the other federal regulatory agencies, was considerably more sympathetic to economic liberalism than was the I.C.C. What is of particular interest here is the extent to which the justices of the Supreme Court agreed and disagreed, with the I.C.C. and with the other agencies, depending upon (1) whether the decisions of the federal agencies were economically liberal or conservative, and (2) the ranking of the justices themselves on the E scale. Douglas, the respondent with the highest rank on the E scale, invariably voted to affirm E+ and to reverse E— decisions of federal regulatory agencies, irrespective of whether it was the I.C.C. or another agency; and with a single exception for each, both Frankfurter and Whittaker, the respondents who ranked lowest on the E scale, always voted the opposite from Douglas. Again, with only a single exception, Douglas and Black and Warren, the three respondents with the highest ranks on E, voted together to affirm E+ and to reverse E— decisions of both the I.C.C. and other agencies; and with two exceptions, Harlan and Frankfurter and Whittaker (the three respondents with the lowest ranks on E) voted together to reverse E+ and to affirm E— decisions of all five agencies. Table 22 shows that generally, respondents who were economic liberals disagreed with the I.C.C. and agreed with the decisions of other agencies; while economic conservatives agreed with the I.C.C. and disagreed with the other agencies.

TABLE 23

Outcomes of Decisions by Federal Regulatory Agencies, and by the Supreme Court Reviewing Federal Agency Decisions, in Relation to Economic Liberalism and Conservatism

Decision-maker Source of Initial Decision:	Regulatory Agencies				Supreme Court		
	I.C.C.	*Other*	*Total*		*I.C.C.*	*Other*	*Total*
Outcome: E+	1	6	7	Outcome: E+	4	6	10
E—	6	2	8	E—	3	2	5
Total	7	8	15	Total	7	8	15

This finding is confirmed by the rank correlation of —.56 between the two sequences of respondent ratios of agreement, and it also is in strict accord with the conclusion reached by other analysts.[3]

The third component involves the identification of the liberal position with the interest of *unions,* as distinguished from a "pro-labor" attitude.[4]

---

[3] *Idem.* The Supreme Court probably has forced the I.C.C. to pursue a more liberal economic policy than would have resulted if there had been no Supreme Court review of I.C.C. decisions. I hypothesize that the reason for this is that during the past quarter of a century, there has been a higher proportion of economic liberals on the Supreme Court than on the I.C.C. An empirical investigation of the attitudes of regulatory commissioners lies beyond the scope of the design for the present research, but I think it is clear that investigations similar to mine could be made of the attitudes and ideologies of these administrative decision-makers, and by using theories and methods similar to those that I have employed in this study. Cf. Stuart Nagel and Martin Lubin, "Regulatory Commissioners and Party Politics," *Administrative Law Review,* Vol. 17 (1964), pp. 39–47.

[4] Cf. Harold J. Spaeth, "An Analysis of Judicial Attitudes in the Labor Relations Decisions of the Warren Court," *Journal of Politics,* Vol. 25 (1963), pp. 290–311.

Thus, for example, E+ means to uphold the union in union disputes with management; to uphold the union over individual workers in disputes over dismissals, as for non-payment of dues, or because of seniority rules, or even because of the personal and malicious bias of union officials against particular individual laborers.

Under the fourth subcomponent, which also involves (like the second) freedom of competition, both parties litigant are private, so the liberal position is to favor small business over large corporations; individuals over corporations (such as life insurance companies); and defendants in patent infringement suits (and the government rather than claimants in patentability suits). The volume of fourth subcomponent decisions is quite small, because these are the kinds of questions that historically have been construed to lie within the jurisdiction of state courts, and the Supreme Court has not chosen to interpret its own appellate jurisdictional authority and responsibilities in such a way as to bring more than one or two such cases before the Court for decision per term. (Perhaps a Court with a more liberal economic orientation might have chosen to increase the volume of decisions on these issues.) Finally, the fifth subcomponent deals with cases in which state taxation is challenged on such federal constitutional grounds as Fourteenth Amendment due process or equal protection, and those of the commerce clause. Students of constitutional history will recognize these cases as one of the primary concerns of the Court's decision-making during the half-century prior to the Court-packing struggle in 1937; during the period covered by this study, however, the volume of such cases was as small as for the fourth subcomponent—one or two per term, at the most. This is an area of constitutional law that has been well worked-over by legal and historical scholars, and there has been no confusion as to which is the liberal and which the conservative position in such decisions: [5] just as in the days of Holmes and Brandeis, the economic liberal upholds the constitutionality of such state taxation, while conservatives use any constitutional pegs that are convenient in order to limit the economic base for state programs of business regulation and social service.

An examination of the data for recent terms showed that the volume of cases for each of the fourth and fifth subcomponents was so low that the drawing of a useful sample was impossible—the set of respondents tended to increase as rapidly as the set of stimuli (an almost inevitable conse-

---

[5] See, *e.g.*, Arnold M. Paul, *Conservative Crisis and the Rule of Law: Attitudes of Bar and Bench, 1887–1895* (Ithaca: Cornell University, 1960); or Wallace Mendelson, *Capitalism, Democracy, and the Supreme Court* (New York: Appleton-Century-Crofts, 1960).

quence of pooling the data for more than four or five terms) so that the high proportion of non-response precluded the possibility of constructing a scale with respondent ranks in which an analyst could place enough confidence to justify comparisons with the rank order of respondents on scales for the other subcomponents. However, the quasi-scales that were constructed for the fourth and fifth subcomponents were quite compatible with the universe scale for E, and also with the scales for the first three subcomponents, to be discussed below. I conclude that, although the content of the dimensions postulated as the fourth and fifth subcomponents properly is included within the E-scale universe, the hypothesis that they represent distinctive attitudinal semantic subcomponents of economic liberalism cannot be proved, on the basis of the data for this study.

For the first three subcomponents, there was no problem encountered in pooling data, with a volume adequate in the technical sense to permit scaling. A sample of 25 decisions, which constituted all relevant decisions on the merits for the five terms 1956–60, was drawn of F.E.L.A. cases alone; and another sample of 30 decisions, for the same period, was drawn of other fiscal claims decisions. Thus, there were two samples, together totaling over 50 cases, which were drawn to test the hypothesis in regard to the first subcomponent; and the specific hypothesis was that there would be no difference between the scales resulting from the analysis of the two samples. It was also hypothesized that the correlation between the scale for the first and that for the second and third subcomponents would be positive and high, but *less than* +.90, which I established as a criterion level of scale equivalence. That is, if any two of these scales correlated at +.90 or better, I would assume that they were the same scale, and any manifest differences between them were due to sampling or other error variance; if the intercorrelation for any pair of the scales was less than the criterion level, then I should have to consider the possibility that these scales represented distinctive subcomponent differences in the attitude of economic liberalism. The period 1956–60 was selected, in part because it was most recent but primarily because of the stability of personnel during the three terms 1958–60: only one more respondent was added to the group by adding the 1957 Term, and an eleventh was required in order to pick up the 1956 Term, for the study of the two samples for the first subcomponent. Only the four terms 1957–60 were required in order to produce samples of thirty-four and thirty-nine cases, respectively, for the second and third semantic subcomponents.

The results are summarized in Table 24:

TABLE 24

Scales for Hypothesized Semantic Subcomponents of Economic Liberalism

Justice	I. (FELA)	Subcomponent Content I. (other fiscal claims)	II. (anti- business)	III. (pro- union)
D	1.00	1.00	1.00	1.00
Bl	1.00	1.00	.82	.90
Wa	.89	.87	.71	.74
Br	.89	.87	.53	.28
C	.63	.67	.32	−.23
S	.47	.00	−.38	−.03
Bu	.05	.07	−.47	.23
H	−.79	−.63	−.76	.08
F	−1.00	−.90	−.82	−.51
Wh	−.89	−.97	−.94	−.95
R coefficient	.98	.96	.97	.95
S coefficient	.88	.72	.81	.83
N	25	30	34	39
Percent pro decisions	84	83	68	59

The rank correlation between the two samples for the first subcomponent is perfect, including the correspondence of the two sets of tied scores, except for the trivial differences (on "other") between Stewart-Burton and Frankfurter-Whittaker. Actually, there is no inconsistency between the voting of Burton and the justice who succeeded him on the Court; to the contrary, the adjacent columns on both the F.E.L.A. and other fiscal claims scales for these two respondents would merge laterally like hand in glove; and the scale score differences between these two reflect nothing other than the effect of my arbitrary rule for scoring non-response. Similarly, another (necessarily) arbitrary rule for scoring jurisdictional dissents—of which Frankfurter had many in the F.E.L.A. scale[6]—is the basis for the slight differences between the scores of Frankfurter and Whittaker on these two scales. I conclude that these two scales measure the same attitudinal content; *viz.,* there is no difference, in the attitudes of the justices, toward F.E.L.A. and towards similar types of fiscal claims.

[6] The significance of Frankfurter's jurisdictional dissents in these cases is discussed at length in my *Quantitative Analysis of Judicial Behavior* (New York: The Free Press, 1959), pp. 221–227, 251–253, and "Policy without Law: An Extension of the Certiorari Game," *Stanford Law Review,* Vol. 14 (1962), pp. 284–327.

I had not expected to find any difference between the two samples of the first semantic subcomponent. But I had hypothesized that there would be a difference between the first and the second subcomponent scales. Is there? Evidently, as Table 24 shows, there is no basis for such an inference in the data of these samples. The rank order between the "other fiscal claims" and "anti-business" scales is identical, except that on the latter, Douglas-Black and Warren-Brennan are in their normal E-scale order, instead of being grouped in pairs of ties—and clearly, we are not justified in attaching any significance to the ties, since they merely inform us that the fiscal claims stimuli were not sufficiently extreme and diverse to distinguish adequately among the extremely liberal respondents. Again, I conclude that there is no difference; that the postulated attitudinal difference between the first and second subcomponents, reflecting the manifest difference in their semantic content, cannot be proved with my data. Moreover, the sample of responses for the fourth and fifth subcomponents, although (as noted above) too small to permit the construction of independent scales, is most consistent with the second component scale.

The question remains whether the third subcomponent scale is different. Evidently, the correlation between the anti-business and the pro-union scales, as shown in Table 24, will be positive but not as high as that between the fiscal claims and anti-business scales. The correspondence between the first four and the last two ranks is perfect, but the transpositions among the four middle ranks (#5–8) reduce the rank correlation (tau) to .78 for the *complete* sequence of ten respondents (cf. Table 27, below). Under the criterion that I had postulated, I have to conclude that most of the justices—and in particular, the extremists at both ends of the E scale—make no significant distinction between their attitude of hostility to business and their attitude of sympathy for unions; but the more moderate justices do make such a distinction. We might infer from Table 24, for instance, that Burton is almost as pro-union as Brennan, although Burton is considerably less anti-business than Brennan appears to be. Clark, to the contrary, appears to be more anti-business than he is pro-union; while Harlan appears to be neutral toward unions and sympathetic toward business. How much confidence we ought to place in such findings, and in the conclusion that they support, is another matter. Burton, who is among the moderates, participated in only one term, and therefore in fewer than 20 percent of the decisions in this sample. Spaeth reports a scale, evidently designed to measure the same attitudinal content, and for a period

(1953–59) that overlaps substantially with that for my own sample (1957–60); my pro-union scale disagrees with the one reported by Spaeth, and specifically in regard to these four middle ranks, while his equivalent scale of anti-business attitudes correlates perfectly with scale II in Table 24,[7] except for the transposition of Harlan and Frankfurter. It should also be reported that it is possible to transpose the rank order of nine of the stimuli on my pro-union scale, with the consequence that the present sequence for ranks #6–8 (*i.e.*, H, S, C) becomes reversed to the normal E-scale sequence of C, S, and H. Doing this results in five additional scale errors, and reduces the R coefficient from .95 to .93, and the S coefficient from .83 to .78. All five additional inconsistent votes occur in cases involving a direct conflict between the interests of unions and their members: one was a case of embezzlement of union funds by a union official; and the other four were cases of union discrimination, in employment practices, against workers (including the union's own employees). In these cases, both Stewart and Harlan voted to uphold the union (*i.e.*, the *ad hoc* management) interest, while Clark voted in support of the workers' interest. The more usual conflict of interest to which this scale appertains, it should be recalled, is unions against employ*ers*, not against employ*ees*. Since these are the cases which discriminate among the middle ranks, on my pro-union scale, one might question whether they belong in the scale, on the ground that they may be tapping an attitudinal content different from the rest of the scale. Spaeth's scale does not include the five cases in question: four of them were decided in the 1960 Term, to which his sample does not extend; and why he did not include the remaining (the embezzlement) case I do not know, but presumably, this reflects either a difference between Spaeth's definition of the semantic content of the subcomponent, or the subjectivity of such judgments about content (which I have pointed out in the previous chapter). I mention this not to focus attention upon the question whether Spaeth is or I am "right" about the inclusion of this particular case, or about the order of the middle ranks in the relevant scale; to the contrary, I think that such questions are really meaningless, as well as inconsequential. What I do wish to underscore is that very slight differences in the sample analyzed can have an important influence upon conclusions and interpretations; and considerably more research needs to be done, by different persons using different methods, before we are entitled to repose high confidence in the validity and reliability of our

[7] Spaeth, *op. cit.*, fn. 1, *supra*, p. 89.

knowledge about judicial attitudes. In the meantime, while exploratory research proceeds, only persons who do not comprehend the methodology [8] will assume that once a scale has been constructed, it can serve as a substitute for the judgment of the analyst about his data. As I have tried to illustrate in various places in this work, scales and coefficients and factors and other quantified paraphernalia are useful guides to, but never substitutes for, the scientific intelligence (*i.e., uncommon* sense) of the analyst—for which the Straussians' "Common Sense" [9] is no substitute either.

Before leaving the question of the correlation between the anti-business and the pro-union scales, there is one final bit of contradictory evidence that ought to be considered. As the 1958 Term scale in Figure 3 indicates, the embezzlement case (359 U. S. 419) attributes inconsistent votes to Clark and to Douglas, with a normal rank order of respondents; similarly, in the 1960 Term scale, Clark is attributed four inconsistent responses—and these are the only inconsistent responses attributed to him in this scale—in the other cases discussed above, and, again, when the order of respondents is the usual one. From a statistical point of view, it is readily understandable that such stimuli, if scattered among several term scales, would be sublimated by the other content; while, if concentrated in a scale of narrower semantic but broader temporal scope, a few such stimuli might indicate a difference in rank order for some of the more moderate respondents. From a psychological point of view, it is not inconsistent with, but to the contrary it is quite in accordance with the theoretical model described in Chapter 2 that there should be differentials in the attitudes of moderate respondents toward subcomponents of E, which might distinguish between those who were primarily pro- or anti-worker, and those who were primarily pro- or anti-union, in their attitudes.[10]

[8] John P. Roche, "Political Science and Science Fiction," *American Political Science Review,* Vol. 52 (1958), pp. 1026–1029; Wallace Mendelson, "The Neo-Behavioral Approach to the Judicial Process: A Critique," *American Political Science Review,* Vol. 57 (1963), pp. 593–603; Wallace Mendelson, "The Untroubled World of Jurimetrics," with comment by Fred Kort and response by Mendelson, *Journal of Politics,* Vol. 26 (1964), pp. 914–928; Theodore L. Becker, "Inquiry into a School of Thought in the Judicial Behavior Movement," *Midwest Journal of Political Science,* Vol. 7 (1963), pp. 254–266, and "On Science, Political Science, and Law," *American Behavioral Scientist,* Vol. 7, No. 4 (December 1963), pp. 11–15; and Theodore L. Becker, *Political Behavioralism and Modern Jurisprudence* (Chicago: Rand McNally, 1965).

[9] Walter Berns, "Law and Behavioral Science," *Law and Contemporary Problems,* Vol. 28 (1963), pp. 185–212.

[10] Cf. the factorial analysis of two such subcomponents of the E scale, EL-L [pro-union] and EL-L-WC [pro-worker], in my article, "A Solution to the Indeterminate Factorial Resolution of Thurstone and Degan's Study of the Supreme Court," *Behavioral Science,* Vol. 7(1962), pp. 454–457.

My tentative conclusion, on the basis of the available evidence that we have reviewed, is that there may be two distinctive subscale components of economic liberalism: a general subscale (which includes the fiscal claims, anti-business, pro-competition, and state taxation semantic subcomponents) and a pro-union component. Since there are typically over twice as many cases accepted for decision which appertain to the anti-business subcomponent alone, as to the pro-union subcomponent, the effect of combining the general and the pro-union scale subcomponents is to produce a scale of economic liberalism which corresponds to the scale for the larger content (pro-fiscal claims, anti-business, pro-competition, and pro-state taxation), and to produce a lower coefficient of reproducibility for E than for either subcomponent scale, since there will be some inconsistencies manifest in the E scale which will not appear as inconsistencies on either subcomponent scale. Evidently, many such inconsistencies will result from the transposition of the middle ranks of the pro-union scale, to make them conform to the rank order of the general subcomponent scale. And finally, it should be noted that we can distinguish only two, not five, subcomponent scales of economic liberalism. I shall henceforth identify the general subcomponent scale as B (anti-business), and the other as W (pro-union).

We can now turn to an analysis of the hypothesized five semantic subcomponents of political liberalism. To facilitate more summary reference to these, I shall refer to them as PE (the first subcomponent, political equality); PF (the second, political freedom); RF (the third, religious freedom); FP (the fourth, fair procedure); and RP (the fifth, the right to individual privacy). Samples were drawn from recent terms, as follows: PE, all seventeen cases from the 1958–62 Terms; PF, all thirty-two cases from the 1960–62 Terms; RF, the eight cases from the 1957–62 Terms—and extending the sample back to earlier terms would have done no good, since it would have been necessary to go back six more terms in order to pick up an additional case, and it is clear that non-response (due to personnel turnover) would increase so much more rapidly than the size of the stimuli sample that there would be no possibility of producing a valid scale; FP, thirty-one cases drawn from the 1960 and 1962 Terms—here the opposite problem was present, with an ample volume of cases in each term, so the 1961 Term was deleted (except for two cases) in order to avoid the large volume of decisions in that term in which less than a full Court participated; and RP, all eighteen cases from the 1958–62 Terms. I shall postulate the equivalent hypothesis, and the same statistical criterion for judgment, for these semantic subcomponents of political liberalism as were used in the preceding analysis of the semantic subcomponents of economic liberalism. Because of the small size of the sample, it was not possible to construct a scale for RF; the results of scaling the samples for the other four variables are summarized in Table 25:

TABLE 25

Scales for Hypothesized Semantic Subcomponents of Political Liberalism

Justice	PE	Subcomponent content: PF	FP	RP
D	1.00	1.00	1.00	1.00
Bl	.88	1.00	.87	.44
Wa	.88	.94	.81	.83
Br	.76	.88	.35	.67
G	.88	.62	.32	.33
BW	.24	−.38	.10	−.50
S	.18	.12	−.03	−.06
Wh	−.18	−.38	−.48	−.46
F	−.71	−.75	−.81	−.78
H	−.76	−.75	−.81	−.46
C	.53	−.94	−.94	−.33
R coefficient	.95	.99	.97	.98
S coefficient	.78	.85	.84	.91
N	17	32	31	18
Percent pro decisions	88	62	55	56

In view of the necessarily large proportion of non-response for both Goldberg and White, neither of whom participated in the decision of as many as 30 percent of the cases in any of these four scales, it seems preferable to eliminate them from consideration in making decisions about the interrelationships among the scales. If this is done, we have the set of rankings shown in Table 26, to which I have added the corresponding rankings, for the same set of respondents during the same approximate period, for the C and E scales; Table 27 also excludes Bu, Bw, and G.

Evidently, FP and PF are adequately represented by the C scale, since these two hypothesized subcomponents differ from each other and from C only in tied ranks. RP also seems generally to resemble the C scale, but Black is lower and Clark is higher than on C, and there is a transposition between Frankfurter and Harlan as well as the tie between Whittaker and

Harlan. PE, however, resembles E as much as C: except for the tie, the first four ranks are (of course) the same as for both C and E, but the fifth and sixth ranks are the same as for E, while the sequence of the three lowest ranks is like C rather than like E. This is a surprising observation, because it is doubtful that, on the basis of the semantic content, one would have predicted on logical grounds that the political equality subcomponent is as closely related to economic as to political liberalism; at least, no one appears to have ventured such an opinion. Nor is it clear, from this table, whether RP is closer to C than to E; and here again, the assumption of constitu-

TABLE 26

Scale Rankings for Political and for Economic Liberalism, and for Hypothesized Semantic Subcomponents of Political Liberalism

			Scales			
Ranks:	C	FP	PF	RP	PE	E
1	D	D		D	D	D
1.5			D, Bl			
2	Bl	Bl		Wa		Bl
2.5					Bl, Wa	
3	Wa	Wa	Wa	Br		Wa
4	Br	Br	Br	Bl	Br	Br
5	S	S	S	S	C	C
6	Wh	Wh	Wh	C	S	S
7	F				Wh	H
7.5		F, H	F, H	Wh, H		
8	H				F	F
9	C	C	C	F	H	Wh

tional law scholars (which I have shared, heretofore) has been that the right to privacy is an integral part of the values associated with the C scale. It should, however, be noted that Justice Jackson used to complain frequently, in his opinions, that the dominant majorities of the Court had relegated "Fourth Amendment rights" to an inferior constitutional position, and I have previously pointed out certain peculiarities in Black's apparent attitude toward the right to privacy, which differed sharply from his attitude toward FP and PF.[11] Table 26 shows that at least three other justices, in addition to Black, have in recent terms responded differently in

[11] Schubert, *Constitutional Politics* (New York: Holt, Rinehart, and Winston, 1960), p. 611; ch. 12 of that book discusses physiological and psychological privacy, ch. 11 (except for the erroneous classification of Fourth Amendment materials) discusses fair procedure; ch. 10, political and religious freedom; and ch. 9, political equality (in part).

their voting, when the question for decision has related to the right to privacy rather than to fair procedure or political freedom. So I infer from this table that both PE and RP represent attitudes that differ, for many of the respondents, from what they associate with the C scale; so the question arises how we can examine the way in which RP and PE relate to both C and E.

In order to investigate more precisely the relationships between PE and RP and the two major scales, I have computed the tau rank correlations among PE and RP, both C and E and their semantic subcomponents, and also F. The resulting matrix is reported in Table 27.

TABLE 27

Correlation Matrix for Scales and Subscales of Political and of Economic Liberalism, and for the Fiscal Authority Scale

	C	PF	FP	RP	PE	W	E	B	FC	F
C		.97	.99	.65	.76	.67	.61	.61	.57	−.06
PF	.97		.99	.66	.72	.69	.63	.63	.68	−.06
FP	.99	.99		.69	.74	.70	.65	.65	.61	−.09
RP	.65	.66	.69		.83	.70	.76	.76	.67	.03
PE	.76	.72	.74	.83		.65	.82	.82	.78	.14
W	.67	.69	.70	.70	.65		.83	.83	.80	.13
E	.61	.63	.65	.76	.82	.83		1.00	.97	.20
B	.61	.63	.65	.76	.82	.83	1.00		.97	.20
FC	.57	.68	.61	.67	.78	.80	.97	.97		.23
F	−.06	−.06	−.09	.03	.14	.13	.20	.20	.23	

As my theoretical model indicates they should be, both the major scales and all of their subcomponents are positively intercorrelated, with the lowest correlation (+.57) between any pair of these liberalism scales and subscales that for C (general political liberalism) and FC (fiscal claims of workers against employers). From this we might infer that there is indeed a universe of psychological content that might be called liberalism, but that it is not sufficiently homogenous to permit us to speak of an *attitude* of liberalism—if we postulate the technical criteria associated with cumulative scaling for our operational definition of attitude—even though we might well speak of an *ideology* of liberalism. We shall consider the latter question in greater detail in the next chapter.

The matrix confirms our earlier conclusion that the semantic subcomponents B and FC are equivalent to each other and to E: these are all the same attitude. Similarly, both PF and FP are so highly correlated with C that, whatever the distinctive content we might associate with the value of political freedom and fair procedure from a *semantic* point of view, we must conclude that from a *psychological* point of view, we cannot meaningfully distinguish among them: in Guttman's language, both of these semantic values constitute a homogeneous body of psychological content for the single attitudinal universe represented by the C scale. Or, in methodological terms, we stand to learn more if we treat these values as though they were identical than we do if we attempt to treat them as though they were different. The *minimal* rank correlation, among E-B-FC, and among C-PF-FP, is +.97, which is much larger than the postulated criterion level of .90. By the same criterion, however, W does represent a distinctive attitudinal subcomponent of E (with which it is correlated at .83). And what of PE and RP? Both PE and RP are more highly correlated with E than with C—indeed, if W with a tau of .83 is to be considered a subcomponent of E, then PE with a tau of .82 must also be so considered. PE is also correlated almost as highly with C, at .76, however, so the most reasonable inference is that from a geometric point of view, PE lies in a loose cluster with C and E, and slightly closer to the latter. RP, it will be noted, is about as closely correlated with E (!) as PE is with C; and RP is not much more highly correlated with C than is E itself. Consequently, these subscales cannot lie in a plane, but must lie in a space of higher dimensionality than two, and RP must be loaded differently from C in *substantial* measure upon at least one reference dimension and *differently from E* upon at least one of the other reference dimensions. The latter inference is reinforced by the observation that RP is rather highly (.83) correlated with PE, which apparently lies almost midway between C and E, but not in the same plane with them.

I have included the F scale in the matrix for two reasons. In the first place, F scaled in 1957, 1959, and 1960; so we happen to have the most complete and reliable information available on this variable for a period that coincides with that for which I have scaled the semantic subcomponents of C and E. Beyond the question of feasibility, it should be of interest to discover how F is related to the two scales of liberalism, since these three attitudinal variables together constituted, during the period of the 1956–62 Terms, an average of 88 percent of the total content of dissensual decisions on the merits. If we know the relationship between C and E and their semantic components, and between them and F, then we know all but a small proportion of the relevant attitudinal relationships, at least during the period of these samples.

The negative correlation of F with C (and with the two semantic subcomponents, PF and FP, which I have now assimilated with C) is so small that I infer that F is virtually independent from C; this finding does correspond to one's logical expectations, in view of the difference between the content of C and F. On the other hand, one would expect a small but positive correlation between F and E, since both relate to questions of property rights; and FC, in particular, might be thought to share with F the function of the reparation of obligations through monetary transfers. In any event, the correlation between F and E (and B and FC) is low but positive; and F is only slightly (although positively) correlated with the W subcomponent of E, a finding which is consistent with my earlier inference that W (unlike B and FC) does represent a distinctive attitudinal subcomponent of E. Also consistent is the slight correlation between F and PE, since I have inferred that PE lies in some manner between C and E. Finally, the substantially zero correlation between F and RP confirms the earlier inference that RP itself is loaded differently from C and E upon at least one of the reference dimensions; so we can infer from the relationship between F and the other variables in the matrix that F is substantially orthogonal to both C and RP, which are oblique to each other.

Even after making allowance for the large amount of probable error variance inherent in any attempt to translate the ordinal relationships represented by a rank correlation matrix, into a set of spatial relationships among vectors, it seems clear that this matrix represents a three-dimensional rather than a two-dimensional structure. If we conceptualize this structure, in accordance with the theoretical model discussed in Chapter 2, as a fan of vectors, then the two major scale vectors (C and E), with an angle of separation of about 50 degrees between them, will define a plane which intersects the space of the cube defined by a set of three orthogonal reference axes. Let us assume that C (including FP and PF) lies above and that E (including B and FC) lies in front of the first (abscissal) reference axis, as depicted schematically in Figure 5. In order to fulfill the requirement that it be orthogonal to both C and RP, F must be maximally negative on the second reference axis, moderately negative on the third, and moderately positive on the first; and all of the C and E scales and subcomponent scales that are represented in the correlation matrix must be maximally positive on the first reference axis.

In such a structure, C would lie in the same vertical plane with PE, which has less than C of whatever may be the psychological dimension equivalent to the third reference axis; and E would lie in the same

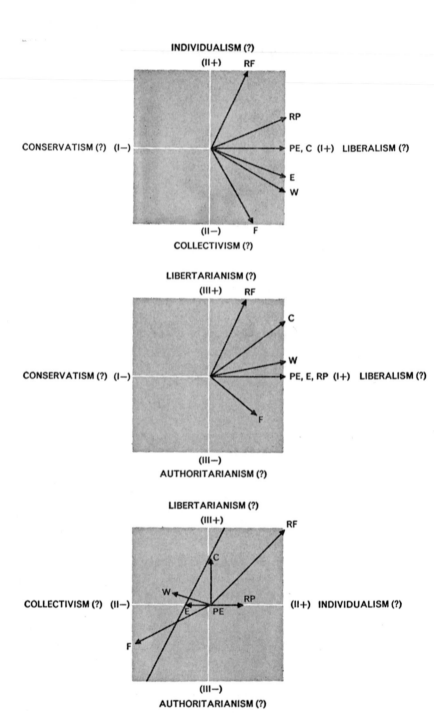

FIGURE 5. Scale and Subscale Vectors in Three-Dimensional Space (schematic)

horizontal plane with PE, which has less than E of whatever may be the psychological dimension represented by the negative segment of the second reference axis. The C and E vectors themselves will define, of course, an oblique plane; and in Figure 5, a line has been drawn through the points of the vectors for the two major variables: this line represents the trace (or the cutting edge) of the intersection of the C/E plane with the reference plane II/III. In the latter plane, the reference axes are assumed to represent (as I shall hypothesize presently) psychological dimensions *other than* liberalism or conservatism; therefore, we can observe in Figure 5 the extent to which the other vectors differ among themselves, as well as from both C and E, in relationship to what are postulated to be the secondary and tertiary (as well as the primary) dimensions.

Evidently, F and W are located on one side of the C/E plane, and PE and RP are on the other side. Although F and W share relatively high negative loadings on the second dimension, F is more negative than W, and they also are separated on the third dimension. E and PE and RP all are neutral to the third dimension, but they are separated by the second; C and PE both are neutral to the second dimension, but separated by the third; and PE, therefore, is loaded exclusively on the first dimension.

The eight decisions of the religious freedom (RF) semantic subcomponent of C, during the 1957–62 Terms, are insufficient to meet the requirements for a cumulative scale; but the cases do form a quasi-scale, on the basis of which very tentative judgments can be made. The rank order of the set of respondents for Tables 26 and 27 is as follows: D; Br, S; F; Bl, H, Wh; Wa; C. The rank correlations of this quasi-scale for RF, with the variables of Table 27, are as follows: with the C cluster, .36 to .41; with RP, .18; with PE, .09; with the E cluster, .18 to .24; and with F, —.53. Evidently, on the basis of this evidence, we should have to conclude that RF is *not* an attitudinal subcomponent of the C scale, but that it represents an attitude that is closer to C than to any of the other variables in this matrix. It is most different from F, and substantially independent from PE, which appears to be the core value of liberalism. This inference, though tentative, is also surprising, since constitutional law scholars long have assumed that religious freedom is closely associated with the value of political freedom, perhaps because of the close verbal association between RF and PF in the First Amendment to the Constitution. A modest correlation of .36 does not signify a very close association, and although my data are such that I do not have as much confidence in the findings about RF as in those previously discussed, I conclude that the aggregate attitude of Supreme Court justices toward religious freedom during the period of this sample was from a psychological point of view only moderately related to the issues of the C scale.

An examination of the quasi-scale sequence listed above helps to explain both why the relationship is positive, and why it is only moderate. Actually, six of the justices (D, Br, S, F, H, C) are in precisely the same sequence on RF as on C. And the transposition for Whittaker, from the rank (as on C) above Frankfurter to a tie with Harlan on the rank below him, does not constitute very much of a change. It is the sharp drop in rank for Black and Warren, from the second and third ranks (respectively, on C) to a tie for sixth and to eighth, that makes RF so different from C. In translating the correlation matrix into the geometric model depicted in Figure 5, it is quite clear that RF must be positive and higher than C on the third reference dimension; and in view of the high negative correlation between RF and F, I have assumed that RF has a moderate positive loading on the first reference dimension and a maximal positive loading on the second. In the next chapter, we shall be in a position to examine the empirical point configurations in the factor spaces for this period, and it will then be possible to check and see whether the positions of the i-points correspond to the kind of differentiation (as in reducing the ranking of Black and Warren) that would result for a vector in the position specified above for RF.

We can now turn to the psychological structure of the three-dimensional space that Figure 5 represents. According to Table 27, the PE vector is the closest to all of the others in the correlation matrix. In finding PE congruent with the first reference axis, I have in effect defined PE to be the core value of general liberalism. We can also see from the figure that this would not necessarily be a scalable value, *if* most of the stimuli are selected from the area of the C and E vector clusters; that is, if the distribution for the stimuli is two-peaked (*i.e.,* where the tails would be in a normal distribution, instead of being one-peaked in the middle). We might also note that since almost all of the term scales were constructed some time before the subcomponent analysis was even contemplated, much of the inconsistent response that we can observe in the term C scales reported in Figure 1 undoubtedly can be attributed to the inclusion, in these scales, of cases dealing with the semantic content of political equality and of the right to privacy. The religious freedom cases, which also appear in the term C scales, would also result in considerable manifest error in the scales, except for the fact that there are so relatively few such cases; in the 1960

Term, for example, there are 23 inconsistent responses for 51 cases, and 5 of these inconsistencies are due to two of the Sunday Closing Cases (which appear in the middle of the term scale). Similarly, much of the inconsistent response in the term E scales can be attributed to the spread between W and the rest of the E vector cluster. (These inferences readily could be treated as hypotheses, and tested by [1] rescaling the term data for C, with PE, RP, and RF cases excluded; and by [2] substituting the PE cases for the W cases, in the data for the E scales: the resulting scales should show higher consistency than the ones reported in Figure 3, because PE correlates the same as W does with E, and there are fewer PE than W cases to reduce the high consistency in the other E cases [*i.e.,* in FC and B]).

Figure 5 shows that neither RF nor F is part of the cluster of vectors maximally correlated with the first reference axis. There is, however, the same ordinal ranking of RF, C, E, and F on both the second and third axes. Evidently, the second reference dimension distinguishes RF and RP from W and F, as well as C from E; and at its extremities it defines religious freedom as opposite to support for governmental fiscal authority. Religious freedom and the right to privacy both place a higher valuation upon the interests of the individual than upon the interests of the group; while a pro-union bias and fiscal support for the service state both imply empathy for group or collective interests.

The third dimension serves primarily to distinguish RF and C from F. We might infer that this dimension has to do with the difference between personal and property rights, with freedom of conscience at one extreme and the power to collect taxes at the other.

One might postulate very tentatively because of the hypothetical nature of the space and also because of the ordinal character of the measurements, that the C and E and F scales are interrelated in a multidimensional space, the major reference axes for which are equivalent to the psychological dimensions of liberalism/conservatism, individualism/collectivism, and libertarianism/authoritarianism. Such a postulate could then be used as a hypothesis which could be tested with more empirical data; and this is what I shall do in the next chapter.

The preceding analysis of the subcomponents of political and of economic liberalism bears directly upon what have been the most conspicuous semantic overtones of the public-policy making of the Supreme Court during the period of this study: we can now see why the issues of political equality and of the right to privacy have emerged as the most dynamic component in the Court's policy output. That the equality value represents the most externally controversial and substantively important aspect of the Court's policy-making, during the past decade, hardly requires proof.[12] The consequences of the Court's policy of racial integration continue to pre-empt the attention of the nation: in autumn 1962, it was Oxford, Mississippi; in the summer of 1963 it was the march on Washington. Similarly, the Court's policy of legislative reapportionment emerged in 1963 and 1964 as an issue of major political implications in every state of the union. The explicit policy which has been the basis of practically all of the Court's decisions of the past decade, holding unconstitutional congressional legislation, has been the equality of citizenship status.[13] All three of these are major issues of public policy, and they are the principal constituent elements of the political equality value. The right to privacy is in effect a new civil liberty that the Court has created as a matter of constitutional policy in its decisions of the past few terms.[14] Our subcomponent analysis, and in particular the geometric interpretation of the vectorial structure, suggests that these emerged as the Court's major policy concerns, precisely because these were the values for which the highest consensus was possible, given the then obtaining respondent composition (*i.e.*, attitudinal structure) of the Court. No matter how externally controversial these values may have been, within the Court it was possible for clear and consistent majorities to form in their support.

Let us return to the subcomponent scales to see why this was so. The only important difference between the rankings for PE and E involves Whittaker, who is two ranks higher on PE than on E; the transposition between Frankfurter and Harlan is trivial, resting upon the scoring of nonresponse. The only difference between the rankings for PE and C involves Clark, who is four ranks higher on PE than on C. We cannot explain why this occurs for Whittaker and Clark, until we examine the factorial space point-configuration data to be discussed in the next chapter; but we can observe that on political equality questions, Whittaker, the lowest-ranking justice on the E scale, responds as though PE raised a C-scale issue; while Clark, the lowest-ranking justice on the C scale, responds as though to an E-scale question; while all other justices respond in the same way as they do on *both* scales. In short, the effect of raising the political equality issue,

---

[12] See, however, Alan P. Grimes, *Equality in America: Religion, Race, and the Urban Majority* (New York: Oxford University Press, 1964); and Glendon Schubert, *Reapportionment* (New York: Charles Scribner's Sons, 1965).

[13] See Schubert, "Civilian Control and Stare Decisis in the Warren Court," ch. 3 in Schubert, *op. cit.* fn. 1, *supra*, p. 56.

[14] Schubert, *op. cit.* fn. 11, *supra*, ch. 12, and pp. 609–620.

which all the justices perceived to lie *between* the issues of political liberalism and those of economic liberalism, was to convert both Whittaker's extremely negative attitude toward E and Clark's extremely negative attitude toward C to more moderate attitudes, without affecting significantly the attitudes of the remaining justices. The effect of this, as we can verify in Table 25, is that five justices have a relatively positive attitude toward political equality (D, Bl, Wa, Br, C), two have a relatively moderate attitude (S, Wh), and only two have a relatively negative attitude (F, H). Such an attribution of attitude certainly is in perfect correspondence with the manifest content of the voting and opinion behavior observable in *Baker* v. *Carr,* 369 U. S. 186 (1962), the first major legislative reapportionment decision (see the middle of the 1961 Term C scale, in Figure 1).[15]

The only differences between the rankings for RP and E involve Black and Clark, who are lower on RP than on E, and Whittaker, who is higher. The only differences between the rankings for RP and C involve Black and Frankfurter, who are lower, and Clark, who now is *higher,* on RP than on C. To produce such an effect obviously requires the influence of the second dimension mentioned above, although the result is very similar to that for PE: both Clark and Whittaker show a relatively moderate negative attitude toward the right to privacy, in lieu of Clark's extremely negative attitude toward C and Whittaker's extremely negative attitude toward E. But Black, whose attitude is extremely positive on both C and E, shows only a moderately positive attitude toward RP; and such a consequence, in the context of our correlational measurements and geometric interpretation, can be explained only in terms of the effect of another dimension. (Presumably, Black, Clark, and Whittaker would be strongly influenced by the second dimension's ideological context.) The general effect of the less negative attitude of Clark and Whittaker compensated for the less positive attitude of Black; and a Court composed (toward this issue) of three justices with a relatively positive attitude (D, Wa, Br), five justices with a relatively moderate attitude (Bl, S, C, Wh, H), and only one justice with a relatively negative attitude (F), was more consensual in its attitude than toward either C or E. In regard to both C and E, there were generally during the period of these samples a total of three justices who were strongly negative in their attitude: Frankfurter, Harlan, and Clark,

---

[15] The stability of these additudinal relationships is further demonstrated by the Court's 22 reapportionment decisions of the 1963 Term: see Schubert, *Judicial Behavior: A Reader in Theory and Research* (Chicago: Rand McNally, 1964), pp. 585–586.

in regard to political liberalism; and Harlan, Frankfurter, and Whittaker, in regard to economic liberalism.

My conclusion, therefore, is that the Court's collective attitude toward what can perhaps best be described as these two subcomponents of general liberalism—political equality and the right to privacy—is more moderate than toward questions of either *political* liberalism or *economic* liberalism per se; and that the reason for this is that several justices—and notably, Clark, Whittaker, and (on RP) Black—are less extreme in their attitude when the core questions of general liberalism are to be decided. I think that this is why the central issues of public policy formulated by the Supreme Court during the past decade and at present relate to the semantic content of political equality and the right to privacy, rather than to either political liberalism (defined as political freedom and fair procedure) or economic liberalism (defined as pro-workers' fiscal claims, anti-business, and pro-union). The Court's policy-making was moving in a liberal direction, but in the (relatively) middle-of-the-road direction made possible by the accommodation of the attitudinal differences among the justices who composed the Court at the time.

Chapter 7 · THE DIMENSIONS OF LIBERALISM

I N THE TWO previous chapters, we discussed the relationships among the justices when their attitudes are analyzed, first through linear scaling, and then further through the subcomponents of the linear scales. In my model, a linear scale of either political or economic liberalism is an artifact; that is to say, I conceive of such a linear scale as a line in the sense that a vector is a line in multidimensional space. A vector is a function of its correlations with the dimensions that define the space. Similarly, the cumulative scales are hypothesized to be vectors in three-dimensional space. The space contains a relatively large number—typically, about a hundred for the average term sample—of stimuli or j-points, and a smaller number (usually, nine) of respondent or i-points. Typically, all of the respondents are correlated with both of the two major scale variables, but the stimuli are partitioned among subsets, each of which is significantly correlated with only one of the scale variables (although it is possible, of course, for a case to be so located as to have high correlations with both major scale variables).[1] The scale variables contain (by definition) points which correspond to the intercepts of projections from both i- and j-points. A vector representing a scale variable can be defined as the line closest to all of the j-points in a subset. My observations, however, consist of measurements of characteristics of respondents (their responses to stimuli) rather than of characteristics of stimuli. Therefore, it is necessary to infer the locations of the (unknown) stimuli points, on the basis of the observations and measurement of responses. In cumulative scaling, we infer the location of sub-subsets of stimuli points within segments of the scale con-

---

[1] An examination of the opinions filed in *Machinists* v. *Street,* 367 U. S. 740 (1961), or in the *Sunday Closing Law Cases,* 366 U. S. 420 *et seq.* (1961), indicates that most of the participating justices considered these cases as raising issues of both political and economic liberalism.

tinuum bounded by pairs of the *i*-points, whose location in ordinal sequence we can determine by the scaling technique. Similarly, we can (according to my theoretical model) determine the location of the scale variable vector in three-dimensional space, by identifying a line upon which the projections from *i*-points correspond in ordinality to the ranking of the same *i*-points on the linear cumulative scale. Although we still cannot locate individual stimulus-points in the three-dimensional space (because, as pointed out above, we have not directly observed their characteristics), we can make rough distinctions among sub-subsets of *j*-points, and we can estimate the probable relationships among their vectors, through subcomponent analysis such as that which we undertook in Chapter 6.

The major hypothesis that we shall examine in this chapter is that the cumulative scales, representing the major scale variables, can be recovered as lines imbedded in the three-dimensional factor space. I shall assume that this hypothesis cannot be refuted, on the basis of my data, providing that the average rank order correlations between the two major cumulative scales and their analogue vectors is not less than +.90 (with an associated chance probability of not more than .01) for the seventeen terms of my sample.

It will be recalled that the same universe of raw data is observed as the basis for the cumulative scaling and the factorial measurements, but that the observations, for these two purposes, are quite different. For the cumulative scaling, the stimuli are partitioned into subsets, according to their major semantic content, in the subjective judgment of the analyst. The items in each subset are then classified nominally, in relationship to the directionality that has been assigned to the scale variable—that is, each case is classified as either C+ or C— if assigned to the political liberalism subset, or as E+ or E— if assigned to the economic liberalism subset, depending upon whether the decision (the majority of responses) was or was not in support of the positive value of the variable. Consequently, the subset of majority responses, for any decision, may be classified as either positive or negative in relation to one of the major scale variables, depending upon the outcome of the decision, and vice versa for the subset of minority responses; or else none of the responses, for a decision, may be assigned to either major scale variable. But in factor analysis, there is no *a priori* partitioning of decisions according to the inferred semantic content of the stimuli; all of the raw data for a term are pooled. For the set of responses constituting each decision, one observes the set of all dyadic relationships, and scores each pair of variables in terms of two dichotomous criteria: (1) whether each respondent was in the majority or in the minority; and (2) whether the pair agreed or disagreed in their responses. The resulting four-fold table is the basis for the computation of a phi correlation coefficient, which purports to measure the extent to which any pair of respondents tends—over all of the decisions for a term—to agree in their voting responses. But, agree in their responses to what? My theory is that this coefficient of agreement is a measure of the similarity of the attitudes of the two respondents. If there are, consistently term after term, only two major scale variable components of respondent attitudes, then it follows that the degree of similarity of the attitudes of any pair of respondents will be a direct function of their attitudes toward the two major variables. Hence, according to this theory, factor analysis of the phi correlation matrix should yield a configuration of i-points whose location is determined primarily by the respondents' attitudinal differences toward the political liberalism and economic liberalism variables. This is because the two scale variables are the latent cause of most of the manifest differences observable among the factorial configuration of i-points. The identification of the analogue vectors for these scale variables, in the factor space, makes manifest these latent causes underlying the factorial structure.

In the usual parlance of factor analysis, what I have just described as the "identification of analogue scale vectors" is called the rotation of the factorial reference axes to positions that are psychologically meaningful. Obviously, there is nothing incompatible between the concept of rotation of axes and the concept of identification of vectors. Each approach seeks to transform a manifest structure, which has been produced by statistical computations, into a latent structure which (it is assumed) supports a "better" psychological explanation than does the manifest structure. The explanation keyed to the latent structure is "better" because it presumably focuses upon more significant variables that affect decision-making behaviors and because it provides a more consistent and complete explanation than would be possible, if one were to observe only the manifest structure. (Indeed, one working with too small a sample, and without a well-developed theory of behavior appropriate to the empirical data, might be unable to interpret either the manifest structure, or the "rotated" structure—if rotation were keyed to a statistical rather than to a psychological criterion.[2]) The usual factorial approach assumes, however, that no attempt should be made to interpret the manifest structure, which is perceived as an intermediate computational stage, a sort of waystation along the route to the desired destination. Thus, the orthogonal "reference" axes, which define the manifest structure, are perceived to be "merely statistical constructs," which are without meaningful psychological significance. My work in this study contradicts such assumptions.

We may start our consideration of this question with the recollection that the i-point configuration remains invariant under any rotation of factorial axes; all that changes are the point coordinates, or (alternatively) the projections from the points to any of the infinite number of lines or planes (if our space is three-dimensional) that we may seek to observe as manifest structures imbedded in the factorial space. Now, when the factor analysis stipulates the loadings for a set of respondents on the reference axes (in, let us say, three-space), what has been done to produce this result? We can consider two answers, the one statistical and the other psycho-logical, to this question. From a statistical point of view, as Thurstone (and others) have so admirably explained, the computations differentiate among the respondents according to a set of statistical variables which, successively, partition the respondents into ordered subsets (of positive and negative loadings) on each of several independent reference dimensions. The first factor will identify the respondent with the highest total of net negative correlation (that is, the absolute sum of both his positive and negative correlations with other respondents is negative and his negative total is higher than that of any of the other respondents), and he will be assigned the highest negative loading on that factor. The computational process then makes the temporary assumption that this respondent with the highest negative loading is a respondent with an equivalent positive sum of correlations (by reversing the sign of all of his individual correla-tions with the other respondents). The revised totals for the remaining respondents then are re-examined, and the one who now has the highest negative total is identified as a member of the subset to receive negative loadings on the first factor; usually, this respondent will receive the second highest negative loading, and he will also usually be the person with whom the respondent first identified (the one with the highest negative loading) had the highest positive correlation in the original correlation matrix. The

[2] Cf. Louis L. Thurstone and James W. Degan, "A Factorial Study of the Supreme Court" (University of Chicago, Psychometric Laboratory *Report No. 64,* March 1951).

individual correlations for this second respondent, with the remaining respondents (excepting the one who was first identified), are then reversed, the correlation totals for the remaining respondents are re-examined, and the process continues until the correlation totals for all respondents are positive.

From a geometric point of view, the initial set of correlation totals can be conceived of as two subsets of vectors, of differing length corresponding to the size of the correlation totals. These vectors are aligned in either a positive or a negative direction from a point of origin on a line (which represents the factorial reference dimension), depending upon the sign of the correlation totals. The computational process has the effect of reversing, successively, the direction of all negative vectors until all vectors lie in the positive direction of the line. The vectors that had to be reversed to make them positive are the ones that are assigned negative loadings on the factor.

All correlations between respondents whose loadings on the first factor are opposite in sign are reversed in sign; and all correlations in the original factor matrix then are reduced by subtracting from them the cross-products of the absolute values of first factor loadings, for each pair of respondents. The process of factoring then is repeated to "extract" the loadings for the second factor from the reduced or residual correlation matrix; the respondent with the highest negative total of residual correlations is the first to be identified and to have his correlation total reversed to positive, but the sign of loadings to be assigned on this factor now depends not only upon whether vectors are reflected in the extraction of the second factor, but also upon whether or not the vectors were reflected in the extraction of the first factor as well.[3] Otherwise the process is similar to that which I described for the first factor; and I hasten to add that it is not my purpose here to describe the complete centroid method of factor analysis in detail or completely: this has been well done by Fruchter[4] and in the related references which I cited in Chapter 2. I do, however, intend to have said

---

[3] I have reversed *all* loadings on the factors identified with asterisks in Figure 10, thus (in effect) changing the polarity of these reference axes. My purpose in doing this was to make possible consistent graphic portrayal of the geometric relationships, over the seventeen terms of the study. This is a permissible procedure, since the statistical procedures are guided solely by the consideration that a particular subset of respondents are negatively correlated with another subset; the resulting assignment of polarity to the axis is psychologically arbitrary. I have attempted to make the reassigned axis polarities psychologically significant and consistent.

[4] Benjamin Fruchter, *Introduction to Factor Analysis* (Princeton: D. Van Nostrand, 1954), pp. 61–85.

enough about the mechanics of the centroid method to lay the groundwork for the psychological interpretation that I shall now present.

At least with regard to the data of our sample, what is happening when the process for extracting the first factor identifies the respondent with the highest negative total of correlations, as the justice to be assigned (by the statistical process) the highest negative loading on the first factor? As we readily can see by examining the four-fold tables for any of the terms (Table 5), a justice becomes highly negatively correlated with another justice only when they are in disagreement most of the time. More specifically, it is necessary that (1) both cells of the minor diagonal ($+/-$ and $-/+$) contain relatively large frequencies, and that (2) the cell signifying joint agreement in dissent ($-/-$) contain a very small or zero frequency. In order for this to occur, it is clear that the first justice must frequently dissent when the second justice is in the majority on—as I shall now assume, and presently will prove—one type of issue; the second justice must frequently dissent while the first justice is in the majority on another type of issue; ergo, there is no major issue on which these two justices are sufficiently in agreement for them to agree in dissent when a majority of the justices take a contrary position. Furthermore, we readily can see that if there were two major issues raised for decision by the Court, and one subset of justices were to assume an extreme (as distinguished from moderate) position on both issues—and for the moment, the question of the direction of their extremeness is irrelevant—while the remaining justices took inconsistent (or, at least, less consistently extreme) positions on the two issues, then the first factor necessarily would differentiate the consistently extreme justices from the others. (Whether, as usually happens, the statistical process should happen to assign negative loadings to the extreme subset depends upon empirical considerations that are psychologically irrelevent, as explained in footnote 3, *supra*.) If, within the extreme subset, justices are ordered equivalently on both issues, then the first factor also would rank them in the same sequence: the justice who was most extreme on both issues would receive the highest loading of the subset, and so on, with the member of the subset who was most moderate in his attitude toward both issues receiving the lowest loading—in the same direction, of course; all other justices would receive loadings in the opposite direction, with the size of the loadings depending upon the relative extremity of their (mixed) attitudes toward the two issues.

We can readily infer what would be likely to happen, in the extraction of the second factor, in terms of the psychological parameters of the respondents. The second factor is going to focus upon whichever of the groups supplies the dominant content (in the sense of number of dissents) in any term sample; and it will differentiate into two sub-subsets those justices who were in the non-extreme or mixed subset on the first factor. One sub-subset will consist of those justices who are relatively extreme in their attitude toward one selected issue, and the other sub-subset will consist of the remaining justices who are relatively moderate on this issue. As for the other first factor subset, which consists of justices who are extreme in the opposite (*e.g.,* positive) direction, they may or may not be divided into sub-subsets on the second factor, depending upon the range of the attitudinal differences among this group toward each of the selected issues; but the extremity of their loadings on the first factor might well lead us to anticipate relatively moderate correlations for them with either the second or the third factor. The third factor similarly will differentiate the justices with the most extreme attitudes (in either direction) on the other major issue (which provides the lesser content, in number of dissents) in the particular term sample.

We now have both a statistical and a corresponding psychological explanation for the observable structure of a configuration of ideal-points, representing the attitudinal syndromes of Supreme Court justices, in three-dimensional factorial space. The statistical explanation is merely a summary description of how the computing routine manipulates the data of a correlation matrix; the psychological explanation is a theoretical model of how attitudinal dimensions, which have been measured by a correlation matrix, may be interrelated to the dimensions of the factorial space—providing that certain very rigid restrictions be placed upon the psychological types into which the respondents are classified. Obviously, this theoretical model would not fit all kinds of empirical attitudinal data; it presumes an exceptionally high degree of cognition and of consistency in both the attitudes and the behavior of the respondents. It may not be unreasonable to anticipate that such restricted and rigid types of attitudinal syndromes may be discovered to exist empirically among United States Supreme Court justices, when one considers the unusual combination of education, training, and skill that is common among the justices, but which probably is very uncommon among the general populace. Consequently, I would not venture to assume that this model would fit response data for a class of undergraduates in the beginning course in psychology—although it certainly would be of interest to inquire whether this is so. In any case, we may learn something from study of an exceptional group (such as the justices) that can contribute to our understanding of attitudinal structure in the less exceptional populations ordinarily sampled for work in attitudinal analysis.

One other implication of the above model should be noted. If the theory correctly describes the behavioral relationships that can be observed to occur empirically in the voting of Supreme Court justices in the cases sampled, then we may be willing to accept the probable validity of the general hypothesis that the justices' voting differences are determined primarily by their attitudinal differences. In that event, we can say that the factor analysis is locating judicial ideal-points in the factor space, according to the attitudinal differences among the justices. Can it be inferred, if this should be true, that the factorial axes, as these are extracted by the computing process, have no psychological significance? As we have noted, the usual assumption in factor analysis is that the orthogonal axes are merely statistical constructs, useful for defining a frame of reference within which the configuration of points can be determined, but of no psychological consequence until after they have been rotated to meaningful positions. We already know, from Chapters 5 and 6, that our two major scale variables, political liberalism and economic liberalism, are positively correlated, because the same subset of justices has the highest positive scores on both scales. The model discussed in Chapter 2 specified that these two scales would provide the criteria for the rotation of the reference axes, or at least for the rotation of two such axes of each set of three. Since two axes define a plane, one might say that the two scale variables together provide the basis for the best two-dimensional interpretation of the attitudes of the justices, and I shall undertake such an analysis in Chapter 8. There remains the question what psychological meaning, if any, should be associated with the three orthogonal dimensions that define the reference space.

The two scale variable axes can be located, according to my general hypothesis, as geometric functions of the three reference axes. And the psychological theory of factor extraction, sketched above, hypothesizes that the factors are functions of the attitudinal differences among the justices toward the same two variables that the cumulative scales purport to measure. In short, my theory is that both the reference axes before rotation, and the "rotated axes" which are equivalent to the linear cumulative scales, are alternative modes of measurement of the same manifest differences in voting behavior and latent differences in attitudes. Indeed, my general hypothesis rests explicitly upon this assumption. Therefore, the reference axes also must be psychologically meaningful, although we can expect that the semantic attitudinal content of the three reference axes will be different from that of the two scale variables (or, equivalently, their analogue axes). If three rather than two reference axes are required in order to determine the i-point configuration, so that analogue scale axes are maximally equivalent to cumulative scales, then it is both possible and necessary to define the two analogue scale axes as functions of the three reference axes. Consequently, we may infer that the three reference axes represent psychological dimensions on a more basic level than that of attitudes, and that political liberalism and economic liberalism themselves may be functions of these more fundamental psychological dimensions.

Attitudes and Ideologies

As a guide to the psychological relationship between the attitudinal and factorial dimensions, I shall summarize the theory of the organization of social attitudes that has been presented by Hans J. Eysenck. In so doing, I am aware of the reputation that Dr. Eysenck enjoys among American social psychologists.[5] I am also aware that Eysenck's work has provided the basis of the first national survey of judicial attitudes in the United States,[6] and that he is the author of a much better and more useful introductory text in political psychology[7] than any of his American colleagues has produced during the past generation. In that book, Eysenck suggests that:

Roughly speaking, we can discriminate four different degrees of organization or structure [of social attitudes]. Right at the bottom we have opinions which

[5] See, *e.g.*, the following examples of trans-national psychological debate: "Measurement and Prediction: A Discussion of Volume IV of Studies in Social Psychology in World War II," in *International Journal of Opinion and Attitude Reserach,* Vol. 5 (Spring 1951), "I. Review," by Hans J. Eysenck, pp. 95–102, and "II. Scale Analysis, Factor Analysis, and Dr. Eysenck: A Reply," by Louis Guttman, pp. 103–120; Milton Rokeach and Charles Hanley, "Eysenck's Tender-mindedness Dimension: A Critique," *Psychological Bulletin,* Vol. 53 (1956), pp. 169–176; Hans J. Eysenck, "The Psychology of Politics: A Reply," *ibid.,* pp. 177–182; Charles Hanley and Milton Rokeach, "Care and Carelessness in Psychology," *ibid.,* pp. 183–186; Richard Christie, "Eysenck's Treatment of the Personality of Communists," *ibid.,* pp. 411–430; Hans J. Eysenck, "The Psychology of Politics and the Personality Similarities Between Fascists and Communists," *ibid.,* pp. 431–438; Richard Christie, "Some Abuses of Psychology," *ibid.,* pp. 439–451.
[6] See Stuart S. Nagel, "Off-the-Bench Judicial Attitudes," ch. 2 in Schubert (ed.), *Judicial Decision-Making* (New York: The Free Press, 1963), pp. 29–53.
[7] Hans J. Eysenck, *The Psychology of Politics* (London: Routledge and Kegan Paul, 1954).

are not related in any way to other opinions, which are not in any way characteristic of a person who makes them, and which are not reproducible in the sense that if the same or a similar question were asked again under different circumstances, the answer might be different. Such purely ephemeral opinions are of no great interest or value; they do not go beyond themselves and they do not throw any light either on the personality or on the ideologies of the people holding them.

A higher level is reached when we come to opinions which are reproducible and which form a relatively constant part of an individual's make-up. In other words, these are opinions which are voiced in the same or a similar manner on different occasions, and which are not subject to sudden arbitrary changes, such as are opinions at the lowest level. In terms of . . . statistical concepts . . . these opinions are *reliable* in the sense of being *stable*.

At the third level, we have what we may call attitudes. Here we find not only that an individual holds a particular opinion with regard to a particular issue with a certain degree of stability; we also find that he holds concurrently a large number of other opinions on the same issue which in combination define his attitude towards that issue. . . . At this level . . . we have the first indication of structure. Opinions do not occur in isolation any more; they are closely related to other opinions on the same issue and thus give rise to our third level.

But even attitudes of this kind are not independent. . . . [A]ttitudes themselves are correlated and give rise to what we might call super-attitudes or ideologies. . . . It will be noticed that we have used the term *opinion* for the lowest two levels, the term *attitude* for the third level, and the term *ideology* for the highest level. . . . This usage links up conveniently with the various distinctions in opinion and attitude measurement. . . . Public opinion polls are practically always at the level of single opinion statements, i.e. at the lowest levels; attitude measurements by means of uni-dimensional scales are concerned with the third level; factor analysis and the more complex statistical procedures are mostly concerned with the ideological level. Thus our levels are differentiated not only with respect to their status in the hierarchy, but also with respect to the most frequently used methods of investigation.

It will have been noticed that the definition of our levels, as well as proof for their existence, depends entirely on the empirical fact of correlation. When we find that a specific opinion as voiced on one occasion is also voiced on another, i.e. when the two correlate, then we speak of opinion measurement proper. When we find that certain opinions are inter-correlated in a certain way, we speak of attitudes, and when we find that certain attitudes are inter-correlated in a certain way, we speak of ideologies.[8]

It should be noted that Eysenck is a factor psychologist, and his model of hierarchical structure, in which attitudes mediate between habitual opinion and ideologies, is explicitly a factorial model; that is, it corresponds

[8] *Ibid.*, pp. 111–114.

psychologically to the statistical processes which factor analysis employs. Of course, this makes it all the more appropriate for our own purposes, since our own discussion in this chapter has similarly been directed to a pyschological interpretation of factor analytic processes, in relation to our own empirical data. In terms of our own data and concepts, we do not deal with what Eysenck calls specific opinions. His "habitual opinion level" describes the judicial votes which constitute our basic universe of data. Guttman's cumulative scaling also presumes a deterministic hierarchical structural model [9] of social attitudes; and so the organization of votes into linear cumulative scales of judicial attitudes corresponds strictly to Eysenck's model, in which habitual opinions are organized into attitudes. My own use of subcomponent analysis, as in Chapter 5, has introduced two levels of attitude measurement, while Eysenck speaks of only one level; [10] we might distinguish the two levels of attitude, in relation to Eysenck's model, by referring to the subcomponent scales as microattitudes and to the major scale variables (such as political liberalism or economic liberalism) as macroattitudes. Certainly, there is nothing incompatible with a hierarchical model such as Eysenck's, if I introduce two levels where he found it convenient to generalize with only one. His ideological level, which he explicitly identifies with factor measurement, would correspond, therefore, to the "more fundamental psychological dimensions" which I have inferred are represented by the factorial reference axes in my own model of Supreme Court attitudes.

Eysenck's model provides a supporting theoretical explanation for my own major hypothesis. I had hypothesized—and long before I ever had heard of Eysenck, it must in all candor be admitted—that the attitude scales would have to be implicit, and could be made explicit, in the factor space. That hypothesis was a logical deduction from Coombs's work in the theory of data; it has not yet been proved, but I shall do so presently in this chapter. In the introductory pages of this chapter, I deduced from an analysis of how factor analytic procedures must be manipulating my empirical data (the major attitudinal parameters of which we already are familiar with through the linear scaling work discussed in Chapter 5 and 6), that the factorial reference axes with which the attitudinal scales are correlated must have psychological as well as statistical significance. Eysenck's model suggests that it is appropriate to conceive of our factorial

[9] Warren S. Torgerson, *Theory and Methods of Scaling* (New York: Wiley, 1958), ch. 12.

[10] Cf., however, Louis Guttman, "A New Approach to Factor Analysis: The Radex," ch. 6 in Paul F. Lazarsfeld (ed.), *Mathematical Thinking in the Social Sciences* (Glencoe: The Free Press, 1954), p. 325.

reference dimensions as ideologies, and that ideologies are reciprocally related to attitudes. Certain combinations of attitudes imply certain corresponding ideologies; and certain combinations of ideologies imply certain corresponding attitudes. What ideologies do our attitudinal scales imply? To answer this question, we must return to the empirical data.

It should be noted that it is explicit in Eysenck's hierarchical model that ideologies, as the more general structures, are even less numerous than attitudes; as he himself put it, "only very few concepts will be found" at the level of ideology. It may seem incongruous, therefore, that we are proposing that three ideologies (factorial dimensions) are needed in order to explain the relationship between only two attitudinal scales. This seeming incongruity disappears, however, once we recall that the three-dimensional factor space is based upon the measurement of all of the data in a term sample; and under our assumption that factors beyond the third are not psychologically meaningful, the factor space is measuring all of the data. Each of the two cumulative scales typically measures only about a third of the data in each term sample, however; so it is apparent that there are several other minor scales which, as we discussed in Chapter 5, are almost always present but rarely in samples adequate to fulfill the technical requirements of cumulative scaling. So we must assume that our three reference dimensions have an influence upon other (and in this study, otherwise largely unmeasured) scale variables than C and E. Our discussion of how the scale types (on C and E) lead to specifiable factorial results should be understood, therefore, as an alternative statement about the major sources of influence which lead to the factorial structure that we shall presently observe. Three types of respondents result in three reference dimensions, and the differing combinations of three ideologies define the three attitudinal types of respondents.

Table 21 reported the proportion of the total content, for each term sample, that was accounted for by the two major scales. On the average, this was about two-thirds, with the remainder divided about equally between the F and N scales and quasi-scales, and the other minor variables (A and J, and F and N when these formed neither scales nor quasi-scales). As that table also shows, F scaled in only four terms, but it was either a scale or a quasi-scale in all except two of the seventeen terms. N scaled only once but formed a quasi-scale in four other terms. Evidently, voting differences that appertain to all six variables (at least) are operating upon the definition of the factorial axes and point configuration in each term, so we may conceptualize the phi correlation matrices (from which the factorial ideologies are deduced) as functions of all six variables, although the two major variables will provide the principal influence upon the factorial structure. Alternatively, the factor ideologies can be conceptualized as functions of the ideologies of the nine individual respondents. We therefore can draw the further distinction that to conceptualize the factors as functions of the scale variables is to hypothesize about the latent basis for the factorial structure, while to conceptualize the factors as the statistical counterpart of the ideologies of individual respondents is to hypothesize on the basis of the manifest structure of the factorial space.

If we observe that portion of the scaling data in which the reliability seems to be highest, empirical ideological types then can be defined in terms of respondent interrelationships with the two major scales. It would be preferable, of course, to define individual ideologies on the basis of an individual's consistent position on scales for all six variables, because such individual ideologies would then be more analogous to the factor ideologies; but this cannot be done with the present data. When individual ideologies are defined on the basis of the two major scales alone, we are capturing (on the average) only about two-thirds of what we might call the individual's "true" ideology. It will be convenient to work with a limited number of empirical ideological types, instead of with eighteen individual ones; so I shall adopt the classification of scale types that was developed in Chapter 5 (Tables 16 and 18). If these are combined, the following matrix of empirical ideological types results:

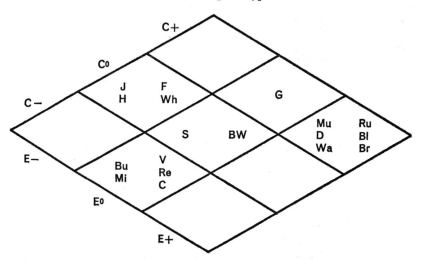

FIGURE 6. Joint Classification of Linear Scale Types

Since Goldberg participated in only one term sample, he can have little influence upon the general analysis; and apart from the two moderates of recent terms, the remaining fifteen respondents are partitioned among only three cells of the matrix: six are in the C+/E+ cell; five are in the C—/Eo cell; and four are in the Co/E— cell. For the present, we can identify these three ideological types by their corresponding joint scale-categories: the political-liberal/economic-liberal group we shall call (tentatively) "liberals"; the political-conservative/economic-moderate group we shall call "political conservatives"; and the political-moderate/economic-conservative group we shall call "economic conservatives."

The condition that the liberal type be highly positively correlated with both scales requires that the scales themselves be positively correlated; the correlation between the scales must be only moderate, however, because if it were very high, we can anticipate that only a single scale would have emerged in at least some of the term samples. We can assume, therefore, that the relationship between the scales can be depicted as geometrically similar to the structure shown in Figure 6, above; and we can, of course, redraw that structure and shift the denoted position of the scales—not their relationship—by placing the origin of the space at Co, Eo instead of at C—, E— (as in Figure 6). The resulting typal structure is shown in Figure 7, below:

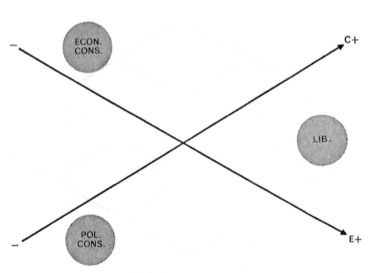

FIGURE 7. Linear Scales and Empirical Attitudinal Types

According to my theory of the factor extraction process, the first factor will pass through the liberal type if they are the dominant subset, in the sense that there are more respondents in this type than in either of the other two types. If there are more political conservatives than economic conservatives, then the second factor will be as much as possible in the direction of the political conservative type, subject to the statistical restriction of orthogonality; and the third factor similarly will be in the direction of the economic conservatives, to the extent that this is possible while remaining orthogonal to the first two factors. If, for example, there were four respondents in the liberal type, three in the political conservative type, and two in the economic conservative type, then we might anticipate the following kind of factorial structure:

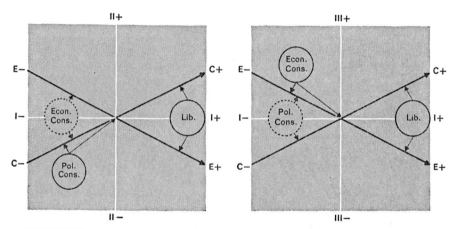

FIGURE 8. Scale Axes and Empirical Attitudinal Types

The economic conservatives do not, in this three-dimensional geometric model, lie in the plane defined by the first and second axes, but rather they project upon it from above; similarly, the political conservatives project from a frontal position upon the plane defined by the first and third axes. The same relationships can be summarized algebraically as follows:

TABLE 28

Scale Axis and Factorial Correlations of Empirical Attitudinal Types

Empirical Types	Scales		Factors		
	C	E	I	II	III
Liberals	+	+	+	0	0
Political conservatives	−	0	−	−	0
Economic conservatives	0	−	−	0	+

We can see that the liberals are the only "pure" or ideal factorial type; both the political conservatives and the economic conservatives are mixed types, in relation to the factorial axes, since they each have loadings upon more than one factor. We can, however, readily depict the ideal factorial types, to which our empirical mixed types most closely correspond: the liberals would remain as they are, the political conservatives would be loaded exclusively upon the second factor, and the economic conservatives would be loaded exclusively upon the third factor.

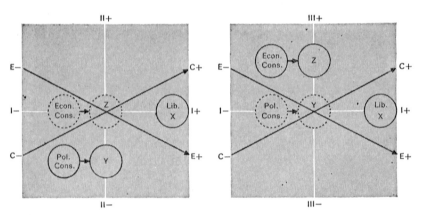

FIGURE 9. Scale Axes and Ideal Attitudinal Types

From an algebraic point of view, the ideal types, which we shall temporarily designate as X, Y, and Z, may be summarized algebraically as follows:

TABLE 29

Scale Axis and Factorial Correlations of Ideal Attitudinal Types

Ideal	Scales		Factors		
Types	C	E	I	II	III
X	+	+	+	0	0
Y	−	+	0	−	0
Z	+	−	0	0	+

Only the liberals, among the *empirical* ideological types, are extreme in their attitude toward both scale variables; but all three of the ideal ideological types are attitudinally extreme toward both issues. It might seem that only two factors would be required, since the X type would have no occasion to be in the minority and dissent; but we shall assume that there remain intensity differences among the types, and in the position in which the scales are shown in Figure 9, above, the X type would be more extremely positive on political liberalism than would the Z type, and the X type would be more extremely positive on economic liberalism than would the Y type; hence, Y and Z might combine to form majorities with X in dissent, on either issue, if extreme claims are raised.

The ideal types are intuitively plausible, if we assume that they represent distinctive ideologies. We might expect that a person who is extremely committed to any ideology—say, X—cannot be heavily committed to competing ideologies and remain an extremist in his attachment to ideology X. An equivalent statement, in factorial terms, would be that a respondent who was very heavily loaded on the first factor would have such small residual coefficients of correlation (with the other respondents), after the extraction of the first factor, that there would be insufficient of his variance left for him to be strongly correlated with any of the remaining factors; it would, in other words, be statistically impossible for any respondent to be extremely loaded on more than one factor. (To make the above statement more precise, we might recall that a factorial loading of $\pm.7$ or greater accounts for half or more of a respondent's total variance, and a respondent with a loading as great as .71 on one factor could not have as high a loading [in any direction, of course] on any other factor; so we might accept $\pm.71$ as our criterion for an "extreme" factorial loading.) Correspondingly, we should expect our empirical ideological types to show moderate loadings on two factors and a low loading on a third factor—excepting, of course, the liberals who correspond to pure type X, and who therefore should be extremely loaded on the first factor and should have low loadings on both of the other two factors.

We can inquire into the semantic content of types X, Y, and Z. The X type, we know, consists of repondents who are liberal in their attitude toward both the political and the economic variables; we might well designate the first factor as "liberalism," signifying broad sympathy for socio-economic and political change. On the other hand, we can recall from Chapter 6 that subcomponent analysis revealed that the issue that was most clearly common to both of the major scales was that of equality; I had hypothesized this issue, on the basis of its manifest semantic content, to be one of *political* equality but analysis showed that this was something of a misnomer, at least from the point of view of Supreme Court justices. The underlying issue was revealed to be both political equality (in an instrumental sense) and economic equality (as an end-value); and in the more recent integration cases relating to golf courses, swimming pools, and lunch counters in five and ten cent stores, the issue is clearly one of social equality. Social equality seems to be a more useful concept for the additional reason that it is broad enough to encompass also the contributing values of political and economic equality. We might also recall that the specific issues of social equality, and in particular racial integration and legislative reapportionment, have been the central issues of public policy which the Supreme Court has decided during the 1950's and 1960's; from a qualitative point of view, these have been the issues with the most profound and pervasive implications for the restructuring of American society in general, and of the American polity and economy in particular. In quantitative terms, the most important issue has consisted of the claims of indigent state prisoners to fair procedure;[11] and this is also an issue of social equality, because these "inferior litigants" characteristically claim that their underprivileged economic, social, or political status has deprived them of a fair trial, with the result that they have been illegally convicted and confined.[12] We might, therefore, prefer to designate X as the Equalitarian ideology, continuing to reserve the concept "liberalism" for use to describe relationships directly referring to either or both of the major scales (rather than to use the liberalism concept to denote the issue which is central to both scales). For convenience in reference, we might refer to the negative direction on the first factor as Traditionalism, rather than to employ the more awkward term "Anti-Equalitarianism." So I suggest that the first factor in our ideal structure is a dimension of *social* ideology.

Y is an ideology which is held (as I have hypothesized) by respondents who are conservative on political issues but liberal on economic issues, and whose closest empirical analogue consists of a type of respondent whose attitude toward the political scale is more extreme than his attitude toward the economic scale. What does being politically conservative have in common with being economically liberal? Both attitudes require a respondent to have little sympathy for claims of either economic, political, or religious freedom, but instead to believe strongly in the necessity for upholding the authority of the government in cases in which "law and order"—with

[11] Schubert, *Quantitative Analysis of Judicial Behavior* (Glencoe: The Free Press, 1959), pp. 28–36; Schubert, *Constitutional Politics* (New York: Holt, Rinehart, and Winston, 1960), pp. 94–97.

[12] Cf. *Gideon* v. *Wainwright*, 327 U. S. 335 (1963); *Douglas* v. *California*, 327 U. S. 353 (1963); *Lane* v. *Brown*, 372 U. S. 477 (1963); *Draper* v. *Washington*, 327 U. S. 487 (1963). See Anthony Lewis, *Gideon's Trumpet* (New York: Random House, 1964).

the emphasis upon "order"—conflict with petitioners' claims to be free from enforced regulation of their behavior in regard to questions of belief, conscience, and economic competition. Such a person believes that society should be protected against the possibility of repetitive depradations by socially maladjusted individuals, while his opposite believes that it is preferable that a guilty person be freed rather than to risk having an innocent person falsely convicted. Conflict between freedom and authority is perhaps the most fundamental of political issues, and it certainly does no violence to the usual understanding of political philosophers for us to assume that an ideological dimension of this content represents the political factor in Supreme Court decision-making. I denote the positive direction of this dimension as Libertarianism, and the negative direction (which corresponds to type Y) as Authoritarianism.

Z is the ideology of respondents who are political liberals and economic conservatives. Since we already have identified a social factor and a political factor, we might well assume that the remaining factor will represent an economic ideology. If we ask what economic ideology is reflected by attitudes of what (by contemporary standards) is conservatism in economics but liberalism in politics, the writings of Mill and Spencer come readily to mind; and if we think of a counter-ideology to economic and political *laissez-faire*, Karl Marx is the obvious spokesman. But the content of liberal ideology has been transformed;[13] the man who today believes with equal staunchness in the log-cabin myth of political liberty and in the Horatio Alger myth of rugged individualism is something of an anachronism; he is a *Nineteenth* (not a Twentieth) Century liberal. We may well call him an Individualist, and his counterpart (in the opposite direction of this dimension) a Collectivist. The Individualist admires eagles, the Collectivist admires colonies of ants. The Individualist admires the stock boy who rises from humble beginnings to become president of a giant corporation; the Collectivist admires labor unions and seniority systems for advancement in status.

Since Z is an ideology held by respondents whose attitudinal position is opposite to that of the Y type, we might question the necessity for identifying a third ideology, and consider designating the Z type as Libertarian. Stated otherwise, both Libertarians and Individualists are attitudinally $C+/E-$; and both Authoritarians and Collectivists are $C-/E+$. We know, however, that our empirical types (the political

[13] Kenneth R. Minogue, *The Liberal Mind* (New York: Random House, 1964), especially pp. 14–15 and Chapter 7.

conservatives and the economic conservatives) are not opposites; they are differentiated from each other by the content of the attitudinal variables. And we have assumed that Authoritarianism is a political ideology, while Individualism is an economic ideology: even though the two dimensions do have similar implications for attitudinal postures, it is not implausible that some respondents may conceptualize issues in terms of political relationships, while other respondents conceptualize the same issues in terms of economic relationships. Correspondingly, there is no inconsistency in the assumption that both the economic and the political scales are correlated with both the political and the economic factors; it has long been recognized that political ideologies have economic as well as political implications, and that economic ideologies have political as well as economic implications. Moreover, we can assume that the minor scales do not correlate as symmetrically with these two factors as do the major scales.

I now have described an ideal structure, or model of the structural relationships of respondents, their attitudes, and their ideologies in three-dimensional factorial space. We can summarize this model, in terms of the factorial dimensions, as follows: Equalitarianism/Traditionalism is the first reference axis, and it measures the extent to which justices believe in the desirability of changing the status quo in order to bring about a society in which there is greater equality of opportunity for all persons. (I pass over the question of the extent to which "natural" inequalities [defining "natural" as biological parameters] can limit the capacity of humans to take advantage of the expanded opportunities that could be made available through a more open society; in the ideology of social Equalitarianism, this, too, is a question which merits scientific investigation.) A second factorial dimension is Libertarianism/Authoritarianism, and this measures the extent to which justices believe in the importance of extending the scope of freedom as opposed to authority. The libertarian believes in both freedom of enterprise *and* freedom of speech, while the authoritarian believes in the desirability of a governmentally regulated market for both material goods and ideas. The other factorial dimension is Individualism/Collectivism, and this measures the extent of the belief that the most important ultimate interest is that of the individual human being, as distinguished from the interests of societies composed of interacting individuals.

Evidently, these three ideologies derive from the major conflicts in social theory of the past three centuries. The oldest ideology is Libertarianism, which reflects the credo of the Declaration of Independence and the French Revolution; Individualism is most conspicuously a product of the

Industrial Revolution and the Nineteenth Century; and Equalitarianism is the ideology of the social revolution of the Twentieth Century. Our three ideologies are also the counterparts of the three values which comprised the slogan of the French Revolution: *Liberté, Égalité, Fraternité*. It is not surprising that the sequence is different in Twentieth Century America; in part the change in emphasis may reflect the fact that the battles for political freedom and economic collectivism have largely been won in the United States, while the struggle for social equality remains the more controversial; or in part it may reflect the greater importance that Americans now place upon social equality and economic security over political freedom. If either or both of these assumptions should be true, we should expect that Supreme Court justices, as Americans and men of their age, would reflect, in their own ideological conflict within the Court, the major ideological conflicts to be found in American society.

Empirical Observations of the Factor Space

The model of the factorial space describes an ideal structure which is static and untroubled by errors of measurement or sampling differences. It may nevertheless be very useful as a guide to our understanding of the set of empirical factor spaces which we shall now examine, although we should recognize that these empirical observations are functions of several sources of variance which are not present, of course, in the model. For one thing, we deal now with a shifting population of eighteen respondents, not a static population of nine; and the real respondents who comprise the decision-making subset that we observe are a very different group at the end of the period from the groups that formed either at the beginning or during the middle of the period. Consequently, the empirical attitudinal types represented vary in their relative size and strength, and these variations naturally affect both the attitudinal and the ideological structure of the factor space. There were also changes in the political context of the society within which the Court acted during this period, as the nation moved from the close of World War II through the Cold War, the Korean War, McCarthyism, the school segregation crisis, the congressional attempts to "curb the Court" in 1957, the initial period of space exploration, and the brief era of the New Frontier. I am aware of such events, and I have every confidence that the justices were probably even more aware; but the only effect that they could have, in terms of the design of this research, is that of an additional source of variance. Sampling differences are another source of variance, since both the proportionate content and the relative

TABLE 30

Reference Factor Loadings for Judicial Ideal-Points, 1946–1962 Terms *

I	V	Wa	Bl	Re	F	D	Mu	J	i-points Ru	Bu	C	Mi	H	Br	Wh	S	BW	G
1946	−409		727	−229	−611	568	808	−476	611	−422	−467	−332						
1947	−347		741	−315	−455	712	783	−548	801	−476	−302	−490						
1948	−542		682	−467	−418	553	711	−663	779	−619	−291	−689						
1949	−177		658	−293	−578	952		−682		163	−510	−443						
1950	−555		202	−459	278	276		124		−201	−487	−116						
1951	−691		495	−350	439	401		122		068								
1952	−569		483	−311	366	615		−248		−269								
1953		−280	712	−624	111	607		−123		−632	162	−350						
1954		306	471	−334	−327	755				−648	150	−515	−404					
1955		837	882	−373	−268	801				−609	−248		−515					
1956		666	802	−514	−307	843				−673	−413		−608	371				
1957		822	870		−526	785				−559	−351		−658	458	−639			
1958		791	733		−684	874					−198		−655	596	−518	−495		
1959		689	776		−707	766					−519		−653	569	−745	−442		
1960		699	769		−736	754					−392		−714	578	−665	−289		
1961		769	689		−627	883							−668	514	−571	−267	−196	
1962		604	570			539					−313		−744	599	−430	−450	−493	159
II																		
1946	171		227	−453	207	−325	317	430	−133	−222								
1947	209		287	157	390	−375	340	113	317	−307								
1948	−418		−077	−503	520	−181	108	328	−053	−072								
1949	−388		092	−612	581	−246		547		−294	−336	−174						
1950	−349		−458	071	335	−444		434		218	−329	301						
1951	−160		−479	384	189	−219		310		392	−185	−057						
1952	−282		−063	173	422	−505		592		−193	−280	−154						
1953		−632	−469	122	371	−435		382		160	−567	152						
1954		−128	295	−785	523	280				061	−265	−465	769					

204

TABLE 30 (continued)

Reference Factor Loadings for Judicial Ideal-Point, 1946–1962 Terms*

i-points = columns J and Ru

II	V	Wa	Bl	Re	F	D	Mu	J	Ru	Bu	C	Mi	H	Br	Wh	S	BW	G
1955		−181	−124	−638	481	111				−430	−361	−542	576					
1956		247	147	−523	488	−051				295	−604		511	299	531			
1957		−173	−162		602	268				−187	−409		372	327	−124			
1958		−219	−091		−283	062					−287		−407	−137	231	313		
1959		−401	−293		−400	357					−359		−149	−227	094	211		
1960		−456	−259		−338	283					−245		−373	−298	065	126		
1961		074	149		370	−193					−514		485	138	268	280	−591	
1962		−541	−257			216					−550		100	−367		227	−244	456

III	V	Wa	Bl	Re	F	D	Mu	J	Ru	Bu	C	Mi	H	Br	Wh	S	BW	G
1946	−402		108	311	−271	−118	−026	475	−199	−166	−220							
1947	−441		−348	−493	535	−064	060	387	−071	−302	075							
1948	−222		−094	159	−046	086	−304	−171	−171	−274	194							
1949	−387		−325	215	171	−274		−187		243		118						
1950	−059		−347	368	−259	255		302		−152		−360						
1951	−155		−088	−368	178	−321		204		−134		235						
1952	420		306	−248	215	−171		330		−095	295	−253						
1953		−096	−208	−499	190	257		239		231	300	103						
1954		274	112	−281	333	−203				−154	137	261	271					
1955		317	302	−317	226	061				285	−265	146	105					
1956		−366	100	−174	132	240				−192	−447		184	−324	130			
1957		358	242		267	−201				−098	−343		336	−152	150			
1958		198	−191		111	−174					−248		053	458	218	309		
1959		149	062		081	061					−341		328	341	071	424		
1960		089	−130		270	170					−309		226	291	−108	363		
1961		−053	195		−217	−177					−222		−616	−136	487	147	186	
1962		395	−237			−266					−021		253	499		445	120	383

NOTE * Decimal points have been omitted; all values are three-place decimals. Since the direction of orthogonal factor axes extracted by the complete centroid method is arbitrary, the polarity has been reversed for the indicated factors in the italicized terms, in order to facilitate uniformity in inter-term comparisons of scale axis relationships in the factor spaces shown in Figure 10.

extremity of the stimuli fluctuated from term to term. Not least, there are all of the sources of measurement variance that I previously have denoted, and particularly in Chapter 4.

In accordance with my stated assumption that there may be changes in both the attitudinal and ideological structure of the empirical factor space, the task of interpretation will be to examine such changes in relationship to the ideal structure postulated by the model. For example, the identification of the first factor as Equalitarianism, and the denoted correlations between the two major scales and this factor, depended upon the assumption that there would be four justices who were liberal on both scales; we could hardly expect the first factor to be the same if there were only one or two such justices on the Court. Consequently, we shall discuss the construction of the factor spaces, initially, in terms of numbered factors (rather than in terms of designated ideologies), because the association of factors with particular ideological dimensions must await analysis of the relationships manifest in the term factor spaces.

Let us first consider the loadings of the justices upon the factorial reference axes. These are reported in Table 30: The factors are designated by Roman numerals (*I, II, III*). As the footnote to the table explains, I have reversed the direction of all loadings on those factors for which the year numeral is italicized; this, in effect, reverses the direction of these axes, and is necessary in order to give them psychological consistency, since the directions assigned by statistical criteria have no psychological significance. The extent to which the statistical criteria for directionality really is arbitrary is exemplified by observing that, of the total of fifty-one axes, twenty-six had to be reversed; it would be impossible to come closer to a chance division. Each respondent is uniquely represented by an ideal-point in the factor space for each term, by the loading that he has on each of the three factorial reference axes for the term. So the loadings of Table 30 uniquely determine the configuration of *i*-points in the factor space for each of the seventeen terms, in relation to an orthogonal set of reference axes. The factor loadings are the result of the analysis of the phi correlation matrices, by the complete centroid method of factor analysis, as explained in Chapter 3.

The next step in building the structure of the factor space is to determine the position of the scale axes which are analogues to the cumulative scales discussed in Chapter Five. The procedure by means of which the position of the scale axes is determined was explained in Chapter 3, and requires the solution of Equation (5) for alpha, beta, and gamma values. These values, for both the C and E scales in every term, and for the F and N scales in selected terms, are reported in Table 31.

TABLE 31

Coordinates for Scale Axis Termini, 1946–1962 Terms *

Term	C+			E+					
	I/α	II/β	III/γ	I/α	II/β	III/γ	I/α	II/β	III/γ
1946	1.00	.20	.50	1.00	−.20	−.13			
1947	1.00	.00	.90	1.00	−.20	−.30			
1948	1.00	.20	−.10	1.00	−.30	−.20			
1949	.60	1.00	.00	1.00	−.50	−.75		*N+*	
1950	1.00	−.20	−.25	.20	−1.00	−.18	−.45	−.85	1.00
1951	1.00	−.65	−.30	.10	−1.00	−.65		*F+*	
1952	1.00	−.15	.40	.50	−1.00	−.20	−1.00	−.25	.10
1953	1.00	.10	.60	1.00	−1.00	−.75			
1954	1.00	1.00	.40	1.00	−.35	.00			
1955	1.00	.60	.20	1.00	−.50	−.85			
1956	1.00	.50	1.00	1.00	−.50	−.30			
1957	1.00	.70	.39	1.00	−.65	−.85	.60	−1.00	−.40
1958	1.00	1.00	−.20	1.00	.10	−.30			
1959	1.00	.05	.30	1.00	−.10	−.10	−.10	−1.00	−.22
1960	1.00	.15	.43	1.00	−.86	−.47	.08	−1.00	−.25
1961	1.00	.30	.25	1.00	−.80	−.50			
1962	1.00	.10	−.35	1.00	−.65	−1.00			

NOTE * These are equivalent to the weights for solving Equation (5).

We can observe that both C and E are maximally correlated with the first factor *(I)*, in all terms except during the four-year period 1949–52: this in itself suggests that the ideological content represented by *I* may be different during that period from what it was both prior and subsequent to then. We may also note that, except during that four-year period, C is usually positively correlated with both *II* and *III:* in none of the remaining dozen terms is C negatively correlated with *II,* and in only three of these terms does C correlate negatively with *III.* E, on the other hand, is negatively correlated with *II* in all except a single term, and it is maximally negatively correlated with *II* only in the four terms 1950–53; E also is negatively correlated with *III* in all except one of the seventeen terms. In the three terms in which F scales (other than during the 1952 Term), it is maximally negatively correlated with *II,* and negatively correlated with *III,* although it maintains no consistent relationship with *I.*

The empirical factorial structures consist of three elements, in each instance: a set of three orthogonal reference axes, a set of nine (or, in two terms, ten) ideal-points which represent the attitudinal positions of the justices, and a set of two (or, in five terms, three) scale axes. The judicial ideal-points are designated by the initial of the respondent's surname, and where more than one respondent would have the same initial, the second letter of his surname is added: this differentiated among all of the justices at the time the research was designed, but the appointment of Byron White in place of Whittaker posed a problem which was resolved by using for White both his first and last initial. I would have preferred to have constructed physical models of the seventeen factorial structures, and to have photographed them in color; lacking the means to do this, I have fallen back upon two-dimensional perspectives of such a three-dimensional physical structure; these are photographed, but in black-and-white. It requires three such two-dimensional perspectives to attempt to represent each factorial structure, since each axis can be paired with each of the others. All of the data necessary for the construction of the two-dimensional perspectives are reported in Tables 30 and 31; these same data, incidentally, would of course suffice also for the construction of a physical three-dimensional model.

I shall henceforth refer to the two-dimensional perspectives and the three-dimensional structure as "factor spaces." The set of three views of the factor space, for each of the seventeen terms, is presented in Figure 10. In each set, the sequence of perspectives is as follows: *I* and *II*, *I* and *III*, and *II* and *III*. These perspectives are equivalent to what one could expect to observe if he were to examine a cubical physical structure from three points of view: from the top, from the (front) side, and from the (right) end. Characteristically, as in the 1946 Term, the C-scale axis passes from a point in the front of and below *I* through the origin to a point to the rear of and above *I;* that is, from the third through the fifth octants. The E-scale axis passes from a point to the rear of and above *I* through the origin to a point in the front of and below *I;* that is, from the sixth through the fourth octants. In ten of the terms, including the first one, the first factor is approximately the centroid (or arithmetic mean) of the C and E scale axes.

Before proceeding to an interpretation of the factor spaces, it is necessary to establish a basis for confidence that the denoted scale axes are indeed the equivalent of the linear cumulative scales that were discussed in Chapter 5. I have posited a statistical test of this relationship, by means of rank correlation. In order to make that test, it is necessary to calculate precisely

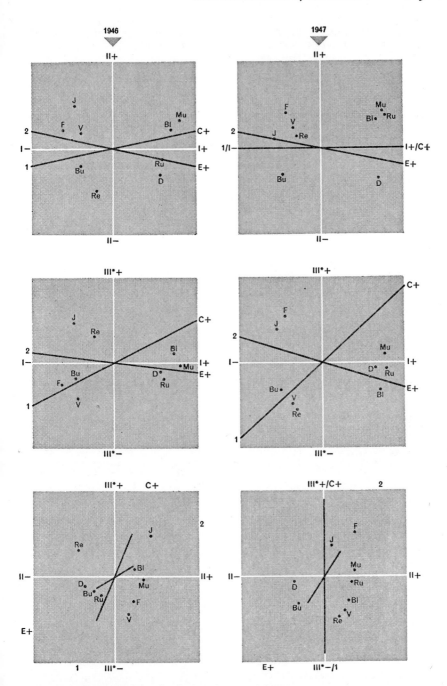

FIGURE 10. The Factor Spaces, 1946–1962 Terms

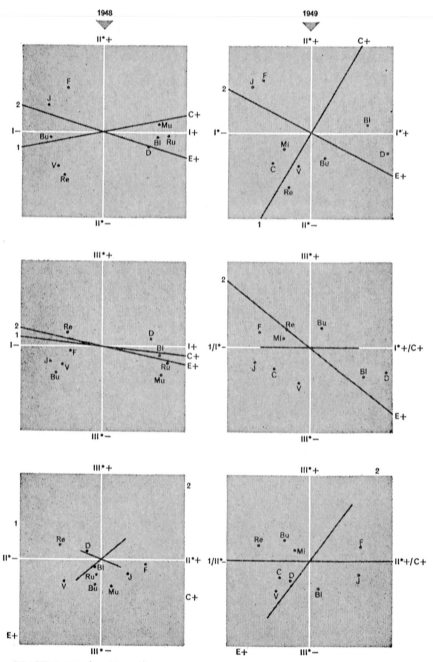

FIGURE 10. (continued)

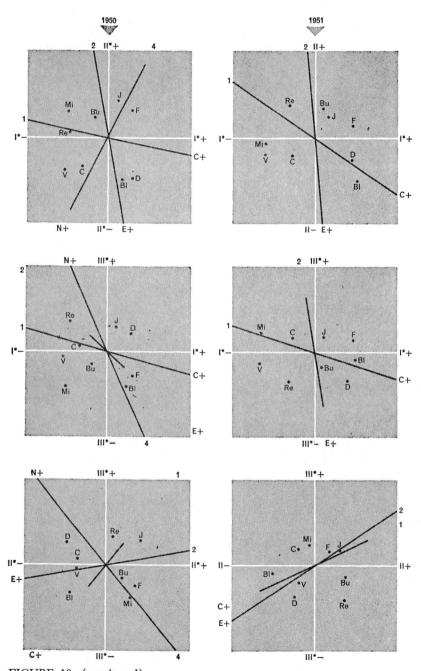

FIGURE 10. (continued)

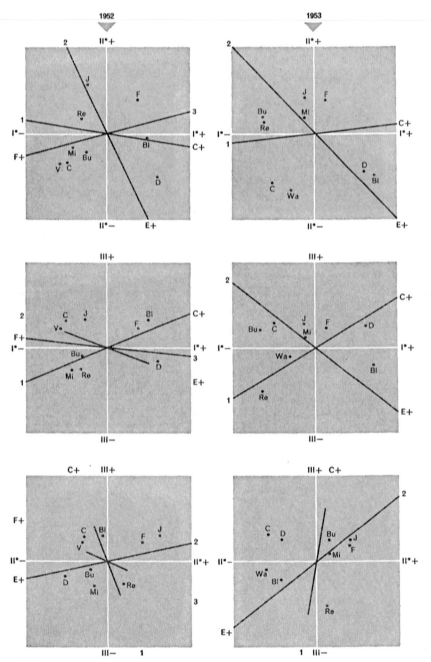

FIGURE 10. (continued)

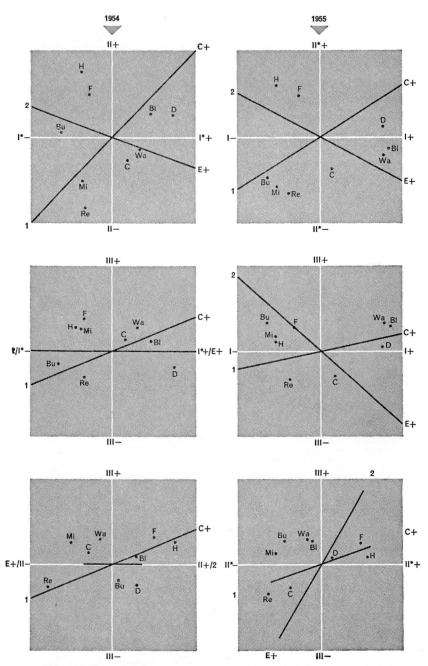

FIGURE 10. (continued)

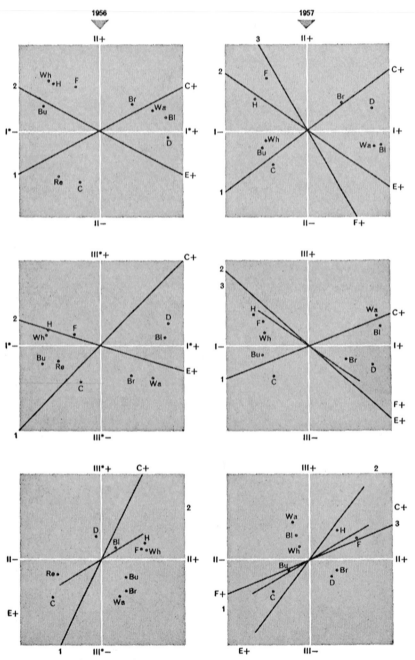

FIGURE 10. (continued)

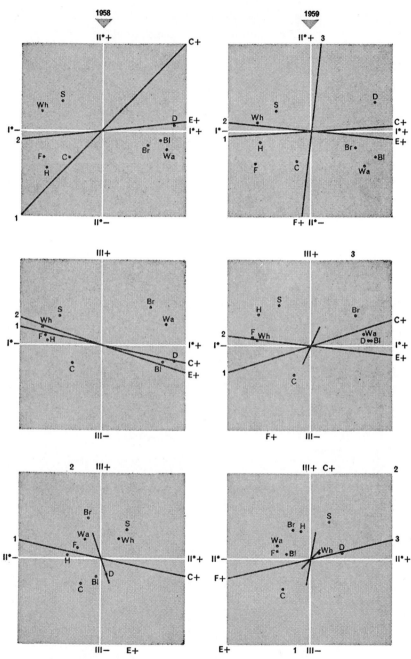

FIGURE 10. (continued)

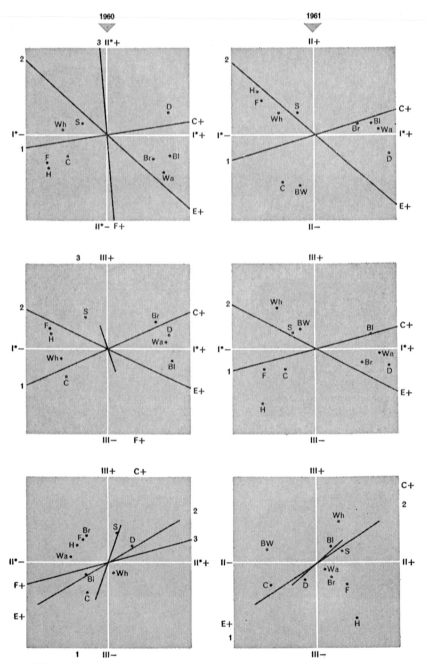

FIGURE 10. (continued)

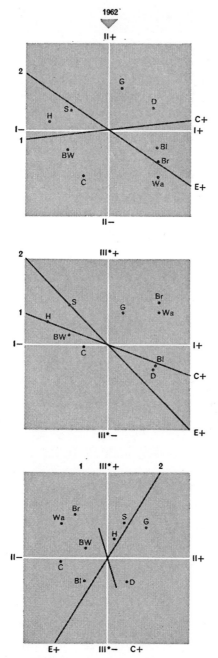

FIGURE 10. (continued)

TABLE 32

Ideal-point Projections on Scale Axes, 1946–1962 Terms *

C+

	Mu	Ru	D	Bl	Wa	Br	G	S	BW	Wh (i-points)	F	J	H	Bu	Mi	Re	C	V
1946	756	427	391	428							−621	−134		−484		−144		−507
1947	622	548	486	318							020	−148		−556		−564		−553
1948	745	767	496	660							−302	−566		−591		−569		−589
1949			279	417							201	118		−168	−320	−676	−528	−424
1950			287	362							263	−036		−197	−438	−538	−243	−448
1951			520	677							214	−114		−119	−587	−398	−186	−439
1952			572	565							357	−188		−256	−479	−491	−322	−396
1953			613	462	−342						224	050		−408	−033	−778	−311	
1954			649	552	196						224		322	−441	−484	−838	−033	
1955			744	734	669						056		−125	−685	−685	−692	−101	
1956			705	650	282	131				−162	046		−112	−478		−633	−665	
1957			702	658	643	494		−171		−430	−008		−218	−564			−638	
1958			679	476	373	257		−291		−391	−693		−751				−412	
1959			767	746	683	631		−104		−611	−673		−538				−304	
1960			791	614	609	599		−136		−553	−610		−612				−627	
1961			727	729	725	486		−548	−304	−212	−531		−630				−560	
1962			614	589	387	364	066		−526				−773				−339	

E+

	Mu	Bl	Ru	D	Wa	Br	C	V	BW	G	S	Mi	Re	Bu	F	J	H	Wh
1946	728	649	645	631				−380					−174	−346	−600	−607		
1947	656	741	714	758				−241					−187	−305	−652	−646		
1948	696	681	780	555				−350					−327	−510	−531	−684		
1949				951			−100	084				−248	−110	095	−740	−606		
1950				438			246	240				−323	−221	−223	−225	−448		
1951				391			025	160				−138	−150	−249	−218	−360		
1952				745			−030	−044				−015	−246	068	−248	−689		
1953				531	265		−091					−216	−232	−603	−251	−427		
1954				619	331		240					−177	−056	−631	−481		−635	

TABLE 32 (continued)

Ideal-point Projections on Scale Axes, 1946–1962 Terms *

E+	Mu	Bl	Ru	D	Wa	Br	C	V	BW	G	S	Mi	Re	Bu	F	J	H	Wh
1955		489		494	469		396					−262	153	−453	−499		−635	−815
1956		603		688	563	275	162						−173	−659	−510		−810	−386
1957		525		534	430	256	099							−242	−781		−809	
1958		745		889	677	424	−291				−531				−711		−678	−751
1959		791		717	707	552	−127				−500				−668		−664	−674
1960		752		308	749	498	−116				−406				−409		−357	
1961		344		819	536	343	095		134		−411				−592		−544	−411
1962		626		427	360	218	039		−292	−334	−670						−682	−646

F+	V	C	Wa	Bl	Br	Re	Mi	Wh	S	Bu	F	J	H
1952	648	595		−426	237		445		300	−494	−440	130	−731
1957		242	424	476	007		−200			230	−831		
1959		441	291	196	092	−253	−043		−089	−434	440		138
1960		272	474	341	263	−232	−081			−256	205		251

N+	Re	D	C	V	Bl	J	Bu	Mi	F
1950	371	366	354	351	−035	−088	−178	−285	−482

NOTE: * Decimal points have been omitted; all values are three-place decimals.

the intercepts where the ideal-points will project upon the scale axes in the three-dimensional factor spaces. It is also of interest to observe how they will project in the two-dimensional spaces, although none of these perspectives, taken alone, conveys an impression of depth; but it is possible to perceive the three-dimensional relationships by comparing the three views of the structure for each term. (As I stated in Chapter 3, the two-dimensional spaces are useful, prior to the determination of the positions of scale axes, for making initial estimates of the alpha, beta, and gamma values for which a solution is sought.) The calculation of the projections from the ideal-points is a by-product of the determination of the position of the scale axes, since the factor loadings for the justices are the known values of x, y, and z that are substituted in the set of simultaneous equations (each of which is in the form of formula [4]) that must be solved for alpha, beta, and gamma: the procedure is to compute the *d* values, one for each of the justices, using estimated values of alpha, beta, and gamma. The *d* value for each justice is the point on the scale axis at which his ideal-point is closest to (projects orthogonally upon) the axis. The ranking of the justices, according to their *d* values, then is compared with the scale ranking; the alpha-beta-gamma values are then modified in order to improve the correlation between the two sets of rankings, and a new set of *d*'s is computed. This process continues until no further positive increase in the rank correlation appears to be possible. The data for the criterion cumulative scales are reported in Figures 1 and 3; the final sets of *d*'s, which result from the use of the factor loadings reported in Table 30 and the scale axis coordinates reported in Table 31, are reported in Table 32.

The rankings of the respondents on the scale axes can easily be determined from observation of Table 32, and I shall not bother to list them. Similarly, the rankings of the respondents on the corresponding term scales can be determined by observing Figures 1 and 3. Kendall's tau was used to compute the rank correlation coefficients, with the results reported in Table 33.

The table shows that the average correlation for both scales is about the same, and is well above the criterion level of .90 that I had postulated. The correlation for the C scale was above the criterion level in twelve of the individual terms, and that for E was above it in ten terms. In only one instance (C in 1959) did the correlation for either scale variable fall below .80; while in four terms, the correlation for C was either prefect or within a single tie in ranks of being so, with values of 1.00 or .99; and E had

TABLE 33

Correlations between Respondent Ranks on Scales and Scale Axes, 1946–1962 Terms *

Variable: Term:	C Tau	C Significance level	E Tau	E Significance level	Tau	Significance level
1946	89	0^312	99	$<0^425$		
1947	97	0^425	89	0^312		
1948	87	$<0^343$	93	$<0^312$		
1949	94	0^425	86	0^343	*N*	
1950	93	$<0^312$	83	0^343	90	$<0^343$
1951	94	0^425	86	0^343	*F*	
1952	99	$<0^425$	89	0^312	74	0^229
1953	94	0^425	100	0^528		
1954	97	0^425	92	0^312		
1955	97	0^425	99	$<0^425$		
1956	99	$<0^528$	96	0^528	*F*	
1957	100	0^528	94	0^425	65	<012
1958	89	0^312	100	0^528	*F*	
1959	78	0^212	94	0^425	75 *F*	0^229
1960	99	$<0^425$	82	$<0^212$	78	$<0^229$
1961	91	0^415	87	0^458		
1962	83	0^343	99	$<0^425$		
Average	93		92		73 (*F*)	

NOTE * Decimal points have been omitted; the rank correlations all are two-place decimals, and the initial zero of each probability index is preceded by a decimal.

correlations of .99 or 1.00 in five terms. In none of the terms did both scales fall below the criterion level of .90; while there are several terms in which both are quite high—e.g., 1955, when C was .97 and E was .99.

It should be noted that the occasional instances in which the Court grouped for common disposition sets of cases, the decisions of which led to scale error, tended to bias the factor spaces more than the cumulative scales. The result was to lower the correlation between the relevant scale/scale-axis pairs. In two instances which I shall use to exemplify the problem, the distortion produced by the multiple-case decisions was enhanced by my own (analyst) error, when the decision was represented by only a single case on the cumulative scale (although the set of cases for each of these decisions was included in the four-fold tables) : these instances are 329 U. S.

14:12, in the 1946 C Scale; and 333 U. S. 683:23, at the bottom of the 1947 E scale. The first decision entailed scale errors for both Rutledge and Jackson, and there were seven other cases (329 U. S. 14:13–19) which should have been included in the scale; their inclusion would bring about a slight drop in both the R and S coefficients, and it would make even more extreme the differences between positive and negative scale scores, but it would not affect the scale ranks other than to transpose Black and Rutledge. The second decision was one in which Burton dissented alone; and there were eleven other cases in the decision set (333 U. S. 683:24–34) : here the result of including these cases in the scale would be to put Burton in the last rank, leaving the R coefficient the same and raising slightly the value of S. Douglas and Jackson each would receive eleven additional asterisks for non-participation; and the scale scores for the three most negative respondents (Jackson, Frankfurter, and Burton) would be further separated from those of the others. But the effect of the inclusion of these multiple cases can be observed as much more dramatic in the factor plots of Figure 10: it will be observed that the three C+ dissenters in the 1946 decision (Murphy, Black, and Jackson) are assigned the highest positive loadings on Factor *II;* while in the 1947 decision, the E— dissenter (Burton) and the two non-participants (Douglas and Jackson) are assigned the two negative loadings and the lowest positive loading on *II*. Although I erred in not following my own prescribed procedure by including in their respective scales the complete sets of cases for these decisions, what I am really questioning here is the wisdom of the procedure in view of the distorting effect it can produce upon the factorial measurements.[14]

There is no particular point in dwelling upon the significance data; all of the probabilities are quite small, with the largest value for chance occurrence, for either scale, about one in a thousand, and the smallest less than one chance in thirty thousand. Since we observe the simultaneous sets of rankings for both scales, in relationship to the same configuration of *i*-points, the probability in which we are more interested is the likelihood that both scale axes could have been so positioned by chance, and this joint probability is the product of the probability for the C-scale variable, and for the E-scale variable, for each term. In the 1950 Term, when N scaled as well as C and E, the joint probability for having a configuration of *i*-points, produced by chance, that would project simultaneously upon all three scale axes so that the resulting rankings would be as consistent, with the scale

---

[14] For a statement of the considerations in favor of the procedure, see Schubert, *Quantitative Analysis of Judicial Behavior*, pp. 164–166.

ranks, as we can observe, would be less than $.0^{10}2$, or between one in a billion and one in a trillion. If we had an unlimited supply of four-digit numbers, ranging from $+1.000$ through 0.000 to -1.000, and were to draw ordered sets of twenty-seven numbers (to use as the Cartesian coordinates, one for each of three factors, for each of nine justices) to define the i-point configuration, no human being could expect to live long enough to draw as well-fitting a point configuration by chance, even if we assume that he draws one number a second from the moment of his birth until his death seventy years later, and never sleeps, eats, et cetera; seventy years is only about 2.2 billion seconds, and a person would have to exist 2,500 *times* longer in order to expect to match the probability. Evidently, this is the kind of mundane task which, if it were to be done at all—as I seriously doubt—should be done by an electronic computer. Obviously, these joint probabilities are very small numbers, and it hardly seems possible to me that anyone would accept the chance hypothesis, in relationship to these data. My conclusion is that I cannot reject my major hypothesis, which is that the scale axes in the factor spaces are the same psychological dimensions, and represent the same attitudinal measurements, as the corresponding linear cumulative scales of political liberalism and economic liberalism.

In the next chapter, I shall present further evidence, based upon curvilinear relationships between scales and the point configurations, which supports the finding that the scale axes measure the same psychological relationships among the respondents, and in the same way, as do the scales. But I am going to assume that the finding has been sufficiently supported already so that we can proceed to interpret the factorial reference axes in terms of their ideological significance. I have accepted the hypothesis that the point configuration is a function of the attitudinal syndromes of the justices. Empirically, two-thirds of the variance among the respondents' attitudinal syndromes can be accounted for by the measurements of their attitudes toward political liberalism and economic liberalism. The question now is, working primarily with the two major scales, which I have added to the point configuration in the factor spaces, can we fit these empirical data to the ideal structure which consists of ideological dimensions, scale axes, and the (X, Y, and Z) respondent types discussed earlier in this chapter?

Table 34 presents our findings, which we shall now discuss. In the ensuing discussion I shall use the concept "scales" to refer to both cumulative scales and scale axes, since I have assumed these to provide equivalent

TABLE 34

Factor Ideologies, 1946–62 Terms

Term	Equalitarianism	Libertarianism	Individualism
1946	I+	III+	II+
1947	I+	III+	II+
1948	I+	III+	II+
1949		II+	I−
1950		I+	II+
1951		I+	II+
1952		I+	II+
1953		I+	II+
1954		II+	I−
1955	I+	II+	III+
1956	I+	III+	II+
1957	I+	II+	III+
1958	I+	II+	III+
1959	I+	II+	III+
1960	I+	II+	III+
1961	I+	III+	II+
1962	I+	II+	III+

sets of measurements, and that either will lead to the same interpretation of the factor spaces. The most obvious relationship in the factor spaces is one to which we already have referred: (1) the positive first-factor correlations of justices who have the highest scores on both scales and (2) the negative first-factor correlations of all other justices, except during the period 1949–55. All of the justices whom I classified in the liberal scale type (Murphy, Rutledge, Douglas, Black, Warren, and Brennan) are always positively correlated with Factor *I,* with the solitary exception of Warren during his first term (1953) on the Court. Moreover, these positive correlations always are moderate or high, except for the 1950 Term, when Douglas, Black, Frankfurter, and Jackson all had low positive correlations with Factor *I.* Both of the above exceptions occurred during the period 1949–55; the other instances of positive correlation with Factor *I,* by justices whom I have classified in the other two scale types, also occur during this period and are as follows: two of the economic conservatives, Frankfurter in 1950–53 and Jackson in 1950–51 only; and two of the political conservatives, Burton in 1949 and 1951, and Clark in 1954–55. The Clark and Warren exceptions, however, can be seen in a quite different light from the others. The exceptions involving Frankfurter, Jackson, and Burton all result from the circumstance that Factor I does not represent the same ideology during 1949–54 as it does during the other terms; while the exception involving Clark in 1954 and 1955 reflects what was certainly a change in his behavior, what was probably a change in his attitudes, but which I very much doubt was due to any change in his ideology. Indeed, it is precisely because ideologies, although more generalized structures of belief, are also more stable structures even than attitudes, that I explain Clark's aberrant behavior during these two terms as his flirtation with Warren during the latter's honeymoon with the Court. (The ideological incompatibility was too great for this affair to last, contrary to several other conspicuously enduring affinities, such as Frankfurter with both Jackson and Harlan, or Douglas with Black.) I count Warren's as the same kind of an exception as Clark's, because of the change in his attitudinal position toward political liberalism during 1953–55.

I have inferred that the first factor, during 1946–48 and 1955–62, was the Equalitarian ideology. During all of these terms, both C and E are maximally correlated with Factor I, and except during 1955, there were four liberals on the Court, and the liberals formed the plurality subset of justices. During 1946–48, the four liberals gave consistent (though generally unsuccessful) support to the positive values of both major scales, and during this period, the second factor was Individualism and the third was Libertarianism. However, several of the minor variables have a much larger influence upon the factorial structure in these first three terms than they had in subsequent terms. The C scale was especially weak in its influence in the first term, when there were more cases on F and over twice as many on E; and evidently the F scale is highly and negatively correlated with the second factor, and it is negatively correlated with the third factor. Otherwise stated, Individualism implies a considerable amount of hostility to governmental fiscal authoritary in this term, and Authoritarianism is reflected not only in upholding the government (state or national) in cases raising claims of political freedom, but also it is reflected in attitudes favoring the government against fiscal claims. In 1948, F, N, and A together include more cases than either C or E.

During 1955, there were only three liberals (Douglas, Black, and Warren), and there were three political conservatives and two economic conservatives, but Clark's moderate behavior during this term generally supported the new liberal ideological subset of three; and under these circumstances, a subset of three liberals plus one protégé was sufficiently influential, in the decision-making in these terms, to cause Equalitarianism to re-emerge, after six terms of sublimation, as the dominant ideology on the Court.

What had happened, during the hiatus of the 1949–54 terms, to cause the temporary disappearance of Equalitarianism as a significant dimension of the Court's decision-making? Chance events had occurred in such a way as to redefine drastically and suddenly the parameters of the attitudes represented on the Court. Both Murphy and Rutledge, probably the two most liberal justices ever to be members of the Court, died during the summer vacation between the 1948 and 1949 Terms; while Douglas, who was seriously injured in a fall from horseback during the vacation, was absent during most of the 1949 Term, participating in only a fifth of the decisions measured by the term C and E scales. So the most important attitudinal type in June 1949 was the type represented by the fewest votes in October 1949: only Black remained, while there were two economic conservatives and no fewer than *five* political conservatives, as a consequence of additional Truman accretions to the Court—four of these five were appointees of President Truman. It is hardly surprising, under these circumstances, that a drastic change should have taken place in the factorial structure. Collectivism became the new dominant ideology of the Court; and it emerged because Black joined with the political conservatives—who were moderate in their attitude toward the economic variable—to have the Court decide an exceptionally large proportion of cases whose attitudinal content was economic and fiscal rather than political. As Table 21 shows, this was the only term in which C and E together provided less than half of the total semantic content; and C provided less than either E or F in this term. I infer that with no chance of getting the Court to advance the cause of political liberalism, Black quite rationally decided to exercise as much influence as he could by directing the built-in majority to as favorable a course as possible on the economic issue. There were only four decisions in the entire term in which majorities favorable to political liberalism formed; and the technical reason why F could not be scaled—there was an ample number of decisions—was that fifteen of the twenty-one F scale decisions consisted of divisions in which Black dissented alone, or with Douglas, against the rest of the Court. Quite to the contrary, sixteen of the twenty-two E-scale cases were decided liberally, and Black voted in favor of every one of them. And a comparison of the C scale with the factor space for 1949 shows just as clearly that Factor *II* is Libertarianism: Frankfurter and Jackson have high positive correlations, while the remaining justices who were negative on Factor *I* are also negative on Factor *II;* and Black is positive while Burton is negative.

There certainly is room for more error variance in the denotation of Douglas' *i*-point than for the other respondents, in view of his low degree of response; his exceptionally high loading on Factor *I* doubtless reflects his 6–0 voting record on the E scale, but we should expect his 3–0 voting in C scale cases to result in his being positively correlated with Factor *II,* and the apparent reason that this does not occur is that Factor *II* also is a function of the minor scales, and Douglas happened to participate in more such decisions than in those on C and E. His three C+ votes certainly were outweighed, in the factor extraction, by his fifteen votes in cases that did not relate to either of the two major scales.

The available evidence is insufficient to guide an inference as to the ideological content of Factor *III*. Clearly, it is not Equalitarianism. I perceive no consistent relationship between Factor *III* and the two major scales (either in this term, or in the next five that follow). Since only two scales for minor variables are available during the period 1949-54—N in 1950 and F in 1952—and quasi-scales cannot be assumed to provide reliable evidence, I conclude that the ideological content of the third factor during this period is unknown, and probably is unascertainable on the basis of my data. It is possible, of course, that during these half dozen terms the third factor represents another ideology (or other ideologies) relating to the minor scale variables. We might assume that when Equalitarianism disappeared because too few respondents were present effectively to raise the issue of social change it implied that then the justices gave greater emphasis to Libertarianism-Authoritarianism and to Individualism-Collectivism and turned to other issues which involved different ideological implications. In order to make this point explicit, let us take the 1949 Term as an example: in accordance with the interpretation of his behavior that I already have stated, Black could not remain overtly committed to the Equalitarian ideology and cooperate effectively with the five political conservatives; so he had to sublimate that issue—not in terms of his beliefs, but in terms of his overt behavior—during the 1949 Term, at least. Most emphatically, the ideologies that I impute to the factors are not direct measurements of the beliefs of the justices; they are approximations which I have induced as logical correlates of judicial attitudinal measurements; and the latter measures are inferences based upon direct observations of the behavior of the justices. So we can identify factor ideologies

only as functions of manifest behavior; we can note their temporary disappearance from the factorial structures, and explain this in terms of the
Newtonian concept of balance and the Freudian concept of sublimation;
and we can infer from the reappearance of such a factor ideology, just
as soon as the manifest behavior makes *statistically* possible its presence,
that our interpretation probably is correct. I cannot prove that Black and
Douglas continued to believe in Equalitarianism (and the remaining justices in Traditionalism) during the several terms in which Black and
Douglas could do nothing much to advance their belief—and during
which the Traditionalists *did not have to do anything* in order to advance
their belief; however, I think the evidence in support of this interpretation
is persuasive.

During the 1949 and 1954 Term, E+ was maximally correlated with
$I+$, and C+ was maximally correlated with $II+$; during the intervening
four terms, it was C+ that was maximal with $I+$ and E+ with $II-$. I
have inferred that the $I+$ represents Libertarianism and that $II+$ represents Individualism during the 1950–53 Terms; and that $I+$ is Collectivism and $II+$ is Libertarianism, in 1954 just as in 1949. A detailed
comparison of the scales with the factors for each of the 1950–53 terms
shows that $I+$ is differentiating among respondents according to their E-
scale scores. During the 1950 Term, the N scale is maximally loaded on the
third (and unknown) factor, and it is also highly correlated with $II-$ and
moderately correlated with $I-$. It certainly is intuitively plausible that an
attitude of preference of national over state interests should be highly
collectivistic and moderately authoritarian in its implications; and the fact
that such an attitude is loaded primarily on the third factor might lead us
to infer that whatever other ideology that may represent, it is not one of
the principal ideological components of the contemporary liberal mind.
The maximal correlation of F+ with $I-$ in 1952, and the low correlations
of F+ with the other two factors, suggests that at this time, the Authoritarian ideology was the major influence upon the attitudes of the justices
who voted to uphold the position of the government in conflicts with
citizens over the administration of federal taxation. The justices most
sympathetic to the government's position were the political conservatives
who also upheld the position of the government in conflicts with civil liberties claimants.

If we compare the factor spaces for the first two factors in 1952 and 1953,
it is notable that the eight respondents who were on the Court in 1952 are
in about the same relative positions in 1953: Douglas and Black are alone

in the fourth quadrant; Frankfurter is alone in the first; Jackson is in the second; Clark is in the third; and Burton, Minton, and Reed are negative on Factor I and have very low loadings on Factor II. In 1952, Vinson is in the third quadrant and closest to Clark; and in 1953, Warren (who replaced Vinson as Chief Justice) also is in the third quadrant and closest to Clark. To be in the third quadrant, with the ideologies that I have identified with the first two factors for both of these terms, classifies a respondent as an authoritarian collectivist. These may seem harsh words to apply to a Chief Justice who in recent years has been roundly and widely assailed, by practically every leading conservative spokesman in the United States, as a militant liberal for whom horse-whipping would probably be too good, and impeachment only just. But we are concerned here not with Warren's public reputation as Chief Justice, or even (at the moment) with his behavior in recent terms. He ranked third on the E scale in 1953, and there has been no indication of any subsequent change in his quite liberal attitude toward the economic variable. But he also ranked seventh on the C scale in 1953, and voted to uphold the claims of only four petitioners in the nineteen decisions involving the political variable in which he participated. Such a voting record accords precisely with the attribution of ideological attachment that is denoted for Warren by his position in the 1953 I/II factor space: primarily a collectivist with strong authoritarian leanings. If such a description does not reflect his true beliefs at that time, it does describe the inference that one ought logically to make about his ideology, judging on the basis of his voting behavior. It may be that the attitudes that he expressed in his behavior were inconsistent with his self-image of his ideology, and that he was the first to discover this after a term or two of experience during which he came better to understand the implications of his new role. He came to the Court with considerable political experience, but the closest he had previously come to being a judge was his service as Attorney General of California. Clark, incidentally, was the Attorney General of the United States at the time of his promotion to the Court, so he and Warren had at least one thing in common: both had been public prosecutors. One might even say, in Veblenian terms, that experience as a public prosecutor could result in a trained incapacity to oppose the government in criminal cases, at least until the subject had experienced a period of retraining. But too much should not be made of this speculation: Murphy also had been Attorney General, Reed had been Solicitor General, and Jackson had been both Solicitor General and then Attorney General; Murphy ranks at the top, Jackson in the middle, and Reed at the bottom of the general scale of political liberalism. It is also possible that in spite of his extensive political experience, Warren never had had a previous occasion to construct for himself a consistent ideology that was relevant to making decisions on the kind of issues that characteristically confront the Supreme Court, and that when we observe his position in the spaces defined by the first and second factors for the 1953–55 Terms, we are accorded a glimpse into the dynamics of the building of the judicial character of a politician—or, as some might prefer to put it, the political character of a Chief Justice of the United States Supreme Court. But all of the above remarks are mere speculation, since the reasons for Warren's change lie beyond the scope of my design, investigation, and data. What is significant here is that Warren clearly did change, permanently (within the time limits of this study), and that Clark changed, but only temporarily, for the next two terms. Thus, the factorial structures confirm in detail the findings, based upon analysis of the C scale in Chapter 5, concerning Warren's conversion to political liberalism and Clark's diversion from political conservatism. When we observe the first and second factor spaces for 1949–52, we can see that Vinson always was close to Clark, and that Vinson's position always was more politically conservative than Clark's; so to the extent that Chief Justice Vinson had any influence upon Clark's attitude toward civil liberties, it must have been to pull Clark toward the authoritarian pole of the axis (*II*— in 1949, and *I*— in 1950–52). When we observe the equivalent spaces for 1953–56, we see that Warren initially assumed in 1953 a position next to Clark (but, contrary to that of Vinson, in the more politically liberal direction); in 1954 Warren and Clark remained about as close together as in the previous term, but now both had moved to a positive position on the first factor—and the whole factorial structure, including the other *i*-points and the scale axes, appears to have rotated counter-clockwise, as though in accommodation to the apparent change in the attitude of Warren and Clark in the direction of a more moderate posture toward political liberalism. Although Warren's and Clark's change was in the right direction to bring about the reappearance of the Equalitarian ideology, it was not sufficiently extreme to bring about that result in 1954. Instead, the quarter-turn counter-clockwise rotation of the structure was reciprocal to the clockwise quarter-turn that had occurred in 1949, and resulted in the same ideological relations as obtained in that term. Collectivism changed from *II*— (in 1953) to *I*+, and Libertarianism changed from *I*+ (in 1953) to *II*+. It should be noted that the general relationships of scales to *i*-points and ideologies did not change in these two terms; but evidently the change of two justices, from moderate to positive support for economic liberalism and from negative to moderate support for political liberalism, was enough to change the factorial structure back to a position in which it would be appropriate for Equalitarianism to emerge—provided the other condition, an increase in the number of justices who were liberal on both scales, were to be met. In short, I view the factorial structure of the 1949 and 1954 terms as transitional between the relatively conservative structure of the 1950–53 Terms (in which the Authoritarian ideology was dominant), and the relatively liberal structures of 1946–48 (in which the Traditionalist ideology was dominant) and 1955–62 (in which the Equalitarian ideology was dominant).

In 1955, Warren and Clark both remained positive in their support of economic liberalism and Clark remained moderate toward political liberalism, but Warren increased his support for political liberalism to a positive position; and in this term, the first three ranks on both scales were filled by Douglas, Black, and Warren. As the space for the first two factors for this term shows, the resulting structure was (in relationship to the two most important dimensions) almost perfectly balanced, except for Clark: the three liberals (Douglas, Black, and Warren) all had high loadings on $I+$ and are bunched midway between the scales; the three political conservatives are clustered in the third quadrant near the middle of the negative segment of the C scale, and the two economic conservatives are together in the second quadrant, near the middle of the negative segment of the E scale. Clark is the respondent closest to the origin (and therefore the one who was most moderate toward both scales in this term), and his position in the fourth quadrant is such that he projects positively on E and near the center of C. This structure shows that the only negative respondents were the two economic conservatives on E and the three political conservatives on C; Clark's moderation had the effect of neutralizing his effect upon the relationship among the three groups; and under this very special set of circumstances, with the five conservatives divided and neither subset of them more numerous than the liberal group, the latter three were in a position to re-establish Equalitarianism as the dominant ideology on the Court.

In 1956, Brennan joined the Court in place of Minton, and Reed served only the first half of the term, his position during the second half being filled by Whittaker. Consequently, the factor spaces for this term include ten *i*-points. Although Reed and Whittaker never participated together in decisions, we can make a direct comparison of their relationships with the same reference group; and through the vehicle of the factor spaces, we can compare Reed and Whittaker directly with each other (just as, in the general scales for C and E, we made direct comparisons among the attitudes of several justices who never were contemporaries on the Court). Evidently, Reed was a political and Whittaker an economic conservative.

The group of political conservatives, who had numbered five as recently as 1952, had been reduced to three during 1953 and 1954, as the result of Vinson's replacement by Warren, and Clark's temporary defection. Two of the three left during 1956, Minton at the beginning and Reed during the middle of the term. On the other hand, Clark returned to his normal position in 1956, with a negative loading on all three factors. The change in his behavior toward the political variable was quite dramatic: from a moderate position and the fifth rank in 1955—which was *after* Warren had completed his change—Clark appeared in 1956 in the tenth rank, and he voted in support of a C-scale claim in only four out of forty-four cases. Clark's support of economic liberalism remained positive in 1956, but by 1957, it was moderate, and by then, we might say, he had completed the journey that he began in the 1953 Term, which can be summarized as follows:

TABLE 35

Clark's Attitudinal and Ideological Positions 1952–57 Terms

Term	C+	E+	Libertarianism	Individualism	Equalitarianism
1952	−	−	− (I+)	0 (II+)	
1953	−	0	− (I+)	− (II+)	
1954	0	+	0 (II+)	0 (I−)	
1955	0	+	− (II+)	0 (III+)	0 (I+)
1956	−	+	− (III+)	− (II+)	0 (I+)
1957	−	0	− (II+)	− (III+)	− (I+)

+ = positive
0 = moderate
− = negative

Clark's maximal support for political liberalism came in the 1954 Term, and by 1956, he had returned to his normal position on this issue; on economic liberalism, however, his maximal support came in the 1955 and 1956 Terms, and it was only after Brennan joined the Court in the latter term that Clark returned to his normal position.

Brennan's consistent liberalism on both scales assured the dominance of the Equalitarian ideology after 1956, and it is of interest to observe his relationship to Clark in the factor space for that term. Although they are the two closest respondents on the first factor, they are not very close on that dimension, since they are separated by a segment equivalent to about a third of the length of the factor (.248 + .371). They are considerably further apart on the second factor, with Brennan scoring as an individualist and Clark as a collectivist; but on the third factor, they are much closer, since Clark appears to be only slightly more authoritarian than Brennan (and Warren, too, for that matter). One might well conclude from an observation of the three-dimensional factor space for the 1956 Term, that Brennan had come between Warren and Clark, in a figurative as well as in a literal sense.

During the eight terms beginning with 1955, Equalitarianism was the dominant ideology associated with the first factor, Libertarianism was the second factor and Individualism was the third, except during the two terms (1956 and 1961) when there were ten respondents; in these two terms, Individualism was the second factor and Libertarianism was the third. A set of ten respondents differs from the normal set of nine in two principal respects. The necessarily large proportion of non-response, for the two justices who served only part of the term (with one succeeding the other), results in some distortion of the correlation coefficients in which these two are involved because each has participated in only about half (or less) of the sample of decisions, and the content and extremity differences of the stimuli in the two subsamples are unknown; this affects sixteen of the forty-five cells of the phi matrix for the term, and in addition, an arbitrary correlation of zero is entered as the correlation between these two justices. There is further error due to sampling variance, and the smaller frequencies in the four-fold tables for these correlations can result in more extreme correlations than would have been likely, if these tables could have measured the larger number of decisions for the entire term. (In 1961 this problem is magnified by Frankfurter's *de facto* retirement in mid-term, which meant that the bases for over half of the correlations—twenty-two, plus the arbitrary zeroes for White/Frankfurter and White/Whittaker— were different than for the other correlations.) The other principal way in which a set of ten respondents affect the factorial structure involves the spurious weighting of attitudinal types, as these necessarily are treated by the factor analysis. In the 1956 Term, there were four liberals, three political conservatives, and two economic conservatives during the first half of the term; and four liberals, two political conservatives, and three economic conservatives during the latter part of the term. The preceding statement was based upon the attitudinal types defined by the general scales. In fact, such a description is misleading for this term, because Clark still voted as an economic liberal, with the consequence that there was only one moderate (Burton) on the economic scale during the last half of the term, and only two during the first half. Clark's strong support for economic liberalism made possible an absolute majority in most E-scale decisions of the term, so that the effective division of the Court on this issue tended to be between two groups instead of three; and the same kind of explanation applies to the 1961 Term, when Clark ranked ahead of Brennan on the E scale. In short, the Collectivist ideology dominated that of Libertarianism, and hence appeared as the second factor, in those terms in which there was more attitudinal cohesion in support of economic liberalism than in support of political liberalism. (Clark's support for economic liberalism was high in 1962 also, but in that term, Goldberg and the four liberals provided even stronger support for political liberalism.)

To summarize, three basic empirical factorial structures have been denoted in the preceding analysis. The first and most common structure was observed in eleven terms (1946–48, and 1955–62) when the first factor was Equalitarianism/Traditionalism. The second most common structure occurred during 1950–53, when the first factor was Libertarianism/Authoritarianism. The third structure was transitional between the other two, occurring in the 1949 and 1954 Terms, when the first factor was Collectivism/Individualism. We can further note that although the first factor represented the same ideology during the 1946–48 and 1955–62 periods, the negative ideology dominated in the earlier period (when the average percentage of pro decisions on C and E was 33 and 47) while the positive ideology dominated in the later period (when the equivalent percentages are 53 and 60). The following dominant ideologies, therefore, can be associated with the major types of factorial structure:

TABLE 36

Factor Structures and Dominant Ideologies

Period	Importance	Dominant Ideology
1946–48	Primary	Traditionalism
1949	Transitional	Collectivism
1950–53	Secondary	Authoritarianism
1954	Transitional	Collectivism
1955–62	Primary	Equalitarianism

Although there were four liberals on the Court during the first period, the negative ideology of Traditionalism dominated because of the consistency with which the two groups of conservatives adhered to their own attitudinal positions and the exceptional degree to which they supported each other. The Collectivist ideology was dominant during the transitional terms when the group was in the process of adjusting to either (1) a sudden decrease in the number of liberals, as in 1949, or else (2) an increase in the number of liberals, as in 1954. The Authoritarian ideology dominated during the four terms 1950–53 when there were only two liberals on the Court and the five political conservatives constituted an absolute majority of the justices. Beginning in the 1955 Term, the four liberals, faced with a divided opposition on the two major issues, emerged as the dominant group; and therefore their ideology, Equalitarianism, was established as the dominant ideology of the Court for the period of the 1955–62 Terms.

Chapter 8 · THE CIRCUMPLEX OF LIBERALISM

ACCORDING to Louis Guttman, there is a much more simple and direct approach than factor analysis provides to the analysis of the interrelationship between attitudes.[1] Guttman has suggested that if two attitudes represent perfect or quasi-simplexes, the mathematical relationship between the attitudes will be curvilinear. (By a simplex, Guttman means a matrix in which the correlations are highest in the main diagonal, and they become successively smaller moving in the direction of the upper-right/lower-left corners of the matrix, and least in the corners; this is equivalent to saying, for our data, that the judicial respondents can be ranked in such an order that each is in highest agreement with the persons closest to him in rank, and the maximum disagreement is between the persons occupying the highest and lowest ranks.)[2] The simplex matrix is the mathematical equivalent of the relationships measured by a linear cumulative scale and hence of our political liberalism and economic liberalism scale variables. Guttman hypothesizes that if two cumulative scales are correlated, because of intersection in (*i.e.,* overlap between) the "super universe" of substantive content which they represent, then the joint relationship of the two scales can best be conceptualized as a circle; and Guttman calls this kind of an attitudinal structure a circumplex. Simplexes measure differences in the intensity of respondents' attitudes towards relatively homogeneous bodies of content; a circumplex

[1] Louis Guttman, "A New Approach to Factor Analysis: The Radex," ch. 6 in Paul F. Lazarsfeld (ed.), *Mathematical Thinking in the Social Sciences* (Glencoe: The Free Press, 1954), pp. 258–348.

[2] On the analysis of simplex matrices, see Edgar F. Borgatta, "On Analyzing Correlation Matrices: Some New Emphases," *Public Opinion Quarterly*, Vol. 22 (Winter 1958–59), pp. 516–528.

provides a frame of reference in which the differences (or intransitivities) of respondents' attitudes toward both variables can be measured. The latter cannot be done unless there are *consistent* differentials in respondents' attitudes such as those which we observed empirically in the respondent scale types discussed in Chapter 5. Guttman further distinguishes a structure which he calls the radex; it differs from the circumplex in that the radex is the more complex structure, since one observes the enclosed space as well as the circumference of the circle. In the radex the center of the circle represents the point of minimal intensity and the circumference represents an infinite set of points of maximal intensity toward the included attitudes. The circumplex is a curved line, and it can therefore provide a basis for measuring more than one variable, which I shall assume to be the joint substantive content of the scales. The radex is a two-dimensional structure which measures the intensity of attitudes towards the joint substantive content.

Before proceeding further with this discussion, I feel obliged to emphasize that the preceding paragraph represents my own very free translation of what Professor Guttman wrote in the cited reference, and it does not purport to be a complete or adequate statement of his theory. It is possible that he might himself disagree with my interpretation, and particularly with my statements about the intensity dimension. His own discussion is couched in a mathematical context, and makes much of what he considers to be the inadequacies of conventional factor analysis. Guttman talks about differences in the "complexity" of content items, as the underlying basis for the structure of a simplex; and he defines as "complexity" the dimension that the radex adds to the circumplex. I think, however, that the apparent difference between Guttman's concept "complexity" and that of attitudinal intensity reflects primarily the fact that he is talking about stimuli and I am talking about respondents. Almost all of his examples relate to educational psychology and the field of mental testing, so that his attention is focusing not upon the responses to questions but rather upon the interrelationships among the items that might enter into a questionnaire that was designed to measure several scale variables. My own position is that, from a psychological point of view, the complexity of stimuli content is the equivalent of the intensity of respondents: in relation to a joint scale, both concepts—complexity and intensity—refer to the *same* ordering. Complexity is an attribute of inanimate items, and it measures the differentials in feeling that we *expect* respondents to experience as they perceive hierarchically ordered differences among the stimuli. It might be considered the most blatant anthropomorphism to attribute intensity—a form of affect—to questionnaire items, although it might also be noted that we commonly speak of differences of intensity in regard to such stimuli as noise and light, when our ultimate meaning necessarily is: anticipated, normal, human perceptions. (The deaf man will not hear—although he may feel—the intense noise of an explosion; the blind man will not see the intense flash of accompanying light; and the man with normal perceptions will not hear the supersonic wave or see the ultra-violet ray.) However, for present purposes it is enough to observe that Guttman's item complexity dimension and my own attitudinal intensity dimension are isomorphic functions of a scale, although I also think it would be less confusing if convention were to accept the use of the concept "intensity" to refer to the stimuli differences as well as to those among the respondents.

In addition to his theory of the radex, Guttman has advanced a theory of the curvilinear relationships for the ranks of a cumulative scale, and his theory describes the successive transformations of this rank order implicit in the principal mathematical components of the simplex matrix for the scale.[3] This is the set of intensity curves discussed in Chapter 2. These principal components constitute an alternative mathematical approach to factor analysis for the reduction of the variance of a correlation matrix, and its restatement in terms of a set of common dimensions. So, in this sense, the first three principal components are analogous to the three factors which defined the multidimensional space that we considered in the preceding chapter. Guttman, however, does not use the principal components to define a greater than two-dimensional space; instead he plots each against the rank order of the scale, and thus derives sets of curves similar to those summarized in Table 37. I have not attempted to calculate the mathematical solutions for the principal components of the C and E scales of this study; such internal relationships *of* the scales are of less interest to me than the interrelationship *between* the scales. I do think, however, that Guttman's set of curves can usefully be employed to facilitate the study of the kind of relationships in which I am interested. The factor axes are equivalent to the principal components of the quasi-simplex phi matrices, and one way to conceive of the scale axes is to consider them to be rotated factor axes. One might also hypothesize a scale axis to be equivalent to the

[3] Louis Guttman, "The Principal Components of Scalable Attitudes," ch. 5 in Lazarsfeld, *op. cit.*, pp. 216–257.

first principal component of the simplex matrix for the scale variable; and under this assumption, the correlational test made in Chapter 7 between scales and their counterpart scale axes is functionally equivalent to plotting the first principal component curves for the *scales*—and each such curve, according to Guttman, should be a straight line. From a statistical point of view, a rank correlation of $+1.00$ between a scale and its scale axis would imply a perfectly straight line; one of $+.90$ or better would imply no bends, just a slight wave or two in the line. But how would one plot second and third component curves?

During part of 1962, Professor Guttman was a visiting professor and colleague of mine at Michigan State University. I discussed my scale data with him, and he suggested that if pairs of scales were plotted together, the result should be elementary component curves analogous to the second and third order principal component curves of a simplex matrix. For example, if the C and E scale ranks for a term were plotted, using one scale to define an abscissal coordinate axis and the other to define the ordinate coordinate axis, the resulting curve should resemble either that for a second principal component (U or J-shaped) or for a third principal component (N-shaped), depending upon which of the scales supplied the greater quantity of votes for the term. Let us assume a term when C supplied the greater content and E was secondary: with the E scale as ordinate and the C scale as abscissa, there would be a second component-type curve; and with the scales in reverse position, a third component-type curve.

If we were to accept Guttman's own interpretation of the psychological meaning of the curves, then we should have to assume that the respondents who were most negative on E would be moderates on C, since this is where the zero or bending of the U- or J-shaped curve would lie. (In actuality, my data do not provide a bad empirical fit to such a curve, since my economic conservatives *are* political moderates.) However, we would also be required to assume that in the third component curve, with C as the ordinate and E as the abscissa, the respondents with positive scores on C would have closed minds on E-scale issues, while the respondents with the lowest scores on C would have an open mind toward E-scale issues. (Again, this makes some sense when applied to my empirical data, since the political conservatives, who are moderate toward E, would fall at the second [or lower] bending point, while both the economic conservatives and the liberals would, in an ideal N-shaped curve, show closure toward E. Evidently, however, the suggested interpretation makes little sense when applied to imperfect empirical curves such as the 1959 E curves [page 249], in which the economic conservatives would have to be characterized as the most open-minded respondents toward E-scale issues.)

What Professor Guttman had suggested to me, however, was that the cumulative scales could be conceptualized as the major *semantic* components of the phi correlation matrix, and that plots of pairs of the scales would yield *elementary* component curves for the phi matrix (analogous to the *principal* component curves of a simplex matrix). However, according to his own theory, "only perfect scales will have the *law of formation* . . . with each component having one more bend in it than the preceding component"[4]—and, of course, the associated psychological interpretation that Guttman has proposed for such components. A phi correlation matrix for my data is a quasi-simplex but it does *not* represent a perfect scale or only one acceptable cumulative scale. If this were true, there would be only one cumulative scale for each term, and all respondents would be aligned in the same rank order on all issues. It is clear, therefore, that the curves produced by plotting pairs of scales together cannot be principal component curves but rather are elementary component curves for the phi correlation matrices.

The curves for plots of C and E scales do resemble second and third principal component curves, and it is possible to explain why this is so by examining the curvilinear relationships implicit in our empirical scale types. The liberal type, it will be recalled, consists of a subset of respondents who have the same rank order on both the C and E scales. Assuming the stability of the liberal type, then whether a J- or U-shaped, or an N-shaped, curve will result from a plot of a C and E scale pair will depend upon whether the respondents in the other two scale types are ranked, within each of the two subsets, in the *same* or in an *opposite* way on the two scales. In Chapter 5, we defined political conservatives as respondents who were negative on C and moderate on E, and economic conservatives as negative on E and moderate on C, but we did not require any particular order of ranking for either political conservatives or economic conservatives on the two scales. Now, in addition to specifying the segments of the scales in which the ranks of these respondent types must be found, we must distinguish the internal rank order of the respondents in these subsets. Assuming that such subsets are consistently ordered, there are four possibilities, which are depicted in Figure 11. The first column of charts shows the E scale plotted against C, and the second column shows the opposite.

[4] *Ibid.*, p. 227.

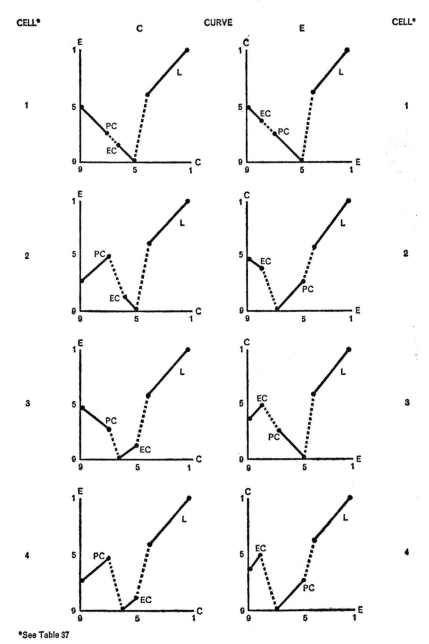

FIGURE 11. How the Ordering of Respondents, within Scale-Type Sets, Determines Elementary Component Curves

Each row contains a pair of charts depicting the corresponding relationships for a given set of assumptions about the respondent scale types. In all of the charts, I have assumed that there are four liberals, three political conservatives, and two economic conservatives (which would correspond to the initial period, 1946–48) and that the liberals are ranked identically on both scales. The variance occurs in the ranking of the scale segments for the political conservatives and for the economic conservatives; and I have assumed that each such ranking may be either the same on both scales (S) or else the opposite on one scale from the other scale (D). In the first pair of charts, both PC and EC are ranked D, and in the second pair one is D and the other S—it makes no difference which, since the critical condition for the appearance of a J-shaped curve, given the other restrictions that I have established for the data, is that the respondent-type ranking lowest on the abscissal scale be inverted in sequence upon the other scale (where it covers the middle ranks). These four charts make it clear that the consistency of ranking for the respondent-type which occupies the *middle* segment of the abscissal scale is immaterial to the appearance of a J-shaped curve, although the first pair of curves—when both respondent types are D—is smoother than the second pair. In the fourth pair of charts, both types are S, and an N-shaped curve results. The third pair of charts show that the critical condition for N-shaped curves is the same as for J-shaped curves: whether the type with the lowest ranks on the abscissal scale are S or D. We can, therefore, conclude that *the shape of the elementary component curve for a scale depends upon the consistency of the ranking, of the respondents most negative toward the scale value, on the other scale.*

Figure 11 can be summarized, as in Table 37. It should, perhaps, be noted that if the two major scales are plotted together, as orthogonal axes, it makes no difference which is placed in the abscissal and which in the ordinal position, except from the point of view of the perspective from which the curves for C and E are viewed: there is only one configuration of points, and both curves necessarily are determined by this single configuration. There would of course be greater empirical variation in the configurations (and therefore in both curves as well) if scale scores were used as the scale metric instead of ranks; I have used ranks in the above example in order to simplify the portrayal of the ideal structure depicted in Figure 11 and in Table 37.

The term scales reported in Figures 1 and 3 (Chapter 5) provide the empirical data needed to prepare charts of the elementary component

TABLE 37

Ideal Types of Elementary Component Curves, as a Function of the Ordering of Respondent Scale-Types

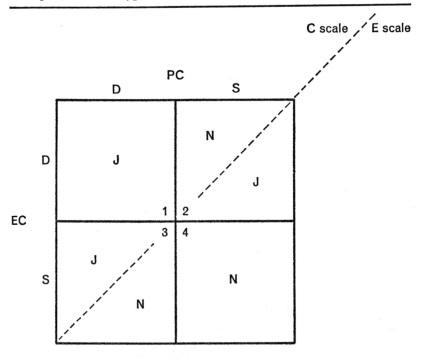

C = Political Liberalism Abscissal Scale
E = Economic Liberalism Abscissal Scale
PC = Political Conservative respondent scale-type
EC = Economic Conservative respondent scale-type
D = Different respondent order on C than on E scale
S = Same respondent order on C as on E scale
J = J- or U-shaped elementary component curve
N = N-shaped elementary component curve

curves for each term. We can anticipate some error variance in the consistency of the relationships within, as well as between, respondent types, when we re-examine these empirical data from the point of view of their joint curvilinear relationships. But we can use the above typology of elementary component curves as a model, and classify the empirical curves according to their similarity to the ideal curves. The results of that analysis are reported in Table 38, below:

TABLE 38

Term Pairs of Empirical Elementary Component Curves

		Abscissal Scale:	
		C	E
Term	Cell *	Curve	Curve
1946	2	N	J
1947	1	J	J
1948	4	N	N
1949	2	N	J
1950	1	J	J
1951	3	J	N
1952	1	J	J
1953	4	N	N
1954	3	J	N
1955	3	J	N
1956	3	J	N
1957	1	J	J
1958	1	J	J
1959	3	J	N
1960	1	J	J
1961	1	J	J
1962	3	J	N

* See Table 37

As we know from Chapter 5, there were several changes in the size of the subsets of respondents whom I have classified as the political conservative and economic conservative types. These changes are summarized in Table 39:

TABLE 39

Sizes of Subsets of Respondents, by Joint-Scale Types

Terms	Liberals	Political Conservatives	Economic Conservatives	Non-type
1946–48	4	3	2	0
1949–52	2	5	2	0
1953–54	2	3	2	2
1955	3	3	2	1
1956	4	3	3	0
1957	4	2	3	0
1958–60	4	1	3	1
1961	4	1	3	2
1962	4	1	1	3

We are familiar with the fact that there were four liberals in ten of the seventeen terms, and with the implications for the factorial structure when there were fewer than four respondents of this type. There were two economic conservatives during the first ten terms, then three for the next six terms, but only Harlan remained in the 1962 Term. The initial group of three political conservatives was increased to five by the appointments of Clark and Minton, and then reduced to three during 1953–55 by Vinson's death and Clark's defection; and Clark's return in 1956 was offset by the retirement of Minton and Reed, so that Clark and Burton were the only political conservatives remaining during 1956–57, and after that there was only Clark. The non-type respondents were Warren and Clark in 1953–54, Clark in 1955, Stewart beginning in 1958, White in 1961 and 1962, and Goldberg in 1962.

As the above table implies, the classification of the C curve after 1957, in Table 38, is more tenuous than for the preceding period, since a type that consists of a single respondent necessarily renders immaterial the question of the internal consistency of ranks within subsets, and classification must depend upon the observation of the other two types and the general shape of the curve. In the 1962 Term, when there was only a single respondent in the economic conservative type as well, the general shape of the curve was the only basis for classification of the curve. It should also be noted that the respondents who were moderates on both scales do not fit the curves. This remark does not apply to Warren and Clark, during the transition of 1953–55, but it does apply to Stewart and White. A respondent with a moderately negative attitude toward the economic variable would have to have been more negative than Stewart was toward the political variable, in order for him to have fit the J curve for E in 1958, 1960, and 1961; but he did fit the curve for E in 1959, which was then an N curve since the economic conservatives were in the same sequence on both scales. White, on the other hand, was too sympathetic toward economic liberalism to fit the C-scale curve; with a lower score on the E scale, he would have fit as an economic conservative in 1961 and 1962. In both 1959 and 1962, when Stewart did fit the curves, it was because he then voted as an economic conservative.

An examination of the cell types in Table 38 shows that seven terms are type 1 and six are type 3; only two terms were type 4 and the remaining two terms were type 2. The only difference between the type 1 and the type 3 patterns lies in whether or not the economic conservatives are in the same or in the opposite sequence on the two scales. I interpret this shifting of sequence among the economic conservatives, from term to term, to reflect the closeness of the attitudinal positions among these justices, toward both issues. In the average scores on the general scales for C and E (Tables 17 and 19), such variation would tend to cancel out, and we do find that Harlan and Whittaker are tied on E and that Frankfurter and Harlan are substantially tied on C. For reasons that will become clear when we consider the circumplex structure, I think that the more fundamental pattern is type 1, with both political conservatives and economic conservatives ranking in opposite ways on the two scales: the political conservative who is least sympathetic to C+ is most sympathetic to E+, and vice versa; similarly, the economic conservative who is least sympathetic to E+ is most sympathetic to C+, and vice versa. In other words, the typical curve for both C and E is J-shaped, as in the first cell type, with the political conservatives and economic conservatives aligning in reversed direction, in opposition to the liberals, on the two issues: the economic conservative who ranks highest on C is lowest on E, and the political conservative who ranks highest on E is lowest on C.

Given the classification of curvilinear relationships between scales for each term, it is possible to raise another question about the relationship between the scales and the factorial space. These elementary component curves can be used as the basis for extending the correlational test, which we made in Chapter 7, between scale and scale axis rankings. If the scale axes are functionally isomorphs of the scales, then it follows logically that plots of the pair of scale axes for a term ought to result in the same pattern of C and E elementary component curves as the scales themselves produce. This would be a less objective but a more rigorous test of isomorphism than the correlation of ranks which we already have observed. It will be more rigorous because it will involve comparisons of the joint scores of each respondent on both scales, and because the use of scale scores and loadings on the scale axes instead of ranks makes possible considerably more variation in the possible shape of curves.

I do not include a table to report the observations of the term pairs of empirical curves for C and E, based upon plots of pairs of scale axes and using respondent loadings rather than ranks, as the counterpart of Table 39. The reason is that the chart patterns, and therefore the curves, are identical in every term, with those reported in that table for the scales, with the single exception of the 1950 Term. In the latter term, the scale axes show type 3 while the scales showed type 1; stated otherwise, the scales showed the economic conservatives to be ranked in opposite sequence on C than on E, while the scale axes show them in the same sequence on the two scales. The set of economic conservatives, in this term, consisted of two respondents, Frankfurter and Jackson. Figure 10 shows that Frankfurter clearly projects more positively than does Jackson on both scale axes for the 1950 Term; and the C scale for this term confirms that Frankfurter (+.36) scores more positively than does Jackson (—.09). On the E scale, however, the difference between Frankfurter's —.87 and Jackson's —.81 is two non-participations for Jackson which, as a consequence of my arbitrary rule for scoring non-participations, gives him a higher scale score than Frankfurter. In short, the basis for the only apparent difference between the scale and scale axes curves turns out to be an arbitrary rule of procedure rather than any substantive evidence. So I conclude that a comparison of the scale curves with the corresponding scale axis curves strongly supports the confirmation, already given by rank correlation, to my basic hypothesis: that the factor space measures the same attitudinal differences as the scales, and that the same relationships that are explicit and implicit in the scales also are explicit and implicit in the scale axes imbedded in the factorial space.

I have made plots of both scale and scale axis curves, for all terms; the preceding analysis could hardly have been made if the data had not been so organized. Rather than to present all of these curves for all of these terms—the total would be 68 curves—I have selected two terms to illustrate the basis upon which the comparisons were made. I picked the 1956 and 1959 Terms, because 1956 was a term in which the *II/III* factor axis pattern was Individualism/Libertarianism, while it was Libertarianism/Individualism in 1959. In both terms, the C curve is U or J-shaped, and the E curve is N-shaped. As Figure 12 shows, there can be no mistaking the similarity of the two sets of curves. The C curves in 1956 are alike except for the technical constraint upon the extremity of the axis loadings, which results in a curve that is smoother and that does not extend to the extremities of the space. In the 1959 C curves, there is a transposition between Frankfurter and Whittaker, who are closely clustered with Harlan at the bending (zero) point of the curve; Clark appears in the proper rank on the curve, but his axis loading on C is too high—I believe that the cause of this lies in the idiosyncracies of the phi correlation coefficients, due to the constraint on the range of the coefficient. The E curves for 1956 also correspond exceptionally well while the 1959 E curves again exemplify the extent to which the scale and scale axis curves typically differ, when they are not identical. As we observed for the C curves for this term, Frank-

C

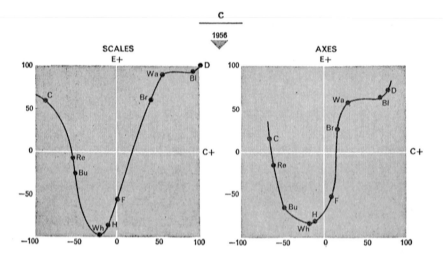

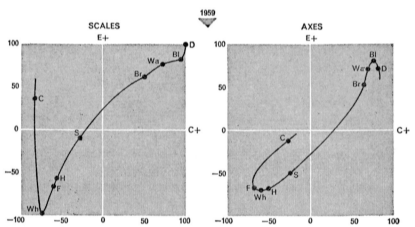

FIGURE 12. Elementary Component Curves for C- and E-Scale Pairs and Scale-Axis Pairs, 1956 and 1959 Terms

furter and Whittaker are transposed on the scale axis curve, and in this instance Douglas and Black also are transposed. Examination of the C scale for the 1959 Term shows that although Frankfurter's score is higher than Whittaker's, the latter's marginals (7–25) show greater support for C than do Frankfurter's (5–27); and it is of course the marginal differences to which the phi coefficient will respond—so the Frankfurter-Whittaker transposition on both scale axis curves for this term can be explained as the result of scale errors in the C scale. I have no ready explanation for the

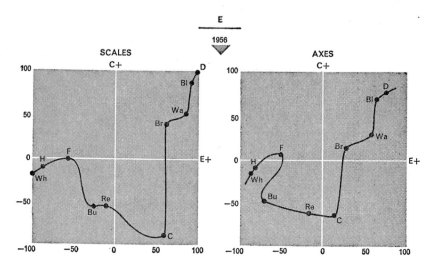

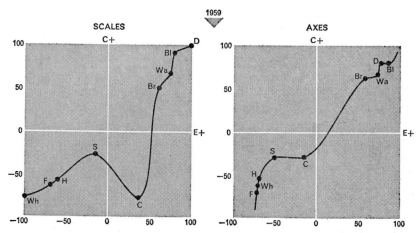

FIGURE 12. (continued)

Douglas-Black transposition, but I assume that it must be due to the influence of voting in decisions in other content areas than C and E—probably it was F—upon the location of the *i*-points for these two respondents in the factor space.

The elementary component curves can be used in yet another way, in order to analyze their joint relationships in the factor spaces. The loadings on the scale axes, it will be recalled, are projections upon lines, from *i*-points in fixed configurations in the three-dimensional spaces. When a pair of scale axes is plotted together (as in Figure 12), what we are in effect observing is the curve connecting the projections upon the plane defined by the two scale axes, after the axes have been rotated from what is usually an oblique position in the factor space to an orthogonal position. The C and E curves that we observe in such plots, in other words, are two-dimensional projections of the relationships among the *i*-points in the three-dimensional space. It follows, therefore, that we ought also to be able to observe the C and E curves as direct functions of the configuration of *i*-points. In order to do this, we must return to the factor spaces presented in Figure 10 (Chapter 7).

We can predict, from our knowledge of the positions of the scale axes in the factor spaces (as shown in Figure 10) and from our knowledge of the systematic relationships to the scale curves of respondent types (as discussed above) where we ought to be able to observe the C and E elementary component curves, in the factor space for each term. In 1946, for example, the negative end of the C curve starts with Vinson; passes generally to the front and upward through Frankfurter, Burton, and Reed; crosses over to the rear to Jackson and reaches a peak in height with him; and then moves downward and to the front to Douglas, Black, and Rutledge, ending with Murphy slightly above and somewhat to the rear of Rutledge. Obviously the path described is not a perfect parabola, nor could we expect this, since the C scale itself is marginally reproducible in this term, and the relative influence of this scale upon the configuration was least for the entire period of this study—only 17 percent of the total content for the 1946 Term consisted of C-scale cases. Nevertheless, the path of the curve that we can observe in the factor space, connecting the *i*-points in the sequence of the C scale, is roughly that of a parabola which bends to the front and upward and then descends through the liberals. We might say that the best perspective for viewing the curve is that provided by the *I/III* factor space, which denotes a C curve that bends around Jackson in an inverted U. (Such an observation accords with the designation of *III* as Libertarianism, in Table 34.) The E curve, on the other hand, clearly appears as an almost perfect U-shaped curve in the *I/II* factor plot for 1946, starting with Jackson in the upper left quadrant, passing downward and bending around Reed, and turning upward through Douglas, Rutledge, Black, and Murphy. If we consider the effect of the third factor, we can see that the three-dimensional curve for E is more an inverted N, because of the downward bend around Vinson from Jackson and Frankfurter. We might infer that the first two dimensions are those primarily influential upon E, since it is in the *I/II* factor space that the E curve appears most clearly; and that the first and third dimensions are the ones primarily influential upon C, since it is in the *I/III* factor space that the C curve appears most clearly. (Again, this agrees with Table 34, which denotes Individualism as the second factor.) In short, our examination of the factor space for the 1946 Term suggests that both C and E curves are imbedded in the three-dimensional space, but that the C curve is primarily a function of the configuration of *i*-points as that configuration has been determined by the influence of the third factor upon the first; while the E curve is primarily a function of the configuration as determined by the influence of the second factor upon the first. It is this observation of the C and E curves in the factor space which was the basis for my denotation of the factor ideologies in Table 34 of Chapter 7; so the correspondence of the findings reported in that table should not be considered a confirmation of the present analysis of the scale curves in the factor space, but rather they are the result of that analysis.

I shall not undertake to report a similar detailed analysis of the subsequent terms, but I shall summarize what such an analysis would show. Except during the period 1949–1954, which is atypical for reasons that we already have explored in Chapter 7, the C curve can be seen in the factor spaces as an inverted U, and the E curve as an upright U. The C curve appears in that factor space, for each term, which is defined by the first factor and by the factor (either *II* or *III*) which represents Libertarianism; Table 34 specifies when the Libertarianism factor is *II* and when it is *III*. In these same terms the E curve appears in the space defined by the other factor plus the first factor. During 1949 and 1954, both the C and E curves appear in the space defined by factors *I* and *II*—there is no general (equalitarian) factor in these and the intervening terms—and C is an inverted U tilted to the left while E is an upright U, also tilted to the left, in 1949; while in 1954, E is an upright U while the C curve is an M tilted to the left, with the middle bend necessary because of the anomalous position of Warren and Clark in this term. During the four intervening terms, the E curve is a U turned sideways (⊂) bending around the negative segment of the first factor in the *I/II* space; while the C curve, in the same space, is an inverted N (ᴖ): the curve during these terms differs from the normal inverted U curve for C primarily in the lower bend, which reflects the positive scores on the second factor of the respondents who were most negative toward C. During this period, several of the justices whom I have classified (on the basis of their overall performance) as political conservatives were quite conservative toward E as well as toward C; in these terms they deviated from the expected behavior of the respondent-types (which results in the normal inverse U curve). In general, when the decision-making group includes one or more respondents who do not fit the joint-scale types, then one of the curves will be distorted in order to pass through the *i*-points for such respondents, although they usually will fit the curve for the other scale. The reason why such non-type respondents will fit one of the curves is this: the joint-scale types fall in only three of the nine cells of the matrix defined by the segments of the two scales (Figure 6), so there are twice as many opportunities for respondents to be non-type as for them to fall within the joint-scale types; on the other hand, any non-type respondent necessarily will have the score of one of the joint-scale types on one of the scales, and he will therefore fall on the expected curve for *that* scale, but not for the other scale. Stewart provides an example of the non-type respondent, in the factor spaces for the 1958–60 Terms: his *i*-point is so positioned that he fits the C curve (which associates him with the economic conservatives, because of his moderate score on C); but since his score on E is also moderate (instead of highly negative), he is much too high on the second factor to fall on the E curve, which is an upright U in the *I/II* factor space.

Several concluding observations can be made about the relationships of the elementary component curves in the factor space. The modal C curve appears to be an inverted U tilted to the left, when viewed from a two-dimensional factor perspective; and the modal E curve appears, when viewed from a different but also two-dimensional factor perspective, to be an upright U tilted to the left. But these curves are projecting upon different planes in the factor space: when *II* is individualism and *III* is Libertarianism, the C curve is perceived to lie in the vertical plane, and the bend is at the top of the space, while the E curve appears to lie in the horizontal plane, and the bend is at the near (*II*—) edge of the space. We must remember, however, that such perspectives merely aid us to perceive the characteristic shape of the curves, both of which pass through the same fixed configuration of *i*-points in three-dimensional factor space. In the three-dimensional space, the C curve is not so much an inverted U as it is an inverted J, with a downward platykurtic skew for the positive tail; while the E curve is either an upright J or an N—and in either case, with an upwards platykurtic slope to the positive tail. The shape of the curves is determined by the consistency of the directionality of the typal sequences of respondents, in their attitudes toward both scales. That is, we observe the same curves reported in Table 38 (except that the C curves are inverted, because of the relationship between the scale axes), and for the same reason: in thirteen of the seventeen terms, the liberals are in the same sequence on both scales, the political conservatives are in opposite sequence, and the economic conservatives (because of respondent ties in scores on one or the other of the scales) are in the same sequence in half of these terms and in opposite sequence in the other half of the terms. When the economic conservatives are in opposite sequence, the three-dimensional E curve is a J, and when the economic conservatives are in the same sequence, the three-dimensional E curve is an N. The two possible patterns of C and E curves, in the three-dimensional space, are schematically portrayed in the figure below, using the 1956 and 1957 terms as examples, and using a two dimensional representation which shows how both curves project upon the plane defined by the C and E scale axes.

Although Douglas' *i*-point does not fit precisely the scale sequence for either the C or the E curve in 1957—and he voted without exception affirmatively in all 36 E cases and all 56 C cases in that term—this can be attributed to the influence, upon the location of his *i*-point, of his attitude toward the F scale, on which he was the most negative of the four liberals. What is more significant is that the configuration of the *i*-points for Frankfurter, Harlan, Whittaker, Burton, and Clark is very similar in both terms, notwithstanding the change from 1956 in the shape of the E curve. From this we might well infer that there was no change in the basic ideological positions of these respondents between the two terms—nor should we expect such a change to have occurred. Rather, the change in the shape of the criterion E scale curve represents the failure of the E scale adequately to distinguish the "true" attitudinal differences among these economic conservatives during the 1956 Term. And examination of the E scales for 1956 and 1957 confirms such an inference: E scales in 1957 with a scalability coefficient of .90, and an R of .99, and both of these indices indicate exceptional consistency in the measurement of attitudes toward economic liberalism in this term; while in 1956 (a ten-respondent scale), both Frankfurter and Whittaker have frequent non-participations, there are many errors in the scale (including half a dozen for the three economic conservatives), and the scalability coefficient drops to .60. We certainly ought to have greater confidence in the validity of the 1957 scale. And I think that the same explanation will generally apply when the E curve is an N instead of a J: that the N is due to scale errors, and the configuration of points provides the more reliable guide to the attitudinal differences, toward E, among the economic conservatives.

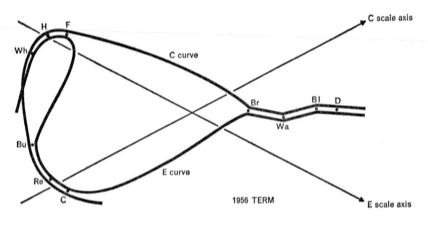

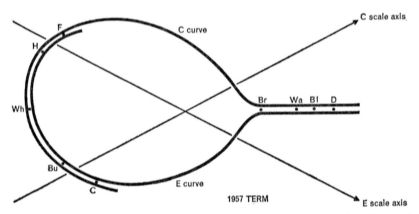

FIGURE 13. The Circumplex of Curvilinear Projections upon the Plane of the C- and E-Scales Axes, 1956 and 1957 Terms (schematic)

If the conclusion just stated is correct, however, then the most fundamental relationship between the elementary component curves is that suggested by Figure 13, for the 1957 Term: the two J curves overlap so as to form together a circular (or perhaps elliptical) joint elementary component curve.

Secondly, we can observe that there is no necessary inconsistency in the several ways in which we have described the appearance of the C and E curves, from the viewpoint of different perspectives. C appeared to be an upright U or J curve, in orthogonal plots of the scales themselves; but that perspective is distorted in at least two respects: (1) in the factor space, C +

is above E $+$, not below it (as it is in the C scale plots); and (2) in the factor space, the correlation between the scale axes is oblique, not orthogonal (as it is in the scale plots); and all of these comments apply equally to the curves based upon orthogonal plots of pairs of scale axes. In the two-dimensional perspectives afforded by the *I/II* and *I/III* factor spaces, the three-dimensional curves are projecting upon different planes from when we viewed them (Figure 13) as projecting upon the plane defined by the scale-axes; so it is not surprising that curves which appear as "J"s in the scale-axes plane appear as "U"s in the factor-axes planes. The three-dimensional curves are more like "J"s than like "U"s, because of the long positive tail for both curves, as they pass through the cluster of *i*-points for the liberals.

Thirdly, the characteristic position of the scale axes is for the positive terminus of the C axis to be "above" the positive terminus of the E axis in both the *I/II* and *I/III* factor space; in three-dimensional factor space, the C axis passes beyond the origin upward and to the rear, while the E axis passes downward and to the front. This is what accounts for both the inversion of the U of the C curve, and the tilting of both curves to the "left" in the two-dimensional factor space perspectives. The C curve bends around the negative segment of the E-scale axis, while the E curve bends around the negative segment of the C axis. This is the way it looks in the two-dimensional factor space perspectives; and if one calculates the bending point of the curves in the three-dimensional space, he discovers that the bend of one curve does occur on or very near to the negative segment of the axis for the *other* scale, as Figure 13 exemplifies.

This is a very important principle, although it is one that might well have been anticipated. The scale axes characteristically pass through the centroid of the cluster of *i*-points (in the three-dimensional point configuration) of the appropriate respondent type: *i.e.,* the negative segment of the E-scale axis passes through the center of the cluster of *i*-points for the economic conservatives, and the C-scale axis passes through the center of the political conservatives. (Both the technical and theoretical explanations for this were given in the introductory section of Chapter 7.) Consequently, when the C curve bends around the negative segment of the E-scale axis, it is bending around the respondents who are economic conservatives, and fitting them as moderates on the C curve—since the point of the bend is, according to Guttman's theory of the second component curve and also in accord with intuitive expectations, the zero point of intensity for the elementary component curve. At the same time, both the liberals (aligned along the positive segment of the curve) and the political conservatives (aligned along the negative segment) will be increasingly intense in their attitudes toward C, as their positions become closer to either the positive or the negative tail of the J-shaped curve. The converse holds for the E curve and the C-scale axis. So when the scale axes are considered in relationship to each other in the factor space, attitudes toward E provide a measure of intensity toward C, and attitudes toward C provide a measure of intensity toward E. We can, therefore, consider the pairs of elementary component curves to be C and E *intensity* curves.

The discovery of these systematic curvilinear relationships, which seem to depend most directly upon the relationships between the i-points and the scale axes, suggests the possibility of working directly with the plane defined by the scale axes, which is imbedded in the three-dimensional factor space in each term, in order to develop a single measure of the joint scale relationships among all respondents. The respondent scale-types, upon which I necessarily have leaned quite heavily thus far, permit us to talk about such relationships for groups of justices, but now we seek a metric which will make it possible for us to classify respondents as individuals on the basis of their conjoint attitude toward both variables. Since we have strong reason to suspect that the underlying metric will be curvilinear in form, and perhaps will be a circle or an ellipse, Guttman's theory of the circumplex and the radex comes to mind as a possible model. The circumplex, it will be recalled, is a curve which combines two (or more) attitudes in a common line; and the radex adds an intensity dimension to the content differences measured by the circumplex. We shall examine my data from the point of view of both of these models in the discussion that follows; but first we must consider what is implied by the isolation of the scale-axes plane from the factor space in which it is imbedded.

The C- and E-scale axes (as I have called them) are technically vectors in the space defined by three orthogonal factor reference axes. I hypothesized in Chapter 2 that these two vectors themselves defined an imbedded plane which contained the genotypic attitudinal content in which we are primarily interested, assuming that we wish to focus our attention exclusively upon the interrelationships between the two major variables, political liberalism and economic liberalism. Much of the empirical evidence that we have examined in Chapters 5–8 supports the plausibility of our thus focusing attention upon the attitudinal content that is most important to most of the respondents.

Since the C-scale axis typically is positively loaded, and the E scale axis typically is negatively loaded, upon both the second and third factor reference axes, we can consider the possibility of folding these reference axes together, to form a single new reference dimension that would remain orthogonal (as each had been individually) to the first reference axis. We can conceptualize such enfolding as taking place in the following manner. Axis $II+$, which defines a horizontal plane with $I+$, is rotated 45 degrees upward to coincide with Axis $III+$, which is rotated 45 degrees but downward. Since the point of origin does not change, we might alternatively conceive of the rotation as follows: I is an axle which we view from the positive end, and there is a wheel supported by four spokes emerging like this⊕from a sleeve (the point of origin) encasing the axle; while the right horizontal spoke is rotated 45 degrees upward, the left horizontal spoke rotates the same angle downward, the upper vertical spoke rotates 45 degrees to the right and the lower vertical spoke rotates 45 degrees to the left, so that our wheel now is supported by only two (each double) spokes, and looks—from the front of the axle—as follows⊗. One who viewed our paradigm from a 10:30 o'clock perspective on the rim of the wheel would see a plane, with the composite rotated axis as the ordinate and the first factor reference axis, I, remaining in the abscissal position.

In effect, the ideological axis of Individualism is superimposed upon the ideological axis of Libertarianism, and such a folding of the space is a possible means of simplifying the attitudinal structure because of the rough but substantial equivalence of the C- and E-axis loadings on the two factors which are folded together. But what is the dimension that has been eliminated, when our factorial sphere is compressed into a circle? We are eliminating the content other than C and E, I suggest—and this other content is, on the average, about a third of the total content, as Table 21 shows—when we enfold axes II and III to isolate the genotypic plane, this other content affects the position of the configuration of i-points, and it affects the association of ideologies with factors, but it confuses rather than clarifies our perception of the respondents' attitudes towards the two major variables, as these are measured by the factorial space. So we can anticipate a simplified and clarified picture of the relationships between political and economic liberalism,[5] as these are measured in the genotypic plane as

---

[5] Guttman has remarked that: ". . . in a radex with empirically distinguishable simplexes, centroids of the simplexes will tend to be the [rotated] reference axes of a Thurstone-type analysis. Thus, the number of common factors . . . will tend to correspond to the number of simplexes employed." *Ibid.*, p. 347.

distinguished from the three-dimensional factorial space. Henceforth, I shall refer to the genotypic plane as the plane of liberalism, since it is now clear that we are discussing only the relationships between political and economic liberalism when we view the attitudinal structure in that plane.

Of course, the method of isolating the liberalism plane, as I described it above, is schematic and was intended only as an illustration of what in general occurs. Two vectors always will define a plane, and the i-points will project onto, but only coincidentally will lie upon, the plane space. Such a plane does not necessarily include factor axis I as the centroid of the vectors: during the period 1949–54, there is no relevant reference axis of this sort, since I during this period is equivalent to either II or III during the other terms, and I therefore folds with II to form the composite ordinal axis of the liberalism plane. The abscissal reference axis of that plane is a statistical artifact, since the Equalitarianism ideology is so weak during these terms that it cannot be associated primarily with any one of the factorial reference factors. However, we can conceive of I as the composite dimension which results from the folding together of the C and E vectors, and this is precisely what it represents, functionally, during the 1946–48 and 1955–62 terms; so defined, the abscissal reference dimension of the plane is also a composite dimension, and it clearly represents the attitudinal content of general liberalism. So, in the intervening terms when there is no corresponding factor, it is still possible to speak of the enfolding of the two vectors to a median position, in which case the "statistical artifact" mentioned above becomes infused with substantive content. During the remaining terms, II and III always can be folded to form a composite ordinal reference axis for the plane, but the angles of rotation are not necessarily 45 degrees for each of the two factor reference axes—the precise angles will vary, depending upon the empirical loadings of the scale axes upon the factor reference axes. Moreover, I shall assume that after II and III have been folded together, an orthogonal rotation takes place for the resulting composite axis, and for I so that I is rotated to a position where it is the median between C + and E +, and the composite axis is rotated so as to remain orthogonal to I. After the folding of II and III to form a composite axis, and the orthogonal rotation of I and the composite axis, they can be redesignated as II' and I'; and these latter symbols will be more convenient to use in subsequent discussion.

In terms of their attitudinal content, I' is now defined as a dimension of general liberalism, and II' is defined as an integration of the Individualism and Libertarianism ideologies. Both Individualism and Libertarianism are ideologies which strongly emphasize the freedom of the individual—the one in his economic rights and the other in his political rights—while the counter-ideologies of Collectivism and Authoritarianism strongly emphasize the socialization of compulsion to delimit individual freedom; we now need to define a super-ideological dimension, which is independent of general liberalism and which stands for a philosophy of individual freedom as opposed to socialized limitations upon personal freedom. Such a dimension seems to have much in common with the psychological studies of my colleague, Milton Rokeach, in the open and closed mind.[6] It also resembles Eysenck's dimension of the "tender-minded" versus the "tough-minded" (and cf. Guttman's third principal component, "closure"). My own reading of the works of both Rokeach and Eysenck, including the periodical literature in which they criticize each other,[7] convinces me that both were studying the same psychological dimension. Both deal with the same question that we now face: what is the psychological dimension which, although typically closely associated with attitudinal structures that include political and economic liberalism and conservatism, deals with fundamental personality attributes rather than (like liberalism and conservatism) with the more externalized values implicit in social attitudes? The component which figures most prominently, in the work of both Rokeach and Eysenck, is that of dogmatism versus pragmatism; and the studies of both of these social psychologists make it quite clear that the question of the open (tough) versus the closed (tender) mind is quite independent from the question of the liberal versus the conservative mind. I am going to assume that the belief in individual freedom can reasonably be identified with pragmatism, and the belief in the socialization of compulsion with dogmatism. Therefore, I shall define $II'+$ as Pragmatism, and $II'-$ as Dogmatism. So the reference dimensions of the liberalism plane are Liberalism/Conservatism and Pragmatism/Dogmatism, and we shall examine, in the circumplex and the radex, the overlapping relationship of the political and economic liberalism attitudinal curves within a frame of reference of the ideologies of Liberalism/Conservatism and Pragmatism/Dogmatism.

Now that we have described the ideal structure of our attitudinal circumplex, we must develop a method for integrating the empirical data provided by the term observations, of either the scales or the factor space,

[6] Milton Rokeach, *The Open and Closed Mind; Investigations into the Nature of Belief Systems and Personality Systems* (New York: Basic Books, 1960).

[7] See the references cited in fn. 5 of Chapter 7, *supra.*

into a synthetic structure which will employ a single common curvilinear metric. In thus combining the term data, what we must in effect do is to superimpose upon each other seventeen term circles (or ellipses); necessarily, we shall have to use some system of averages in order to smooth out the error and sampling variances in these empirical data for individual terms, and in order to define the positions most typical for the individual respondents.

There are several ways in which this might be done. In my initial attempts to develop a metric, I assigned scores to the respondents (as +, 0, or −) on each scale, by observing the elementary component curves for the major scales (such as in Figure 12) for each term: for the J- or U-shaped curves, those respondents in the right tail were scored as positive, those in the left tail as negative, and those at or very close to the bend as moderate; for N-shaped curves, the tails were scored in the same way as for J or U curves, and those respondents in or between the bends were scored as moderates. This resulted in a score for each respondent for each term on each curve; the joint scores located each respondent, in each term, in one of the nine cells of a matrix identical in form to that employed for the generation of empirical scale types in Chapter 7 (Figure 6). The procedure for averaging the term matrices is the same, irrespective of the way in which the data are observed for the matrix, so I shall postpone briefly an exposition of that procedure until I can exemplify it, below, in regard to the method which I finally settled upon for the analysis of the empirical data. The circumplex which resulted from the observation of the elementary component curves is very similar to the one subsequently produced by the use of what I think is a better method; its rank correlation, with the one to be presented below (and omitting White, since the available observations are inadequate to classify him on the basis of the elementary component curves), is a tau of .88. However, the observation of these curves necessarily entails a subjective judgment, and the procedure of plotting the curves—if it were to be done only for this purpose—would be time-consuming and laborious.

I had tried the elementary component curves first, because I thought that the entirely relativistic criterion provided by the bends in these intensity curves would result in observations less subject to sampling variance, from term to term, than would the use of scale scores. Scale ranks were clearly too relativistic a criterion, depending as they so largely do upon changes in personnel. But later experimentation with a system of classification using scale scores to generate the matrix convinced me that the effect of sampling variance tended to cancel out for respondents with long tenure; and for the others, the distortion attributable to this source was not much greater than the error variance for the intensity curves. The term scales for C and E can be used by establishing cutting points at $\pm.33$: scale scores of $+.34$ or above are classified as $+$, those of $-.34$ or below are classified as $-$, and those within the range $\pm.33$ as 0. The resulting circumplex also is very similar to the one to be presented below, and (again, excluding White) correlates with it at a tau of .90. One reason for not basing the circumplex upon the data provided by joint scale scores is this: the cumulative scales are completely independent, statistically, from each other, while the scale axes are intercorrelated; and as we have observed earlier in this chapter, the curves in the factor space are smoother than the scale curves. And an even better reason is this: the joint scale-axis scores for C and E are functions of the dimensions that define the genotypic plane, which I have postulated as, in theory, the space in which we can expect to observe the ideological circumplex for political and economic liberalism.

In order to classify the scale-axis scores, cutting points of $\pm.30$ are established; I have used .30 rather than .34 as in the instance of the scale scores, because the axis loadings—unlike the scale scores—rarely attain extreme values. (The only loading in excess of $\pm.89$ was for Douglas on E in 1949, the term in which his phi correlations were extremely biased by his exceptionally high nonparticipation.) The matrix then assumes the form indicated in Figure 14 below, in the cells of which the ideological values associated with the rotated reference axes (I' and II') also have been specified.

It is convenient to assign numbers to the cells, and the procedure for computing the circumplex index values is as follows. Ten columns are set up, the first to identify the terms, and each of the others for a cell of the matrix in the sequence 0–8–1–2–3–4–5–6–7–8. Each row then contains the data for a single term, which consists of a listing of the respondents in the columns where they are placed by their joint scale-axis loadings. A respondent's average score is then computed as follows: his frequencies of appearance in each column are totaled; the column with the highest total is selected (and if two are tied, either can be selected) as his reference column; multiply $+1$ times the frequency of the column for the next higher cell in the sequence, $+2$ times the columnar frequency of the second higher cell, $+3$ times the third higher, but 0 times the fourth higher; and multiply -1 times the columnar frequence for the next lower cell, -2 times the columnar frequency for the second lower cell, -3 times the third lower,

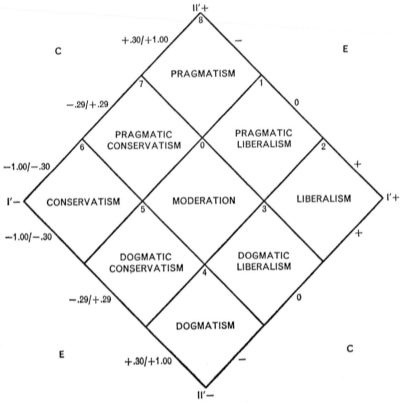

FIGURE 14. Ideological Types Defined by Scale Axes Scores

but 0 times the fourth lower; also multiply 0 times the frequencies for *both* the reference column and the "Moderation" cell column; sum all weighted columnar frequencies, and divide by the unweighted sum of the frequencies for columns 1–8. The result will be either zero or a positive or negative decimal fraction, which specifies the location on the circumplex of the respondent's *i*-point, in relation to the reference column.

More formally, the Circumplex Index (C) is defined by the equation below,

$$
(14) \quad C = M + \frac{\pm(1 \xrightarrow{d} 3) \sum dXn}{Xm + \sum_{1-8} Xn} + 0X_m + 0X_o + 0\sum_{4}^{d} dX_n = M + \frac{\pm(1 \xrightarrow{d} 3) \sum dXn}{Xm + \sum_{1-8} Xn}
$$

when X = the frequency of observations of any matrix cell (corresponding to Figure 14); m = the non-zero modal cell, for any respondent; n = any non-zero non-modal cell, for any respondent; M = the matrix sequence number for m; and d = the minimal algebraic difference between *the rank* of any non-modal cell, and *the rank* of the modal cell, in the circular sequence . . . 8–1–2–3–4–5–6–7–8–1–2–3–4 . . . , with clockwise rank differences defined as positive and counterclockwise rank differences defined as negative. For example, Reed served for eleven terms, from 1946–1956; in 1946 his classification was under the column headed by the numeral zero; in 1948, he was classified under column six; and in the other nine terms, under column five; his circumplex index is equal to:

$$5 + \frac{(1 \times 1)}{10} + (0 \times 9) + (0 \times 1) + (0 \times 4 \times 0) = 5.1.$$ The observations for each term are reported in Table 40, and the circumplex is depicted in Figure 15 below.

The table is of some interest, simply because it conveys an impression of the very substantial consistency with which these eighteen justices adhered to similar joint-positions on the scale axes; with the previously noted exception for Warren, the respondents' attitudes may fluctuate within a circumscribed range, but they do not change. (The zero or Moderation column, it should be remembered, is in the center of the matrix, and therefore is adjacent to all of the others, which otherwise are adjacent to only the columns on either side of each.) Since the columns correspond to points which divide the circumplex into eight segments, we can say that the span equivalent to each pair of columns is a segment of the circumplex, three adjacent columns correspond to a span of two segments, and so forth; the neutral M column does not help to define a segment, but rather defines a transitional space which is contiguous to all segments. Warren—for reasons with which we are familiar—has the broadest attitudinal range, extending over the three segments between the fifth and second columns. Several other justices, such as Frankfurter and Clark, have a range of two segments, although it should be noted that the normal range for these respondents is smaller than this: Frankfurter is confined to the segment between six and seven except during the 1952 Term, when he is in column one, signifying the limit of the more liberal salient which he ventured during the period of politically conservative domination of 1949–53, when he appeared to define for himself the role of political counterweight, by voting most liberally (for him) when the representation of the liberal

TABLE 40

Circumplex Observations of Joint Scale-Axis Loadings, by Terms

Term	M 0	P 8	PL 1	L 2	DL 3	D 4	DC 5	C 6	PC 7	P 8
1946	Re			Mu Ru Bl D				Bu V F	J	
1947				Mu Ru Bl D			Re V	Bu	F J	
1948				Mu Ru Bl D				Re V Bu F J		
1949	Bu			Bl	D		Re V Mi C		F J	
1950	Bu F C			Bl	D		Re V	Mi	J	
1951	Bu F C			Bl D			Re V Mi		J	
1952	Bu		F Bl	D			Re V Mi C		J	
1953	Mi F			Bl D			Re Wa C	Bu	J	
1954	C	H		Bl D	Wa		Re Mi	Bu	F	H
1955				Bl D Wa	C		Re Mi	Bu	F H	
1956	Br			Bl D	Wa		Re C	Bu	F H Wh	
1957			Br	Bl D Wa			C Bu	Wh	F H	
1958				Bl D Wa	Br		C	Wh F H	S	
1959				Bl D Wa Br			C	Wh F H	S	
1960				Bl D Wa Br			C	Wh F H	S	
1961				Bl D Wa Br			C BW	F H	Wh S	
1962			Br	Bl D Wa			C BW	H S	G	

ideology otherwise was weakest. On the other hand, his seeming liberalism may be better explained by the conservative character of the stimuli to which Frankfurter was responding during the period. Under either interpretation, Frankfurter did serve to check the strength of the dominant conservative ideology during this period, just as during the other periods he served to check the strength of the dominant liberal ideology. Clark's normal range is even narrower: in ten terms, he is in the fifth column, and only once (in 1955) does he appear in the third column. The only respondents who appear in the M column more than once are Burton, Frankfurter, and Clark.

It is notable that throughout the seventeen terms, not a single respondent ever appears in the fourth column, which requires that a justice be politically conservative and economically liberal; and with only a single exception, no respondents appear in the eighth column, which requires that a justice be politically liberal and economically conservative. (The single exception is provided by Harlan, who in 1955—his first term on the Court—had a marginally positive loading on the C-scale axis; throughout the remaining eight terms, his loading on the C-scale axis, like his loadings on the E-scale axis, were negative.) The absence of entries in columns four and eight indicates how secondary the influence of the Pragmatism/Dogmatism dimension is upon the attitudes of Supreme Court justices. Primarily the justices are influenced by the para-ideology of Liberalism/Conservatism, and Pragmatism/Dogmatism has an important, but strictly secondary influence, upon their attitudes in relationship to the major content of Supreme Court decision-making which the circumplex measures. (Of course, in regard to the minor scale variables, we should expect that Pragmatism/Dogmatism—and hence also its constituent factor ideologies, Libertarianism/Authoritarianism and Individualism/Collectivism—will have more influence that Liberalism/Conservatism.)

The table also shows that respondents who are primarily liberals are much less influenced by Pragmatism and Dogmatism than the respondents who are primarily conservatives: the liberals are concentrated in the second column, while the conservatives are partitioned among three columns, 5–7, and with total columnar frequencies in that order of magnitude. Moreover, the sum of the frequencies of the liberal columns (1–3) is 57, while that for the conservative columns (5–7) is 50 percent greater. This means that the conservative ideology had considerably more representatives than did the liberal ideology, during the period of this study, but the conservatives were

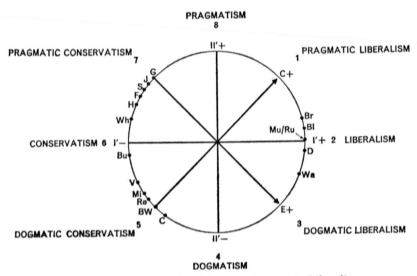

FIGURE 15. The Circumplex of Political and Economic Liberalism

divided among themselves along a second ideological dimension, while the liberals were not so divided. Hence, the liberal ideology had the more effective representation, because it received more cohesive support.

Figure 15 presents the circumplex. Since the index values, which determine the positions of respondents along the curve, represent the average positions of the respondents, the circumplex should be construed to indicate the usual relationships among them. Since the curve is a circle, the scale axes are shown in an orthogonal relationship to each other; this, of course, involves some distortion, since we know that the scale axes are positively correlated in the factor space. It might seem that a second source of distortion could be attributed to the elimination of the intensity component, due to the procedure which has the effect of projecting all *i*-points to the perimeter of the circle, so that they lie upon the circumplex. However, the circumplex does provide some measure of intensity, since it can be viewed as consisting of the fusion of the two elementary component curves; thus a circumplex is a higher-order curve in the set of elementary component curves for a phi matrix. With directionality extending from — to +, the C component is the following curve: 5–6–7–8–1–2; while the E component is: 7–6–5–4–3–2. The C-component curve is an inverted J which bends around the E— axis terminus; and the E-component curve is an upright J which bends around the C— axis terminus; both curves are tilted to the left. This accords with my general description of the way in which these curves project upon the genotypic plane defined by the scale axes in the factor space. When we relate these component curves to the axes, we see that the liberal respondents will project positively and with high intensity upon both scale axes; the pragmatic conservatives will project generally negatively but with low intensity upon the C axis while the dogmatic conservatives will project very negatively and with high intensity upon C; and the dogmatic conservatives will project generally negatively but with low intensity upon the E axis, and the pragmatic conservatives will project very negatively and with high intensity upon E. Of course the two curves overlap in the circumplex only where there are respondents' i-points, that is, from 5 through 7 and at or near 2. They do not overlap in the segments of 8 and 1 or 3 and 4, which defines possible attitudinal combinations for which there were no empirical examples during the period of this study. There were no pragmatists or dogmatists on the Court at this time. Goldberg, on the basis of the evidence of a single term, appears to come closest to representing the pragmatic ideology; and among those for whom we have more adequate data, Jackson is next; for the circumplex defines a pragmatic conservative (as an ideal type) as a respondent for whom the ideologies of pragmatism and conservatism were of equal importance. Clark comes closer to being a dogmatist than any of the other respondents. And Burton is the only justice who served during the period studied who appears to have been a consistent conservative, although Whittaker also is classified as predominately a conservative.

Although the subject lies beyond the scope of this study, I should like to suggest that further work in the influence of the ideological dimension of Pragmatism/Dogmatism may shed considerable light upon the importance of what lawyers call *"stare decisis,"* as an attitudinal variable. The extent to which a belief in the obligation of justices to follow precedents, in either the personal or institutional sense,[8] is an important component of the attitudes of judges, is virtually unknown. This is largely because lawyers have attempted to study *stare decisis* by using logical rather than socio-psychological tools of analysis. But the relationships depicted by the circumplex are not inconsistent with the small beginning that has been made, in attempts to study from a behavioral point of view the belief in "following precedent."[9] For example, in my study of the attitudes of the Warren

---

[8] See Reed C. Lawlor, "What Computers Can Do: Analysis and Prediction of Judicial Decisions," *American Bar Association Journal*, Vol. 49 (1963), pp. 337–344.

[9] Fred Kort, "Content Analysis of Judicial Opinions and Rules of Law," ch. 6, and Glendon Schubert, "Civilian Control and Stare Decisis in the Warren Court," ch. 3, in Schubert (ed.), *Judicial Decision-Making* (New York: The Free Press, 1963), pp. 133–197, and 55–77.

Court toward civilian (versus military) control and *stare decisis,* I arrived at findings that are strictly compatible with the more general structure arrived at in the present study, although I did not then appreciate the extent to which the findings of the earlier study—based upon an analysis of only half a dozen decisions dealing with a relatively narrow content area—would have general implications. I think it requires no argument to support the judgment that to believe in the authority of precedent, that rules should be followed until they are formally changed, etc., corresponds with the Dogmatic ideology; while a concern for the present and future consequences of decisions, and a willingness to manipulate precedents to achieve results deemed desirable now, should be associated with the ideology of Pragmatism. So Dogmatism is pro-*stare decisis,* and Pragmatism is anti-*stare decisis.* My earlier study concludes with a figure—a two-dimensional factor space—with $I+$ defined as "an attitude favoring civilian rather than military control" and $II+$ defined as "an attitude favoring *stare decisis.*" [10] So defined, $I+$ is a subcomponent of the ideology of liberalism, and $II+$ is a subcomponent of the ideology of Dogmatism. If the polarity of $II+$ were reversed in that figure, so that it was turned upside down, it would then correspond almost precisely with the relationships shown here in the circumplex (a structure of which I was, at the time the earlier study was made, quite unaware). In the earlier figure, Douglas, Black, Warren, and Brennan are in a position equivalent to that of 2 in the circumplex; Frankfurter and Harlan are at a position equivalent to about 7.5, Stewart and Whittaker at about 6.5, and Clark at about 5. The conclusion reached by the earlier study was that the basic difference was between liberals and conservatives, but that the conservatives were differentiated by their attitudes toward *stare decisis,* with Clark ranking exceptionally high in his regard for *stare decisis,* and Frankfurter and Harlan ranking exceptionally low. Students of judicial behavior may find it particularly fruitful if they attempt to link their empirical work with the research, in dogmatism and authoritarianism as personality variables, which has been undertaken by such social psychologists as the Berkeley group, Rokeach, and Eysenck. If this is the second most important ideological dimension in Supreme Court decision-making, it probably merits much more careful attention and study than it has received in the past, on the hypothesis that this is a major dimension of judicial behavior generally. It is certainly plausible to assume, for example, that on other courts—or on the Supreme Court at other times—Pragmatism/Dogma-

[10] *Ibid.,* p. 74.

tism is a dimension which divides liberal as well as conservative judges. (I would speculate, for example, that Holmes was a pragmatic liberal while his colleague John H. Clarke was a dogmatic liberal.)

The final attitudinal structure which I wish to present is that which corresponds to Guttman's radex, which I have interpreted to be different from the circumplex primarily in that the ideal points of the respondents, instead of being projected to the perimeter of the joint attitudinal curve, are located within the enclosed space, thus providing an explicit measure of intensity as well as a measure of the substance of their attitudes toward the two substantive variables. We should expect that the relationships in the radex will be very similar to those shown by the circumplex, the difference being that we shall have a much more refined metric for measuring intensity differences: the entire enclosed space, instead of general positions on the intensity curves for the overlapping simplexes. The radex to be depicted here also differs from the circumplex in that the scale axes are shown as correlated in the radex, just as we know them to be correlated in the genotypic planes about which the radex purports to present a generalized or average replication. Since the scale axes are correlated, the enclosed space is better represented as an ellipse rather than as a circle.

One method which might be employed to generate the data for the radex would be to use the average scale scores, as reported in Tables 17 and 19. As in the instance of the circumplex, however, and for the same reasons, I have preferred to use average loadings on the scale axes. The term loadings are reported in Table 32, and the average loading for each respondent on each scale is reported in Table 41. Evidently, these average loadings can be used, and I have used them, as a system of coordinates to position the i-points of respondents in the plane of the axes; since the axes are oblique, the i-points project, in the radex, obliquely upon the scale axes (rather than, as in the circumplex structure that we examined, orthogonally). The radex that could be constructed, by using average scale scores, would be very similar to the structure resulting from the use of average axis loadings. This finding is probably best supported by citing the rank correlations between the sequences of average scale scores and average axis loadings, for each variable; and it should be noted that such a test is a generalization of the similar tests for the term sequences, which are reported in Table 33. The correlation of the average rankings is, in a sense, an even more rigorous test of the degree of correspondence between the cumulative scales and the factor-space configurations than that provided by the term correlations, because of the much larger effect that sampling variations in content,

TABLE 41

Average Loadings on the Scale Axes for Political and for Economic Liberalism, and Ideological Types

Respondent	Scale Axis: C	E	Ideological Types
Murphy	.708	.693	
Black	.589	.589	
Douglas	.585	.617	Liberals
Rutledge	.581	.713	
Brennan	.423	.367	
Warren	.422	.509	
Goldberg	.066	−.334	
Frankfurter	−.115	−.507	Pragmatic Conservatives
Jackson	−.127	−.558	
Stewart	−.250	−.504	
Harlan	−.382	−.646	
Whittaker	−.393	−.614	Conservatives
Burton	−.412	−.338	
Clark	−.376	.039	
White	−.415	−.079	
Minton	−.432	−.197	Dogmatic Conservatives
Vinson	−.479	−.076	
Reed	−.566	−.157	

and differences in length of tenure, can have upon the average sequences; so we should not expect the present correlations to be as high as the averages for the term correlations, which were 92 for C and 91 for E. For the average sequences, including all respondents, tau for C is .82, and for E it is .83. The principal reasons for these correlations not being higher are that White has too high an average scale score on C to correspond well to the position of a dogmatic conservative, to which he is assigned by the axis measurements. Similarly, Goldberg has too high a scale score on E to be consistent with the position of a pragmatic conservative. The available data for these two respondents, however, are much less adequate than for any of the other sixteen respondents, since Goldberg served for only a single term, and White for less than two out of the total period of seventeen terms. Dropping Goldberg and White from consideration, the rank correlation for C becomes .89, and for E it is .86. These seem to me to be surprisingly high, when one considers the many sources of error and other variance to which the average scale scores and axis loadings are subject. In any event, these correlations certainly confirm my earlier findings that the cumulative scale and factorial measurements are equivalent; and they support the remark above, to the effect that a radex based directly upon the average scale scores would resemble closely the radex based upon axis loadings.

Tables 17 and 19 would also produce a circumplex very similar to that of Figure 15, and the only respondent who would be classified differently would be Harlan, who is slightly closer to PC than to C in Figure 15, but who would be classified as a conservative (together with Burton and Whittaker) on the basis of Tables 17 and 19. (Such a circumplex would be produced by extending the vectors for each of the respondents [as in Figure 16] to the perimeter of the circle.)

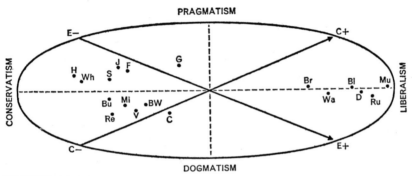

FIGURE 16. The Radex of Political and Economic Liberalism

The radex of Figure 16 defines the same ideological types as does the circumplex of Figure 15. Four clusters of respondents are clearly manifest: the six liberals, all of whom lie on or very close to the liberalism axis ($I'+$); the four pragmatic conservatives, who are clustered near the middle of the E— axis; the three conservatives, who are closest to the conservatism axis ($I'-$); and the five dogmatic conservatives, who are clustered near the middle of the C— axis. We can also, however, now make direct comparisons among these types in regard to the relative intensity or moderation of their attachment to their respective ideologies. As a group, the liberals are much more intense in their belief than are either the pragmatic or the dogmatic conservatives. Clearly, Brennan is the least committed of the liberals, but he is further from the point of attitudinal and ideological indifference—the origin of the space where the axes intersect—than all except two of the remaining justices, Harlan and Whittaker; and four of the liberals are considerably more intense in their liberalism than these two conservatives in their conservatism. So, although Brennan is the most moderate of the liberals, ten of the twelve conservatives (of the three types combined) are more moderate in their views than he. So we can now add an important supplement to our previous finding about the relationship between the liberals and the conservatives: not only are the liberals more cohesive in their attitudes than the conservatives, they also are much more intense in their attitudes than are the conservatives. Finally, it is also possible to use the radex (or the circumplex) as the basis for an even more general classification of the respondents. Since the scale axes partition the radex into four segments which correspond to two pairs of ideologies, we can classify the justices on this basis. If we do so, we can say that there are the same six liberals, one pragmatist (Goldberg), and one dogmatist (Clark), and that the ten remaining justices all are conservatives. In terms of this system, we could observe that the pragmatist and the dogmatist are the most moderate of all in their attachment to their ideologies, and that among the conservatives, White is the most moderate, while Harlan and Whittaker are the most intense. My most general conclusion is that during all except the most recent of the seventeen terms studied, the attitudinal differences of Supreme Court justices toward political and economic issues have reflected the para-ideological division of the justices between a minority of liberals and a majority of conservatives; and since the conservatives, but not the liberals, were further divided ideologically between pragmatists and dogmatists, the more cohesive and intense ideology of the liberal minority tended to be the dominant ideology of the Court throughout the latter half of the period of this study.

Chapter 9 · CONCLUSION

IN THIS concluding chapter, I shall discuss three subjects: (1) the major substantive findings that have been presented in this book; (2) the principal questions of methodology with which we have been concerned; and (3) the theoretical implications of the work.

The Substance of the Liberal Mind

This study of Supreme Court justices during the past generation suggests three paradoxes involving interrelationships between political attitudes and political ideologies. It is possible that some of these paradoxes may apply to a much larger population than the elite group of judicial obligarchs who act as the super-ego of the popular sovereigns of the American system of constitutional democracy.

The first paradox can be simply described: there is both a liberal ideology and a liberal attitude, and there is a conservative ideology but there is no conservative attitude. The reason why we can say that there is a liberal attitude is found in the relatively high degree of both homogeneity and intensity with which a substantial minority of Supreme Court justices have perceived and responded to issues of political, social, and economic policy. Because of the high homogeneity and intensity of their attitude, the liberals are affected hardly at all by the competing ideology of dogmatism/pragmatism. But it is precisely because the judicial respondents who were *not* liberals *were* divided between those who were relatively pragmatic and those who were relatively dogmatic, that it is not possible to speak of a conservative *attitude* as characterizing more than one or two of the Supreme Court justices in my sample. Instead, we find that the conservative ideology spans two quite disparate conservative attitudes: a conservative attitude toward political issues, and a conservative attitude toward

273

economic issues. Thus, the eighteen justices who constituted my sample are partitioned, by their attitudes, into three groups of approximately equal size: liberals, pragmatic (economic) conservatives, and dogmatic (political) conservatives. Only Harold Burton, a Republican crony of Southern Democrat Harry Truman in the most exclusive club in Washington, can best be described as a justice with an unmixed and moderately intense conservative attitude. I say "unmixed" advisedly, because the paradox can be restated in the following alternative form: in order for a respondent to be either a liberal or a conservative, and irrespective of the degree of intensity of his attitude, it is essential that he maintain a balanced attitude toward political and toward economic policy issues. (A balanced attitude toward the two major scale variables is the functional equivalent, at the level of manifest attitudes, to an insignificantly low correlation with the pragmatism/dogmatism dimension, at the level of latent ideology.)

It happens that for my empirical data, the respondents can be classified just about as well, in terms of manifest attitudinal types, as they can be in terms of latent ideological types: there is no need to distinguish for the liberals; and for the conservatives, the adjectives "economic" and "political" denote attitudinal types, while "pragmatic" and "dogmatic" denote the equivalent ideological types. Although there were no such respondents in my sample, we can contemplate the hypothetical possibility that Presidents might appoint to the Court justices who are *either* economic-conservative and political-liberal *or* political-conservative and economic-liberal, thus corresponding to the pragmatic or to the dogmatic ideological types. It is a matter of more than incidental interest that not a single such person was a Supreme Court justice during the past generation. I assume that it is not because of the absence, among lawyer-politicians who might be considered eligible for appointment to the Supreme Court, of persons who would fit the psychological types of relatively "pure" pragmatism, or of dogmatism—provided one is willing to extend the time dimension, for sampling purposes, back to include the entire period of a century and two-thirds of the Supreme Court's existence. The pragmatic ideology defines a combination of attitudes which was characteristic of the classical liberalism of an earlier age; the man who believes in freedom of the individual, in both his personal and his property rights, is a Nineteenth Century liberal. But the person who believes in the authoritative socialization of both personal and property rights is the exponent of an attitudinal syndrome that is much closer to that of the modern totalitarian ideologies of the Twentieth Century, such as communism and fascism. Hence, the counterpart, in political ideology, to the psychological dimension of pragmatism/dogmatism, is the liberalism of John Stuart Mill and the totalitarianism of Josef Stalin; and an alternative interpretation of the radex of Figure 16 is that the ideologies of modern liberalism and conservatism both offer a middle way, poised between classical liberalism on the one hand, and modern totalitarianism on the other. Such an interpretation certainly accords with our intuitive expectations: we should hardly expect that either Franklin Roosevelt or Harry Truman or Dwight Eisenhower or John Kennedy would appoint to the United States Supreme Court exponents of either Nineteenth Century individualism or Twentieth Century totalitarianism. Neither did they, nor is Lyndon Johnson likely to do so. But we should certainly expect to find many justices on the Supreme Court, as it was composed during and prior to 1937, who would fit the ideological type of classical liberalism; and whether there have been any justices on the Court, whose attitudinal syndromes correspond best to the ideological type of modern totalitarianism, is a question that might well be of interest in future research.

The above analysis also implies that conservatives, at least among the judicial respondents in my sample, tend to be attracted by the competing ideologies of classical liberalism and modern totalitarianism, but that liberals do not. From an attitudinal point of view, and in the vernacular of factor analysis, conservatives tend to be "loaded" on either one or the other of the two scale variables, while liberals are loaded to about the same degree on both scales. Thus, from both the perspective of ideology and that of attitude, the liberal point of view seems to afford a more stable and attractive middle way than does conservatism.

A second paradox is found in the dynamic consistency of judicial attitudes and ideologies. On the one hand, we found considerable evidence in support of the proposition that there is exceptional consistency in the structure and in the articulation of both the attitudes and the ideologies of Supreme Court justices; and on the other hand, we found that attitudes and ideologies are subject to change—or, at least, so it appears at certain levels of analysis. In order to explain this paradox, it is necessary to distinguish three levels of attitudinal and ideological analysis: that of the Court, that of the subgroups who correspond to attitudinal and ideological types, and that of the individual respondents.

At the sociological level of analysis, we examined changes in the attitude of the Court in Chapter 5. We found that during the initial three terms when Murphy and Rutledge were members of the decision-making group, there was a slight conservative bias in the aggregate attitude of the Court toward both scale variables, and consequently in the dominant political ideology of the Court as well. This was followed by a change in the Court's attitudes consequent upon personnel changes involving the substitution of Clark and Minton for Murphy and Rutledge: for six terms beginning in 1949, the Court's attitude toward the C scale became much more conservative, while its attitude towards the E scale was one of moderation. During this second period, the dominant ideology of the Court was that of dogmatic (or authoritarian) conservatism. The third and final period begins with the 1955 Term; and during the final eight terms included in this study, the Court's attitude became increasingly liberal toward both political and economic issues. After 1955, liberalism was the dominant ideology of the Court. So it is clear that there was continuing and substantial change in both the attitudes and the ideology of the Court. Nevertheless, the Court also manifested very considerable consistency in its attitudes, as demonstrated by the fact that both of the major attitudinal variables were scalable in every term, and also by the narrow range of fluctuation for the index of consensus (Table 1).

The Court can be conceptualized, in the alternative, as consisting of an aggregate group of no more than nine individual justices; and I have defined the attitudes and dominant ideology of the Court exclusively in terms of the most frequent majority of the individual justices. Accordingly, attitudes and ideologies have been analyzed as characteristics of individual judicial respondents at the psychological level of analysis. In Chapters 5, 7, and 8, I assigned various scores to these individual respondents, and examined various of the many individual differences in their attitudes toward both scale variables, and in their ideologies. My analysis showed that there was very high consistency in the attitudes of the individual respondents. Only two of the eighteen individuals—Clark and Warren—manifested any attitudinal change; and both of them changed only in their attitude toward the political variable. Clark's change was temporary, while Warren's was permanent (within the time dimensions of this study.) There were many minor fluctuations in ideological type for almost all of the individual respondents, but I have interpreted these to be a consequence of sampling variation, rather than as indicants of changes in ideology. The only individual whose ideology appears to have changed was Warren, from dogmatic conservatism to liberalism.

Evidently, both attitudes and ideologies appear to be most dynamic when viewed from the perspective of the sociological level of analysis; and they appear to be most consistent when seen from the psychological level of analysis. But the level of analysis which proved to be most fruitful for comprehension of the multivariate relationships and the latent psychological dimensions was the socio-psychological level, in which we examined the attitudes and ideologies of subsets of the Court—that is, of subgroups of individual respondents. We found that there was continuing change in the size of such subgroups, as individual respondents joined or left the Court; but the relationship of the subgroups to the attitudinal scales was highly consistent. Indeed, I defined the manifest attitudinal respondent-types on the basis of the empirical differentiation among subgroups, in relation to the scales, and my entire analysis of the latent ideological structure, in Chapters 7 and 8, is based upon inferences from the manifest behavioral (voting) differences among the three principal subgroups of respondents. Subgroup study links psychological constructs, statistical measurements, and individual behavior. This middle level of socio-psychological analysis is the key to the understanding of the attitudes and ideologies of Supreme Court justices.

Although most changes in the attitude of "the Court" (to return to the sociological level) can be traced directly to personnel changes or to nonparticipation by incumbent justices, and pseudo-changes frequently can be traced to sampling variation from term to term, the data of this study also support the hypothesis, which frequently has been investigated in earlier research, that responses to external stimuli also can result in changes in the attitudes of the Court. In 1937, there was a permanent change (in the sense that it has continued without further change since then) in the Court's attitude toward economic issues [1]—"permanent" because it was quickly followed by personnel changes which precluded the possibility of backsliding. A generation later, the Court again changed its attitude in response to external stimuli, but this time the issue was the C scale, and the change was only temporary. (The fact that this kind of change occurs no more often than once in a generation testifies to the extent to which the appointed justices of the United States Supreme Court are *relatively* immune to direct influence from "outside political pressures," [2] as does also the temporary duration of the recent attitudinal change—which was *not* nailed down by

---

[1] Glendon Schubert, *Constitutional Politics* (New York: Holt, Rinehart, and Winston, 1960), pp. 159–168.

[2] Cf. Kenneth N. Vines and Herbert Jacob, *Studies in Judicial Politics* (New Orleans: Tulane University Studies in Political Science, Vol. VIII, 1962).

personnel changes, because of Kennedy's electoral victory over Nixon in 1960.)

The crisis of 1937 was brought on by external political attacks on the part of economic liberals, who successfully sought to curb the economic-conservative trend of the Court's decisions. The crisis of 1958–59 was brought on by external political attacks on the part of political conservatives, who sought (but failed) to curb the politically liberal trend in the Court's "civil liberty" decisions. As my data show, the trend was perceived (and with considerable accuracy) to have begun with the conversion of Earl Warren, an event which occurred on the heels of the Court's decision in the School Segregation Cases. The complaints of the political conservatives were that the Court had substituted "egg-headed social science evidence" for law, that the justices were writing into the Constitution their own biases on the race question, that the Court was endangering national security by its softness toward Communists, and that its centralizing policies were undercutting the American federal republic by destroying the power of the states. It is not pertinent to my purpose, in this particular book, to discuss the content of discrete decisions and opinions; but Pritchett has done an excellent job of summarizing both the relevant decisions of the Court and opinions of the justices, and also the events that transpired in Congress, where the nation-wide movement to "curb the Court" came to a focus.[3] An examination of the term C scales (Figure 1) shows the following: the volume of C-scale decisions doubled in 1956 and 1957 in comparison to 1954 and 1955, then dropped sharply during 1958 and 1959 (when Congress actively was considering the Jenner bill, Eastland's motion to impeach the Chief Justice, and similar measures), and then rose sharply again in 1960 (after the political storm in Congress had subsided, and after Kennedy had defeated Nixon for the Presidency). It is interesting to note that the proportion of C-scale decisions, to total content, dropped from a high of 57 percent in 1957 to a low of 34 percent in 1958, but bounced back to 48 percent in 1959; this suggests that the jurisdictional decision-making of the Court was even more sensitive to the external stimuli than was the substantive decision-making on the merits—evidently, at least one of the four liberals was reluctant, during the fall and summer of 1957, to have the Court consider the decision of a large volume of civil liberties cases. In this regard, we might note that it was Frankfurter,

[3] C. Herman Pritchett, *Congress versus the Supreme Court, 1957–1960* (Minneapolis: University of Minnesota, 1961).

in particular, who was both articulate about, and apparently very sensitive to, the implications of fluctuations in the Court's jurisdictional decision-making.[4] In any event, it is clear from the term C scales that, to the extent that the Court temporarily changed its attitude toward political liberalism during the period of the 1957–1960 Terms, this was not due to any change in the voting, on the merits, of the four liberals, or of Clark. The change came exclusively from among the individual respondents whom I have classified as pragmatic (or economic) conservatives. This makes perfect sense, because these are the respondents who are least intense in their attitude toward the C-scale issues; and we should expect that if any Supreme Court justices are going to respond to external stimuli, it will most likely be the moderates on the scale, not those who are psychologically committed to relatively extreme positions of either favor or disfavor. The scales show that Whittaker was moderate in 1956, and progressively more negative from 1957 through 1959, returning to a marginally negative score in 1960. Frankfurter and Harlan had moderate scores in 1955–57, and negative scores thereafter. Stewart, however, had a moderately negative score in 1958 and a moderate positive score in 1959, 1960, and thereafter. All four of these respondents are classified as pragmatic conservatives in Figures 15 and 16. When personnel changes did come in 1962, the replacement of Whittaker by White was reinforced by the replacement of Frankfurter by Goldberg; and both of the new justices appeared to be more liberal, on both scales, than the men whom they replaced. This is why the effect of the election of 1960 was to preclude the possibility of the "civil liberties recession" of 1958–59 from becoming a more enduring change. But, as my analysis has shown, the Court itself (just as in 1937) already had changed, but this time back to a more politically liberal position, and *before* the personnel changes took place. More specifically, the swing toward political conservatism in 1958 and 1959 was due primarily to the change in voting behavior of Frankfurter, Harlan, and Whittaker, both in decisions on the merits and, perhaps, in their influence in jurisdictional decision-making as well. But the swing back to a more liberal attitude of "the Court" in 1960 can be attributed directly to the change in the attitude of Potter Stewart opposite to that of Frankfurter, Harlan, and Whittaker on C-scale issues. Stewart occupied the middle rank on the C scale and consequently was the key decision-maker in civil liberties issues during the period of the crisis of 1958–59.

[4] See his dissenting opinion in *Ferguson* v. *Moore-McCormack Lines*, 352 U. S. 521 (1957).

A third paradox constitutes my most important finding with regard to the substance of the liberal mind among Supreme Court justices during the past generation: *neither* of the two major attitudes (the political scale and the economic scale) constitutes the core of the liberal ideology. The central component of liberalism is equalitarianism; and for my sample of respondents and cases, equalitarianism is defined by the issues of racial integration, legislative reapportionment, and the right to citizenship. There can be no doubt that these were among the most important issues of public policy decided by the Supreme Court during the period of my study, if we are to measure importance in terms of the pervasiveness of impact upon the American polity. My analysis of the relationship between the configuration of ideal-points of the respondents, in three-dimensional space, and the factorial dimension which represents the ideology of equalitarianism, showed that the condition that made it possible for equalitarianism to emerge as the most important dimension of the Court's decision-making was the higher degree of consensus that was possible toward equalitarianism than toward either the C or E or F scale. Higher consensus was possible because the most intensively negative (*i.e.,* extreme) conservatives on both of the major attitudinal scales, political and economic, projected much more moderately upon the centroid equalitarianism dimension than upon either scale. My explicit conclusion was that given the ideological positions of the various justices who constituted the Supreme Court during the period of this study, the basic explanation for decisions such as *Brown* v. *Board of Education,*[5] and *Trop* v. *Dulles*[6] or *Kent* v. *Dulles,*[7] and *Baker* v. *Carr*[8] is that these issues of equalitarianism were the ones upon which it was possible, during the middle years of the Twentieth Century, for the Supreme Court to achieve substantial consensus. The core of modern liberalism, therefore, is equivalent to the area of highest communality for the attitudes of most of the Supreme Court justices who served during this period.

Some Methodological Aspects of Modern Liberalism

Most of the earlier attempts to measure, in some systematic way, the attitudes of Supreme Court justices, have been based upon rather crude attempts to denote patterns of association and disassociation in matrices of

[5] 347 U. S. 483 (1954).
[6] 356 U. S. 86 (1958).
[7] 357 U. S. 116 (1958).
[8] 369 U. S. 186 (1962).

agreement scores.[9] Although it is possible to use more sophisticated techniques to make more elegant analyses of this type of data,[10] there seems to be no compelling argument against the slight additional investment required in order to convert the raw data into correlation matrices which then can be examined by techniques of cluster analysis.[11] The chief argument against the latter approach, and the main reason why I rejected it as a methodology for use in the present study, is that it can partition respondents into types, but it provides much less information than does factor analysis, about the attitudinal-ideological content of the types and about how these are related to each other. In earlier attempts to study the attitudes of Supreme Court justices, both Pritchett and I assumed that our bloc analyses were arraying groups of justices along a single dimension of general liberalism and conservatism. If there were only one general liberalism dimension represented by the phi matrices, then the rank order of the matrix itself in the form of a simplex would be a liberalism scale (or a single factor of liberalism). As I have just pointed out above, what such a rank order really denotes is the approximate ranking of the justices on equalitarianism, which is the most important single dimension of the Court's decision-making, but which accounts (as a manifest scale) for only a very small proportion of the decisions on the merits in any term. Such a ranking is not equivalent to either the C or the E scale, although, as we discussed in Chapter 6, there necessarily is a fairly high positive correlation between both of the major attitudinal scales and the equalitarianism dimension. If there were no C and E and F scales, and if equalitarianism were as significant in quantitative as it is in qualitative terms, then there would be no need for either scale analysis or factor analysis, or for analyses of principal component curves, circumplexes, or radexes. My own task in this book would have been greatly simplified if only it were true that the attitudes of Supreme Court justices can adequately be analyzed in terms of a single dimension of general liberalism. Unfortunately, from the point of view of research parsimony, the collective judicial mind is not that simple.

The analysis in Chapter 6 of the semantic subcomponents of the two

[9] *E.g.,* C. Herman Pritchett, *The Roosevelt Court* (New York: Macmillan, 1948), pp. 32–45 and 242–247; and Glendon Schubert, *Quantitative Analysis of Judicial Behavior* (New York: The Free Press, 1959), pp. 144–163.

[10] See, for example, Louis L. McQuitty, "Elementary Linkage Analysis for Isolating Orthogonal and Oblique Types and Typal Relevancies," *Educational and Psychological Measurement,* Vol. 17 (1957), pp. 207–229; and also his "Hierarchical Syndrome Analysis," *ibid.,* Vol. 20 (1960), pp. 293–304; and cf. Schubert, *op. cit.* fn. 9, *supra,* pp. 167–172.

[11] Benajmin Fruchter, *Introduction to Factor Analysis* (New York: Van Nostrand, 1954), ch. 2; Edgar F. Borgatta, "On Analyzing Correlation Matrices: Some New Emphases," *Public Opinion Quarterly,* Vol. 22 (1955–59), pp. 516–528.

major scales does show, however, that there are degrees of positive association, ranging from moderate to maximal, among all of these subcomponents. Those subcomponents that are most highly intercorrelated define the content of the political and the economic scales, in the manner that I think these ought to be redefined for purposes of future research in judicial attitudes. As Table 27 demonstrated, it is readily possible to identify other components of attitudinal content (such as that of the F scale), for which the association with the subcomponents of the two major scales ranges from low positive to negative. We found that the revised semantic content of political liberalism includes only the political freedom and fair procedure subcomponents. The revised economic liberalism scale includes fiscal claims, anti-business, and pro-labor subcomponents. The frequencies for the other two postulated subcomponents of the economic scale, freedom of competition and the constitutionality of state taxation, were so small that it was possible to conclude (and then only tentatively) that these probably should continue to be included as part of the semantic content of the E scale. Two other postulated semantic subcomponents of the C scale, political equality and the right to privacy, are located between the two major scales; and one of the most surprising findings was that both of these subcomponents are more closely related to E than to C; indeed, the correlation between political equality and some of the subcomponents of E is so high that we must conclude that political equality is perhaps better understood to be a subcomponent of economic rather than of political liberalism! On the other hand, the postulated religious freedom subcomponent of the C scale appeared, on the basis of the inadequate evidence available, to share only a low positive association with the C scale, but to be maximally positively correlated with the independent reference dimensions —independent, that is, of the dimension that was the centroid for the other postulated subcomponents of the C and E scales—with which the F scale also was highly (although negatively) correlated. In sum, the use of subcomponent analysis made it possible to demonstrate:

1. more precisely, the semantic content of the two attitudinal scales—the political scale and the economic scale;
2. that the subcomponents of the two (revised) scales, plus two other subcomponents that lay between the scales, together defined the semantic content of liberalism as an ideological dimension;
3. that the two non-scale subcomponents (political equality and the right to privacy) define the semantic core of the liberal ideology;
4. that religious freedom probably is not a subcomponent of either the

political liberalism attitudinal scale (with which it has a low positive correlation) or of the ideological dimension of liberalism (from which it is statistically independent), but rather appears to be most closely related to another ideological dimension, that of pragmatism/ dogmatism. (Religious toleration is highly positively correlated with pragmatism, and religious conformity is highly positively correlated with dogmatism.)

A point that cannot be overemphasized is that in making interpretations of ordinal scales, changes in rank order on term scales do not necessarily indicate attitudinal change; indeed, they rarely signify that. If two or more ideal-points are densely clustered in the phenotypic space, then rank changes usually will reflect errors, which may be due to the respondents' perceptions, sampling variance, computational routines and other measurement sources, or to mistakes in judgment on the part of the analyst—in classifying a respondent with considerable non-participation, for example. A more usual cause of rank changes will be a consequence of changes in the composition of the decision-making set (*i.e.,* the Court); and these are not errors at all. For example, Douglas and Black ranked on the C scale below Murphy and Rutledge during the 1946–1948 Terms; and throughout the next fourteen terms, Douglas and Black ranked as the two most extreme political liberals on the Court—but extreme in what sense? Clearly, there is no basis for assuming that Douglas and Black became more sympathetic to political liberalism *after* Murphy and Rutledge left the group. The attitude of Douglas and Black must be evaluated, not merely on the basis of their ranks on the C scales of 1949 and thereafter, but also in relationship to an even more extremely liberal political position that disappeared from the Court after the end of the 1948 Term. Similarly, it is conceivable that one who observed Frankfurter's ranking on the C scales from 1946 through 1961 might infer—and such an inference would be erroneous—that Frankfurter had been following a migratory orbit during this period. Or one might infer that Frankfurter's ranks provide dubious evidence for a frequently iterated hypothesis: that judges tend to become more conservative, as their tenure increases. Assuming, as I do, that minimal confidence should be reposed in the 1946 C scale generally, and in Frankfurter's rank in particular—he is credited with 25 percent of the scale errors—I shall take the 1947 and 1948 C scales to be probably more reliable indicators of Frankfurter's attitude. He ranked fifth in 1947–48; third for the next half-dozen terms; and then his rank increased to fourth in 1955, fifth again in 1956–57, seventh in 1958–60, and eighth in 1961. But did *he* change? He became third after 1948 simply because Murphy and Rutledge both were no longer members of the decision-making group; and Douglas and Black moved up from the third and fourth to the first and second ranks while Frankfurter's relationship to Douglas and Black and his other surviving colleagues was precisely the same in 1949 *et seq.* as it had been before then. His increase in rank after 1954 was explicitly due to the appointment to the Court of several justices in succession whose attitudes toward the political scale variable were more liberal than his: Warren, Brennan, Whittaker, Stewart, and White. (And to the extent that the circumplex of Figure 15 and the radex of Figure 16 do not completely confirm this finding, they suffer, I believe, from error due to sampling variance and the measurement processes associated with these highly schematic models.)

A closely related point has to do with my analysis of the functional basis for the elementary component-type curves which result from plotting together the two major scales. We discovered in Chapter 8 that the latent intensity curve for each of the major scales is parabolic, and that the frequent appearance of sine-type curves can be attributed to transpositional errors involving the economic-conservative type of respondents. These errors, I have inferred, are due to the dense clustering of the ideal-points of the economic conservatives. A sample which includes a dense cluster of ideal-points is equivalent, from a statistical point of view, to having multiple empirical observations of the same attitudinal syndrome; points that were scattered in the phenotypic space, representing different attitudinal syndromes (even though they were in the same sub-universe of the space) would be less likely to create confusion in the empirical measurements. With a better (in the statistical sense) sample of respondents, such transpositions should not occur, and therefore it should not be possible to observe the N-shaped intensity curves.

My original intention was to include in this book a chapter on the psychological distance separating the ideal-points of the justices in the configuration in the three-dimensional genotypic space. Given the reference factor coordinates for the *i*-points (Table 30), the computation of the distance between each pair of points, using Equation 4, is a simple matter. There are two reasons why I have not included such a chapter. The first reason, but not the most important one, is that I do not have the computations at hand; but I do have the *i*-point coordinates on punch cards, and a computer could calculate the seventeen distance matrices in a minute or two. I do have also the calculations for distance matrices of the configurations in *five*-dimensional space; this reflects a mistaken assumption, made early in the research activities, that the fourth and fifth factors represent minor scale variables rather than (as I am now persuaded) merely error variance. Interpretations of distance matrices for five-dimensional space configurations have been published in preliminary reports on this research,[12] and they exemplify the method. There is probably no greater difference between the distances reported in the cited articles, and those that would result from computations omitting the fourth and fifth factors, for the same terms: the reason is that the loadings on the fourth and fifth factors were, generally speaking, very small. A second and more important reason for not presenting and analyzing a set of distance matrices is that they add very little information to what can be inferred from the phi matrices. In interpreting phi matrices, one should infer that the higher the positive correlation, the closer together are the attitudes of two respondents; and in interpreting the distance matrices, one should infer that the smaller the index (All values must be positive, ranging in theory from zero to two and in practice from about .10 to less than 2.00.) the more similar the attitudinal syndromes. Hence, high negative phi correlations correspond to high positive distance index values. About the only inference that one can make directly from the distance matrices, that one cannot make directly from the phi matrices, is the comparison of the *i*-points of respondents who did not participate in decisions together. In the phi matrices, it is necessary to report arbitrary zero correlations for such dyads. But since their relationships with the other respondents in the term set makes it possible to locate the *i*-point of each in the factorial space, it is also possible to measure directly the distance between the *i*-points of the pair. However, there are only three such dyads that arise empirically (out of a total of 630 for the seventeen terms of this study): Reed and Whittaker in 1956, Whittaker and White in 1961, and Frankfurter and White in 1961. All three of these instances were due to mid-term retirements (Reed's and Whittaker's *de jure,* and Frankfurter's *de facto*) and appointments of successors (Whittaker for Reed, and White for Whittaker). It hardly seems warranted to pursue the analysis in order to discuss this rather refined question, particularly since I happen to have reported the data for the more recent dyads, which involve Byron White, in my article on the 1961 Term.

[12] Glendon Schubert, "The 1960 Term of the Supreme Court: A Psychological Analysis," *American Political Science Review,* Vol. 56 (1962), pp. 106–107; and "Judicial Attitudes and Voting Behavior: The 1961 Term of the United States Supreme Court," *Law and Contemporary Problems,* Vol. 28 (1963), pp. 135–137.

The Theory of the Liberal Mind

A point of criticism that is almost certain to be levied against this research is that it is based upon the S-R (stimulus-response) model of behaviorist pyschology and learning theory; and that, as a consequence, I have greatly oversimplified the true attitudinal relationships of and among the justices. I think that the most appropriate response to such an accusation is to point out that the model of the atom may also be said to greatly oversimplify the physical universe; and doubtless the concepts of gene and chromosome do violence to the intricate complexities of heredity, particularly in a context of environmental influences. The test of the value of a scientific model, concept, or theory is not *whether* it oversimplifies empirical reality; but rather, what effect it has upon our understanding of that reality. The lawyer's model of judicial decision-making, which is based upon traditional logic and depends upon the *stare decisis* norm for its *deus ex machina,* is also a vast oversimplification of empirical reality. If we must choose between S-R and *stare decisis* conceptualism, our criterion should be: Which helps us the better to acquire valid and reliable understanding about how and why judges make their decisions?

Even if we assume that a psychometric model is appropriate, there is still the question: Which, among competing concepts of factorial interpretation, ought to be prefered by lay analysts—such as myself—of judicial psychology? My own approach has been eclectic. I have not hesitated to employ the traditional factorial concept of rotation, and Coombs's alternative concept of enfolding the space, when either of these provided a shorthand way to describe relationships or operations. Similarly, I have borrowed freely from Guttman's work in linear cumulative scaling, and from his concepts of principal and of elementary component curves, the circumplex, and the radex. But so far as I know, my basic procedures for identifying scale axes in factorial space are, like my basic model of the psychology of the decision-making process of the United States Supreme Court, original. My methodology was constructed to help resolve the theoretical questions in which I was interested.

As I see it, the phenotypic space (the empirical field of observed events) is fundamental; all of the various genotypic spaces I have postulated, as differing perspectives of the empirical data, are distinctly of secondary importance. The three-dimensional factor space discussed in Chapter 7 is most certainly an artifact, and a rather abstruse one, at that; but so is the two-dimensional circumplex or radex of Chapter 8 an artifact; and so are the linear scales of Chapter 5. Neither attitudes nor ideologies have any essence; such dimensions are strictly hypothetical constructs which are invoked to help explain the manifest observable regularities and discontinuities in the voting behavior of United States Supreme Court justices. I do not for a moment delude myself in thinking that I have boxed the compass of Supreme Court decision-making, by offering an interpretation exclusively in socio-psychological terms, and at that, one confined to judicial attitudes toward policy values. Other studies of human behavior indicate a high probability that their attitudes toward and relationships with each other, with wives, with secretaries, with friends, and so on, have an influence upon their decisions; and although such influences necessarily are within the scope of what is measured by the phi matrices, they are *dehors* the attitudinal scales, and they certainly are *dehors* the strictly psychological interpretation that I have provided in this book. It seems likely that the health—both physical and mental—of the justices has an influence upon their decisions; also their ethnic origins, religion, political affiliation, indeed, their whole life experience. But every one of these other sources of variance can be conceptualized as an indirect influence upon a respondent's attitudes toward policy values, and hence, an appropriate subject for future research into the question: What are the factors which condition attitudes and ideologies? [13] In focusing as I have done upon attitudes and ideologies that are oriented toward issues of public policy, these other influences have been sublimated rather than lost; they are omitted from my analytical framework, but not from the empirical field of potentially observable events. This is why, as I said, the phenotypic space is primary; interpretations necessarily are based upon the postulation of some kind of genotypic space, and they are necessarily theoretical—otherwise, they do not explain—and they are necessarily incomplete.

My study of the judicial mind, subject to these caveats, shows that modern liberalism as a political ideology has as its primary content two scalable attitudinal dimensions. One of these, the political scale, measures attitudes toward personal rights; and the other, the economic scale, measures attitudes toward property rights. The combinations of attitudes of Supreme Court justices—that is, their ideologies—are such that the attitudinal relationship among the justices characteristically is not linear but rather is elliptical. This elliptical structure of judicial attitudes is of fundamental importance, because it makes possible the relatively high degree of con-

[13] For a more extended development of this point of view, see my *Judicial Behavior: A Reader in Theory and Research* (Chicago: Rand McNally, 1964), pp. 4–5, 445–447.

sensus that is prerequisite to the Court's performance of its role in the larger political system. The fact that there are two major attitudinal dimensions means that differently constructed majorities can and do form on different issues; if there were only a single major dimensions, it would be much more likely that the Court would be divided between a permanent majority and a permanent minority. Moreover, about a third of the issues resolved by the Court are *not* closely related to liberalism and conservatism; and the elliptical structure of ideologies makes it possible for the extremes of liberalism and conservatism to meet on common ground—as they do—when the issue is (for example) freedom of religious belief, or its opposite: rendering what is due unto Caesar, the collection of the public tithe through the income tax. My finding that the structure of the attitudes of Supreme Court justices is elliptical may afford a certain glow of momentary pleasure to those critics of the Court who have been saying for years that the liberal mind is egg-shaped. More mature reflection should give them pause, however. It is the conservatives rather than the liberals on the Supreme Court who are primarily responsible for the curvilinear context in which we have observed the judicial mind.

INDEX